A HISTORY OF OUR TIME

A HISTORY OF OUR TIME
Readings on Postwar America

Edited by

William H. Chafe
DUKE UNIVERSITY

Harvard Sitkoff
UNIVERSITY OF NEW HAMPSHIRE

New York   Oxford
OXFORD UNIVERSITY PRESS
1983

Library of Congress Cataloging in Publication Data
Main entry under title:

A History of our time.

1. United States—History—1945–
—Addresses, essays, lectures. I. Chafe,
William Henry. II. Sitkoff, Harvard.
E742.H57   973.92   82-3590
ISBN 0-19-503174-1 (pbk.)   AACR2

Printing (last digit): 9 8 7 6 5 4 3 2

Printed in the United State of America

Preface

For most students reading this book, the matters analyzed may well seem like ancient history. Hiroshima and Nagasaki, McCarthyism, the bus boycott in Montgomery, *The Feminine Mystique*—all of these evoke an age different from our present one. To many people born in the 1960s, events like the American Revolution and the Civil War are more familiar, tangible, and immediate than occurrences of the last thirty years.

Yet to a remarkable extent, our own history is a direct product of changes that transpired since the beginning of World War II. In 1940 the nation had not yet emerged from the Great Depression. Barely 15 percent of all young people attended college. American foreign policy was based on a posture of neutrality and noninvolvement in foreign ventures. Black Americans lived predominantly in the South, could not vote, were denied use of the toilet facilities of public restaurants, and suffered systematic brutality with no recourse before the law. Women—at least middle-class white women—were expected to marry, raise children, and devote themselves to homemaking. The idea of combining marriage and career was frowned upon, and most professional schools—especially those in law and medicine—excluded women.

Today, that world has been transformed. Nearly 50 percent of all young people attend college of some kind. Despite persistent poverty among some, the two-car family has become typical, with ribbons of four-lane highways linking regions which forty years ago seemed worlds apart. American foreign policy is premised upon the United States serving as a guardian of American interests everywhere, with hostility to the Soviet Union providing the basis for U.S. involvement in virtually every country of the world. In the 1950s and 1960s, a massive movement of black Americans insisted upon equal justice for the children of all races, and set in motion the most far-reaching drive for social change that America had ever seen. In family life the norm for most households has become two wage earners; women apply in nearly equal numbers with men to many professional schools; and in theory, at least, most Americans subscribe to the value of sex equality. In the midst of all this, Americans had their first experience of losing a war, and their first experience of seeing a president resign in disgrace.

Clearly, not every development since World War II has involved change. Many of the political and social themes discussed in this book have origins that go far back in our history. McCarthyism, for example, bears a strong resemblance to the Red Scare after World War I, the nativism of the 1850s, and the xenophobia of the 1790s. Despite major changes in legislation, black Americans continue to suffer from discrimination based on racism that the law does not correct. Nevertheless, it seems accurate to conclude that the period since 1940 represents a distinctive era in our history, its events shaping to a remarkable degree the lives of those who now prepare to assume leadership roles in the 21st century.

This book represents an effort to come to grips with some of the major themes and issues of the postwar period. Although the material presented occurs in a chronological framework, the organization is thematic. Such issues as the Cold War, civil rights, and changes in sex roles—extending over more than one decade—can best be viewed as a coherent entity, rather than being parceled out according to who was President at a given time. Furthermore, while much of the material presented involves traditional political history, there is also a major emphasis on developments in social history.

The book is structured so that students will have the basis for asking critical questions and arriving at independent judgments on major issues. It is our belief that the best learning occurs when different points of view are presented and individuals have the means for comparison. Consequently, each section of the book contains historical interpretations of a given problem, plus at least one primary document from an involved participant. In this way, we hope that students can achieve understanding of, and empathy with, those who influenced the events being discussed, as well as the retrospective view of scholars.

It is our hope that readers of this volume will come away from it with a new understanding of the developments that have brought us where we are today, as well as sensitivity to the agenda of unresolved questions that confront us as we face the next century. This promises to be one of the most turbulent and exciting eras of world history: It calls for a particularly perceptive understanding of how we have arrived at our contemporary situation.

Durham, N.C.   W.H.C.
Durham, N.H.   H.S.
September 1982

Contents

Part Nine *Where Do We Go from Here?*

A HISTORY OF OUR TIME

Part One

THE SOURCES
OF THE COLD WAR

Probably no event has been more decisive in shaping the world of postwar Americans than the Cold War. Prior to the 1940s, the United States had studiously refrained from involvement in international alliances. World War I represented an exception to that policy. Inspired by the apocalyptic rhetoric of Woodrow Wilson that this would be a war "to end all wars" and to "make the world safe for democracy," Americans had participated with fervor in a European war. But in the aftermath of that experience—particularly the sense of betrayal that wartime ideals were abandoned at Versailles—Americans had retreated again to isolationism.

World War II brought a permanent end to that phenomenon. For reasons of both self-interest and moral commitment, fascism had to be fought. But even as the wartime alliance between Great Britain, the Soviet Union, and the United States successfully attacked Hitler's tyranny, there were questions as to how the postwar world would be organized. Americans had traditionally expressed a bitter hostility toward Bolshevism. Russia, in turn, resented America's refusal to acknowledge the Soviet regime through diplomatic recognition, and believed that western failure to join in a collective pact against Germany prior to 1939 represented a not so subtle effort to make the Soviet government vulnerable to German aggression.

These problems of suspicion and division continued even during the war. Russia bore the brunt of the battle, losing over twenty million lives. A second front in western Europe was crucial to her own survival, and Roosevelt and Churchill repeatedly promised that such a front would be initiated, first in 1942, then in 1943. Resentment that the Normandy invasion did not occur until June

1944 clearly provided an ongoing source of tension. Similarly, Russia and her western allies split over who would control occupation governments in Italy, Rumania, and other conquered territory. Underlying all of these problems was a basic conceptual conflict over the purposes for which the war was being fought. The primary goal of the Soviet Union was security on her borders and control over those governments closest to Russia. The United States, in contrast, articulated the more universalistic principles of the Atlantic Charter, insisting that the war was fought for self-determination, democracy, territorial integrity, and traditional western freedoms. This underlying conflict of sphere of influence versus universalist principles during the war meant conflict over priorities and values in a postwar world.

These problems came to a head over five specific issues. The Polish question—the first—symbolized to both sides the primary purpose for which they had fought the war. A friendly Polish government meant everything to the Soviet Union since, on three occasions, the Polish corridor had been the path through which invasions of Russia had occurred. Self-determination for Poland was also the immediate pretext why Britain had gone to war, and a democratically elected government there represented, in the purest possible form, a test of the principles of the Atlantic Charter. Who would control Poland thus constituted a profound point of contention for both sides. A second issue involved the fate of other occupied nations. American wishes for democratic elections clashed with the division of authority that Churchill and Stalin had agreed upon for Greece, Rumania, and other occupation governments.

The fate of Germany presented a third point of conflict, with the allies divided over reparations from Germany, whether that country should remain industrialized, and whether it should be permanently divided. Control over atomic energy constituted a fourth point of division, with many Russians believing that the U.S. monopoly over atomic weaponry represented an effort to intimidate the world. America, in turn, insisted that only after everyone else had agreed to United States proposals would she turn over control of nuclear secrets. Fifth, and finally, was the conflict over economic reconstruction of Europe, and particularly, whether the United States would provide loans to eastern as well as western Europe for the purpose of rehabilitation. What form

European economies would take was clearly an underlying source of stress.

The following selections address major questions of the origins of the Cold War. Martin Sherwin carefully analyzes the intertwining of atomic bomb policies and diplomatic objectives during the Roosevelt and Truman administrations, and shows how wartime assumptions and decisions contributed to the emergence of the Cold War. Similarly emphasizing the consequences of wartime problems and policies, John Gaddis examines the development of the American strategy of containment toward the Soviet Union and provides a valuable perspective on the inevitability of Cold War conflicts. Clark Clifford, Truman's closest personal aide, summarizes the views of most American foreign policy officials in his confidential memorandum to the President in September 1946. Based largely upon George F. Kennan's diplomatic cables from Moscow, Clifford's report reflects the assumptions behind the steadily developing "get tough" containment policy in Washington.

Students examining this period will want to consider such questions as: Was the Cold War inevitable? If so, what made it a necessity? Were the primary differences ideological? Economic? Political? If the Cold War was not inevitable, how could it have been avoided? Was there room for compromise in eastern Europe along the lines of the Churchill/Stalin agreement? What diplomatic considerations affected the decision to drop the atomic bomb on Japan, and what were the diplomatic consequences of that decision? Would it have made any difference if Roosevelt had lived? Finally, are we perpetual victims of the Cold War, or does there remain any posibility of finding the basis for mutual accommodation?

The Atomic Bomb and the Origins of the Cold War

Martin J. Sherwin

The deaths from incineration and radiation of some 200,000 residents of Hiroshima and Nagasaki in August 1945 dramatically ushered in the atomic age, surely one of the most significant developments in recorded history. Among its more profound consequences, the destruction of these two cities contributed to the origins of the Cold War. The American possession of a monopoly on atomic power and the subsequent effort of Secretary of State James F. Byrnes to practice atomic diplomacy rapidly catalyzed Soviet-American disagreements into an implacable confrontation.

Assessments of the motives behind the decision to drop the bombs have tended to cluster diplomatic historians into opposing camps. Those labeled "traditionalist" or "orthodox" echo Secretary of War Henry L. Stimson's contention that the use of the bomb was militarily necessary to force Japan's surrender as quickly as possible and with the least possible loss of American lives. Contrarily, "revisionists" generally argue that the bombs were not vital to defeating Japan but were utilized to influence Soviet behavior.

Martin J. Sherwin forges a synthesis of these clashing interpretations. In the article from which this selection is excerpted, and in greater detail in his A World Destroyed: The Atomic Bomb and the Grand Alliance (New York, 1975), Sherwin contends that the bombs were dropped to bring a speedy conclusion to the war with Japan, but also that American leaders understood the potential diplomatic value of the bombs and viewed them as a lever against the Soviet Union. He particularly stresses the implications of Franklin D. Roosevelt's wartime atomic policy decisions. The President recognized the bomb both as a legitimate weapon of war against the Axis and as a possible diplomatic weapon against the

Soviet Union. Perhaps most fatefully, Roosevelt permitted the British a junior partnership in the Manhattan Project but totally excluded the Russians.

During the Second World War the atomic bomb was seen and valued as a potential rather than an actual instrument of policy. Responsible officials believed that its impact on diplomacy had to await its development and, perhaps, even a demonstration of its power. As Henry L. Stimson, the secretary of war, observed in his memoirs: "The bomb as a merely probable weapon had seemed a weak reed on which to rely, but the bomb as a colossal reality was very different." That policymakers considered this difference before Hiroshima has been well documented, but whether they based wartime diplomatic policies upon an anticipated successful demonstration of the bomb's power remains a source of controversy. Two questions delineate the issues in this debate. First, did the development of the atomic bomb affect the way American policymakers conducted diplomacy with the Soviet Union? Second, did diplomatic considerations related to the Soviet Union influence the decision to use the atomic bomb against Japan?

These important questions relating the atomic bomb to American diplomacy, and ultimately to the origins of the cold war, have been addressed almost exclusively to the formulation of policy during the early months of the Truman administration. As a result, two anterior questions of equal importance, questions with implications for those already posed, have been overlooked. Did diplomatic considerations related to Soviet postwar behavior influence the formulation of Roosevelt's atomic-energy policies? What effect did the atomic legacy Truman inherited have on the diplomatic and atomic-energy policies of his administration?

To comprehend the nature of the relationship between atomic-energy and diplomatic policies that developed during the war, the bomb must be seen as policy makers saw it before Hiroshima, as a weapon that might be used to control postwar diplomacy. For this task our present view is conceptually inadequate. After more than a quarter century of experience we understand, as wartime policy

From the *American Historical Review*, 78 (October 1973). Reprinted by permission of the author.

makers did not, the bomb's limitations as a diplomatic instrument. To appreciate the profound influence of the unchallenged wartime assumption about the bomb's impact on diplomacy we must recognize the postwar purposes for which policy makers and their advisers believed the bomb could be used. In this effort Churchill's expectations must be scrutinized as carefully as Roosevelt's, and scientists' ideas must be considered along with those of politicians. Truman's decision to use the atomic bomb against Japan must be evaluated in the light of Roosevelt's atomic legacy, and the problems of impending peace must be considered along with the exigencies of war. To isolate the basic atomic-energy policy alternatives that emerged during the war requires that we first ask whether alternatives were, in fact, recognized.

What emerges most clearly from a close examination of wartime formulation of atomic-energy policy is the conclusion that policy makers never seriously questioned the assumption that the atomic bomb should be used against Germany or Japan. From October 9, 1941, the time of the first meeting to organize the atomic-energy project, Stimson, Roosevelt, and other members of the "top policy group" conceived of the development of the atomic bomb as an essential part of the total war effort. Though the suggestion to build the bomb was initially made by scientists who feared Germany might develop the weapon first, those with political responsibility for prosecuting the war accepted the circumstances of the bomb's creation as sufficient justification for its use against any enemy.

Having nurtured this point of view during the war, Stimson charged those who later criticized the use of the bomb with two errors. First, these critics asked the wrong question: it was not whether surrender could have been obtained without using the bomb, but whether a different diplomatic and military course from that followed by the Truman administration would have achieved an earlier surrender. Second, the basic assumption of these critics was false: the idea that American policy should have been based primarily on a desire not to employ the bomb seemed as "irresponsible" as a policy controlled by a positive desire to use it. The war, not the bomb, Stimson argued, had been the primary focus of his attention; as secretary of war his responsibilities permitted no alternative.

Stimson's own wartime diary nevertheless indicates that from

1941 on, the problems associated with the atomic bomb moved steadily closer to the center of his own and Roosevelt's concerns. As the war progressed, the implications of the weapon's development became diplomatic as well as military, postwar as well as wartime. Recognizing that a monopoly of the atomic bomb gave the United States a powerful new military advantage, Roosevelt and Stimson became increasingly anxious to convert it to diplomatic advantage. In December 1944 they spoke of using the "secret" of the atomic bomb as a means of obtaining a *quid pro quo* from the Soviet Union. But viewing the bomb as a potential instrument of diplomacy, they were not moved to formulate a concrete plan for carrying out this exchange before the bomb was used. The bomb had "this unique peculiarity," Stimson noted several months later in his diary; "Success is 99% assured, yet only by the first actual war trial of the weapon can the actual certainty be fixed." Whether or not the specter of postwar Soviet ambitions created "a positive desire" to ascertain the bomb's power, until that decision was executed "atomic diplomacy" remained an idea that never crystallized into policy.

Although Roosevelt left no definitive statement assigning a postwar role to the atomic bomb, his expectations for its potential diplomatic value can be recalled from the existing record. An analysis of the policies he chose from among the alternatives he faced suggests that the potential diplomatic value of the bomb began to shape his atomic-energy policies as early as 1943. He may have been cautious about counting on the bomb as a reality during the war, but he nevertheless consistently chose policy alternatives that would promote the postwar diplomatic potential of the bomb if the predictions of scientists proved true. These policies were based on the assumption that the bomb could be used effectively to secure postwar diplomatic aims; and this assumption was carried over from the Roosevelt to the Truman administration.

Despite general agreement that the bomb would be an extraordinarily important diplomatic factor after the war, those closely associated with its development did not agree on how to use it most effectively as an instrument of diplomacy. Convinced that wartime atomic-energy policies would have postwar consequences, several scientists advised Roosevelt to adopt policies aimed at achieving a postwar international control system. Churchill, on the other hand, urged the president to maintain the Anglo-American atomic monopoly as a diplomatic counter against the postwar ambitions of other nations—particularly against the Soviet Union. Roosevelt fashioned his atomic-energy policies from the choices he made between these conflicting recommendations. In 1943 he rejected the counsel of his science advisers and began to consider the diplomatic component of atomic-energy policy in consultation with Churchill alone. This decision-making procedure and Roosevelt's untimely death have left his motives ambiguous. Nevertheless it is clear that he pursued policies consistent with Churchill's monopolistic, anti-Soviet views.

The findings of this study thus raise serious questions concerning generalizations historians have commonly made about Roosevelt's diplomacy: that it was consistent with his public reputation for cooperation and conciliation; that he was naive with respect to postwar Soviet behavior; that, like Wilson, he believed in collective security as an effective guarantor of national safety; and that he made every possible effort to assure that the Soviet Union and its allies would continue to function as postwar partners. Although this article does not dispute the view that Roosevelt desired amicable postwar relations with the Soviet Union, or even that he worked hard to achieve them, it does suggest that historians have exaggerated his confidence in (and perhaps his commitment to) such an outcome. His most secret and among his most important long-range decisions—those responsible for prescribing a diplomatic role for the atomic bomb—reflected his lack of confidence. Finally, in light of this study's conclusions, the widely held assumption that Truman's attitude toward the atomic bomb was substantially different from Roosevelt's must also be revised.

Like the grand alliance itself, the Anglo-American atomic-energy partnership was forged by the war and its exigencies. The threat of a German atomic bomb precipitated a hasty marriage of convenience between British research and American resources. When scientists in Britain proposed a theory that explained how an atomic bomb might quickly be built, policymakers had to assume that German scientists were building one. "If such an explosive were made," Vannevar Bush, the director of the Office of Scientific Research and Development, told Roosevelt in July 1941, "it would be thousands of times more powerful than existing explosives, and its use might be determining." Roosevelt assumed nothing less. Even before the atomic-energy project was fully organized he assigned it the highest priority. He wanted the program "pushed not only in regard to development, but also with due regard to time. This is very much of the essence," he told Bush in March 1942. "We both felt painfully the dangers of doing nothing," Churchill recalled, referring to an early wartime discussion with Roosevelt about the bomb.

The high stakes at issue during the war did not prevent officials in Great Britain or the United States from considering the postwar implications of their atomic-energy decisions. . . .

It can be argued that Roosevelt, the political pragmatist, renewed the wartime atomic-energy partnership to keep relations with the British harmonious rather than disrupt them on the basis of a postwar issue. Indeed it seems logical that the president took this consideration into account. But it must also be recognized that he was perfectly comfortable with the concept Churchill advocated—that military power was a prerequisite to successful postwar diplomacy. As early as August 1941, during the Atlantic Conference, Roosevelt had rejected the idea that an "effective international organization" could be relied upon to keep the peace; an Anglo-American international police force would be far more effective, he told Churchill. By the spring of 1942 the concept had broadened: the two "policemen" became four, and the idea was added that every other nation would be totally disarmed. "The Four Policemen" would have "to build up a reservoir of force so powerful that no aggressor would dare to challenge it," Roosevelt told Arthur Sweetser, an ardent internationalist. Violators first would be quarantined, and, if they persisted in their disruptive activities, bombed at the rate of a city a day until they agreed to behave. The president told Molotov about this idea in May, and in November he repeated it to Clark Eichelberger, who was coordinating the activities of the American internationalists. A year later, at the Teheran Conference, Roosevelt again discussed his idea, this time with Stalin. As Robert A. Divine has noted: "Roosevelt's concept of big power domination remained the central idea in his approach to international organization throughout World War II."

Precisely how Roosevelt expected to integrate the atomic bomb into his plans for keeping the peace in the postwar world is not clear. However, against the background of his atomic-energy policy decisions of 1943 and his peace-keeping concepts, his actions in 1944 suggest that he intended to take full advantage of the bomb's potential as a postwar instrument of Anglo-American diplomacy. If Roosevelt thought the bomb could be used to create a more peaceful world order, he seems to have considered the threat of its power more effective than any opportunities it offered for international cooperation. If Roosevelt was less worried than Churchill about Soviet postwar ambitions, he was no less determined than the prime minister to avoid any commitments to the Soviets for the international control of atomic energy. There could still be four policemen, but only two of them would have the bomb.

Harry S. Truman inherited a set of military and diplomatic atomic-energy policies that included partially formulated intentions, several commitments to Churchill, and the assumption that the bomb would be a legitimate weapon to be used against Japan. But no policy was definitely settled. According to the Quebec Agreement the president had the option of deciding the future of the commercial aspects of the atomic-energy partnership according to his own estimate of what was fair. Although the policy of "utmost secrecy" had been confirmed at Hyde Park the previous September, Roosevelt had not informed his atomic-energy advisers about the *aide-mémoire* he and Churchill signed. Although the assumption that the bomb would be used in the war was shared by those privy to its development, assumptions formulated early in the war were not necessarily valid at its conclusion. Yet Truman was bound to the past by his own uncertain position and by the prestige of his predecessor. Since Roosevelt had refused to open negotiations with the Soviet government for the international control of atomic energy, and since he had never expressed any objection to the wartime use of the bomb, it would have required considerable political courage and confidence for Truman to alter these policies. Moreover it would have required the encouragement of his advisers, for under the circumstances the most serious constraint on the new president's choices was his dependence upon advice. So Truman's atomic legacy, while it included several options, did not necessarily entail complete freedom to choose from among all the possible alternatives.

"I think it is very important that I should have a talk with you as soon as possible on a highly secret matter," Stimson wrote to Truman on April 24. It has "such a bearing on our present foreign relations and has such an important effect upon all my thinking in this field that I think you ought to know about it without further delay." Stimson had been preparing to brief Truman on the atomic bomb for almost ten days, but in the preceding twenty-four hours he had been seized by a sense of urgency. Relations with the Soviet Union had declined precipitously during the past week, the result, he thought, of the failure of the State Department to settle the major problems between the Allies before going ahead with the San Francisco Conference on the United Nations Organization. The secretary of state, Edward R. Stettinius, Jr., along with the department's Soviet specialists, now felt "compelled to bull the thing through." To get out of the "mess" they had created, Stimson wrote in his diary, they were urging Truman to get tough with the Russians. He had. Twenty-four hours earlier the president met with the Soviet foreign minister, V. M. Molotov, and "with rather brutal frankness" accused his government of breaking the Yalta Agreement. Molotov was furious. "I have never been talked to like that in my life," he told the president before leaving.

With a memorandum on the "political aspects of the S-1 [atomic bomb's] performance" in hand and General Groves in reserve, Stimson went to the White House on April 25. The document he carried was the distillation of numerous decisions already taken, each one the product of attitudes that developed along with the new weapon. The secretary himself was not entirely aware of how various forces had shaped these decisions: the recommendations of Bush and Conant, the policies Roosevelt had followed, the uncertainties inherent in the wartime alliance, the oppressive concern for secrecy, and his own inclination to consider long-range implications. It was a curious document. Though its language revealed Stimson's sensitivity to the historic significance of the atomic bomb, he did not question the wisdom of using it against Japan. Nor did he suggest any concrete steps for developing a postwar policy. His objective was to inform Truman

of the salient problems: the possibility of an atomic arms race, the
danger of atomic war, and the necessity for international control
if the United Nations Organization was to work. "If the problem
of the proper use of this weapon can be solved," he wrote, "we
would have the opportunity to bring the world into a pattern in
which the peace of the world and our civilizations can be saved."
To cope with this difficult challenge Stimson suggested the "establishment of a select committee" to consider the postwar problems
inherent in the development of the bomb. If his presentation was
the "forceful statement" of the problem that historians of the
Atomic Energy Commission have described it as being, its force
inhered in the problem itself, not in any bold formulations or
initiatives he offered toward a solution. If, as another historian
has claimed, this meeting led to a "strategy of delayed showdown," requiring "the delay of all disputes with Russia until the
atomic bomb had been demonstrated," there is no evidence in the
extant records of the meeting that Stimson had such a strategy in
mind or that Truman misunderstood the secretary's views.

What emerges from a careful reading of Stimson's diary, his
memorandum of April 25 to Truman, a summary by Groves of
the meeting, and Truman's recollections is an argument for over-
all caution in Amercan diplomatic relations with the Soviet Union:
it was an argument against any showdown. Since the atomic bomb
was potentially the most dangerous issue facing the postwar world
and since the most desirable resolution of the problem was some
form of international control, Soviet cooperation had to be secured. It was imprudent, Stimson suggested, to pursue a policy
that would preclude the possibility of international cooperation on
atomic-energy matters after the war ended. Truman's overall impression of Stimson's argument was that the secretary of war was
"at least as much concerned with the role of the atomic bomb in
the shaping of history as in its capacity to shorten the war." These
were indeed Stimson's dual concerns on April 25, and he could
see no conflict between them.

Despite the profound consequences Stimson attributed to the
development of the new weapon, he had not suggested that Truman reconsider its use against Japan. Nor had he thought to
mention the possibility that chances of securing Soviet postwar
cooperation might be diminished if Stalin did not receive a commitment to international control prior to an attack. The question

of why these alternatives were overlooked naturally arises. Perhaps what Frankfurter once referred to as Stimson's habit of setting "his mind at one thing like the needle of an old victrola caught in a single groove" may help to explain his not mentioning these possibilities. Yet Bush and Conant never raised them either. Even Niels Bohr had made a clear distinction between the bomb's wartime use and its postwar impact on diplomacy. "What role it [the atomic bomb] may play in the present war," Bohr had written to Roosevelt in July 1944, was a question "quite apart" from the overriding concern: the need to avoid an atomic arms race.

The preoccupation with winning the war obviously helped to create this seeming dichotomy between the wartime use of the bomb and the potential postwar diplomatic problems with the Soviet Union raised by its development. But a closer look at how Bohr and Stimson each defined the nature of the diplomatic problem created by the bomb suggests that for the secretary of war and his advisers (and ultimately for the president they advised) there was no dichotomy at all. Bohr apprehended the meaning of the new weapon even before it was developed, and he had no doubt that scientists in the Soviet Union would also understand its profound implications for the postwar world. He was also certain that they would interpret the meaning of the development to Stalin just as scientists in the United States and Great Britain had explained it to Roosevelt and Churchill. Thus the diplomatic problem, as Bohr analyzed it, was not the need to convince Stalin that the atomic bomb was an unprecedented weapon that threatened the life of the world but the need to assure the Soviet leader that he had nothing to fear from the circumstances of its development. By informing Stalin during the war that the United States intended to co-operate with him in neutralizing the bomb through international control, Bohr reasoned that its wartime use could be considered apart from postwar problems.

Stimson approached the problem rather differently. Although he believed that the bomb "might even mean the doom of civilization or it might mean the perfection of civilization" he was less confident than Bohr that the weapon in an undeveloped state could be used as an effective instrument of diplomacy. Until its "actual certainty [was] fixed," Stimson considered any prior approach to Stalin as premature. But as the uncertainties of impending peace became more apparent and worrisome, Stimson,

Truman, and the secretary of state-designate, James F. Byrnes, began to think of the bomb as something of a diplomatic panacea for their postwar problems. Byrnes had told Truman in April that the bomb "might well put us in a position to dictate our own terms at the end of the war." By June, Truman and Stimson were discussing "further *quid pro quos* which should be established in consideration for our taking them [the Soviet Union] into [atomic-energy] partnership." Assuming that the bomb's impact on diplomacy would be immediate and extraordinary, they agreed on no less than "the settlement of the Polish, Rumanian, Yugoslavian, and Manchurian problems." But they also concluded that no revelation would be made "to Russia or anyone else until the first bomb had been successfully laid on Japan." Truman and Stimson based their expectations on how they saw and valued the bomb; its use against Japan, they reasoned, would transfer this view to the Soviet Union.

Was an implicit warning to Moscow, then, the principal reason for deciding to use the atomic bomb against Japan? In light of the ambiguity of the available evidence the question defies an unequivocal answer. What can be said with certainty is that Truman, Stimson, Byrnes, and several others involved in the decision consciously considered two effects of a combat demonstration of the bomb's power: first, the impact of the atomic attack on Japan's leaders, who might be persuaded thereby to end the war, and second, the impact of that attack on the Soviet Union's leaders, who might then prove to be more cooperative. But if the assumption that the bomb might bring the war to a rapid conclusion was the principal motive for using the atomic bomb, the expectation that its use would also inhibit Soviet diplomatic ambitions clearly discouraged any inclination to question that assumption. . . .

Thus by the end of the war the most influential and widely accepted attitude toward the bomb was a logical extension of how the weapon was seen and valued earlier—as a potential instrument of diplomacy. Caught between the remnants of war and the uncertainties of peace, scientists as well as policy makers were trapped by the logic of their own unquestioned assumptions. By the summer of 1945 not only the conclusion of the war but the organization of an acceptable peace seemed to depend upon the success of the atomic attacks against Japan. When news of the successful atomic test of July 16 reached the president at the

Potsdam Conference, he was visibly elated. Stimson noted that
Truman "was tremendously pepped up by it and spoke to me of it
again when I saw him. He said it gave him an entirely new feeling
of confidence." The day after receiving the complete report of the
test Truman altered his negotiating style. According to Churchill
the president "got to the meeting after having read this report
[and] he was a changed man. He told the Russians just where they
got on and off and generally bossed the whole meeting." After the
plenary session on July 24 Truman "casually mentioned to Stalin"
that the United States had "a new weapon of unusual destructive
force." Truman took this step in response to a recommendation
by the Interim Committee, a group of political and scientific advisers organized by Stimson in May 1945 to advise the president
on atomic-energy policy. But it is an unavoidable conclusion that
what the president told the premier followed the letter of the
recommendation rather than its spirit, which embodied the hope
that an overture to Stalin would initiate the process toward international control. In less than three weeks the new weapon's destructive potential would be demonstrated to the world. Stalin
would then be forced to reconsider his diplomatic goals. It is no
wonder that upon learning of the raid against Hiroshima Truman
exclaimed: "This is the greatest thing in history."

As Stimson had expected, as a colossal reality the bomb was
very different. But had American diplomacy been altered by it?
Those who conducted diplomacy became more confident, more
certain that through the accomplishments of American science,
technology, and industry the "new world" could be made into one
better than the old. But just how the atomic bomb would be used
to help accomplish this ideal remained unclear. Three months
and one day after Hiroshima was bombed Bush wrote that the
whole matter of international relations on atomic energy "is in a
thoroughly chaotic condition." The wartime relationship between
atomic-energy policy and diplomacy had been based upon the
simple assumption that the Soviet government would surrender
important geographical, political, and ideological objectives in exchange for the neutralization of the new weapon. As a result of
policies based on this assumption American diplomacy and prestige suffered grievously: an opportunity to gauge the Soviet
Union's response during the war to the international control of
atomic energy was missed, and an atomic-energy policy for deal-

ing with the Soviet government after the war was ignored. Instead of promoting American postwar aims, wartime atomic-energy policies made them more difficult to achieve. As a group of scientists at the University of Chicago's atomic-energy laboratory presciently warned the government in June 1945: "It may be difficult to persuade the world that a nation which was capable of secretly preparing and suddenly releasing a weapon as indiscriminate as the [German] rocket bomb and a million times more destructive, is to be trusted in its proclaimed desire of having such weapons abolished by international agreement." This reasoning, however, flowed from alternative assumptions formulated during the closing months of the war by scientists far removed from the wartime policy-making process. Hiroshima and Nagasaki, the culmination of that process, became the symbols of a new American barbarism, reinforcing charges, with dramatic circumstantial evidence, that the policies of the United States contributed to the origins of the cold war.

Containment Before Kennan

John Lewis Gaddis

Similar to the conflicting interpretations of the decision to drop the atomic bombs, the historical debate on the causes of the Cold War has largely followed the disagreements voiced by the leading actors in the drama. Whether stressing Communist ideology, Russian expansionism, Soviet totalitarianism, or Stalin's paranoia, "traditionalists" tend to restate the official explanations of the Truman Administration. They place responsibility for the conflict squarely in Moscow and suggest that the United States did only what was prudent and necessary in the face of Soviet aggression and intransigence. Heeding the criticism of such Administration foes as Walter Lippmann and Henry Wallace, most "revisionists" focus on the rigidity of American policy, its rejection of legitimate Soviet needs, and its hypocritical employment of a double standard of international behavior. While they differ on the selective importance of various cultural, economic, personal, and political determinants, "revisionists" largely agree that the United States sought to use its overwhelming power after the Second World War to establish a Pax Americana.

Like Sherwin, John Lewis Gaddis in this selection seeks to circumvent the simplistic dualism of this debate on Cold War origins. His interpretation synthesizes what is best in the opposing arguments. Moreover, Gaddis also strongly emphasizes the consequences of wartime decisions and developments. Rather than seeking to apportion or assign "blame," he depicts an intricate web of interrelated phenomena over an extended period of time. After reading the selection one may well reflect on the implications of a theory of historical inevitability, on how to assign weight to assorted causative factors, and on what it means to seek the "origin" of an historical event.

Excerpted from *Strategies of Containment: A Critical Appraisal of Postwar American National Security Policy* by John Lewis Gaddis. Copyright © 1982 by Oxford University Press, Inc. Reprinted by permission.

Footnotes omitted.

"My children, it is permitted you in time of grave danger to walk with the devil until you have crossed the bridge." It was Franklin D. Roosevelt's version of an old Balkan proverb (sanctioned by the Orthodox Church, no less), and he liked to cite it from time to time during World War II to explain the use of questionable allies to achieve unquestionable objectives. In all-out war, he believed, the ultimate end—victory—justified a certain broad-mindedness regarding means, nowhere more so than in reliance on Stalin's Russia to help defeat Germany and Japan. Allies of any kind were welcome enough in London and Washington during the summer of 1941; still the Soviet Union's sudden appearance in that capacity could not avoid setting off Faustian musings in both capitals. Winston Churchill's willingness to extend measured parliamentary accolades to the Devil if Hitler should invade Hell is well-known; less familiar is Roosevelt's paraphrase of his proverb to an old friend, Joseph Davies: "I can't take communism nor can you, but to cross this bridge I would hold hands with the Devil."

The imagery, in the light of subsequent events, was apt. Collaboration with the Soviet Mephistopheles helped the United States and Great Britain achieve victory over their enemies in a remarkably short time and with surprisingly few casualties, given the extent of the fighting involved. The price, though, was the rise of an even more powerful and less fathomable totalitarian state, and, as a consequence, an apparently perpetual condition of precarious uncertainty that has now many times outlasted the brief and uneasy alliance that brought it about.

"Containment," the term generally used to characterize American policy toward the Soviet Union during the postwar era, can be seen as a series of attempts to deal with the consequences of the World War II Faustian bargain: the idea has been to prevent the Soviet Union from using the power and position it won as a result of that conflict to reshape the postwar international order, a prospect that has seemed, in the West, no less dangerous than what Germany or Japan might have done had they had the chance. George F. Kennan coined the term in July 1947, when he called publicly for a "long-term, patient but firm and vigilant containment of Russian expansive tendencies," but it would be an injustice to wartime policy-makers to imply, as has too often been done, that they were oblivious to the problem. In fact, "containment" was much on the minds of Washington officials from 1941

on; the difficulty was to mesh that long-term concern with the
more immediate imperative of defeating the Axis. What Roosevelt, Truman, and their advisers sought was a way to win the war
without compromising the objectives for which it was being
fought; it was out of their successive failures to square that circle
that Kennan's concept of "containment" eventually emerged.

One way to have resolved the dilemma would have been to devise
military operations capable of containing the Russians while at the
same time enlisting their help to the extent necessary to subdue
the Axis. Truman himself had suggested a crude way of doing
this after Hitler attacked the Soviet Union in June 1941: "If we
see that Germany is winning the war we ought to help Russia, and
if Russia is winning we ought to help Germany and in that way let
them kill as many as possible." But Truman at the time was an
obscure Missouri senator; his somewhat brutal flash of geopolitical cynicism attracted little attention until he unexpectedly entered the White House four years later. By that time, and with
increasing frequency in the months that followed, questions were
being raised as to whether the United States had not in fact relied
on the Russians too heavily to defeat the Germans too thoroughly.
William C. Bullitt, former ambassador to the Soviet Union and
now one of its most vociferous critics, said it best in a 1948 *Life*
magazine article entitled: "How We Won the War and Lost the
Peace."

Bullitt himself had advocated an alternative strategy five years
earlier in a series of top secret memoranda to Roosevelt. Stalin's
war aims were not those of the West, he had insisted: those who
argued that participation in an anti-fascist coalition had purged
the Soviet dictator of his autocratic and expansionist tendencies
were assuming, on the basis of no evidence, a conversion "as striking as [that] of Saul on the road to Damascus." The fact was that a
Europe controlled from Moscow would be as dangerous as one
ruled from Berlin, and yet "if Germany is to be defeated without
such cost in American and British lives that victory might well
prove to be a concealed defeat (like the French victory in the war
of 1914), the continued participation of the Red Army in the war
against Germany is essential." The problem, then, was to prevent
"the domination of Europe by the Moscow dictatorship without

losing the participation of the Red Army in the war against the Nazi dictatorship." Bullitt's answer, put forward long before Winston Churchill had explicitly advocated a similar but better-known solution, was to introduce Anglo-American forces into Eastern Europe and the Balkans, for the purpose, first, of defeating the Germans, but second, to bar the Red Army from Europe. "War is an attempt to achieve political objectives by fighting," he reminded Roosevelt in August 1943, "and political objectives must be kept in mind in planning operations."

There are hints that Roosevelt did, from time to time, consider using military forces to achieve something like the political results Bullitt had in mind. The President showed more than polite interest in Churchill's subsequent schemes for Anglo-American military operations in the Balkans, despite the horrified reactions of Secretary of War Henry Stimson and the Joint Chiefs of Staff. He emphasized, at least twice in 1943, the need to get to Berlin as soon as the Russians did in the event of a sudden German collapse. And in April 1945, less than a week before his death, he countered Churchill's complaints about Soviet behavior by pointing out that "our armies will in a very few days be in a position that will permit us to become 'tougher' than has heretofore appeared advantageous to the war effort."

But Roosevelt generally resisted efforts to deploy forces for the dual purposes of defeating the Germans and containing the Russians. He did not do this, though, in a geopolitical vacuum: there were, in his mind, powerful reasons other than a single-minded concentration on victory for holding hands with the Devil to cross the bridge.

One had to do with Roosevelt's conception of the balance of power. American security, he thought, lay chiefly in preventing the coming together of potentially hostile states. He had extended diplomatic recognition to the Soviet Union in 1933 partly to counter-balance, and attempt to keep separate, the growing military power of Germany and Japan. When the Kremlin backed out of that role in 1939, F.D.R., sensitive to the unnatural character of the Nazi-Soviet alignment, carefully left the way open for an eventual reconciliation with Moscow, despite his intense personal revulsion at the Russians' behavior. He moved swiftly when the events of June 1941 made it possible to reconstitute his strategy, even though collaboration with Russia was more difficult to sell in a still ostensibly neutral United States than in embattled England. After Pearl Harbor, one of his persistent concerns was to prevent any new "deal" between Hitler and Stalin, and simultaneously to secure the latter's cooperation in the war against Japan. The geo-political requirements of keeping adversaries divided, therefore, constituted one powerful argument against military deployments directed against Russia as well as Germany.

Coupled with this was an appreciation of the nature of American power. Roosevelt was an early and firm believer in the "arsenal of democracy" concept—the idea that the United States could most effectively contribute toward the maintenance of international order by expending technology but not manpower. Long before Pearl Harbor, he had sought to enlist the productive energies of American industry in the anti-fascist cause: the United States, he thought, should serve as a kind of privileged sanctuary, taking advantage of its geographical isolation and invulnerable physical plant to produce the goods of war, leaving others to furnish the troops required to fight it. Even after active belligerency became unavoidable, Roosevelt and his chief military strategist, General George C. Marshall, retained elements of the earlier approach, limiting the American army to 90 divisions instead of the 215 that had been thought necessary to defeat both Germany and Japan. As Marshall admitted, though, it could not have been done without Soviet manpower. The United States, in this sense, was as dependent on the Red Army as the Russians were on American Lend-Lease—perhaps more so. That fact, too, precluded military operations aimed at containing the Russians while defeating the Germans.

There was yet a third consideration involved, most often attributed to Churchill but very much present in Roosevelt's mind as well: the need to minimize casualties. Averell Harriman has best summarized the President's concern in this regard:

> Roosevelt was very much affected by World War I, which he had, of course, seen at close range. He had a horror of American troops landing again on the continent and becoming involved in the kind of warfare he had seen before—trench warfare with all its appalling losses. I believe he had in mind that if the great armies of Russia could stand up to the Germans, this might well make it possible for us to limit our participation largely to naval and air power.

The United States was new at the business of being a world power, Roosevelt must have reasoned. If the sacrifices involved became too great, especially in a war in which its own territory did not seem directly threatened, then pressures for a reversion to a "fortress America" concept, if not outright isolationism, might still prevail. Letting allies bear the brunt of casualties was a way of ensuring internationalism for the future.

Finally, there was the fact that the United States had another war to wage in the Far East—one in which it was bearing a far heavier share of the burden than in Europe. To be sure, American strategy, even before Pearl Harbor, had been to defeat Germany first. But Roosevelt recognized that support for a major effort against Germany required progress in the war against Japan as well: the American people would not tolerate indefinite defeats in the Pacific while arming to cross the Atlantic. Hence, F.D.R.'s strategy evolved by subtle stages into one of taking on Germany and Japan at the same time; the war in the Pacific became more than just the holding action that had originally been planned. The effects were benefcial in one sense: few would have anticipated that wars against both Germany and Japan could have been brought to roughly simultaneous conclusions with so few casualties. But the price, again, was reliance on Soviet manpower to carry the main burden of the struggle in Europe; had the atomic bomb not worked, the Russians might have been called upon to play a similar role in the Far East as well after Germany's surrender.

It will not do, then, to see Roosevelt's strategy as totally insulated from political considerations. A war plan aimed at making careful use of American resources to maintain a global balance of power without at the same time disrupting the fabric of American society hardly fits that characterization. It is true that Roosevelt did not orient wartime strategy toward the coming Cold War—he foresaw that possibility, but hoped, indeed trusted, that it would not arise. Instead he concentrated on winning the war the United States was in at the time as quickly as possible and at the least possible cost. Given those objectives, it would be hard to have improved on the strategy Roosevelt actually followed.

It is interesting, as a corrective to those who have criticized Roosevelt for ignoring political considerations, to see how Soviet scholars view his conduct of the war. The emphasis here is on the

wholly political nature of his strategy: one recent account even has
it that F.D.R. in fact adopted Truman's 1941 recommendation to
let Russians and Germans kill each other off. Certainly, on the
basis of statistical indices, this would appear to have been the
effect: for every American who died in the war, fifteen Germans
and fifty-three Russians died. It is worth asking whether something like this might not have been a crafty way of ensuring both
full Russian participation in the war and the postwar containment
of the Soviet Union, not by denying that country territory or
resources, but by forcing it to exhaust itself?

With the elusive Roosevelt, one can never be sure. Few statesmen guarded their own counsel more jealously than the decep-
tively loquacious F.D.R.; if this had been his strategy, it is unlikely
that he would have told anyone about it. There is, though, a more
plausible and less sinister explanation. To have done what the
Russians wanted—create an early second front—or what his domestic critics wanted—deploy forces against both Russians and
Germans—would have violated Roosevelt's fundamental aversion
to the use of American manpower to bring about major geopolitical shifts in world affairs. The President fully intended to have an
impact, but he sought to do it in such a way as to neither demoral-
ize nor debilitate the nation. In short, he wanted to keep means
from corrupting ends. It is easy to write off this approach as
naive, as some of Roosevelt's American detractors have done, or
as self-serving, as the Russians have done. What seems more probable, though, is that Roosevelt's strategy reflected the rational balance of objectives and resources any wise statesman will try to
achieve, *if he can*. It was Stalin's misfortune, largely as a result of
his errors of strategy between 1939 and 1941, to have denied
himself that opportunity.

Another reason for doubting that Roosevelt set out deliberately to
contain the Russians by exhausting them is that his postwar plans
seemed to lean in a wholly different direction—that of containment by integration. F.D.R. sought to ensure a stable postwar
order by offering Moscow a prominent place in it; by making it,
so to speak, a member of the club. The assumption here—and it is
a critical one for understanding Roosevelt's policy—was that Soviet hostility stemmed from insecurity, but that the sources of that
insecurity were external. They lay, the President thought, in the

threats posed by Germany and Japan, in the West's long-standing aversion to Bolshevism, and in the refusal, accordingly, of much of the rest of the world to grant the Russians their legitimate position in international affairs. "They didn't know us, that's the really fundamental difference," he commented in 1944. "They are friendly people. They haven't got any crazy ideas of conquest, and so forth; and now that they have got to know us, they are much more willing to accept us." With the defeat of the Axis, with the West's willingness to make the Soviet Union a full partner in shaping the peace to come, the reasons for Stalin's suspicions, Roosevelt expected, would gradually drop away.

The President had never seen in the ideological orientation of the Soviet state a reason not to have cooperative relations at the interstate level. As a liberal, he lacked the visceral horror with which American conservatives regarded the use of state authority to bring about social change. As a self-confident patrician, he discounted the appeal communism might have inside the United States. As a defender of the international balance of power, he distinguished between fascism's reliance on force to achieve its objectives, and what he saw as communism's less dangerous use of subversion and propaganda. But, most important, as an intelligent observer of the international scene, he recognized the significance of a trend in the evolution of the Soviet state many experts on that country were only beginning to grasp: the fact that considerations of national interest had come to overshadow those of ideology in determining Stalin's behavior.

It was within this context that Roosevelt developed his idea of integrating the Soviet Union into a postwar security structure. F.D.R. had long advocated some form of great-power condominium to maintain world order. He was, it has been argued, a "renegade Wilsonian," seeking Wilson's goals by un-Wilsonian means. Chief among these was his conviction that the peace-loving states should band together to deter aggression, first by isolating the perpetrators, and then, if necessary, by using force against them. As early as 1935, Roosevelt had begun talking about an arrangement along those lines to blockade Nazi Germany; two years later he was proposing similarly vague plans for collective resistance against Japan. Nothing came of either initiative, but it is worth noting that Roosevelt had counted on the Soviet Union's cooperation in both of them. It was not too surprising, then, that after June 1941, when Moscow was again in a position to cooperate with the West, F.D.R. should have revived his plan, this time in the form of the "Four Policemen"—the United States, Great Britain, the Soviet Union, and China—who would, as the President described it, impose order on the rest of the postwar world, bombing anyone who would not go along.

The "Four Policemen" concept, it has been argued, reflected an unrealistic assumption on Roosevelt's part that the great powers would always agree, an expectation that seemed painfully at odds with the obviously antagonistic nature of the international system. Again, though, surface manifestations were deceiving. "When there [are] four people sitting in a poker game and three of them [are] against the fourth," F.D.R. told Henry Wallace late in 1942, "it is a little hard on the fourth." Wallace took this to mean the possibility of American, Russian, and Chinese pressures against the British, and indeed the President did make efforts subsequently to impress both Stalin and Chiang Kai-shek with his own anti-imperial aspirations. But Roosevelt was telling others, at roughly the same time, that he needed China as one of the "Four Policemen" to counter-balance Russia. And certainly Churchill, without even being asked, could have been counted upon to join in any such enterprise, should it have become necessary. The picture is hardly one of anticipating harmony, therefore; rather, it is reminiscent, as much as anything else, of Bismarck's cold-blooded tactic of keeping potential rivals off balance by preventing them from aligning with each other.

It is also the case that Roosevelt was not above using what a later generation would call "linkage" to ensure compliance with American postwar aims. His employment of economic and political pressure to speed the dismantling of the British Empire has recently been thoroughly documented. No comparably blatant requirements were imposed on the Russians, probably because Roosevelt feared that the relationship, unlike the one with London, was too delicate to stand the strain. Still, he did keep certain cards up his sleeve for dealing with Moscow after the war, notably the prospect of reconstruction assistance either through Lend-Lease or a postwar loan, together with a generous flow of reparations from Western-occupied Germany, all of which Washington would have been able to control in the light of Soviet behavior. Also, intriguingly, there was Roosevelt's refusal, even after learning they knew of it, to tell the Russians about the atomic bomb, perhaps with a view to postwar bargaining. This combination of counter-weights and linkages is not what one would expect from a statesman assuming a blissfully serene postwar environment: although Roosevelt certainly hoped for such an outcome, he was too good a poker player to count on it.

But Roosevelt's main emphasis was on trying to make the Grand Alliance survive Hitler's defeat by creating relationships of mutual trust among its leaders. The focus of his concern—and indeed the only allied leader not already in some position of dependency on the United States—was Stalin. F.D.R. has been criticized for thinking that he could use his personal charm to "get through" to the Soviet autocrat, whose resistance to such blandishments was legendary. But, as with so much of Roosevelt's diplomacy, what seems at first shallow and superficial becomes less so upon reflection. The President realized that Stalin was the only man in the Soviet Union with the authority to modify past attitudes of hostility; however discouraging the prospect of "getting through," there was little point in dealing with anyone below him. . . .

Like any statesman, though, Roosevelt was pursuing multiple objectives; building a friendly peacetime relationship with the Soviet Union was only one of them. As often happens, other priorities got in the way. For example, Roosevelt's second front strategy, designed not so much to weaken Russia as to avoid weakening the United States, could not help but create suspicions in Moscow that Washington was in fact seeking containment by exhaustion. These dark misgivings survived even the D-Day landings: as late as April 1945 Stalin was warning subordinates that the Americans and British might yet make common cause with the Germans; that same month the Red Army began constructing *defensive* installations in Central Europe.

Another of Roosevelt's priorities was to win domestic support for his postwar plans, and thereby to avoid Wilson's repudiation of 1919–1920. To do this, he became convinced of the need to moderate his own somewhat harsh approach to the task of peacekeeping: the country was not ready, Speaker of the House Sam Rayburn told him late in 1942, for a settlement to be enforced through blockades and bombing. Roosevelt sought, accordingly, to integrate the great power condominium his strategic instincts told him would be necessary to preserve world order, on the one hand, with the ideals his political instincts told him would be necessary at home to overcome objections to an "unjust" peace, on the other. Idealism, in Roosevelt's mind, could serve eminently realistic ends.

It would be a mistake, then, to write off Roosevelt's concern for self-determination in Eastern Europe as mere window-dressing. Although prepared to see that part of the world fall within Moscow's sphere of influence, he expected as well that as fears of Germany subsided, the Russians would moderate the severity of measures needed to maintain their position there. Otherwise, he was convinced, it would be impossible to "sell" the resulting settlement to the American people. But, like Henry Kissinger in somewhat different circumstances thirty years later, Roosevelt thus found himself in a situation in which domestic support for what he had negotiated depended upon the exercise of discretion and restraint in the Kremlin. Those tendencies were no more prevalent then than later; as a consequence, a gap developed between what F.D.R. thought the public would tolerate and what the Russians would accept—a gap papered over, at Yalta, by fragile compromises.

Competing priorities therefore undercut Roosevelt's efforts to win Stalin's trust: to that extent, his strategy was flawed. And even if that had not happened, there is reason to wonder whether F.D.R.'s approach would have worked in any event, given the balefully suspicious personality of the Soviet autocrat. But there are, at times, justifications for directing flawed strategies at inauspicious targets, and World War II may have been one of these. Certainly alternatives to the policies actually followed contained difficulties as well. And there are grounds for thinking that Roosevelt might not have continued his open-handed approach once the war had ended: his quiet incorporation of counter-weights and linkages into his strategy suggests just that possibility. One is left, then, where one began: with the surface impression of casual, even frivolous, superficiality, and yet with the growing realization that darker, more cynical, but more perceptive instincts lay not far beneath.

Whatever Roosevelt's intentions were for after the war, though, dissatisfaction with the strategy he was following during it had become widespread within the government by the end of 1944. American military chiefs and Lend-Lease administrators resented the Russians' increasingly importunate demands on their limited resources, made with little understanding of supply problems or logistics, and with infrequent expressions of gratitude. Career diplomats had always maintained a certain coolness toward the U.S.S.R.; now, with the State Department excluded by Roosevelt from any significant dealings with that country, they brooded in relative isolation over the gap they saw emerging between Stalin's postwar aims and the principles of the Atlantic Charter. But it was officials with direct experience of service in the Soviet Union who developed the strongest and most influential reservations about Roosevelt's open-handedness. Attempts to win Stalin's trust through generosity and good will would not work, they argued: the Soviet dictator was too apt to confuse those qualities with weakness. What was needed instead was recognition of the fact that the Soviet Union was neither going to leave nor lose the war, and that if its Western allies did not soon begin to apply such leverage as they had available, the Kremlin would shape its own peace settlement, without regard to their aspirations or interests. . . .

F.D.R.'s death cleared the way for a revision of strategy he himself would probably have executed in time, but not in as abrupt and confused a manner as was actually done. Harry S. Truman, totally unbriefed as to what Roosevelt had been trying to do, did the natural thing and consulted the late President's advisers. But those most directly associated with Soviet affairs, notably Harriman, had been trying to stiffen Roosevelt's position; now, with a new and untutored chief executive in the White House, they redoubled their efforts at "education." Eager to appear decisive and in command, Truman accepted this instruction with an alacrity that unsettled even those providing it, lecturing the Soviet foreign minister in person, and his distant master by cable, in a manner far removed from the graceful ambiguities of his predecessor. The result was ironic: Truman embraced a *quid pro quo* approach in the belief that he was implementing Roosevelt's policy, but in doing so he convinced the Russians that he had changed it. F.D.R.'s elusiveness continued to bedevil Soviet-American relations even after his death.

In fact (and despite his 1941 remark about letting Germans

and Russians kill each other off), Truman was no more prepared
to abandon the possibility of an accommodation with Moscow
than were Harriman and Deane. He firmly rejected Churchill's
advice to deploy Anglo-American military forces in such a way as
to keep the Russians out of as much of Germany as possible. He
sent Harry Hopkins to Moscow in May of 1945 in part to repair
the damage his own brusqueness had done. Long after relations
with Stalin went sour, he continued to seek the counsel of those
sympathetic to the Soviet Union, notably Henry Wallace and Joseph E. Davies. The new President harbored a healthy skepticism
toward all totalitarian states: ideology, he thought, whether communist or fascist, was simply an excuse for dictatorial rule. But,
like Roosevelt, he did not see totalitarianism in itself as precluding
normal relations. Not surprisingly in the light of his own background, the analogy of big city political bosses in the United States
came most easily to mind: their methods might not be delicate or
fastidious, but one could work with them, so long as they kept
their word.

Truman found a kindred spirit in James F. Byrnes, whom he
appointed Secretary of State shortly after taking office. An individual of vast experience in domestic affairs but almost none in
diplomacy, Byrnes believed in applying to this new realm an assumption that had worked well for him at home: nations, he
thought, like individuals or interest groups, could always reach
agreement on difficult issues if a sufficient willingness to negotiate
and to compromise existed on both sides. A *quid pro quo* strategy
was as natural for Byrnes as for Truman, then; the new Secretary
of State observed that dealing with the Russians was just like dealing with the United States Senate: "You build a post office in their
state and they'll build a post office in our state."

The new administration thought it had leverage over the Russians in several respects. Harriman himself had stressed the importance of postwar reconstruction assistance, which the United
States would be able to control, whether through Lend-Lease, a
rehabilitation loan, or reparations shipments from its occupation
zone in Germany. Roosevelt had been leaning toward use of this
leverage at the time of his death; Truman quickly confirmed that
unconditional aid would not be extended past the end of the
fighting. Lend-Lease would be phased out, and postwar loans and
reparations shipments would be tied, at least implicitly, to future

Soviet political cooperation. Publicity was another form of leverage: the administration assumed that the Kremlin was still sensitive to "world opinion," and that by calling attention openly to
instances of soviet unilateralism, it could get the Russians to back
down. Then there was the ultimate sanction of the atomic bomb:
Byrnes, though not all his colleagues in the administration, apparently believed that the simple presence of this awesome weapon
in the American arsenal would make the Russians more manage-
able than in the past; at a minimum, he wanted to hold back
commitments to seek the international control of atomic energy as
a bargaining chip for use in future negotiations.

But none of these attempts to apply leverage worked out as
planned. The Russians were never dependent enough on American economic aid to make substantial concessions to get it: intelligence reports had long indicated that such aid, if extended, would
have speeded reconstruction by only a matter of months. Another
difficulty was that key Congressmen, whose support would have
been necessary for the passage of any loan, quickly made it clear
that they would demand in return nothing less than free elections
and freedom of speech inside the Soviet Union, and the abandonment of its sphere of influence in Eastern Europe. Publicity, directed against Soviet violations of the Yalta agreements in that part
of the world, produced no greater success: when Byrnes warned
that he might have to make public a report on conditions in Rumania and Bulgaria prepared by the American publisher, Mark
Ethridge, Stalin, with understandable self-confidence, threatened
to have his own "impartial" observer, the Soviet journalist Ilya Eh-
renburg, prepare and release his own report on those countries.
The Russians dealt effectively with the atomic bomb by simply
appearing to ignore it, except for a few heavyhanded cocktail party
jokes by a tipsy Molotov. In the meantime, domestic pressures had
forced Truman to commit the United States to the principle of
international control before Byrnes had even attempted to extract
a *quid pro quo* from Moscow.

By the time of the Moscow foreign ministers' conference in
December 1945, Byrnes had come to much the same conclusion
that Roosevelt had a year earlier: that the only way to reconcile
the American interest in self-determination with the Soviet interest
in security was to negotiate thinly disguised agreements designed
to cloak the reality of Moscow's control behind a facade of demo-

cratic procedures. But that approach, manifested in the form of token concessions by the Russians on Bulgaria and Rumania, came across at home as appeasement: as a result, Byrnes found himself under attack from both the President and Congress, upon his return, for having given up too much. The *quid pro quo* strategy, by early 1946, had not only failed to produce results; it had become a domestic political liability as well.

The *quid pro quo* approach proved unsuccessful for several reasons. One was the difficulty of making "sticks" and "carrots" commensurate with concessions to be demanded from the other side. The "sticks" the United States had available were either unimpressive, as was the case with publicity, or unusable, as in the case of the atomic bomb. The major "carrot," economic aid, was important to the Russians, but not to the point of justifying the concessions that would have been required to obtain it. Another difficulty with the strategy was the problem of coordination. Bargaining implies the ability to control precisely the combination of pressures and inducements to be applied, but that in turn implies central direction, something not easy to come by in a democracy in the best of circumstances, and certainly not during the first year of an inexperienced and badly organized administration. Extraneous influences—Congress, the press, public opinion, bureaucracies, even personalities—tended to intrude upon the bargaining process, making the alignment of conditions to be met with incentives to be offered awkward, to say the least.

But the major difficulty was simply the Soviet Union's imperviousness to external influences. The *quid pro quo* strategy had assumed, as had Roosevelt's, that Soviet behavior could be affected from the outside: the only difference had been over method and timing. In fact, though, experience showed that there was remarkably little the West could do, in the short term, to shape Stalin's decisions: the Soviet dictator maintained tight control in a mostly self-sufficient country, with little knowledge or understanding of, much less susceptibility to, events in the larger world. It was this realization of impermeability—the fact that neither trust nor pressure had made any difference—that paved the way for the revision of strategy set off by George Kennan's "long telegram" of February 1946. . . .

"Patience and firmness" became the watchword for dealings

with the Soviet Union over the next year—if anything, the emphasis, as the Joint Chiefs of Staff had recommended, was primarily on the "firmness." The new approach showed up in the Eastern Mediterranean and the Near East, where the administration not only induced the Russians to withdraw troops from Iran and to give up demands for boundary concessions and base rights from Turkey, but in addition committed itself to support the government of Greece against an externally supplied communist insurgency and to make the presence of the Sixth Fleet in waters surrounding the latter two countries a permanent fixture of the postwar world. It showed up in the Far East, where Washington continued to resist any substantive role for the Russians in the occupation of Japan, while at the same time making clear its determination to prevent a Soviet takeover of all of Korea. It showed up in Germany, where the United States cut off reparations shipments from its zone and began moving toward consolidating it with those of the British and the French, while at the same time offering the Russians a four-power treaty guaranteeing the disarmament of Germany for twenty-five years. It showed up in the Council of Foreign Ministers, where Byrnes firmly resisted Soviet bids to take over former Italian territories along the Mediterranean, while at the same time patiently pursuing negotiations on peace treaties for former German satellites. Finally, and most dramatically, the new strategy manifested itself in the Truman Doctrine, in which the administration generalized its obligations to Greece and Turkey into what appeared to be a world-wide commitment to resist Soviet expansionism wherever it appeared.

Truman's March 12, 1947, proclamation that "it must be the policy of the United States to support free peoples who are resisting attempted subjugation by armed minorities or outside pressures" has traditionally been taken as having marked a fundamental point of departure for American foreign policy in the Cold War. In fact, though, it can more accurately be seen as the ultimate expression of the "patience and firmness" strategy that had been in effect for the past year. Decisions to aid Greece and Turkey, as well as other nations threatened by the Soviet Union, had been made months before. What was new, in early 1947, was Great Britain's abrupt notice of intent to end its own military and financial support to those countries, and the need that imposed for quick Congressional approval of aid to replace it. It was that requirement, in turn, that forced the administration to justify its request in globalist terms; even so, that rhetoric was consistent with the assumption, underlying the "patience and firmness" strategy for almost a year, that the United States could afford no further gains in territory or influence for the Soviet Union anywhere.

American Firmness vs. Soviet Aggression

Clark Clifford

To understand history requires an attitude of historical mindedness. Students must put themselves in the position of other people in other times. They must try to be aware of the frame of reference of others, of the pressures on them, and of the nature of their understanding of a particular problem or development. An analysis of President Harry Truman's actions in the Cold War needs to be rooted in an examination of how he and his closest advisors viewed American relations with the Soviet Union.

This private memorandum for the President, prepared by his Special Counsel, Clark Clifford, just a year after V-J Day, summarizes the attitudes and outlook of the Joint Chiefs of Staff, the Secretaries of State, War, and Navy, and other high level officials, especially George F. Kennan's diplomatic cables from Moscow. It wholly blames the Soviet Union for the emerging Cold War. It urges the President to arm the United States for possible war, to negotiate reluctantly with the Russians, to never compromise for fear that it might be interpreted as weakness, to utilize American economic power to force Soviet concessions, and to employ foreign aid to build a "barrier to communism." Students may wish to compare Clifford's interpretation of Soviet behavior with that of Gaddis, and Clifford's "get tough" recommendations with the reconsideration of Cold War assumptions offered by George Kennan in 1981 (reprinted here in Part IX).

It is perhaps the greatest paradox of the present day that the leaders of a nation, now stronger than it has ever been before,

Excerpted from a Clark Clifford memorandum to President Truman, September 24, 1946, in Clark Clifford Papers, Harry S. Truman Library, Independence, Missouri.

should embark on so aggressive a course because their nation is "weak." And yet Stalin and his cohorts proclaim that "monopoly capitalism" threatens the world with war and that Russia must strengthen her defenses against the danger of foreign attacks. The USSR, according to Kremlin propaganda, is imperilled so long as it remains within a "capitalistic encirclement." This idea is absurd when adopted by so vast a country with such great natural wealth, a population of almost 200 million and no powerful or aggressive neighbors. But the process of injecting this propaganda into the minds of the Soviet people goes on with increasing intensity.

The concept of danger from the outside is deeply rooted in the Russian people's haunting sense of insecurity inherited from their past. It is maintained by their present leaders as a justification for the oppressive nature of the Soviet police state. The thesis, that the capitalist world is conspiring to attack the Soviet Union, is not based on any objective analysis of the situation beyond Russia's borders. It has little to do, indeed, with conditions outside the Soviet Union, and it has risen mainly from basic inner-Russian necessities which existed before the Second World War and which exist today. . . .

The Kremlin acknowledges no limit to the eventual power of the Soviet Union, but it is practical enough to be concerned with the actual position of the USSR today. In any matter deemed essential to the security of the Soviet Union, Soviet leaders will prove adamant in their claims and demands. In other matters they will prove grasping and opportunistic, but flexible in proportion to the degree and nature of the resistance encountered.

Recognition of the need to postpone the "inevitable" conflict is in no sense a betrayal of the Communist faith. Marx and Lenin encouraged compromise and collaboration with non-Communists for the accomplishment of ultimate communistic purposes. The USSR has followed such a course in the past. In 1939 the Kremlin signed a nonaggression pact with Germany and in 1941 a neutrality pact with Japan. Soviet leaders will continue to collaborate whenever it seems expedient, for time is needed to build up Soviet strength and weaken the opposition. Time is on the side of the Soviet Union, since population growth and economic development will, in the Soviet view, bring an increase in its relative strength. . . .

A direct threat to American security is implicit in Soviet foreign policy which is designed to prepare the Soviet Union for war with the leading capitalistic nations of the world. Soviet leaders recognize that the United States will be the Soviet Union's most powerful enemy if such a war as that predicted by Communist theory ever comes about and therefore the United States is the chief target of Soviet foreign and military policy. . . .

The most obvious Soviet threat to American security is the growing ability of the USSR to wage an offensive war against the United States. This has not hitherto been possible, in the absence of Soviet long-range strategic air power and an almost total lack of sea power. Now, however, the USSR is rapidly developing elements of her military strength which she hitherto lacked and which will give the Soviet Union great offensive capabilities. Stalin has declared his intention of sparing no effort to build up the military strength of the Soviet Union. Development of atomic weapons, guided missiles, materials for biological warfare, a strategic air force, submarines of great cruising range, naval mines and mine craft, to name the most important, are extending the effective range of Soviet military power well into areas which the United States regards as vital to its security. . . .

The primary objective of United States policy toward the Soviet Union is to convince Soviet leaders that it is in their interest to participate in a system of world cooperation, that there are no fundamental causes for war between our two nations, and that the security and prosperity of the Soviet Union, and that of the rest of the world as well, is being jeopardized by the aggressive militaristic imperialism such as that in which the Soviet Union is now engaged.

However, these same leaders with whom we hope to achieve an understanding on the principles of international peace appear to believe that a war with the United States and the other leading capitalistic nations is inevitable. They are increasing their military power and the sphere of Soviet influence in preparation for the "inevitable" conflict, and they are trying to weaken and subvert their potential opponents by every means at their disposal. So long as these men adhere to these beliefs, it is highly dangerous to conclude that hope of international peace lies only in "accord," "mutual understanding," or "solidarity" with the Soviet Union.

Adoption of such a policy would impel the United States to make sacrifices for the sake of Soviet-U.S. relations, which would only have the effect of raising Soviet hopes and increasing Soviet demands, and to ignore alternative lines of policy, which might be much more compatible with our own national and international interests.

The Soviet government will never be easy to "get along with." The American people must accustom themselves to this thought, not as a cause for despair, but as a fact to be faced objectively and courageously. If we find it impossible to enlist Soviet cooperation in the solution of world problems, we should be prepared to join with the British and other Western countries in an attempt to build up a world of our own which will pursue its own objectives and will recognize the Soviet orbit as a distinct entity with which conflict is not predestined but with which we cannot pursue common aims.

As long as the Soviet government maintains its present foreign policy, based upon the theory of an ultimate struggle between communism and capitalism, the United States must assume that the USSR might fight at any time for the two-fold purpose of expanding the territory under Communist control and weakening its potential capitalist opponents. The Soviet Union was able to flow into the political vacuum of the Balkans, Eastern Europe, the Near East, Manchuria and Korea because no other nation was both willing and able to prevent it. Soviet leaders were encouraged by easy success and they are now preparing to take over new areas in the same way. The Soviet Union, as Stalin euphemistically phrased it, is preparing "for any eventuality."

Unless the United States is willing to sacrifice its future security for the sake of "accord" with the USSR now, this government must, as a first step toward world stabilization, seek to prevent additional Soviet aggression. . . . This government should be prepared, while scrupulously avoiding any act which would be an excuse for the Soviets to begin a war, to resist vigorously and successfully any efforts of the USSR to expand into areas vital to American security.

The language of military power is the only language which disciples of power politics understand. The United States must use that language in order that Soviet leaders will realize that our government is determined to uphold the interests of its citizens and the rights of small nations. Compromise and concessions are considered, by the Soviets, to be evidences of weakness and they are encouraged by our "retreats" to make new and greater demands.

The main deterrent to Soviet attack on the United States, or to attack on areas of the world which are vital to our security, will be the military power of this country. It must be made apparent to the Soviet government that our strength will be sufficient to repel any attack and sufficient to defeat the USSR decisively if a war should start. The prospect of defeat is the only sure means of deterring the Soviet Union.

The Soviet Union's vulnerability is limited due to the vast area over which its key industries and natural resources are widely dispersed, but it is vulnerable to atomic weapons, biological warfare, and long-range power. Therefore, in order to maintain our strength at a level which will be effective in restraining the Soviet Union, the United States must be prepared to wage atomic and biological warfare. A highly mechanized army, which can be moved either by sea or by air, capable of seizing and holding strategic areas, must be supported by powerful naval and air forces. A war with the USSR would be "total" in a more horrible sense than any previous war and there must be constant research for both offensive and defensive weapons.

Whether it would actually be in this country's interest to employ atomic and biological weapons against the Soviet Union in the event of hostilities is a question which would require careful consideration in the light of the circumstances prevailing at the time. The decision would probably be influenced by a number of factors, such as the Soviet Union's capacity to employ similar weapons, which can not now be estimated. But the important point is that the United States must be prepared to wage atomic and biological warfare if necessary. The mere fact of preparedness may be the only powerful deterrent to Soviet aggressive action and in this sense the only sure guaranty of peace.

The United States, with a military potential composed primarily of [highly] effective technical weapons, should entertain no proposal for disarmament or limitation of armament as long as the possibility of Soviet aggression exists. Any discussion on the limitation of armaments should be pursued slowly and carefully with the knowledge constantly in mind that proposals on outlawing atomic warfare and long-range offensive weapons would greatly limit United States strength, while only moderately affecting the Soviet Union. The Soviet Union relies primarily on a large infantry and artillery force and the result of such arms limitation would be to deprive the United States of its most effective weapons without impairing the Soviet Union's ability to wage a quick war of aggression in Western Europe, the Middle East or the Far East. . . .

In addition to maintaining our own strength, the United States should support and assist all democratic countries which are in any way menaced or endangered by the USSR. Providing military support in case of attack is a last resort; a more effective barrier to communism is strong economic support. Trade agreements, loans and technical missions strengthen our ties with friendly nations and are effective demonstrations that capitalism is at least the equal of communism. The United States can do much to ensure that economic opportunities, personal freedom and social equality are made possible in countries outside the Soviet sphere by generous financial assistance. Our policy on reparations should be directed toward strengthening the areas we are endeavoring to keep outside the Soviet sphere. Our efforts to break down trade barriers, open up rivers and international waterways, and bring about economic unification of countries, now divided by occupation armies, are also directed toward the reestablishment of vigorous and healthy non-Communist economies.

In conclusion, as long as the Soviet government adheres to its present policy, the United States should maintain military forces powerful enough to restrain the Soviet Union and to confine Soviet influence to its present area. All nations not now within the Soviet sphere should be given generous economic assistance and political support in their opposition to Soviet penetration. Economic aid may also be given to the Soviet government and private trade with the USSR permitted provided the results are beneficial to our interests. . . .

Even though Soviet leaders profess to believe that the conflict between Capitalism and Communism is irreconcilable and must eventually be resolved by the triumph of the latter, it is our hope that they will change their minds and work out with us a fair and equitable settlement when they realize that we are too strong to be beaten and too determined to be frightened.

Part Two

THE COLD WAR AT HOME

There has always been a close connection between American foreign policy and American domestic politics. In a democracy, it is difficult to pursue diplomatic positions that do not have broad popular support. Given the distinctive image America has had of its role in the world, that has almost always meant posing foreign policy issues in moralistic or universal terms. During World War I, for example, Woodrow Wilson would not have been able to justify American involvement simply on the basis of economic or military self-interest. Rather, drawing upon America's traditional image as being a beacon of hope, morality, and freedom, Wilson portrayed the war as a crusade to "make the world safe for democracy."

When the Truman administration found itself at loggerheads with the Soviet Union after World War II, it too resorted to a rhetoric of moralism as a means of justifying the massive economic and military aid it deemed necessary to combat the perceived Soviet threat. In 1947 the administration decided to ask Congress for a major program of assistance to Greece and Turkey in what became the Truman doctrine. The Secretary of State and other officials briefing congressional leaders met with a cool response when they simply presented the issue in terms of self-interest. Only when Dean Acheson invoked the specter of Russian tyranny spreading throughout the world in a direct assault on freedom did the congressmen respond. As Arthur Vanderburg, Republican leader of the Senate foreign relations committee, told the President, Truman would have to "scare hell" out of the American people if he wished their support for his program. Consequently, Truman presented the Cold War to Congress as an

issue of freedom against tyranny, democracy against totalitarianism, a struggle between those who believed in God and those who
were atheists.

Eventually, this kind of rhetoric created its own logic—a logic
that inhibited freedom of discussion and amounted to a form of
domestic tyranny at home. Anyone who dared question the wisdom of America's Cold War policies was portrayed as a sympa-
thizer of communism and part of a "fifth column" beholden to
the Soviet Union. If one's own policy was defined as moral, anyone opposing that policy was inevitably immoral. Indeed, when
Truman ran for re-election in 1948, he followed a strategy of
defining his left-wing opponent, Henry Wallace of the Progressive
Party, as pro-communist and hence disloyal.

It was out of such a framework that the phenomenon we call
McCarthyism grew. Many Americans felt beleaguered and threatened in the immediate postwar years, as the Soviet Union asserted
control over eastern Europe, tested an atomic bomb, and put
forward her own rhetoric of ideological confrontation with the
United States. When Chinese communists took over China in
1949, many Americans saw events in the world moving against
them. The fact that Soviet spies had secured atomic energy secrets
from the United States, and that some State Department officials
had predicted the victory of the Chinese communists, gave rise to
a sense, on the part of some, that a communist conspiracy existed
within the ranks of the United States government itself. Responding to such fears, Truman himself instituted a security program to
impose a test of loyalty on government employees. Not satisfied
with that response, the House Committee on Un-American Activities and others in Congress launched what became a witch hunt,
seeking to ferret out anyone and everyone who might be
accused—fairly or unfairly—of less than one hundred percent
loyalty to the most conservative program of patriotism. Those
who had been part of Soviet-American Friendship Societies during World War II while America and Russia were allies, or who
had flirted with communism in the 1930s, or who had participated in various progressive causes including advocacy of civil
rights for blacks or national health insurance, were brought before congressional committees, subjected to harrassing questioning, and treated as pariahs. Hundreds of lives were destroyed by
the insinuation—often never justified—that at some point in the

past, they had said something or belonged to an organization that could be construed as friendly to the Soviet Union or to social democratic policies.

When Senator Joseph McCarthy announced in Wheeling, West Virginia, in 1950 that he had a list of 207 card-carrying communists in the State Department, he simply carried to a new height the hysteria that was already rampant in the country. McCarthy had no such list and most of his charges were made of whole cloth. Nevertheless, he succeeded through the technique of the big lie and the red smear in intimidating the American people in and outside of Congress, as well as destroying careers and lives. So powerful was McCarthy, and so out of control were his charges, that even people as established and invulnerable as President Dwight David Eisenhower refused to attack him or challenge his credibility. McCarthyism cast a pall over the land, chilling political debate for a decade and making it virtually impossible for many Americans to actively espouse any cause, domestic or international, that could be distorted as sympathetic to socialism or communism.

The following selections analyze and illustrate the impact of the Cold War at home. Robert Griffith's assessment indicates that although McCarthy did not represent a new or powerful political force, he was able to impose his own political tyranny due to partisan Republicanism and the agitation of conservative interest groups. The senator's demagoguery is best exemplified by the words which launched his personal crusade against the Democrats for their alleged "softness" on communism. The "Declaration of Conscience" by seven Republican senators and the comments of Margaret Chase Smith represent both a courageous effort to stand up to McCarthy by moderates within his own party and a principled statement against the selfish exploitation of fear and intolerance. Finally, Lillian Hellman, who risked going to jail by taking the position that she would inform the House Un-American Activities Committee about herself but would say nothing about other people, describes her thoughts while being interrogated and the devastating personal consequences of McCarthyism for those who sought to carry forward the American principles of freedom of speech and independent thought.

Among the questions that remain from the McCarthy period are the extent to which Truman himself paved the way for

McCarthyism by his definition of Cold War issues; whether other political leaders could have acted in concert to put a stop to the reckless charges of the anti-communist Right; and how it was possible for such a poison to spread through the body politic in the name of democratic principle. The McCarthy period had a disastrous impact on American political discussion for a generation, and it is imperative to come to grips with that heritage in order to understand the history of the postwar period.

American Politics and the Origins of "McCarthyism"

Robert Griffith

At the height of McCarthyism many critics pictured the junior Senator from Wisconsin as a charismatic demagogue with a special flair for arousing the darkest instincts of the American public. Some compared him to Hitler. Others emphasized the irrationality of the Senator's popular following. Still others, borrowing the insights and terminology of social psychology, described McCarthyism as a mass movement rooted in the status resentments of the lower-middle and working-class Americans. Most commentators on McCarthyism today, however, concentrate on politics rather than social pathology. They stress the role of political institutions and interest groups. They emphasize the actions and inactions of both conservative and liberal elites, down-playing the fears and discontents of the mass of Americans.

Fundamentally, they depict Senator McCarthy as an outgrowth, not the origin, of the Second Red Scare. McCarthy, they aver, was the consequence of an already formed anti-Communist consensus, not its cause. In the following selection, Robert Griffith, winner of the Frederick Jackson Turner Award of the Organization of American Historians for his brilliant analysis of McCarthyism as a political phenomenon, The Politics of Fear, *Joseph R. McCarthy and the Senate (1970), succinctly summarized the views of these historians who interpret McCarthyism not as "mass" but as "interest group" politics. If there is any truth to the dictum "The study of history is the best guarantee against repeating it," the roots and repercussions of McCarthyism ought to be carefully pondered.*

For nearly two decades American scholars and journalists have described "McCarthyism" in terms of a popular uprising, a mass movement of the "radical right" that threatened the very fabric of American society. Inchoate, irrational, it swept across the political landscape like an elemental force of nature carrying all before it. Its sources, these scholars maintained, lay not so much in the emergent cold war, but in the "social strains" and status tensions produced by a century of modernization. McCarthyism, like populism, was seen as an attack by paranoid provincials upon the educated and the wealthy. Politicians, in this view, were but the passive instruments of the popular will, reflecting the hysteria that welled up from the grass roots. McCarthy himself, of course, was something of an exception. Indeed, he was credited with a demonic talent for probing "the dark places of the American mind." He was "the most gifted" demagogue in American history, succeeding where others had failed in arousing the American masses and inciting them to action "outside of and against the established channels of constitutional government."

But was McCarthyism really a popular movement? Probably not. To be sure, anti-Communism was an element in the American polical culture, and popular attitudes toward Communism, conditioned as they were by several decades of misinformation and strident propaganda, were mostly negative. It is also true that public opinion polls showed a rather high level of support for McCarthy (around 35 percent for most of 1953–54), combined with frequently intolerant attitudes toward nonconformists and dissenters. But popular intolerance and anti-Communism, however important, have tended to be constants. Even in the supposedly radical thirties, for example, most Americans seemed to favor denying freedom of speech, press, and assembly to native Communists. What needs to be explained, therefore, is not the mere existence of such attitudes, but how, during the late 1940's and early 1950's, they were mobilized and became politically operational.

Second, as even Seymour Martin Lipset and other proponents of the "radical right" thesis admit, intense negative feelings about McCarthy were usually more common than strongly favorable ones. McCarthy aroused more opposition than support. Third, as

Nelson Polsby has suggested in a critique of the radical right thesis, the most common characteristic of McCarthy supporters was not class, religion, or ethnicity, but political affiliation. Support for McCarthy was strongest among Republicans. Socioeconomic factors were not unimportant—when party affiliation was held constant, those with lower status, less education, and of the Catholic faith tended to support McCarthy disproportionately. But these last factors seem clearly less significant than party. There was, moreover, no continuity between populism and McCarthyism, as some historians have argued. Indeed, as Michael Paul Rogin has shown, nearly the reverse was true—agrarian radicalism, where cohesive, contributed not to the Republican right, but to the constituency of Democratic liberalism.

Fourth, while the polls did show substantial support for McCarthy and extremely negative feelings about Communism, as well as a low level of support for the civil liberties of Communists and other political dissidents, the intensity of these feelings was apparently not very strong. When people were asked, for example, whether they favored allowing Communists to teach in their schools, the response (both in the thirties and in the fifties) was largely and unsurprisingly negative. But in 1953, at the height of the McCarthy era, when people were asked a simple, nondirective question ("What kinds of things do you worry about most?"), less than 1 percent listed the threat of Communism as a major concern and only 8 percent mentioned the tangentially related area of world problems. Even when the interviewer sought to lead the respondent ("Are there other problems you worry about or are concerned about, especially political or world problems?"), the level of concern was not great. The number expressing anxiety about Communism increased only from 1 percent to 6 percent. The number concerned over international affairs rose more substantially, from 8 percent to 30 percent. Significantly, more than half of those so questioned added nothing to their initial response. Thus, as Samuel Stouffer concluded in his 1954 study, *Communism, Conformity and Civil Liberties*, Americans were not very deeply concerned over domestic Communism. The "picture of the average American as a person with the jitters, trembling lest he find a Red under the bed, is clearly nonsense."

Finally, what is all too often overlooked is the congruence between popular attitudes toward Communism and the attitudes of influential public figures. Many prominent Republicans, for example, were constantly accusing the Roosevelt and Truman Administrations of selling out to Communism at home and abroad. Nor were such charges limited to conservatives. Some liberal Republicans, such as Senator Ralph Flanders of Vermont who would later lead the movement to censure McCarthy, believed that "our late departed saint Franklin Delano Roosevelt was soft as taffy on the subject of Communism and Uncle Joe." Even Democrats such as Massachusetts Congressman John F. Kennedy attacked the Truman Administration's foreign policies, charging that "what our young men saved [in World War II], our diplomats and our President have frittered away." The Truman Administration itself used the Red issue against Henry Wallace and the Progressives and occasionally even against the Republicans. McCarthy, the President charged at one point, was the Kremlin's "greatest asset." In denouncing Communism, then, Joe McCarthy, despite his occasional attacks on "the bright young men who are born with silver spoons in their mouths," was adopting a political issue already sanctioned by much of the nation's political leadership.

The commonly accepted portrait of McCarthyism as a mass movement and McCarthy as a charismatic leader is, thus, badly overdrawn. People were less concerned about the threat of Communism and less favorably inclined toward McCarthy than is generally thought. Support for McCarthy, moreover, was closely identified with partisan Republicanism. Finally, popular attitudes about Communism generally mirrored the views of many prominent political leaders, and McCarthy's use of the issue was unexceptional.

But if McCarthyism is not to be understood primarily in terms of popular passion, then how do we explain the contentious and tumultuous politics of the mid-twentieth century? A partial answer to this problem involves a political definition of McCarthyism and, as Michael Paul Rogin has suggested, the actions and inactions of political elites. McCarthyism may not have been only a political phenomenon; it may indeed have reflected the "social strains" of modern American society, as Talcott Parsons and others have maintained. But it was primarily a product of the political system and its leaders. The latter did not simply respond to popular protest, but rather helped to generate the very sense of concern and urgency that came to dominate the decade.

This is not to argue that the politics of McCarthyism was born solely of the postwar period. There was a long history of anti-radicalism in America, a history produced both by conservative resistance to social change and by nativist fears of strangers in the land. It was not a history created by protean mass movements, however, but by the complicated interplay of political manipulation and popular myth and stereotype. . . .

The cold war transformed the climate of American politics, overlaying traditional political issues with a new and emotionally charged set of concerns. The growing power of the Soviet Union and its challenge to American supremacy served to focus previously diffuse fears and anxieties over Communism. So did the arrest of men and women accused of spying for the U.S.S.R. But the anti-Communist protest of the late 1940's was more than a simple response to external events. It also sprang from the goals that American leaders set for postwar foreign policy, the manner in which they perceived the Soviet challenge to that policy, and the methods they chose to meet that challenge.

For a variety of reasons—idealism, self-interest, the hubris of the very powerful—American leaders defined United States policy in sweeping terms: the creation of a global system of stability, peace, and prosperity. The Soviet challenge to this new order was seen as a threat to world peace and to American security, a threat to which the United States was compelled to respond. The character of this response, in turn, helped to create a climate in which anti-Communist politics gained a vastly heightened potency and appeal. In part, this was because the Truman Administration itself couched its policies in a rhetoric of crusading anti-Communism, which stressed American innocence, Soviet depravity, and the necessity for confrontation.

Such views, of course, were scarcely unique to the Truman Administration. Rather they were shared by a broad segment of America's political leadership—liberal and conservative, Democratic and Republican. Both Truman and his conservative critics were influenced to a great extent by the legacy of prewar anti-Communism. Both shared illusions concerning the limits of American power and the nature of Soviet foreign policy. Tru-

man's critics, however, generally proposed more drastic policies
and justified them with greater militance than did the Administration. Even Robert Taft, a frequently incisive critic of containment,
denounced the Administration for being "soft on Communism,"
advocated greater assistance for Chiang Kai-shek, and supported
General Douglas MacArthur in the controversy over the Korean
War. The Truman Administration, committed to an intervention-
ist policy abroad, stressed anti-Communism as a means of winning
support from such nationalistic but fiscally cautious conservatives.
As a result, most conservatives joined the Administration in a
bipartisan anti-Communist consensus, while the rest, including
Taft, were left isolated and impotent. A second, and unintended
consequence of this tactic, however, was the generation of a new
and conservative political climate, resistant to social change at
home and to negotiation and compromise abroad.

The new political climate inspired conservative businessmen,
organized veterans, patriotic societies, and other zealous anti-
Communists and made their efforts appear more plausible and
relevant. The Chamber of Commerce, for example, through its
Committee on Socialism and Communism, prepared and distributed a series of pamphlets designed to expose Communists in
government and labor, to discredit New Deal social legislation,
and to help businessmen reassert themselves at the community
level. The American Legion was even more active. Led by its
Americanism Division and active at both the state and federal
levels, the Legion campaigned vigorously to arouse the nation to
the perils of Communism. The Legion played an important role
in creating and sustaining the Special House Committee on Un-
American Activities and in the establishment of "little Dies Committees" in the states. The Legion lobbied hard for new anti-
Communist legislation, supporting the Mundt-Nixon Communist
registration bill as well as a wide variety of restrictive measures at
the state level. Finally, the Legion became deeply involved in the
colorful crusade against Communism in Hollywood and in the
subsequent spread of blacklisting in the film, radio, and television industries.

The Legion and the Chamber of Commerce were only two
among a welter of anti-Communist organizations, which included
patriotic societies such as the Daughters of the American Revolution, Catholic groups such as the Knights of Columbus and the

Catholic War Veterans, ethnic groups such as the Polish-American Congress, and a host of smaller right-wing organizations. The activities of these groups included lobbying, propaganda, and on occasion picketing and other forms of public protest. The concerns of such groups were amplified by the press. The conservative McCormick, Hearst, and Gannett chains were especially active in this undertaking, though overwrought anti-Communism was not limited to them alone. As early as 1945, for example, *Life* magazine complained that "The 'fellow traveler' is everywhere, in Hollywood, on college faculties, in government bureaus, in publishing companies, in radio offices, even on the editorial staffs of eminently capitalistic journals." From here it was but a short step to the demand that such "fellow travelers" be purged from American life.

This was not, of course, "mass" politics but "interest group" politics, a typical expression of the American political culture and not an aberrational one. The group base of American politics was not aligned, as earlier scholars have suggested, against a mass politics of anti-Communism. Instead, interest groups themselves lay at the heart of the anti-Communist politics of the era.

The aggressive actions of right-wing interest groups were not, moreover, met by countervailing pressures from the left. Instead, the same broad forces that lent strength and legitimacy to the postwar right served to undermine and destroy the postwar left. In 1945 the American left was a relatively large and potentially powerful movement, which included a wide assortment of liberals, socialists, and Communists. Though scarred by the memory of past betrayals and sharply divided among themselves, these leftists nevertheless shared a consensus on two fundamental points: the necessity for radical social change at home and for a conciliatory and pacific foreign policy abroad. The rise of the cold war and the resurgence of conservatism, however, led to bitter divisions within the left over American policy toward the Soviet Union and over the role of Communism in American life. The precarious unity of the popular front was shattered, both by the Communists who repudiated the wartime leadership of Earl Browder and by cold-war liberals who supported the foreign policies of the Truman Administration and sought to purge Communists from labor unions, political parties, and other voluntary associations. The overwhelming rejection of Henry Wallace in the 1948 campaign and the emergence of Americans for Democratic Action (ADA) marked the beginning of a new political era in which the left was in virtual eclipse and in which the distinction between liberals and conservatives became one of method and technique, not fundamental principle. Divided, demoralized, and after 1948 led by men who shared many of the anti-Communist assumptions of the right, the American left was unable to withstand the mounting demands of McCarthyite conservatives.

The political climate of postwar America was thus shaped by the cold war, by the agitation of conservative interest groups, and by the disintegration of liberalism. It remained, however, for politicians to mobilize the support necessary for a politics of anti-Communism. Foremost among such politicians were those Republican and Democratic conservatives who had championed the anti-Communist issues since the thirties and who had maintained all along that Democratic liberalism was leading the country down the road to Communism. After 1945, however, this anti-reformist impulse was joined with the new foreign policy and internal security issues bred by the cold war. Congressional conservatives now charged that the Roosevelt and Truman Administrations were "soft" on Communism abroad and tolerant of subversion and disloyalty at home; and beginning in 1945 they launched a series of investigations in Communist activities designed in part to embarrass the government.

The frequency of such investigations was one measure of the rise of the Communist issue in American politics. There were four investigations during the 79th Congress (1945–47); twenty-two during the Republican 80th Congress (1947–49); twenty-four during the 81st Congress (1949–51); thirty-four during the 82nd Congress (1951–53); and fifty-one, an all-time high, during the Republican 83rd Congress (1953–55). Throughout the forties most of these investigations were conducted by the House Committee on Un-American Activities, led, following the retirement of Martin Dies, by J. Parnell Thomas (Republican-New Jersey) and by John S. Wood (Democrat-Georgia). More important, the focus and character of these investigations changed. Before December 1948 most of HUAC's investigations seemed to be linked to domestic concerns—the committee's primary targets were left-wing

New Deal personnel, New Deal agencies such as the Federal Theatre Project and the Office of Price Administration, trade unions whose leadership included Communists, and Hollywood. But after 1948, the year in which Whittaker Chambers accused Alger Hiss first of having been a Communist and then, later, of having spied for the Soviet Union, the committee began increasingly to emphasize the internal security issues of espionage, subversion, and "Communists in government."

The Communist issue was injected into the 1946 elections and was apparently a factor in the Republican triumph, especially among urban Catholics. In 1947–48 the Truman Administration responded to these pressures by justifying its foreign policies with a crusading anti-Communist rhetoric, by instituting a federal loyalty-security program, by prosecuting Communist party leaders under the Smith Act, and in general by stressing its own firm anti-Communist credentials. Indeed, by 1948 the Administration had succeeded, if only temporarily, in using the Communist issue to its own advantage against both the Progressives and the Republicans. Crusades, however, are more easily begun than halted, and by early 1950 those conservative politicians whom Truman had sought to outflank once again held the initiative, now denouncing the Administration for the "loss" of China and demanding a sweeping purge within the government.

The rise of anti-Communism as an issue in national politics was accompanied by the growth of a derivative anti-Communist politics at the state and local levels. In part this was because many of the organizations that had agitated for restrictive measures at the federal level were also active in the states and in the communities. Some of these groups, the Chamber of Commerce and the American Legion, for example, labored not only to arouse others to the menace of Communism, but also to popularize techniques and methods for combating it. The Chamber sponsored anti-Communist seminars for local businessmen, while the American Legion held conferences for state legislators anxious to learn what the federal government and other states were doing to safeguard the Republic. Catholic Church groups and the conservative Hearst press also helped agitate the issue, as did the coterie of staff and witnesses that surrounded the House Committee on Un-American Activities.

More important, state legislatures responded almost slavishly to

the force of federal law and precedent and to the anxieties
aroused by national leaders. Anti-radical legislation was not, of
course, new to most states. Yet what was remarkable about the
great outpouring of the late forties was that so many legislatures
acted at the same time and in the same way. In 1949, for example,
the Maryland legislature passed a Subversive Activities Act, popularly known as the Ober Law. There was little original in the new
law, however, for it had been drawn from the Smith Act of 1940,
from Truman's Loyalty Program of 1947, and from portions of
the Mundt-Nixon bill then pending before Congress. The Ober
Law was in turn copied in part or entirely by the states of Mississippi, New Hampshire, Washington, and Pennsylvania. In the
case of Pennsylvania, the legislature in 1951 established as the
criteria for dismissing state employees not the Ober Law's standard—"reasonable grounds . . . to believe that any person is a
subversive person"—but instead "reasonable doubt as to the loyalty of the person involved." The Maryland law had followed the
criteria set forth in Truman's March 1947 loyalty order (Ex.
Order 9835); the Pennsylvania legislature incorporated a generally unheralded but highly significant change in that criteria, in
effect reversing the burden of proof, which Truman had ordered
in April 1951 (Ex. Order 10241).

During the late forties, nearly thirty states enacted laws seeking
to bar from public employment those who advocated the violent
overthrow of the government, or who belonged to organizations
which so advocated. In only one instance did such a state statute
predate the Truman loyalty order; all of them, of course, came
after the 1939 Hatch Act, which had provided such restrictions for
federal employment. The Attorney General's list, institutionalized
by Truman's 1947 loyalty order, was quickly adopted as a test of
loyalty by states (including Arizona, New York, Michigan, Texas,
Oklahoma), by municipalities (among them Detroit and New York
City), and even by private employers (including the Columbia
Broadcasting System). Following the passage in September 1950 of
the McCarran Internal Security Act, more than a half dozen states
rushed to enact so-called Communist Control Laws. Even cities
passed municipal ordinances directed against Communists.

Thus state and local anti-Communist legislation, though widespread, is best understood as a reflection, not a cause, of national
priorities. Unlike populism, the impact of which was felt first at

the local and state level and only later at the national level, the politics of anti-Communism originated at the national level and then spread to the states.

By 1950, then, political leaders had succeeded through the manipulation of popular myths and stereotypes, in creating a mood conducive to demagogues such as Joseph R. McCarthy. The Wisconsin senator's crude attacks on American policy and policy-makers resonated through the political system not because of their uniqueness, but because of their typicality. To call this political impulse "McCarthyism," however, is to exaggerate the senator's importance and to misunderstand the politics that he came to symbolize. McCarthy was the product of anti-Communist politics, not its progenitor. Had he never made that speech in Wheeling, West Virginia, had his name never become a household word, what people came to call "McCarthyism" would nevertheless have characterized American politics at the mid-century.

Speech at
Wheeling, West Virginia

Joseph McCarthy

Whatever the deeper causes of the Second Red Scare, few doubt that Senator Joseph R. McCarthy did more than any other individual to turn the concern about domestic disloyalty and security into a form of national hysteria. His name still stirs violent emotions in those who lived through that turbulent period. The words McCarthyism *and* McCarthyite *have become a part of our language.*

"A man without moral perceptions," in the words of one recent biographer, "one who will break all the rules because for him there are none," McCarthy had floundered through four years in the Senate and was desperately searching for an issue that would increase his visibility and would aid his plans for reelection when he appeared before the Ohio County Women's Republican Club in Wheeling, West Virginia, on February 9, 1950. Following the outline of speeches by other Republican anti-communists, McCarthy charged that the United States had lost ground in the world not as a result of foreign aggression, but "because of the traitorous actions of those who have been treated so well by this nation." He claimed, according to press reports of the address, to have in his hands a list of 205 members of the Communist Party and members of a spy ring currently employed by "and shaping the policy of the State Department." When later challenged to produce evidence for his charges McCarthy maintained that he was referring to Communist "party loyalists" or "bad risks" in the State Department, and in the moderated version of the Wheeling speech introduced into the Congressional Record *on February 20, reprinted below, he reduced the number of alleged Communists to 57.*

McCarthy had no list at all. But it didn't matter. In an atmosphere charged by the Communist victory in China, the successful explosion of an A-bomb by the Soviet Union, the Hiss-Chambers confrontations, the Tru-

man Administration's own campaign against subversion, and soon the outbreak of war in Korea, McCarthy had a winning issue which dominated news headlines and the Republican Party had a potent weapon which pummeled the Democrats.

Five years after a world war has been won, men's hearts should anticipate a long peace, and men's minds should be free from the heavy weight that comes with war. But this is not such a period— for this is not a period of peace. This is a time of the "cold war." This is a time when all the world is split into two vast, increasingly hostile armed camps—a time of a great armaments race. . . .

Today we are engaged in a final, all-out battle between communistic atheism and Christianity. The modern champions of communism have selected this as the time. And, ladies and gentlement, the chips are down—they are truly down. . . .

Six years ago, at the time of the first conference to map out the peace—Dumbarton Oaks—there was within the Soviet orbit 180,000,000 people. Lined up on the antitotalitarian side there were in the world at that time roughly 1,625,000,000 people. Today, only 6 years later, there are 800,000,000 people under the absolute domination of Soviet Russia—an increase of over 400 percent. On our side, the figure has shrunk to around 500,000,000. In other words, in less than 6 years the odds have changed from 9 to 1 in our favor to 8 to 5 against us. This indicates the swiftness of the tempo of Communist victories and American defeats in the cold war. As one of our outstanding historical figures once said, "When a great democracy is destroyed, it will not be because of enemies from without, but rather because of enemies from within." . . .

The reason why we find ourselves in a position of impotency is not because our only powerful potential enemy has sent men to invade our shores, but rather because of the traitorous actions of those who have been treated so well by this Nation. It has not been the less fortunate or members of minority groups who have been selling this Nation out, but rather those who have had all the

From *Congressional Record,* 81 Congress, 2nd Session, 1954–57.

benefits that the wealthiest nation on earth has had to offer—the finest homes, the finest college education, and the finest jobs in Government we can give.

This is glaringly true in the State Department. There the bright young men who are born with silver spoons in their mouths are the ones who have been the worst. . . . In my opinion the State Department, which is one of the most important government departments, is thoroughly infested with Communists.

I have in my hand 57 cases of individuals who would appear to be either card carrying members or certainly loyal to the Communist Party, but who nevertheless are still helping to shape our foreign policy. . . .

I know that you are saying to yourself, "Well, why doesn't the Congress do something about it?" Actually, ladies and gentlemen, one of the important reasons for the graft, the corruption, the dishonesty, the disloyalty, the treason in high Government positions—one of the most important reasons why this continues is a lack of moral uprising on the part of the 140,000,000 American people. In the light of history, however, this is not hard to explain.

It is the result of an emotional hang-over and a temporary moral lapse which follows every war. It is the apathy to evil which people who have been subjected to the tremendous evils of war feel. As the people of the world see mass murder, the destruction of defenseless and innocent people, and all of the crime and lack of morals which go with war, they become numb and apathetic. It has always been thus after war.

However, the morals of our people have not been destroyed. They still exist. This cloak of numbness and apathy has only needed a spark to rekindle them. Happily, this spark has finally been supplied.

As you know, very recently the Secretary of State proclaimed his loyalty to a man guilty of what has always been considered as the most abominable of all crimes—of being a traitor to the people who gave him a position of great trust. The Secretary of State in attempting to justify his continued devotion to the man who sold out the Christian world to the atheistic world, referred to Christ's Sermon on the Mount as a justification and reason therefore, and the reaction of the American people to this would have made the heart of Abraham Lincoln happy.

When this pompous diplomat in striped pants, with a phony British accent, proclaimed to the American people that Christ on the Mount endorsed communism, high treason, and betrayal of a sacred trust, the blasphemy was so great that it awakened the dormant indignation of the American people.

He has lighted the spark which is resulting in a moral uprising and will end only when the whole sorry mess of twisted, warped thinkers are swept from the national scene so that we may have a new birth of national honesty and decency in government.

Republican Declaration of Conscience

Margaret Chase Smith

Not all Republicans applauded the accusations of treason that McCarthy hurled at the Democratic Administration. On June 1, 1950, Margaret Chase Smith of Maine presented to the Senate the Declaration of Conscience that she penned and that six other moderate Republican senators had cosigned. Evenhandedly, it criticized the Democratic Administration's "complacency to the threat of communism here at home" while refusing to countenance Republicans who sought party victory "through the selfish political exploitation of fear, bigotry, ignorance, and intolerance." Such a view, however, did not represent a majority of the GOP. In the immediate years ahead Republican red-baiting increased in volume and virulence.

Mr. President, I would like to speak briefly and simply about a serious national condition. It is a national feeling of fear and frustration that could result in national suicide and the end of everything that we Americans hold dear. It is a condition that comes from the lack of effective leadership either in the legislative branch or the executive branch of our Government. That leadership is so lacking that serious and responsible proposals are being made that national advisory commissions be appointed to provide such critically needed leadership.

I speak as briefly as possible because too much harm has already been done with irresponsible words of bitterness and selfish political opportunism. I speak as simply as possible because the

From *Congressional Record*, 81 Congress, 2nd Session, 1954–57.

issue is too great to be obscured by eloquence. I speak simply and briefly in the hope that my words will be taken to heart.

Mr. President, I speak as a Republican. I speak as a woman. I speak as a United States Senator. I speak as an American.

The United States Senate has long enjoyed world-wide respect as the greatest deliberative body in the world. But recently that deliberative character has too often been debased to the level of a forum of hate and character assassination sheltered by the shield of congressional immunity.

It is ironical that we Senators can in debate in the Senate, directly or indirectly, by any form of words, impute to any American who is not a Senator any conduct or motive unworthy or unbecoming an American—and without that non-Senator American having any legal redress against us—yet if we say the same thing in the Senate about our colleagues we can be stopped on the grounds of being out of order.

It is strange that we can verbally attack anyone else without restraint and with full protection, and yet we hold ourselves above the same type of criticism here on the Senate floor. Surely the United States Senate is big enough to take self-criticism and self-appraisal. Surely we should be able to take the same kind of character attacks that we "dish out" to outsiders.

I think that it is high time for the United States Senate and its Members to do some real soul searching and to weigh our consciences as to the manner in which we are performing our duty to the people of America and the manner in which we are using or abusing our individual powers and privileges.

I think it is high time that we remembered that we have sworn to uphold and defend the Constitution. I think it is high time that we remembered that the Constitution, as amended, speaks not only of the freedom of speech but also of trial by jury instead of trial by accusation.

Whether it be a criminal prosecution in court or a character prosecution in the Senate, there is little practical distinction when the life of a person has been ruined.

Those of us who shout the loudest about Americanism in making character assassinations are all too frequently those who, by our own words and acts, ignore some of the basic principles of Americanism—

The right to criticize.
The right to hold unpopular beliefs.
The right to protest.
The right of independent thought.

The exercise of these rights should not cost one single American citizen his reputation or his right to a livelihood nor should he be in danger of losing his reputation or livelihood merely because he happens to know someone who holds unpopular beliefs. Who of us does not? Otherwise none of us could call our souls our own. Otherwise thought control would have set in.

The American people are sick and tired of being afraid to speak their minds lest they be politically smeared as Communists or Fascists by their opponents. Freedom of Speech is not what it used to be in America. It has been so abused by some that it is not exercised by others. . . .

As members of the minority party, we do not have the primary authority to formulate the policy of our Government. But we do have the responsibility of rendering constructive criticism, of clarifying issues, of allaying fears by acting as responsible citizens.

As a woman, I wonder how the mothers, wives, sisters, and daughters feel about the way in which members of their families have been politically mangled in Senate debate—and I use the word "debate" advisedly.

As a United States Senator, I am not proud of the way in which the Senate has been made a publicity platform for irresponsible sensationalism. I am not proud of the reckless abandon in which unproved charges have been hurled from this side of the aisle. I am not proud of the obviously staged, undignified countercharges which have been attempted in retaliation from the other side of the aisle.

I do not like the way the Senate has been made a rendezvous for villification, for selfish political gain at the sacrifice of individual reputations and national unity. I am not proud of the way we smear outsiders from the floor of the Senate and hide behind the cloak of congressional immunity and still place ourselves beyond criticism on the floor of the Senate.

As an American, I am shocked at the way Republicans and Democrats alike are playing directly into the Communist design of "confuse, divide, and conquer." As an American, I do not want a

Democratic administration white wash or cover up any more than I want a Republican smear or witch hunt.

As an American, I condemn a Republican Fascist just as much as I condemn a Democrat Communist. I condemn a Democrat Fascist just as much as I condemn a Republican Communist. They are equally dangerous to you and me and to our country. As an American, I want to see our Nation recapture the strength and unity it once had when we fought the enemy instead of ourselves. . . .

STATEMENT OF SEVEN REPUBLICAN SENATORS

1. We are Republicans. But we are Americans first. It is as Americans that we express our concern with the growing confusion that threatens the security and stability of our country. Democrats and Republicans alike have contributed to that confusion.

2. The Democratic administration has initially created the confusion by its lack of effective leadership, by its contradictory grave warnings and optimistic assurances, by its complacency to the threat of communism here at home, by its oversensitiveness to rightful criticism, by its petty bitterness against its critics.

3. Certain elements of the Republican party have materially added to this confusion in the hopes of riding the Republican Party to victory through the selfish political exploitation of fear, bigotry, ignorance, and intolerance. There are enough mistakes of the Democrats for Republicans to criticize constructively without resorting to political smears.

4. To this extent, Democrats and Republicans alike have unwittingly, but undeniably, played directly into the Communist design of "confuse, divide, and conquer."

5. It is high time that we stopped thinking politically as Republicans and Democrats about elections and started thinking patriotically as Americans about national security based on individual freedom. It is high time that we all stopped being tools and victims of totalitarian techniques—techniques that, if continued here unchecked, will surely end what we have come to cherish as the American way of life.

Scoundrel Time

Lillian Hellman

*"I cannot and will not cut my conscience to fit this year's fashions,"
playwright Lillian Hellman wrote to the chairman of the House Committee
on Un-American Activities when called to testify in 1952. Her refusal to
imitate the behavior of the "scoundrels" of the title of her book, who ruined
the lives of others in their groveling appearances before the Committee,
came at a particularly grim moment in the Second Red Scare. Alger Hiss
had been sent to jail and the Rosenbergs condemned to death. With impunity, Joe McCarthy implicated Democratic officials for every manner of
infamous behavior. And the stalemated war in Korea ground on with little
hope for victory. Fear and hatred of communism were paramount. In an
ugly mood, the American people apparently would brook no interference
with the congressional search for spies and scapegoats. Thus, Hellman's
offer to answer all questions about herself but refusal to name others—"to
bring bad trouble to people"—had an extraordinary impact at the time.
Her moral courage in choosing not to hurt innocent people to save herself
made it easier for others to deny the demand to name names and inspired
still others to speak out for freedom of speech and thought. Although
Congress, to the surprise of many, did not cite Hellman for contempt, the
author paid dearly for her defiance, as her autobiographical account,
Scoundrel Time, makes painfully clear.*

DEAR MR. WOOD:

As you know, I am under subpoena to appear before your
Committee on May 21, 1952.

I am most willing to answer all questions about myself. I have nothing to hide from your Committee and there is nothing in my life of which I am ashamed. I have been advised by counsel that under the Fifth Amendment I have a constitutional privilege to decline to answer any questions about my political opinions, activities, and associations, on the grounds of self-incrimination. I do not wish to claim this privilege. I am ready and willing to testify before the representatives of our Government as to my own opinions and my own actions, regardless of any risks or consequences to myself.

But I am advised by counsel that if I answer the Committee's questions about myself, I must also answer questions about other people and that if I refuse to do so, I can be cited for contempt. My counsel tells me that if I answer questions about myself, I will have waived my rights under the Fifth Amendment and could be forced legally to answer questions about others. This is very difficult for a layman to understand. But there is one principle that I do understand: I am not willing, now or in the future, to bring bad trouble to people who, in my past association with them, were completely innocent of any talk or any action that was disloyal or subversive. I do not like subversion or disloyalty in any form, and if I had ever seen any, I would have considered it my duty to have reported it to the proper authorities. But to hurt innocent people whom I knew many years ago in order to save myself is, to me, inhuman and indecent and dishonorable. I cannot and will not cut my conscience to fit this year's fashions, even though I long ago came to the conclusion that I was not a political person and could have no comfortable place in any political group.

I was raised in an old-fashioned American tradition and there were certain homely things that were taught to me: to try to tell the truth, not to bear false witness, not to harm my neighbor, to be loyal to my country, and so on. In general, I respected these ideals of Christian honor and did as well with them as I knew how. It is my belief that you will agree with these simple rules of human decency and will not expect me to violate the good American tradition from which they spring. I would, therefore, like to come before you and speak of myself.

I am prepared to waive the privilege against self-incrimination and to tell you everything you wish to know about my views or actions if your Committee will agree to refrain from asking me to name other people. If the Committee is unwilling to give me this assurance, I will be forced to plead the privilege of the Fifth Amendment at the hearing.

A reply to this letter would be appreciated.

Sincerely yours,
LILLIAN HELLMAN

The answer to the letter is as follows:

DEAR MISS HELLMAN:

Reference is made to your letter dated May 19, 1952, wherein you indicate that in the event the Committee asks you questions regarding your association with other individuals you will be compelled to rely upon the Fifth Amendment in giving your answers to the Committee questions.

In this connection, please be advised that the Committee cannot permit witnesses to set forth the terms under which they will testify.

We have in the past secured a great deal of information from persons in the entertainment profession who cooperated wholeheartedly with the Committee. The Committee appreciates any information furnished it by persons who have been members of the Communist Party. The Committee, of course, realizes that a great number of persons who were members of the Communist Party at one time honestly felt that it was not a subversive organization. However, on the other hand, it should be pointed out that the contributions made to the Communist Party as a whole by persons who were not themselves subversive made it possible for those members of the Communist Party who were and still are subversives to carry on their work.

The Committee has endeavored to furnish a hearing to each person identified as a Communist engaged in work in the entertainment field in order that the record could be made clear as to whether they were still members of the Communist Party. Any persons identified by you during the course of Committee hearings will be afforded the opportunity of appearing before the Committee in accordance with the policy of the Committee.

Sincerely yours,
JOHN S. WOOD, *Chairman*

... The room suddenly began to fill up behind me and the press people began to push toward their section and were still piling in when Representative Wood began to pound his gavel. I hadn't seen the Committee come in, don't think I had realized that they were to sit on a raised platform, the government having learned from the stage, or maybe the other way around. I was glad I hadn't seen them come in—they made a gloomy picture. Through the noise of the gavel I heard one of the ladies in the rear cough very loudly. She was to cough all through the hearing. Later I heard one of her friends say loudly, "Irma, take your good cough drops."

The opening questions were standard: what was my name, where was I born, what was my occupation, what were the titles of my plays. It didn't take long to get to what really interested them: my time in Hollywood, which studios had I worked for, what periods of what years, with some mysterious emphasis on 1937. (My time in Spain, I thought, but I was wrong.)

Had I met a writer called Martin Berkeley? (I had never, still have never, met Martin Berkeley, although Hammett told me later that I had once sat at a lunch table of sixteen or seventeen people with him in the old Metro-Goldwyn-Mayer commissary.) I said I must refuse to answer that question. Mr. Tavenner said he'd like to ask me again whether I had stated I was abroad in the summer of 1937. I said yes, explained that I had been in New York for several weeks before going to Europe, and got myself ready for what I knew was coming: Martin Berkeley, one of the Committee's most lavish witnesses on the subject of Hollywood, was now going to be put to work. Mr. Tavenner read Berkeley's testimony. Perhaps he is worth quoting, the small details are nicely formed, even about his "old friend Hammett," who had no more than a bowing acquaintance with him.

MR. TAVENNER: ... I would like you to tell the committee when and where the Hollywood section of the Communist Party was first organized.

MR. BERKELEY: Well, sir, by a very strange coincidence the section was organized in my house. . . . In June of 1937, the middle of June, the meeting was held in my house. My house was picked because I had a large living room and ample parking facilities. . . . And it was a pretty good meeting. We were honored by the presence of many functionaries from downtown, and the spirit was swell. . . . Well, in addition to Jerome and the others I have men-

tioned before, and there is no sense in going over the list again and
again. . . . Also present was Harry Carlisle, who is now in the process of being deported, for which I am very grateful. He was an
English subject. After Stanley Lawrence had stolen what funds
there were from the party out here, and to make amends had gone
to Spain and gotten himself killed, they sent Harry Carlisle here to
conduct Marxist classes. . . . Also at the meeting was Donald Ogden
Stewart. His name is spelled Donald Ogden S-t-e-w-a-r-t. Dorothy
Parker, also a writer. Her husband Allen Campbell, C-a-m-p-b-e-l-l;
my old friend Dashiell Hammett, who is now in jail in New York
for his activities; that very excellent playwright, Lillian Hellman . . .

And so on.

When this nonsense was finished, Mr. Tavenner asked me if it
was true. I said that I wanted to refer to the letter I had sent. I
would like the Committee to reconsider my offer in the letter.

> MR. TAVENNER: In other words, you are asking the committee
> not to ask you any questions regarding the participation of other
> persons in the Communist Party activities?

I said I hadn't said that.

Mr. Wood said that in order to clarify the record Mr. Tavenner
should put into the record the correspondence between me and
the Committee. Mr. Tavenner did just that, and when he had
finished Rauh sprang to his feet, picked up a stack of mimeographed copies of my letter, and handed them out to the press
section. I was puzzled by this—I hadn't noticed he had the
copies—but I did notice that Rauh was looking happy.

Mr. Tavenner was upset, far more than the printed words of
my hearing show. Rauh said that Tavenner himself had put the
letters in the record, and thus he thought passing out copies was
proper. The polite words of each as they read on the page were
not polite as spoken. I am convinced that in this section of the
testimony, as in several other sections—certainly in Hammett's
later testimony before the Senate Internal Security Subcommittee—either the court stenographer missed some of what was said
and filled it in later, or the documents were, in part, edited. Having read many examples of the work of court stenographers, I
have never once seen a completely accurate report.

Mr. Wood told Mr. Tavenner that the Committee could not be

"placed in the attitude of trading witnesses as to what they will testify to" and that thus he thought both letters should be read aloud.

Mr. Tavenner did just this, and there was talk I couldn't hear, a kind of rustle, from the press-section. Then Mr. Tavenner asked me if I had attended the meeting described by Berkeley, and one of the hardest things I ever did in my life was to swallow the words, "I don't know him, and a little investigation into the time and place would have proved to you that I could not have been at the meeting he talks about." Instead, I said that I must refuse to answer the question. The "must" in that sentence annoyed Mr. Wood—it was to annoy him again and again—and he corrected me: "You might refuse to answer, the question is asked, do you refuse?"

But Wood's correction of me, the irritation in his voice, was making me nervous, and I began to move my right hand as if I had a tic, unexpected, and couldn't stop it. I told myself that if a word irritated him, the insults would begin to come very soon. So I sat up straight, made my left hand hold my right hand, and hoped it would work. But I felt the sweat on my face and arms and knew that something was going to happen to me, something out of control, and I turned to Joe, remembering the suggested toilet intermission. But the clock said we had only been there sixteen minutes, and if it was going to come, the bad time, I had better hang on for a while.

Was I a member of the Communist Party, had I been, what year had I stopped being? How could I harm such people as Martin Berkeley by admitting I had known them, and so on. At times I couldn't follow the reasoning, at times I understood full well that in refusing to answer questions about membership in the Party I had, of course, trapped myself into a seeming admission that I once had been.

But in the middle of one of the questions about my past, something so remarkable happened that I am to this day convinced that the unknown gentleman who spoke had a great deal to do with the rest of my life. A voice from the press gallery had been for at least three or four minutes louder than the other voices. (By this time, I think, the press had finished reading my letter to the committee and were discussing it.) The loud voice had been answered by a less loud voice, but no words could be distinguished. Suddenly a clear voice said, "Thank God somebody finally had the guts to do it."

It is never wise to say that something is the best minute of your life, you must be forgetting, but I still think that unknown voice made the words that helped to save me. (I had been sure that not only did the elderly ladies in the room disapprove of me, but the press would be antagonistic.) Wood rapped his gavel and said angrily, "If that occurs again, I will clear the press from these chambers."

"You do that, sir," said the same voice.

Mr. Wood spoke to somebody over his shoulder and the somebody moved around to the press section, but that is all that happened. To this day I don't know the name of the man who spoke, but for months later, almost every day I would say to myself, I wish I could tell him that I had really wanted to say to Mr. Wood: "There is no Communist menace in this country and you know it. You have made cowards into liars, an ugly business, and you made me write a letter in which I acknowledged your power. I should have gone into your Committee room, given my name and address, and walked out." Many people have said they liked what I did, but I don't much, and if I hadn't worried about rats in jail, and such. . . . Ah, the bravery you tell yourself was possible when it's all over, the bravery of the staircase.

In the Committee room I heard Mr. Wood say, "Mr. Walter does not desire to ask the witness any further questions. Is there any reason why this witness should not be excused from further attendance before the Committee?"

Mr. Tavenner said, "No, sir."

My hearing was over an hour and seven minutes after it began. I don't think I understood that it was over, but Joe was whispering so loudly and so happily that I jumped from the noise in my ear.

He said, "*Get up. Get up.* Get out of here immediately. Pollitt will take you. Don't stop for any reason, to answer any questions from anybody. Don't run, but walk as fast as you can and just shake your head and keep moving if anybody comes near you."

Life had changed and there were many people who did not call me. But there were others, a few friends, a few half-strangers, who made a point of asking me for dinner or who sent letters.

That was kind, because I knew that some of them were worried about the consequences of seeing me.

But the mishmash of those years, beginning before my congressional debut and for years after, took a heavy penalty. My belief in liberalism was mostly gone. I think I have substituted for it something private called, for want of something that should be more accurate, decency. And yet certain connecting strings have outworn many knives, perhaps because the liberal connections' had been there for thirty years and that's a long time. There was nothing strange about my problem, it is native to our time; but it is painful for a nature that can no longer accept liberalism not to be able to accept radicalism. One sits uncomfortably on a too comfortable cushion. Many of us now endlessly jump from one side to another and endlessly fall in space. The American creative world is not only equal but superior in talent to their colleagues in other countries, but they have given no leadership, written no words of new theory in a country that cries out for belief and, because it has none, finds too many people acting in strange and aimless violence.

But there were other penalties in that year of 1952: life was to change sharply in ordinary ways. We were to have enough money for a few years and then we didn't have any, and that was to last for a while, with occasional windfalls. I saw that coming the day the subpoena was first served. It was obvious, as I have said, the farm had to be sold. I knew I would now be banned from writing movies, that the theatre was as uncertain as it always had been, and I was slow and usually took two years to write a play. Hammett's radio, television and book money was gone forever. I could have broken up the farm in small pieces and made a fortune—I had had an offer that made that possible—and I might have accepted it except for Hammett, who said, "No, I won't have it that way. Let everybody else mess up the land. Why don't you and I leave it alone?", a fine sentiment with which I agree and have forever regretted listening to. More important than the sale of the farm, I knew that a time of my life had ended and the faster I put it away the easier would be an altered way of living, although I think the sale of the farm was the most painful loss of my life. It was, perhaps, more painful to Hammett, although to compare the pains of the loss of beloved land one has worked oneself, a house that fits because you have made it fit thinking you would live in it forever, is a foolish guess-game.

Part Three

THE POLITICS OF
THE AFFLUENT SOCIETY

The 1950s and 1960s are generally seen as very different eras in American history. Under the calm, beneficent, paternal leadership of Dwight Eisenhower, America in the 1950s appeared to be enjoying a time of equanimity. After the immediate postwar tensions of inflation, strikes, and foreign policy conflicts, the era of Eisenhower seemed remarkable for its stability. The first Republican to be elected in twenty years, Eisenhower pledged moderation, peace, and an end to corruption in government. While not extending New Deal social welfare programs, neither did Eisenhower attempt to reverse them. Rather, his was an administration of consolidation. The country appeared prosperous, and happy to have a respite from conflict.

The 1960s, by contrast, represented a new cycle of reform and insurgency. Led by the presidencies of John F. Kennedy and Lyndon B. Johnson, the nation set forth to allievate persistent inequities of racial discrimination, to combat poverty, and to create a new and improved society. "We can do better," Kennedy had said in 1960. "We *will* do better," Johnson promised in 1964. At least on the surface, the two postwar eras seemed radically different, one given to complacency, quietude, and stability, the other to activism, challenge, and change.

In fact, the appearances were as deceptive as they were accurate. The struggles that brought reform in the 1960s were already emerging throughout the "quiet years of the 1950s." Moreover, the policies of the 1960s represented continuity with the past as well as an effort to generate new programs. Both eras, in fact, reflected what Godfrey Hodgson has called the "liberal consensus" in America—the belief that improvement is always possible within a fundamentally sound economic and social system, that right-minded and intelligent people can create a healthy and viable social system, that moderation is preferable to extremism, and that an economy committed to growth will provide the basis for eliminating almost all social problems while assuring prosperity for the middle class.

The selections included here paint in broad strokes the similarities as well as discontinuities in these two eras. Lawrence Wittner describes the emergence of corporate and technological hegemony during the 1950s and 1960s, showing the underlying economic forces at work in the society. Godfrey Hodgson contrasts the promise of Kennedy with the tragedy of Watergate and Nixon. Perhaps most interesting, selections from Eisenhower and Johnson highlight some of the basic forces at work during the two decades. Despite his apparent complacency, Eisenhower clearly recognized the long-range dangers in a society where technology and corporate control could work together with the military to shape and define the options available to the society. His plea for awareness of, and control over, the military-industrial complex represents a wise voice of concern about the dangers of the new forces taking control of the society. Johnson's call for a Great Society, in turn, represents the positive side of the same developments, reflecting LBJ's belief that a country willing and able to harness the forces of technology and economic growth could go on to create a quality existence for virtually everyone.

Among the questions raised by these selections are the extent to which we are controlled by impersonal economic and social forces beyond our ability to shape; whether political leaders are capable of directing these forces; and how and whether it is possible to achieve our goals within the constraints of the existing social and economical order, based as it is on significant class and income differences. One ought to ponder, moreover, why such a false complacency existed in American life and thought, the assumptions of modern American liberalism, and the causes of its successes and failures.

The Rulers and the Ruled: American Society, 1945–60

Lawrence S. Wittner

Rejecting the conventional interpretation of American society in the post-war era, Lawrence Wittner of the State University of New York in Albany depicts the 1945–60 period as years of corporate hegemony. Writing from a radical, "New Left" point of view, Wittner excoriates the privileged elite that selfishly controlled the government to enhance its own power and wealth and that set a tone for the "silent generation" to ignore continuing racial discriminations and the existence of bitter poverty in the midst of the consumer culture.

To the many millions who gained little or nothing from the ever-expanding Gross National Product or from technological progress, no discernible difference existed between Truman's Fair Deal and Eisenhower's Dynamic Conservatism. Although a necessary corrective to the roseate pictures of the United States developed by most commentators in the age of consensus, students may well ask what is omitted or distorted in Wittner's portrait of America. After a decade and a half of depression and war, what did this generation of Americans seek, and why? What meaningful distinctions can be made between modern American liberalism and conservatism? What intelligent generalizations best characterize this period?

"America is a middle-class country," sociologist David Riesman concluded from the vantage point of his Harvard University office. "Perhaps people will soon wake up to the fact that there is no

From *Cold War America: From Hiroshima to Watergate* by Lawrence S. Wittner. Copyright © 1974 by Praeger Publishers, Inc. Reprinted by permission of Holt, Rinehart and Winston.

longer . . . a 'we' who don't run things and a 'they' who do, but
rather that all 'we's' are 'they's' and all 'they's' are 'we's'." Few
ideas were more widely bruited about in the prosperous postwar
years than the notion that substantial inequalities in the distribution of wealth and power in America had ceased to exist. Arthur
F. Burns, Eisenhower's top economic adviser, remarked in 1951
that "the transformation in the distribution of our national income . . . may already be counted as one of the great social revolutions in history." When economist John Kenneth Galbraith's *The
Affluent Society* appeared in 1958, it seemed merely to set the seal
of approval on the prevailing consensus. The "old issues" of inequality, slums, and inadequate wages and medical care were
dead, he contended; instead, the nation now faced the problems
of abundance. All seemed to agree that the crusades against inequality that had marked previous decades in American history
could safely be abandoned. "The fundamental political problems
of the industrial revolution have been solved," sociologist Seymour Martin Lipset announced in 1959, with the "triumph of the
democratic social revolution in the West."

This optimistic assessment owed much to the postwar wave of
prosperity. The gross national product jumped from $212 billion
to $504 billion between 1945 and 1960. In the 1950s alone, per
capita personal income rose 48 percent. In 1953 an estimated 58
percent of American families earned between $3,000 and $10,000
a year compared to 31 percent with similar purchasing power in
1929. . . .

But postwar prosperity obscured the more significant reality of
economic inequality. Although the share of the national income
received by the wealthiest 5 percent of the American population
dropped markedly in the Depression and war years, it stabilized
in 1944 at 21 percent and did not change significantly thereafter.
The poorest 20 percent of American families received 5 percent
of the national income in 1944, and this, too, remained virtually
constant. Even more striking was the increasingly unequal distribution of wealth. According to the National Bureau of Economic
Research, the share of the nation's wealth held by the richest .5
percent of the adult population steadily declined between 1929
and 1949 until it hit 19.3 percent, but thereafter it increased,
reaching 25 percent in 1956. By 1962 the richest 1 percent of the
population held 33 percent of the wealth, the richest 5 percent

held 53 percent, and the richest 20 percent held 77 percent—more than 154 times the share of the nation's wealth (less than .5 percent) held by the poorest 20 percent.

Corporate wealth provided the basis for this inequitable structure. Despite the fanfare given "people's capitalism" by the National Advertising Council and the U.S. Information Agency, almost 95 percent of the American people owned no corporate stock in 1956. Indeed, a study by Robert Lampman, later a top White House economic adviser, revealed that the share of corporate stock held by 1 percent of American adults increased from 61.7 percent in 1945 to 76 percent in 1953. In that same year, 1.6 percent of the population owned 82.2 percent of the corporate stock, 88.5 percent of the corporate bonds, and virtually all of the state and local bonds. If the United States lacked dramatic class conflict from 1945 to 1960, it was nonetheless a class society, based on private ownership of a corporate economy.

Actively managing their businesses or merely reaping the profits, the corporate rich enjoyed a rewarding life in the postwar years. The board chairmen of six American oil companies drew annual salaries ranging from $175,000 to $250,000. Most corporation executives owned large blocks of company stock; indeed, stock and cash bonuses often out-distanced annual salaries. Thus, in 1952, the president of Du Pont received $153,290 in salary and $350,000 in bonuses; the president of Bethlehem Steel received $150,000 in salary and $306,652 in bonuses; and the president of General Motors received $201,000 in salary and $380,000 in bonuses—in addition to dividends. Corporation executives also received a variety of less visible emoluments, including expense accounts, country club privileges, business cars, lavish parties, company credit cards, paid vacations, medical treatment, and sizable pensions. The U.S. Treasury Department estimated in 1957 that expense accounts ran from $5 billion to $10 billion annually; most items charged to credit card companies in 1958 were billed to businesses. Direct income, then, represented only a small fraction of the bonanza enjoyed by the corporate élite, and even this fraction was frequently underestimated on federal tax returns. . . . In 1953 Robert Lampman had estimated that there were 27,000 millionaires in America; nine years later, the Federal Reserve System reported 80,000.

Despite their unprecedented prosperity, the corporate rich introduced few dramatic changes in the well-ordered routine of

American upper-class life. Childhood dancing classes and attendance at prep schools like Exeter, Andover, Choate, Groton, and
Hotchkiss continued to give a young man the proper social training and associates before entering an élite college or university,
joining the "right" campus club or fraternity, and taking up his
place in the appropriate men's club—the Links, the Knicker-
bocker, the Metropolitan, the Racquet, or the Brook. Fashionable
summer resorts, debutante balls, cultural organizations, and recreational activities such as yachting, polo matches, and fox hunts
gave him the opportunity to mingle comfortably with members of
his class. A young lady might attend dancing classes as a child
before "coming out" in society at the crucial debutante ball. . . .

As always, the business élite took a keen interest in the policies
of the American government. "Gulf and every other American
corporation is in politics, up to its ears in politics," a senior vice-
president remarked in 1958. The largest manufacturers and
bankers, primarily white Anglo-Saxon Protestants from families
that achieved prominence between the Civil War and the Depression, controlled the Republican Party. The Democratic Party, on
the other hand, was controlled by very old and very new elements
within the upper class, including Southern aristocrats, a few old
Northern patricians, and the newer ethnic rich. . . .

"Business liberals," usually from the largest, most internationally oriented companies, found their voice in the Council on Foreign Relations and the Committee for Economic Development
and their home in the "moderate" Eastern wing of the GOP or in
the Democratic Party. The "old guard," more right-wing in view-
point, mostly comprised nationally oriented businessmen who
provided the bedrock strength of the National Association of
Manufacturers and the conservative wing of the Republican Party.
"Business liberals" were particularly enraptured by the Eisenhower Administration, but "old guard" elements, such as the new
Texas oil millionaires, lavishly funded right-wing politicians and
causes. Three former presidents of the NAM were among the
first leaders of the John Birch Society.

The political power of the corporate rich is illustrated by the
fact that, although they constituted less than 1 percent of the
population, they dominated the key policy-making posts within
the federal government. Of the ninety-one individuals who served
as Secretaries and Under Secretaries of State and Defense, the

Secretaries of the three military services, the Chairmen of the AEC, and the Directors of the CIA between 1940 and 1967, seventy came from the ranks of big business and finance. Members of the upper class seemed particularly welcome in the State, Defense, and Treasury departments. Of the six Secretaries of State between 1945 and 1960, five were listed in the *Social Register*. Three of the five were corporation lawyers, one was a wealthy general, and one was a Boston aristocrat; the sixth was a powerful Southern Democrat of conservative views. Between 1947, when it was created, and 1960 the Department of Defense was headed by six men, of whom five were listed in the *Social Register;* the exception was the president of General Motors.

During his term of office, President Truman relied heavily upon Wall Street financiers, many of whom were not even Democrats. Twenty-two key posts in the State Department, ten in the Defense Department, and five top positions in other agencies went to bankers who were either registered Republicans or politically unaffiliated. Eisenhower preferred to appoint directors of the nation's major manufacturing concerns. His first Secretary of Defense was a former president of the world's largest industrial corporation; his Secretary of the Treasury had formerly directed a complex of more than thirty corporations; his Secretary of State had been the senior partner of the nation's leading corporate law firm; and every other member of his Cabinet—with the exception of the Secretary of Labor—came from the ranks of the corporate rich. Of the thirty-two members of Eisenhower's subcabinet, only four were not directly associated with the corporate world. . . .

As the business élite moved assuredly through the world of political power, the leading corporations strengthened their grip on the nation's economy. Corporate profits, $19 billion in 1945, hit $50 billion but fifteen years later. In 1950 the share of the business assets held by the nation's 200 largest companies was 48.9 percent; by 1962 it had reached 55 percent. In the latter year, the hundred largest manufacturing corporations drew 57.6 percent of the net profits, while the thousand largest manufacturing corporations accounted for 86.4 percent. . . .

Government solicitude for the rich did much to make such gains possible. A variety of loopholes kept the effective rate of inheritance taxes under 10 percent, while sales taxes, a form of government levy that hardly touched the wealthy, spread to cities and states throughout the nation. The progressive effects of the federal income tax, once the pride of liberals, were gutted in the postwar years by preferential treatment for capital gains, depletion allowances, depreciation allowances, and tax-free privileges for interest on state and municipal bonds. In 1961 seventeen persons with incomes of $1 million or more and thirty-five others with incomes over $500,000 paid no federal income taxes. Reporting on the cumulative impact of taxation on income in 1960, economist Leon Keyserling concluded that those who earned under $2,000 paid out 38 percent of their income in taxes, while those who earned above $10,000 paid out only 31.6 percent.

Similar government beneficence was extended to corporations. A study during the 1950s disclosed that, as a result of the 27½ percent oil-depletion allowance, oil companies deducted nineteen times more for tax purposes than they could deduct under normal cost depletion. Senator Paul Douglas estimated that between 1945 and 1954 twenty-seven domestic oil companies with pretax incomes of $3.25 billion paid federal corporate taxes of only $562 million—an effective rate of 17 percent as compared to the official corporate tax rate of 52 percent. Other tax breaks, such as deductions for depreciation, development costs, and special losses, also favored the oil industry. Thus, Humble Oil, with a pretax income in 1957 of $193 million, paid only $17 million that year in corporate taxes. The Arabian-American Oil Company, with a net income of $272 million in 1955, paid no corporate income taxes.

Even more significant benefits flowed to American corporations—and to the economy as a whole—from the high level of federal military expenditures. Between 1946 and 1960 the Defense Department alone purchased $501 billion worth of goods and services. "National security" expenditures generally accounted for about 70 percent of the annual federal budget. In the half-century prior to 1930 federal military expenditures had averaged less than 1 percent of the nation's annual GNP, and from 1931 to 1939 military outlays averaged only about 1.3 percent. From 1946 to 1960, however, federal military spending averaged about 10 percent of the nation's annual GNP, serving as a sharp stimulus to the economy. . . . Yet the high level of "defense" spending not only spurred sales and employment but altered the very nature of the nation's economy. In the new "contract state," the Pentagon set demand, funding its purchases of corporate equipment with tax dollars. The price of such equipment was generally determined, not through free market competition, but through a "cost plus" arrangement, guaranteeing a corporation a minimum profit agreed upon in advance. Thus, the United States moved away from the "free enterprise" system preached by conservatives and the "mixed economy" proclaimed by liberals toward a government-subsidized private profit system. . . .

Convinced, in the words of the pro-business *U.S. News and World Report*, that the "Cold War is almost a guarantee against a bad depression," American corporations tied their fortunes to the ascending military star. Corporations lobbied furiously for bigger Pentagon contracts. "The aircraft industry," said Senator Barry Goldwater, "has probably done more to promote the Air Force than the Air Force has done itself." Cementing their links to the Pentagon, corporations staffed their hierarchies with unprecedented numbers of retired military officers. A House subcommittee revealed in 1960 that 1,400 retired officers above the rank of major, including 261 generals and admirals, were employed by the hundred leading defense-contract corporations. General Dynamics, ranking first among defense contractors from 1957 to 1960, maintained 186 retired officers on its payroll, while retaining a former Secretary of the Army as chairman of its board of directors. With sales and profits soaring under the reign of Pentagon capitalism, American business showed little enthusiasm for peacetime reconversion. In 1960, when the projected international summit conference collapsed and talk of disarmament faded, the stock market rose dramatically. . . .

American business also gained significantly from its expanding overseas operations, promoted and protected by U.S. foreign policy. Between 1946 and 1960 the value of direct (or controlling) American private investment abroad increased from $7 billion to $32 billion. Total U.S. private investment abroad increased between 1950 and 1960 from $19 billion to $49 billion. During the 1950s the direct investment outflow was $13.7 billion and the returned income $23.2 billion—a handsome profit. . . .

A growing volume of world trade proved equally crucial to American corporations. . . . A 1954 staff report of the President's Commission on Foreign Economic Policy noted that the "transition of the United States from a position of self-sufficiency to one of increasing dependence upon foreign supply is one of the striking economic changes of our time." In return for their vast imports of raw materials, U.S. corporations inundated the markets of the "free world" with the latest manufactured products. From 1950 to 1960 the value of American exports doubled to $20.6 billion, while American imports climbed by almost two-thirds to $14.7 billion. Moreover, these figures reflect only a declining fraction of total U.S. overseas commerce, for America's rapidly growing multinational corporations increasingly produced and sold goods within foreign nations themselves. Little wonder that the corporate élite took a keen interest in American foreign policy. The United States "must set the pace and assume the responsibility of the majority stockholder in this corporation known as the world," declared the treasurer (later chairman) of Standard Oil of New Jersey in 1946. "American private enterprise . . . may strike out and save its own position all over the world, or sit by and witness its own funeral."

Committed to expanding their overseas operations, American businessmen remained equally determined to develop their private markets at home. Widening the base of personal consumption in the United States would have necessitated a redistribution of income; corporate chieftains sought instead to induce those who could already purchase what they wanted to buy still more and, if possible, to waste what they had already bought. Not the fulfillment of need but the creation of desire was the function of advertising, whose annual volume rose in the fifteen years after 1945 from less than $3 billion to almost $12 billion—about three times the nation's annual expenditures on higher education. Consumerism became the true American religion, the "American way of life." Dr. Raymond Saulnier, chairman of the Eisenhower Council of Economic Advisers, proclaimed that the "ultimate purpose" of the American economy was "to produce more consumer goods. This is the goal. This is the object of everything we are working at." Caught up in the mammoth sales campaigns and barraged by the mass media, Americans became increasingly convinced that happiness meant ceaseless acquisition. . . .

The mass media served as the principal disseminators of the ideology of individual acquisition. As one critic noted: "It could almost be argued that the articles in magazines and programs on television are simply a device to keep the advertisements and commercials from bumping loudly together. The message of the media is the commercial." Between 1946 and 1960 the number of families in the United States with television sets rose from 8,000 to 46 million, giving the electronic medium the ability to reach into 90 percent of American homes. With families spending an estimated five hours a day watching television, corporations worked ceaselessly to exploit this market for their products. . . . The primary function of television, then, was commerce, which explains why commercials, filling 20 percent of air time, cost far more to produce and were far more skillfully done than the programs they framed. . . .

Yet television and the mass media also played a crucial political role. As the Defense Department's director of research told a Senate committee in 1961: "We cannot consider our communications systems solely as civil activities . . . but we must consider them as essential instruments of national policy." On news programs events were reported anecdotally, individually, amusingly. Institutional problems were ignored, controversial opinions left unspoken, and the day's events viewed as a hopeless jumble, interesting but purposeless, by a cheery, fatherly commentator; implicitly, the viewer was assured that the nation was in good hands. More subtly, the mass media evaded America's public and private issues and thus, as sociologists Paul Lazarsfeld and Robert Merton observed, "fail to raise essential questions about the structure of society." Television and the movies were filled with escapist tales of violence and exploitative sex. Mass culture did not encourage thought, creativity, or personal expression but, rather, passivity. It channeled the interests of the weary viewer into an unreal world where he could act out fantasies of personal power and freedom. Not religion but television served as the opiate of the masses. . . .

The blackout of critical opinion during the postwar years received still further impetus from the loyalty crusade. Learned men assessed the patriotic merits of movie and television scripts. Performers and newscasters were dropped as "security risks." Charlie Chaplin, once America's best-loved clown and social satirist, surrendered his re-entry permit in 1953, choosing exile from a nation he could no longer endure. "What is the new loyalty?" asked historian Henry Steele Commager. "It is, above all, conformity. It is the uncritical and unquestioning acceptance of America as it is."

In the era of the booster, religion took on a patriotic significance. "Recognition of the Supreme Being is the first, the most basic expression of Americanism," President Eisenhower declared in 1955. Congress added the words "under God" to the nation's "pledge of allegiance" and "In God We Trust" to coins. In Lincoln's day only about one out of five Americans had belonged to a church, but by 1958 church membership had climbed to a record 110 million citizens. Polls found that 95 percent of the respondents considered themselves Protestants, Catholics, or Jews, and that 97 percent believed in God. The Reverend Billy Graham held enormous religious revivals, while fundamentalist sects grew rapidly. Religious books became best-sellers, spreading a message of joyous acceptance. "Don't doubt," pleaded the Reverend Norman Vincent Peale; "doubt closes the power flow." The very source of Communism, claimed Whittaker Chambers, an ardent religious mystic, was the scientific method, with its "rigorous exclusion of all supernatural factors in solving problems." Believing America to be locked in a struggle with "atheistic Communism," American churches faithfully mirrored the Cold War line in the years before 1960. Roman Catholic clergy spearheaded the Anti-Communist Crusade and discussed preventive war against Russia, while fundamentalist Protestant sects portrayed the Cold War in apocalyptic terms, identifying Stalin with the Anti-Christ and discovering descriptions of atomic warfare in the Book of Revelation.

Blessed by the guardians of religion, America's "patriotic" crusade also drew at least the tacit support of most American educators. "The single most important educational frontier," reported the U.S. Commissioner of Education in 1947, was the need to "strengthen national security through education." Responding to pressures for conformity, the National Education Association proclaimed in 1949 that Communist teachers should be dismissed from their posts. Three years later the American Federation of Teachers adopted a similar position, which also became the general outlook of college and university presidents. Only the American Association of University Professors and the American Civil Liberties Union took the stand that competence alone should determine employment. A minority of American educational institutions—exemplified by Harvard University and the University of Chicago—stood firm against the loyalty zealots. Most colleges, however, showed an eager willingness to cooperate with special investigations. Indeed, a group of educators even proposed that the colleges set up their own investigatory procedures to weed out alleged "subversives.". . .

But the American university was a valuable institution, and the corporate élite merely wanted it tamed, not destroyed. Thus, despite the demoralization of the professoriat, its ranks actually swelled from 196,000 to 250,000 between 1948 and 1957 as part of a vast building and expansion program in higher education. A study by the Council for Financial Aid to Education found that in 1956 "corporate investments in education" by 275 firms totaled amost $29 million. University presidents lent a sympathetic ear to the needs of business, promoted the establishment or expansion of engineering and business schools, frequented the conference room of wealthy private foundations and the Pentagon, and managed their growing "plant" like administrators of the great industrial and financial corporations, on whose boards of directors they often sat. Grayson Kirk, president of Columbia University after Eisenhower, served on the boards of Consolidated Edison, IBM, the Socony-Mobil Oil Company, and the Nation-Wide Securities Company, and would soon be one óf the directors of the Institute for Defense Analysis. By the mid-1950s, the Pentagon was supplying approximately $300 million annually for university research, and two major universities—MIT and Johns Hopkins—placed on the list of the nation's top 100 defense contractors. According to a 1961 Harvard University report, "science and defense have brought Government and the educational community together to such an extent that 20% of the total expenditures in higher education in the United States now comes from Federal sources."

Surveys of college students during the 1950s invariably found them conservative, careerist, and conformist. Journalist William H. Whyte contended that younger men "do not wish to protest, they wish to collaborate." Students worked harder, professors agreed, but seemed less "interesting." College girls told pollsters that they preferred having babies to careers, while bright young men asked corporate interviewers about their pension plans. "When a liberal or speculative voice is heard in the classroom, it is more likely than not to be the professor's," noted a faculty member at Queens College. Students, he observed, "matriculate cautious, wanting above all . . . to buy security for themselves in the full knowledge that the price is conformity." From the University of Nebraska, the poet Karl Shapiro reported: "Passivity is the last word we expect to use in connection with a generation of students, but that's the only word that applies."

Loyalty investigators and corporate recruiters did much to encourage this "silent generation." "Personal views can cause a lot of trouble," confided an oil company "guidance" pamphlet widely used in college placement offices. "Remember to keep them always conservative. The 'isms' are out. Business . . . naturally looks with disfavor on the wild-eyed radical or even the moderate pink." But a more immediate stimulus to Cold War orthodoxy developed after 1950, when the CIA began covertly funding the National Student Association, the nation's largest and most influential student organization, providing it in some years with up to 80 percent of its income. By 1966, when the CIA venture was at last exposed by an NSA officer, NSA leaders had accepted $4 million in return for providing information on foreign student leaders and for operating a properly anti-Communist student organization. . . .

Intellectual life in America had taken a profoundly conservative turn. A new generation of historians smoothed over the radical convulsions of the past, writing fondly of an American "consensus" beyond which only fools and neurotics dared to tread. Political scientists talked much of "pluralism"—the alleged equality of power among competing groups in America. Accepting the structure of society as given, they looked to technical experts to solve any problems that might crop up. Sociologists, ignoring class structure and the existence of poverty, focused upon the problems of individual identity in a mass society. In philosophy speculative thought gave way to analysis of existing linguistic practices, in the belief that most—if not all—philosophical difficulties arose from the misuse of language; social distinctions that enforced linguistic usage were not themselves examined or criticized. Increasingly, economists and social scientists argued that big business was both democratic and beneficent. America, they claimed, had a "mixed" economy in which socialist aims—at least those of any value—had been incorporated. While most intellectuals never drifted to the right of the moderate Establishment, a few preached a New Conservatism, drawing their arguments consciously from Aristotle, Saint Thomas Aquinas, Edmund Burke, George Santayana, Irving Babbitt, and T. S. Eliot. "For the radical intellectual who had articulated the revolutionary impulses of the past century and a half," wrote Daniel Bell, there has been "an end to chiliastic hopes, to millenarianism, to apocalyptic thinking—and to ideology."

Not suprisingly, American intellectuals developed considerable affection for a U.S. foreign policy based upon *Realpolitik*. Many, like Reinhold Niebuhr and Walter Lippmann, both former idealists and socialists, criticized what they considered a bankrupt utopianism and urged renewed attention to human greed, ignorance, and depravity. Power, they argued, was what counted in world affairs. In *American Diplomacy, 1900–1950* (1951), George F. Kennan helped set the tone for political scientists and other scholarly appraisers of foreign policy by sharply assailing "the assumption that state behavior is a fit subject for moral judgment." Together with Hans J. Morgenthau—whose *In Defense of the National Interest* (1951) found justice, morality, and "world opinion" irrelevant— Kennan launched an attack upon "idealism," which frequently had the effect of stimulating cynicism and Machiavellianism among intellectuals and policy makers. In these years the "defense of the national interest" invariably coincided with a defense of America's role in the Cold War.

Prized by Washington for their skills as sophisticated weaponeers, American scientists and engineers quickly swirled into the Cold War vortex. President Eisenhower revealed that in 1960 approximately a third of American scientists and engineers were engaged in military work and that half the nation's research and development funds went to military projects. "This symbiosis between science and the military," wrote physicist I. I. Rabi, was "the most important . . . social and political development of this century." By contrast, those scientists with doubts about the arms race encountered a most unsympathetic reception from government loyalty investigators. The scientific community was "demoralized," reported Dr. Vannevar Bush, former head of the Office of Scientific Research and Development, in 1954. Later that year, Albert Einstein declared in a public letter that, if he were young again, he "would not try to become a scientist or scholar or teacher. I would rather choose to be a plumber or a peddler in the hope to find that modest degree of independence still available under present circumstances.". . .

The retreat of intellectuals from social criticism reflected a variety of factors. For some, the failure of American capitalism to collapse and of the Soviet Union to provide a decent alternative lay at the root of their disillusionment with "ideology." Others seemed eager to erase the stigma of a radical past by "confessing" before loyalty investigators or simply by becoming "apolitical." Most significantly, well-paid employment in book publishing, radio, and television, and with universities, foundations, magazines, newspapers, and the federal government took the edge off intellectual alienation. Soothed by comfortable salaries and flattered by the attention of men of power, many intellectuals concluded that their own upper-middle-class problems of affluence, leisure, and suburban existence were the major ones facing American society. . . .

Once the very symbol of life in the lower depths, American labor seemed to thrive in the postwar years. Incomes rose, unemployment remained mild by Depression standards, and union membership increased from 14.3 million to 18.1 million between 1945 and 1960. In 1955 the feud between the CIO and the AFL came to an end when a convention in New York merged the two labor federations. The political-action arms of both groups joined to form the Committee on Political Education, and a staff of 265 organizers and millions of dollars in union pledges were set aside to "organize the unorganized." New labor contracts provided for cost-of-living increases as well as productivity increases, and unions also made breakthroughs on "fringe benefits": holidays and vacations, health and welfare plans, and pension and unemployment benefits. Throughout the 1950s most strikes grew less rancorous than in previous decades. Picketing was sometimes unnecessary, and at other times management would supply pickets with hot coffee and portable washrooms. Taking office in 1955, AFL-CIO president George Meany announced: "American labor has never had it so good."

In fact, however, the labor movement was in serious trouble. It encountered little difficulty in retaining the allegiance of those blue-collar workers it had already organized, but their numbers were steadily dwindling with the over-all decline of blue-collar employment. After 1951 more than a third of American unions suffered membership losses. Nor did the AFL-CIO succeed in reaching many of the unorganized, particularly in service trades, white-collar fields, and agricultural employment. By 1960 unions had organized only 12,000 of the 600,000 engineers, draftsmen, and technicians; 184,000 of the 5 million public employees; 200,000 of the 8.5 million office workers; and 4,000 of the 2 million agricultural workers. Pledges to the AFL-CIO's organizing fund were never met, the size of the organizing staff was cut in half, and the attempt to unionize the South—the nation's anti-union bastion—proved virtually a complete failure. Nonunion companies and areas fought fiercely to smash organizing efforts. "Do you want to work under a Negro foreman?" Southern employers would ask their workers. "Do you want your dues money to go to the NAACP?". . .

Moreover, even organized workers achieved only minimal gains. In part, this reflected the fact that a giant corporation, having agreed to a wage settlement, would simply raise its prices, thus passing along the cost of the settlement to all workers as consumers. Of all labor leaders, only Walter Reuther championed raising wages while freezing prices, and the auto companies refused to consider this prospect. During the 1950s blue-collar workers fell farther behind other groups in terms of income. Laborers and service workers made income gains of 39 percent, while professional and managerial workers made income gains of 68 percent. In addition, by concentrating upon wages and fringe benefits, unions failed to secure many changes in job conditions. Safety features in American coal mines remained abysmal; mine explosions and other lethal disasters were frequent. Every year approximately 100,000 American workers were killed or suffered permanent impairment in industrial accidents. Factory labor remained exceptionally alienating: the work was often physically exhausting; the hours were long and the rest periods few; the assembly line was fast and inexorable; the work was monotonous and unfulfilling; the shop noisy and ugly; the air filled with smoke, dust, or chemicals; and the production goals set by a distant corporate bureaucracy. . . .

One of the most striking developments of the postwar years was the growing centralization of power in the union leadership and the concomitant decline in rank-and-file participation. Lacking left-wing rivals to contest their authority, many labor leaders grew increasingly autocratic and arbitrary, if not actually corrupt. This trend was reinforced by the merger of the AFL and CIO, which ended competition for locals and members and thus precluded escape from domination by the national union's political machine. In the United Mine Workers, one-man control by John L. Lewis and secret bargaining sessions after 1950 between the union and the bituminous coal industry left the membership inactive and uninvolved, learning of contract negotiations only after a settlement had been reached. After 1950 no major strike occurred in the soft coal industry—a far cry from the annual strikes and grass-roots militancy of the past. . . . The story was the same throughout most of the American labor movement. Between 1946 and 1963 the number of striking workers dropped from 4.6 million to 941,000. Union leadership was so stable that by 1958 the average age of the men on the AFL-CIO executive council was in the middle sixties. . . .

Class-conscious politics and anticapitalist fervor had become historical relics. Once a leading American Socialist, David Dubinsky, president of the International Ladies Garment Workers Union, concluded in the postwar years that "trade unionism needs capitalism like a fish needs water." In foreign affairs, few could match organized labor's devotion to the Cold War. Both the AFL and the CIO served as conduits for CIA funds to Washington's favorite overseas unions. Meany headed the American Institute for Free Labor Development, which disbursed an estimated $120 million a year in CIA money to tame labor movements abroad. The AFL-CIO's foreign policy program—written for the most part by Jay Lovestone, the embittered former secretary of the American Communist Party—supported U.S. government actions at every turn.

America In Our Time

Godfrey Hodgson

In the frenetic years between the inauguration of John F. Kennedy and the resignation of Richard M. Nixon, the national mood veered from Augustan confidence to disappointment and disillusion. From an almost limitless belief in the promises of American capitalism and democracy, the United States spurted into an age of limits and insoluble problems. Many view this consequence of the years of protest, war, and violence as a tragic loss. British journalist Godfrey Hodgson disagrees. He interprets this break in the continuity of the American experience as a painful but necessary shedding of false illusions and hubris.

In this selection from his America In Our Time, *Hodgson introduces some of the central themes of his probing examination of the crisis in the mind and spirit of the United States in the 1960s. Although wholly different in their mode of analysis, one should note the parallels in the critiques of Hodgson and Wittner, and account for them. One may also speculate on what new myths have supplanted the old.*

Looking back at the years from Dallas to Watergate, there can be few Americans who do not agree that the age of Kennedy and Nixon has been a time of lost hopes. Making the comparison not between two men but between the climates of two periods, it is hard not to echo Hamlet's horrified sense of moral retrogression:

"Look here, upon this picture, and on this. . . . / . . . that was, to this, / Hyperion to a satyr."

The presidency is so much the master symbol of the public mood and national aspirations that this sense of loss is best measured by one fact and two contrasting images. The fact is that each of the three men who have been elected to the presidency since 1960 has been destroyed by it. The contrasts are those evoked by the words Dallas and Watergate. All nations live by myths. Any nation is the sum of the consciousness of its people: the chaotic infinitude of the experience and perceptions of millions alive and dead. Merely in order to communicate with itself, to function as a conscious organism at all, a nation must distill and simplify this chaos into the ideas and slogans of public debate and politics. One of the essential agents in this crystallization of the national consciousness is myth.

Just as a film director, by optically freezing a single frame, can cause a particular image to etch itself into the viewer's mind, so myth can fix in the national mind a tableau that is instinctively felt to sum up a general truth.

There are old myths which still have the power to express living parts of the American historical experience: Washington at Valley Forge, Lee at Appomattox, John Brown at Harpers Ferry. But in a nation as full of vigor and self-awareness as the United States, new myths are still being created. In a nation that is also deeply divided, not all of these myths, however potent, have universal validity. There are Americans for whom the moon landing epitomizes the essential national qualities: adventure, technological prowess, the drive to go on further than anyone has gone before. There are other Americans for whom the imprisonment and death of George Jackson express a more relevant truth. One man's myth indeed may be, in a society as deeply split as the United States, another man's obscenity.

There is one contemporary American myth, however, that does have an almost universal magic. The force of it is conveyed in two pictures that still have undiminished poignancy.

In the first frame, a youthful President, hatless in the cold air, rededicates a new generation to whom the torch of idealism has been handed.

In the second, the same head is blown to pieces by a bullet. The Kennedy myth has been so potent because it is a myth of hope shattered by absurd, meaningless death. It thus inverts the redemptive promise of the most universal and powerful of all human myths, in which the blameless king dies so that the people may live.

For contemporary Americans, the assassination was specially charged with tragic meaning. Their culture had come to stress achievement before almost all else. For a people who almost worshiped achievement, to see a leader whose personal and family history were an epic of achievement killed by a loser, a nobody, was peculiarly disturbing.

This was the death of a democratic prince, but still the death of a prince. The President had always been the symbolic as well as the executive head of the nation. In 1963, after thirty years of crisis, the mounting intensity of the people's need for leadership had invested the office with the emotional magic of an elective kingship.

John Kennedy had been elected by a slender margin. But, especially after the Cuban missile crisis of October 1962, his stature in the public mind had risen. Many Americans identified with him as the symbol of their own aspirations both for their country and for themselves. The imagination of some had been caught by the austere vision of national duty and national destiny that was one element in Kennedy's complex personality. More were captivated by his chic, his wit, his glamour. Above all, John F. Kennedy appealed to a sense of upward mobility, individual and national.

A great many Americans had come up in the world by the beginning of the 1960s, and a great many more hoped to do so. Many were not quite sure how the good life should be lived; the Kennedys seemed to know. The United States, too, had come up in the world; and John Kennedy seemed to conduct himself as the leader not just of a very rich and powerful country in a hostile world but of an imperial nation with time on its side, the center and the standard of civilization.

Even those who in no way identified with him could still find him a fitting embodiment of their country. There were plenty of people who didn't particularly like his politics, who doubted whether they would vote for his re-election, yet who still felt, when he died, that something of them died with him.

In life, the President had been only beginning to establish his stature. In death, he became overnight the protomartyr of something akin to a religion of national unity and greatness. The National Opinion Research Center found that, even in the group that was most hostile to him, "anti-Kennedy Southerners," 62 percent felt his death as "the loss of someone very close and dear." Kennedy had been elected by 49.7 percent of the popular vote. By June 1963, 59 percent of those surveyed claimed to have voted for him in 1960. Immediately after the assassination, this posthumous landslide swelled to 65 percent. In November 1960, one out of every two voters had chosen Kennedy; three years later, two out of every three believed that they had!

Before the assassination, it seemed that the coming years, the age of Kennedy, would be—as Robert Frost put in in lines specially written for the inauguration in 1961—an Augustan age "of poetry and power." The test-ban treaty and the peaceful March on Washington in the summer of 1963 seemed to confirm his promise of imperial splendor in the world, matched by tranquillity and social progress at home.

The circumstances of the crime contributed, as much as the personality of the victim, to the shock; and fear was involved, as well as the loss of hopes.

There was the fact that it happened in Dallas, a city seething with the anger of the Right against the Supreme Court's desegregation decision. That aroused all the suspicions of liberals, including the oldest specter of disunity, the memory of a nation divided between North and South.

It was generally assumed—for example, even by Chief Justice Earl Warren—that the murder was somehow caused by this rightwing hatred. When the Warren Commission later established that Lee Harvey Oswald had acted alone but that his affiliations had been with Communists rather than anti-Communists, the opposite suspicions of the Right were strengthened.

The assassination was like a crack in the earth in volcanic country. Fumes of suspicion vented to the surface, reminding people of forces they would have preferred to forget: the irrationality, hatred, and violence that lay beneath the glittering structure of liberal, imperial America. In retrospect, people looked back to Friday, November 22, 1963, as the end of a time of hope, the beginning of a time of troubles.

In January 1961, *Camelot* was still a musical.

It was playing at the Majestic, on West Forty-fourth Street, with Richard Burton and Julie Andrews.

Time magazine, that month, chose fifteen American scientists as its collective men of the year. "Statesmen and savants, builders and even priests," intoned *Time*, "are their servants. . . . Science is at the apogee of its power."

Synthetic fabrics were the fashion news that month. Dacron and Lycra in hot pinks and purples, *The New Yorker's* fashion pundit reported, were just the thing to wear with the bouffant hair styles that Mr. Kenneth of Lilly Daché had just invented for Mrs. Kennedy and that women of all ages were rushing to imitate.

The aerosol sprays with which these ponderous helmets were lacquered into place, it was said, were a "spin-off" from the space program. (The crucial patent belonged, in fact, to one Robert Abplanalp, the particular friend in later days of Richard Nixon.) It hardly mattered whether that was literally true. It expressed something most Americans believed instinctively: that the wonders of the American kitchen and the technological might of America's armed forces were profoundly interconnected; that Americans lived better because of the strength of American industry and the inventiveness of American research. Knowledge, it was assumed, was not only power but happiness as well.

It was a time of faith in science and technology, in technique and artifice, in organized innovation and orderly change. The President-elect talked about the New Frontier, giving popular currency to an earlier coinage of the intellectuals. It was a brilliant slogan, because it combined the promise of restless adventure with reassuring undertones of tried and true American tradition.

That was the paradox. For all its belief in innovation, American society at the beginning of the 1960s was still conservative. People wanted change; they did not want to be changed. Or, rather, they changed their clothes, their cars or their homes more easily than they changed their assumptions, their attitudes or their beliefs.

"What will cars be like in 1980?" a journalist asked the head of Chrysler's product-planning team. He answered, much the same as in 1960, but of course longer, wider, more powerful. Would we really still be groping for the dipstick to check the oil in twenty years' time? the reporter persisted. That would depend on cost: "In our business, the economic barrier is the big thing separating dream from reality."

The most exciting dream of all in January 1961 was the possibility that the economic barrier itself need not be a reality forever. In 1960, the United States had just enjoyed the most prosperous year in its history, as it had come to expect to do as a matter of course every year. The gross national product had passed $500 billion for the first time. Yet the economic situation was not good. Growth had been sticky and slow. Unemployment stubbornly refused to drop. People were talking about a recession. Balance-of-payments difficulties and foreign competition were beginning to cloud the future prospect. "This is the first time in my lifetime," said William McChesney Martin, chairman of the Federal Reserve Board, "that the credit of the United States has been questioned. A serious shadow lies over the American business picture."

That was the conservative view of the outgoing administration. The professors of the New Economics who were packing up to come down from Cambridge and New Haven, and a few other places, to join the new administration, were more impressed by the opportunity than by the danger. They believed they knew how to guarantee uninterrupted prosperity, unlimited growth. That was the secret they thought they had divined from the theories of John Maynard Keynes.

American scientists might know how to put a man on the moon; American economists might think they had discovered the secret of everlasting prosperity; the papers might be full of new missiles, new drugs, new products and discoveries of every kind; and yet it was a society careening toward the twenty-first century with many of the beliefs and attitudes of the nineteenth.

"With the kind of technology that is likely to be available in 1969," said a young physicist named Herman Kahn, reaching for the most improbable example to make his point, "it may literally turn out that a Hottentot . . . would be able to make bombs."

"These people are the cream of the crop," Dr. Carl D. Stewart of the Methodist Committee for Overseas Relief told *Newsweek*, contemplating the Cuban refugees pouring into southern Florida. "It's the poorer people and the ne'er-do-wells who are with Fidel."

Forty-eight million Americans, or more than one in every four, were overweight, according to the Metropolitan Life Insurance Company.

A California state agency calculated that the average working girl still needed to budget to buy dinner and breakfast, for one, every day. But now she could afford to buy twenty-seven pairs of stockings every year, up from a dozen ten years earlier. "She must be a dolt," said a secretary telephoned for comment by a reporter.

"Besides," she added, "how is she going to get by with only twenty-seven pairs of stockings?"

An affluent society with growing abundance, and one that was steadily being transformed for the better by science and technology—that was how the great majority of Americans saw their country in January 1961. But that does not mean that the mood was insouciant. On the contrary, the press and television, like the candidates in the presidential election that had just finished, harped ceaselessly on the theme of crisis. On December 29, Ed Murrow was hooked up with CBS correspondents worldwide. *Years of Crisis,* the show was called.

No one needed to be told what the nature of that crisis was. In mid-January *Time* reported grimly that the United States had survived a week "when the underlying conflict between the West and Communism erupted on three fronts": in Cuba, in Laos, and in the Congo.

On January 23 *Newsweek* celebrated the inauguration with a special section. "Around the restive globe from Berlin to Laos," it began, "the Communist threat seethed, and nowhere more ominously than in Cuba," where Fidel Castro, that month, stood down his mobilization because he believed (wrongly, as it turned out) that no invasion was on the way. There were problems at home, too, *Newsweek* conceded, among them "problems of racial violence, schools and housing." But "the greatest single problem that faces John Kennedy—and the key to most of his other problems—is how to meet the aggressive power of the Communist bloc."

The United States was ready. That same month, *Time* devoted a cover story to CINCPAC Admiral Harry D. Felt. "To maintain order and build prosperous trade in a free world," the editors explained, "the U.S. must control the seas and be the guardian of the land areas along the shores." From Singapore to the Diomede Islands in the Bering Strait, it was an imperial responsibility. But a double-page spread showed how the gallant admiral was equiped to meet it, with his carriers and his marines and his hundreds of strike aircraft. "He is prepared," wrote *Time* in that peculiar tone of exultation, barely disguised as a stoic sense of duty, that was characteristic of Washington in the early sixties, "to keep the peace if possible, to win a war if necessary."

The journalists who wrote those articles were briefed by the outgoing Eisenhower administration. But their tone, and their assumption that the United States stood on the verge of global war against "the aggressive power of the Communist bloc," were precisely the theme of John Kennedy's inaugural address.

Kennedy struck a Churchillian note of struggle and sacrifice. He offered blood, sweat, toil and tears:

> We shall pay any price, bear any burden, meet any hardship. . . .
> Now the trumpet summons us again . . . to bear the burden of a long twilight struggle, year in and year out, "rejoicing in hope, patient in tribulation"—a struggle against the common enemies of man: tyranny, poverty, disease and war itself.
>
> Only a few generations have been granted the role of defending freedom in its hour of maximum danger. . . .
>
> The energy, the faith and the devotion which we bring to this endeavor will light our country and all who serve it, and the glow from that fire can truly light the world.

Twelve years later, Richard Nixon's second inaugural address echoed that rhetoric. He, too, wanted to kindle a fire:

> Let us pledge together to make these four years the best four years in America's history, so that on its 200th birthday America will be as young and vital as when it began, and as bright a beacon of hope for all the world.

The theme Nixon had chosen for his second inauguration was the Spirit of 1976. By chance, we have an insight into what that meant for him and those about him. One of the casualties of government secrecy in the Nixon years were the files of the American Revolution Bicentennial Commission, a disciplined instrument of the presidential will as interpreted by that most zealous of its agents, John D. Ehrlichman. The commission had been in existence for some years. But now, under White House direction, it made every effort to turn the bicentennial into a partisan promotion. Leaked documents from the commission's offices reveal just how closely the Nixon administration identified patriotism with military glory on the one hand and corporate profit on the other, especially for its friends.

Each state was to celebrate the bicentennial in its own way. The commission looked with favor on Kansas' plans, for example, to

build a National Military Museum at a cost of $50 million. This
was to be in the shape of a gigantic five-pointed star, visible for
miles, and dedicated to commemorating the battles that "helped
achieve peace through patriotism." However, as the secretary of
the Iowa state bicentennial commission put it, "Principles are nice,
but they don't make the cash register ring." The ARBC concentrated most of its efforts on persuading national corporate business how profitable patriotic principles could be. There were
plans to tie in the anniversary of the American Revolution with
the Orange Bowl parade, the Miss America contest, and the
McDonald hamburger chain (run by one of the President's free-
spending contributor-friends). Such giant corporations as Ford,
AT&T, IBM, and ITT kept in touch. "One of the major efforts of
the American Revolution Bicentennial Commission," its chairman
wrote in one letter, "is to involve as many Americans as possible in
a meaningful observance of our nation's 200th anniversary. With
this in mind, I would like to invite approximately twenty principal
executives of major corporations of our country to a dinner at
Blair House. . . ."

There remained one trifling ideological difficulty before the
Spirit of '76 could be finally appropriated for promotional purposes by these corporate marketing men. It was duly disposed
of, by the bicentennial commission of the President's own home
state, in a way Nixon must have admired if the paper caught his
eye. "The American revolution," it formally resolved, "was not a
'revolution.' "

The style of the two speeches is as different as the minds of the
two men who made them; and John Kennedy and Richard Nixon
were profoundly different men—more different, even, than the
ideas and policies they represented. Language was not the only
difference between the two speeches. Nixon's vision, however taw-
dry, was a vision primarily for the United States, a domestic vision. Kennedy's call was to a struggle that, whatever its wisdom,
would be played out in the whole world.

Nixon spoke about both foreign and domestic affairs. He spoke
proudly and at length about his administration's achievements in
international relations, about its "bold initiatives" and its hopes of
building "a structure of peace" that would last for generations.

But, in one passage, he stated obliquely but unmistakably his sense of priorities. It must be America first.

> Let us accept that high responsibility [to build a structure of peace] not as a burden but gladly—gladly because the chance to build such a peace is the noblest endeavor a people can engage in; gladly also because only if we act greatly in meeting our responsibilities abroad will we remain a great nation, and only if we remain a great nation will we act greatly in meeting our challenges at home.

For Nixon, the United States must be strong in order to embark upon "a new era of progress" at home. For Kennedy, the argument had been exactly the other way around.

Kennedy did not mention domestic issues at all in his 1961 inaugural. He made a conscious decision to exclude them, according to his chief assistant in drafting the speech, Theodore Sorenson. There were several reasons for that decision, of course, including a simple desire to keep the speech short. None the less, it revealed Kennedy's sense of national priorities unmistakably.

The change of emphasis should not be put down to the temperament of the two Presidents. Nixon, in 1961, almost certainly shared Kennedy's view of the primacy of foreign policy. Public-opinion poll data show that the priorities of the American people as a whole had changed in exactly the same way.

In 1972 William Watts and Lloyd Free published a book, *State of the Nation,* that reported the results of a survey conducted specially for their project by The Gallup Organization. Their most startling discovery was precisely the fact that the American public, which as recently as 1964 had been far more concerned about foreign affairs, was now overwhelmingly worried about domestic issues.

The evidence for attitudes in 1964 comes from a similar survey carried out in that year by the Institute for International Social Research. These were the issues that most concerned Americans in 1964, in order of urgency:

1. Keeping the country out of war
2. Combating world communism
3. Keeping our military defenses strong

4. Controlling the use of nuclear weapons
5. Maintaining respect for the United States in other countries.

"Only in sixth place," Watts and Free commented, "did a domestic item surface: maintaining law and order." By 1972 they found these priorities exactly reversed. Rising prices, the cost of living, violence in American life, drugs, water and air pollution, health care, misleading advertising, garbage disposal, the problems of the elderly, unemployment, poverty, and education all ranked above any foreign-policy issue, they found, except one: Vietnam.

The Harvard social scientist James Q. Wilson has written, "The decade of the 1960s began in a mood of contentment with domestic affairs and confidence in international ones; it ended in an agony of bitterness and frustration over both." That way of drawing the contrast seems to me wrongly expressed. It underestimates the genuine anxiety with which Americans looked out at the world at the beginning of the 1960s, and forgets the authentic sense of danger and struggle of which Kennedy's inaugural was the classic expression. By the time of Nixon's second inaugural, too, the principle cause of "bitterness and frustration" abroad had been removed. For most Americans, if not for the Vietnamese, the war was over. It would be truer to join the terms of the formula the other way: Americans entered the age of Kennedy and Nixon contented at home and frustrated abroad. They left it relatively confident about the world abroad, but in an agony of bitterness at home.

The shift of emphasis from the problems of the world to the problems of America was only the symptom of a deeper change. The United States entered the 1960s in an Augustan mood: united, confident, conscious of a historic mission, and mobilized for the great task of carrying it out. The Americans of 1960 felt the maturity of their power. They accepted the legitimacy of their institutions. They believed, not in the perfection, but in the perfectibility, of their society. If they were anxious about danger from abroad, it was because they saw their own society as so essentially just and benevolent that danger could come only from else-where. If they found international affairs frustrating, it was be-cause they found it infuriating that foreigners could not always believe that their only ambition was a generous desire to share the abundance of American capitalism and the promise of American democracy with those less fortunate than themselves.

Some voted for Kennedy, and some for Nixon. But, except for a small fringe of conservatives and an almost insignificant sprin-kling of radicals, political differences were less important in 1960 than the underlying consensus. Most Americans then accepted an ideology of imperial liberalism whose chief tenets were simplicity itself: the American system worked at home, and America must be strong abroad. There was a sense at the beginning of the 1960s that the businessman and the unskilled laborer, the writer and the housewife, Harvard University and the Strategic Air Command, International Business Machines and the labor movement, all had their parts to play in one harmonious political, intellectual, and economic system.

A dozen years later, that system was in ruins. The legitimacy of virtually every institution had been challenged, and the validity of virtually every assumption disputed. Instead of girding themselves for a great mission in the world, Americans seemed increasingly to pray only to be allowed to live peacefully in their habitations.

Two quotations measure the change.

Here is how Professor William L. Langer, holder of a presti-gious chair in history at Harvard and former chairman of the Board of National Intelligence Estimates of the CIA, summed up, calmly and in the manner of one stating indisputable fact, the prevailing orthodoxy in 1960:

> The United States has, throughout its history, cherished ideals of independence, freedom and democracy. The energy and inge-nuity of its people as well as the extent and resources of its territory have enabled it to attain a level of civil liberty, social equality and general prosperity. . . .
> The United States should, at all times, exert its influence and power on behalf of a world order congenial to American ideals, interests and security. It can do this without egotism because of its deep conviction that such a world order will best fulfill the hopes of mankind.

By 1970, it could not be said that there was any prevailing
orthodoxy. But here is the concluding passage from a book that
was at least well certificated at the time. It was written by Professor Andrew Hacker of Cornell University, a regular contributor
to the New York *Times Magazine*. It was respectfully reviewed and
went through half a dozen editions in a year.

> America's history as a nation has reached its end. The Ameri-
> can people will of course survive; and the majority will continue to
> exist quite comfortably.... But the ties that make them a society
> will grow more tenuous with each passing year. There will be
> undercurrents of tension and turmoil, and the only remaining
> option will be to learn to live with these disorders. For they are
> not problems that can be solved with the resources we are willing
> to make available....
>
> The American people will continue to produce new generations
> and carry on with the business of life. Abroad they will either make
> peace with a world they cannot master, or they will turn it into a
> battle ground for yet another century of war. Closer to home, how-
> ever, Americans will learn to live with danger and discomfort, for
> this condition is the invitable accompaniment of democracy in its
> declining years.

From the world of Langer and Kennedy to the world of Hacker
and Nixon, the United States had traveled in just ten years from
the vigorous assurance of mid-Victorian England to something like
the angry confusion and despair of Weimar Germany.

"America is change."

James Bryce wrote that in his *American Commonwealth*, which
was first published in 1888.

More than forty years later, in the month before the Wall
Street market break of 1929, an eminent committee of social scientists reported that the country was still suffering from a nasty
case of change:

> ... Birth control, race riots, stoppage of immigration ... govern-
> mental corruption, crime and racketeering, the sprawl of great
> cities ... imperialism, peace or war, international relations, urban-
> ism ... shifting moral standards, new leadership in business and
> government, the status of womankind, labor child training, mental
> hygiene, the future of democracy and capitalism ... all of these

grave questions demand attention if we are not to drift into zones of danger.

There never has been a time when the United States has not been changing in ways that a great many Americans found disturbing. This very continuity of change hints at the paradox we have already noted.

America has always been change, yes. But at the beginning of the 1960s it was also still a deeply conservative country. It was the only important state in the world to be operating, essentially unchanged, under an eighteenth-century constitution. It was the only nation where nineteenth-century faith in capitalism and suspicion of socialism were still dominant, and the one among all the major societies of the world to have been the least touched by the twentieth-century experience of war and revolution.

Change and stability seemed in 1961 to be married in America in a fruitful partnership. The pace of technological innovation, the spread of education, and the rise of living standards seemed only to confirm the stability of the American system. The stability of institutions, in turn, seemed to guarantee a continuing flow of beneficent change.

What happened in the age of Kennedy and Nixon was something more than a mere acceleration in the pace of change. There was a real break in the continuity of the American experience.

The country was not invaded. On the contrary, on one pretext or another it invaded or otherwise attacked half a dozen foreign countries, with impunity. Its strategic military strength may or may not now be surpassed by that of the Soviet Union: both are so awesome that the question is academic.

There was civil strife in the United States, but on a scale trivial compared to what has taken place elsewhere: in Chile, in the Indian subcontinent or in Northern Ireland, for example, in the same years, and even compared to earlier periods in American history. When a black sniper killed several policemen in New Orleans in 1973, the mayor said it was the worst crime in the city's history. He had forgotten, or did not know, that two dozen Italians were killed there in a riot in 1893 and four dozen Negroes were massacred by the police in the French Quarter in 1866.

Ten thousand Americans have been put under surveillance by the federal government, and a handful imprisoned for what can only be called political crimes. Yet in general the civil liberties of American citizens are as carefully protected as those of any other state.

The economy has performed well, on the whole. There has been poverty, and even hunger: more of both than people supposed there would be twenty years ago, but less than in the past. And nothing to compare with the widespread destitution of the 1930s. American living standards are no longer as far ahead of those of the rest of the world as they used to be. But the gross national product in 1973 had more than doubled since John F. Kennedy's inauguration.

No: the crisis was in the mind and spirit of the country. That does not mean that it was any less real. It was not a "crisis of confidence," in the foolish sense in which that phrase is sometimes used, meaning that if only everyone had whistled to keep his courage up and drown the voices of doubt, the problems would have gone away. There was too much of that kind of confidence, not too little.

Yet in a more serious sense confidence was involved. The crisis of the sixties went deeper than the sum of "the problems." That is what the older generation of liberals, in particular, found so hard to understand. No period has seen a richer crop of "solutions" spring up to match its problems. Too often, indeed, the solution became the problem.

The real crisis of the sixties was that, for the first time since the Civil War and Reconstruction, a generation of Americans were compelled to ask not, as people asked in the Depression, how to solve their problems, but whether problems could be solved. That is why the great conflicts of the age of Kennedy and Nixon challenged the central promise of American life as it was not challenged by a shortage of jobs in the 1930s, or by war in the 1940s and Cold War in the 1950s.

The Military–Industrial Complex

Dwight D. Eisenhower

As a consequence of World War II and the Cold War, the military, once a small part of American life, waxed increasingly influential and powerful. The armed forces, moreover, developed vital ties with the giant corporations and thousands of subcontractors heavily dependent upon government defense spending. Joined by such organizations as the Air Force Association, the Navy League, and the Association of the United States Army, military and industrial leaders campaigned together for the production of more and newer weapons. Abetted by veterans and labor groups, by university scientists eager for a slice of the military's R and D budget, and by congressmen representing districts laden with defense plants and bases, the "military-industrial complex" rarely had difficulty in exerting the pressure on the government necessary for increased defense funds.

In the late 1950s, however, President Eisenhower grew alarmed at the vast enlargement of government spending and its impairment of the economic health of the United States. He sought to curtail the mushrooming power of the "conjunction of an immense military establishment and a large arms industry." As a part of his effort to control its "unwarranted influence," the retiring President issued this fateful warning in his farewell address. Students can surmise what the General might say two decades later as the annual defense budget soars over $200 billion.

We now stand ten years past the midpoint of a century that has witnessed four major wars among great nations. Three of these

From *Public Papers of the Presidents of the United States: Dwight D. Eisenhower, 1960–1961* (Washington, 1961), pp. 1036–1040.

involved our own country. Despite these holocausts, America is today the strongest, the most influential and most productive nation in the world. Understandably proud of this pre-eminence, we yet realize that America's leadership and prestige depend, not merely upon our unmatched material progress, riches and military strength, but on how we use our power in the interests of world peace and human betterment. . . .

Our military organization today bears little relation to that known by any of my predecessors in peacetime, or indeed by the fighting men of World War II or Korea.

Until the latest of our world conflicts, the United States had no armaments industry. American makers of plowshares could, with time and as required, make swords as well. But now we can no longer risk emergency improvisation of national defense; we have been compelled to create a permanent armaments industry of vast proportions. Added to this, three and a half million men and women are directly engaged in the defense establishment. We annually spend on military security more than the net income of all United States corporations.

This conjunction of an immense military establishment and a large arms industry is new in the American experience. The total influence—economic, political, even spiritual—is felt in every city, every State house, every office of the Federal government. We recognize the imperative need for this development. Yet we must not fail to comprehend its grave implications. Our toil, resources and livelihood are all involved; so is the very structure of our society.

In the councils of government, we must guard against the acquisition of unwarranted influence, whether sought or unsought, by the military-industrial complex. The potential for the disastrous rise of misplaced power exists and will persist.

We must never let the weight of this combination endanger our liberties or democratic processes. We should take nothing for granted. Only an alert and knowledgeable citizenry can compel the proper meshing of the huge industrial and military machinery of defense with our peaceful methods and goals, so that security and liberty may prosper together.

Akin to, and largely responsible for, the sweeping changes in our industrial-military posture has been the technological revolution during recent decades.

In this revolution, research has become central; it also becomes more formalized, complex, and costly. A steadily increasing share is conducted for, by, or at the direction of, the Federal government.

Today, the solitary inventor, tinkering in his shop, has been overshadowed by task forces of scientists in laboratories and testing fields. In the same fashion, the free university, historically the fountainhead of free ideas and scientific discovery, has experienced a revolution in the conduct of research. Partly because of the huge costs involved, a government contract becomes virtually a substitute for intellectual curiosity. For every old blackboard there are now hundreds of new electronic computers.

The prospect of domination of the nation's scholars by Federal employment, project allocations, and the power of money is ever present—and is gravely to be regarded.

Yet, in holding scientific research and discovery in respect, as we should, we must also be alert to the equal and opposite danger that public policy could itself become the captive of a scientific-technological elite.

It is the task of statesmanship to mold, to balance, and to integrate these and other forces, new and old, within the principles of our democratic system—ever aiming toward the supreme goals of our free society.

Down the long lane of the history yet to be written America knows that this world of ours, ever growing smaller, must avoid becoming a community of dreadful fear and hate, and be, instead, a proud confederation of mutual trust and respect.

Such a confederation must be one of equals. The weakest must come to the conference table with the same confidence as do we, protected as we are by our moral, economic, and military strength. That table, though scarred by many past frustrations, cannot be abandoned for the certain agony of the battlefield.

Disarmament, with mutual honor and confidence, is a continuing imperative. Together we must learn how to compose differences, not with arms, but with intellect and decent purpose. Because this need is so sharp and apparent I confess that I lay down my official responsibilities in this field with a definite sense of disappointment. As one who has witnessed the horror and the lingering sadness of war—as one who knows that another war could utterly destroy this civilization which has been so slowly and painfully built over thousands of years—I wish I could say tonight that a lasting peace is in sight.

Happily, I can say that war has been avoided. Steady progress toward our ultimate goal has been made. But, so much remains to be done. As a private citizen, I shall never cease to do what little I can to help the world advance along that road.

The Great Society

Lyndon B. Johnson

Suddenly elevated to the presidency on November 22, 1963, Lyndon Baines Johnson sought to use his tremendous powers to impose his personal stamp on national politics and to secure his place in history's pantheon. From the start, he repeatedly assured the American people that "we have the power to shape the civilization that we want." He desired to fulfill the promises of the New Deal, and much more. Johnson stressed that the Great Society "asks not only how much, but how good; not only how to create wealth, but how to use it. It proposes as the first test for a nation: the quality of its people." In May 1964, he spelled out his tenets of "qualitative liberalism" in an address at the University of Michigan reprinted below.

Congress granted most of his far-reaching legislative requests in the next two years, but then the intensifying war in Vietnam undermined the liberal climate of opinion and caused cuts in domestic spending. The Great Society could not survive. Ironically, the President who aimed to promote harmony by concentrating on domestic reform became thoroughly preoccupied with foreign affairs and greatly increased social tension and conflict by promising more than he could deliver. As an index of change, one might consider how the current president would define the Great Society and how his priorities would differ from Johnson's.

. . . For a century we labored to settle and to subdue a continent. For half a century we called upon unbounded invention and untiring industry to create an order of plenty for all of our people.

From *Public Papers of the Presidents of the United States: Lyndon B. Johnson* (Washington, D.C., 1965), I (1963–64), 704–7.

The challenge of the next half century is whether we have the wisdom to use that wealth to enrich and elevate our national life, and to advance the quality of our American civilization.

Your imagination, your initiative, and your indignation will determine whether we build a society where progress is the servant of our needs, or a society where old values and new visions are buried under unbridled growth. For in your time we have the opportunity to move not only toward the rich society and the powerful society, but upward to the Great Society.

The Great Society rests on abundance and liberty for all. It demands an end to poverty and racial injustice, to which we are totally committed in our time. But that is just the beginning.

The Great Society is a place where every child can find knowledge to enrich his mind and to enlarge his talents. It is a place where leisure is a welcome chance to build and reflect, not a feared cause of boredom and restlessness. It is a place where the city of man serves not only the needs of the body and the demands of commerce but the desire for beauty and the hunger for community.

It is a place where man can renew contact with nature. It is a place which honors creation for its own sake and for what it adds to the understanding of the race. It is a place where men are more concerned with the quality of their goals than the quantity of their goods.

But most of all, the Great Society is not a safe harbor, a resting place, a final objective, a finished work. It is a challenge constantly renewed, beckoning us toward a destiny where the meaning of our lives matches the marvelous products of our labor. . . .

Aristotle said: "Men come together in cities in order to live, but they remain together in order to live the good life." It is harder and harder to live the good life in American cities today.

The catalogue of ills is long: there is the decay of the centers and the despoiling of the suburbs. There is not enough housing for our people or transportation for our traffic. Open land is vanishing and old landmarks are violated.

Worst of all expansion is eroding the precious and time-honored values of community with neighbors and communion with nature. The loss of these values breeds loneliness and boredom and indifference.

Our society will never be great until our cities are great. Today the frontier of imagination and innovation is inside those cities and not beyond their borders. . . .

A second place where we begin to build the Great Society is in our countryside. We have always prided ourselves on being not only America the strong and America the free, but America the beautiful. Today that beauty is in danger. The water we drink, the food we eat, the very air that we breathe, are threatened with pollution. Our parks are overcrowded, our seashores over-burdened. Green fields and dense forests are disappearing. . . .

A third place to build the Great Society is in the classrooms of America. There your children's lives will be shaped. Our society will not be great until every young mind is set free to scan the farthest reaches of thought and imagination. We are still far from that goal. . . .

In many places, classrooms are overcrowded and curricula are outdated. Most of our qualified teachers are underpaid, and many of our paid teachers are unqualified. So we must give every child a place to sit and a teacher to learn from. Poverty must not be a bar to learning, and learning must offer an escape from poverty.

But more classrooms and more teachers are not enough. We must seek an educational system which grows in excellence as it grows in size. This means better training for our teachers. It means preparing youth to enjoy their hours of leisure as well as their hours of labor. It means exploring new techniques of teaching, to find new ways to stimulate the love of learning and the capacity for creation. . . .

For better or for worse, your generation has been appointed by history to deal with those problems and to lead America toward a new age. You have the chance never before afforded to any people in any age. You can help build a society where the demands of morality, and the needs of the spirit, can be realized in the life of the nation.

So, will you join in the battle to give every citizen the full equality which God enjoins and the law requires, whatever his belief, or race, or the color of his skin?

Will you join in the battle to give every citizen an escape from the crushing weight of poverty?

Will you join in the battle to make it possible for all nations to live in enduring peace—as neighbors and not as mortal enemies?

Will you join in the battle to build the Great Society, to prove that our material progress is only the foundation on which we will build a richer life of mind and spirit?

There are those timid souls who say this battle cannot be won; that we are condemned to a soulless wealth. I do not agree. We have the power to shape the civilization that we want. But we need your will, your labor, your hearts, if we are to build that kind of society. . . .

So let us from this moment begin our work so that in the future men will look back and say: It was then, after a long and weary way, that man turned the exploits of his genius to the full enrichment of his life.

Part Four

THE BLACK STRUGGLE

No domestic development has been more important to postwar American society than the struggle for racial equality. During the three quarters of a century after the end of Reconstruction, little occurred to improve the status of Afro-Americans. The vast majority lived in the South, were denied the right to vote, suffered the overt and covert consequences of segregation, experienced dire poverty, and were subject—at virtually every moment—to the threat of physical intimidation and violence. Through most of that time, black Americans strove to build the best schools, churches, and homes they could for their children and themselves. Yet in an environment shaped and defined by white supremacy, the possibilities of substantial change were minimal.

The modern civil rights struggle received a major impetus from the New Deal and World War II. Hundreds of thousands of blacks left the rural south to take new jobs that were opening up in the north, the west, and urban areas of the south. The number of blacks in labor unions doubled, some economic improvements occurred, and in the north especially there was the opportunity for political participation. On the other hand, both the New Deal and the war witnessed callous indifference toward racial sensibilities, the perpetuation of Jim Crow, and vicious forms of racism. Black soldiers were not allowed to fight beside white soldiers, black blood supplies were segregated from white blood supplies, and black soldiers in southern training camps were subject to the brutality of southern white racism. Together, the New Deal and Second World War brought some progress, but in a context of continued and pervasive discrimination. The combination spurred black anger and frustration, helping to galvanize a new mood of protest.

In the face of evergrowing black militancy, liberal Democrats and Republicans began to pay more attention to the issue of civil rights. Through much of the postwar era the major theme of race relations in America was the gap between promises of change and the reality of continued oppression. When blacks protested, whites responded with words of concern and promises of change. There then would follow years of inaction until black protest initiated the cycle once more. By the 1960s, it had become evident that only when blacks forced white institutions into action could any substantive change be anticipated.

There are two general interpretations of the developments in race relations since World War II. One emphasizes the importance of external and impersonal factors such as migration, economic progress, a shift in government policies, and the emergence of an environment more conducive toward racial justice. The second interpretation focuses more on the collective demand of black Americans themselves for change, stressing the critical role of black protest in bringing about whatever progress has taken place. The first interpretation accentuates the role of objective and external forces; the second highlights the role of individual and collective activism. Both sources of change are clearly important, and, in most cases, only when the two complement each other does significant progress occur.

The following selections provide the basis for an assessment of the black struggle during the postwar period. Harvard Sitkoff analyzes the consequences of some of the structural changes in the economy, social values and intellectual attitudes, the law and national politics. August Meier emphasizes the activism of blacks, using the vantage point of Martin Luther King, Jr.'s career to analyze the shifting currents of black protest. Stokeley Carmichael brings a first-person perspective to the emergence of black power, and Clayborne Carson attempts to assess the significance of black power ten years after its emergence.

Many questions emerge from these readings: Has the black struggle really brought significant change in race relations? Was black power a repudiation of, or an extension of the civil rights movement? Could America have progressed further and faster than it did, or were the conflicts of the 1960s necessary before significant change could take place? Racial equality remains one of the primary issues on America's national agenda, and these as well as other questions, are crucial to understanding how we have gotten to where we are, and where we need to go.

The Preconditions for Racial Change

Harvard Sitkoff

Although McCarthyism and the ideology of consensus did much to mute black discontent in the first postwar decade, the black quest for justice and equality steadily grew more determined and insistent following the 1954 landmark decision of the Supreme Court in Brown v. Board of Education of Topeka. *In short order, thousands of black families withstood harassment, economic intimidation, and violence to desegregate their local schools; the mass of blacks in Montgomery, Alabama, boycotted city buses for 381 days to topple Jim Crow; and, in 1960, black college students in Greensboro, North Carolina, "sat in" at a white lunch counter and set off a wave of similar challenges to the Southern caste system. But the ruling that "separate educational facilities are inherently unequal," according to Harvard Sitkoff, did not start the modern black freedom struggle. This movement, he contends, stemmed from the basic socioeconomic changes in American society set in motion by the New Deal and, especially, World War II. These structural developments set the stage for black activism and made possible far-reaching racial changes in national policies and legislation.*

Of the interrelated causes of progress in race relations since the start of the Great Depression, none was more important than the changes in the American economy. No facet of the race problem

Excerpted and revised from Harvard Sitkoff, "Race Relations: Progress and Prospects," in James T. Patterson, ed. *Paths to the Present* (Minneapolis: Burgess Publishing Co., 1975). Reprinted by Permission of the Author.

was untouched by the elephantine growth of the Gross National Product, which rose from $206 billion in 1940 to $500 billion in 1960, and then in the 1960s increased by an additional 60 percent. By 1970, the economy topped the trillion dollar mark. This spectacular rate of economic growth produced some 25 million new jobs in the quarter of a century after World War II and raised real wage earnings by at least 50 percent. It made possible the increasing income of blacks; their entry into industries and labor unions previously closed to them; gains for blacks in occupational status; and created a shortage of workers that necessitated a slackening of restrictive promotion policies and the introduction of scores of government and private industry special job training programs for Afro-Americans. It also meant that the economic progress of blacks did not have to come at the expense of whites, thus undermining the most powerful source of white resistance to the advancement of blacks.

The effect of economic changes on race relations was particularly marked in the South. The rapid industrialization of the South since 1940 ended the dominance of the cotton culture. With its demise went the need for a vast underclass of unskilled, subjugated laborers. Power shifted from rural areas to the cities, and from tradition-oriented landed families to the new officers and professional workers in absentee-owned corporations. The latter had neither the historical allegiances nor the nonrational attachment to racial mores to risk economic growth for the sake of tradition. The old system of race relations had no place in the new economic order. Time and again in the 1950s and 1960s, the industrial and business elite took the lead in accommodating the South to the changes sought by the civil rights movement.

The existence of an "affluent society" boosted the fortunes of the civil rights movement itself in countless ways. Most obviously, it enabled millions of dollars in contributions from wealthy liberals and philanthropic organizations to pour into the coffers of the NAACP, Urban League, Southern Christian Leadership Conference, and countless other civil rights groups. Without those funds it is difficult to comprehend how the movement could have accomplished those tasks so essential to its success: legislative lobbying and court litigation; nationwide speaking tours and the daily mailings of press releases all over the country; the organization of mass marches, demonstrations, and rallies; constant, rapid communication and traveling over long distances; and the convocation of innumerable public conferences and private strategy sessions.

Prosperity also increased the leisure time of many Americans and enabled them to react immediately to the changing times. The sons and daughters of the newly affluent increasingly went to college. By 1970, five times as many students were in college as in 1940. What they learned helped lead to pronounced changes in white attitudes toward racial discrimination and segregation. Other whites learned from the TV sets in their homes. By the time Lyndon Johnson signed the Voting Rights Act of 1965, some 95 percent of all American families owned at least one television. The race problem entered their living rooms. Tens of millions nightly watched the drama of the Negro Revolution. The growing majority of Americans favoring racial equality and justice had those sentiments reinforced by TV shots of snarling police dogs attacking black demonstrators, rowdy white hoods molesting young blacks patiently waiting to be served at a lunch counter, and hate-filled white faces in a frenzy because of the effrontery of little black children entering a previously all-white school.

Blacks viewed the same scenes on their TV sets, and the rage these scenes engendered helped transform isolated battles into a national campaign. Concurrently, the conspicuous display of white affluence on TV vividly awakened blacks to a new sense of their relative deprivation. That, too, aroused black anger. And now something could be done about it. The growing black middle and working classes put their money and bodies on the line. In addition, because the consumer economy depended on consumer purchasing, black demands had to be taken seriously. By 1970, black buying power topped $25 billion, a large enough sum to make the threat of boycotts an effective weapon for social change. Afro-American economic advances also made blacks less patient in demanding alterations in their social status. They desired all the decencies and dignity they believed their full paycheck promised. Lastly, nationwide prosperity contributed to more blacks entering college, which stimulated higher expectations and a heightened confidence that American society need not be static.

Most importantly, changes in the economy radically affected black migration. Cotton mechanization pushed blacks off the farms, and the lure of jobs pulled them to the cities. In 1930, three-quarters of the Afro-Americans lived in or near the rural black belt. By 1973, over half the blacks lived outside the South, and nationally, nearly 80 percent resided in urban areas. Indeed, in the two decades prior to 1970, the black population in metropolitan areas rose by more than seven million—a number greater than the total immigration by any single nationality group in American history. Such a mass migration, in conjunction with prosperity, fundamentally altered the whole configuration of the race problem. First, the issue of race became national in scope. No longer did it affect only one region, and no longer could it be left in the hands of Southern whites. Second, it modified the objective conditions of life for blacks and changed their perception of what was right and how to get it. For the first time in American history the great mass of blacks were freed from the confines of a rigid caste structure. Now subject to new formative experiences, blacks developed new norms and beliefs. In the relative anonymity and freedom of the North and the big city, aggression could be turned against one's oppressor rather than against one's self; more educational and employment opportunities could be secured; and political power could be mobilized. Similarly, as expectations of racial equality increased with the size of black migration from the rural South, so the religious faith that had for so long sustained Afro-Americans working on plantations declined. The promise of a better world in the next one could not suffice. The urban black would not wait for his rewards until the afterlife.

Because blacks could vote in the North, they stopped believing they would have to wait. Enfranchisement promised all in this life that religion did in the next. The heavenly city, to put it mildly, was not achieved; but vital legislative and legal accomplishments did flow from the growing black vote. Without the presence of black political power in the North, the demonstrations in the South would not have led to the civil rights laws and presidential actions necessary to realize the objectives of those protesting against Jim Crow in Montgomery, Greensboro, Birmingham, Jackson, and Selma. Although the claim of black publicists that the concentration of Northern black votes in the industrial cities made the Afro-American electorate a "balance of power" in national politics was never wholly accepted by either major party, the desire of every president from Franklin Roosevelt to Lyndon Johnson to win and hold the black vote became a factor in determining public policy. And as the Democratic party became less dependent upon Southern electoral votes, and less able to garner them, it had to champion civil rights more in order to win the populous states of the North and Midwest where blacks were increasingly becoming an indispensable component of the liberal coalition.

The prominence of the United States as a world power further pushed politicians into making race relations a matter of national concern. During World War II millions of Americans became aware for the first time of the danger of racism to national security. The costs of racism went even higher during the Cold War. The Soviet Union continuously undercut American appeals to the nations of Africa and Asia by publicizing American ill-treatment of blacks. As the competition between the United States and international Communism intensified, foreign-policy makers came to recognize racism as the American's own worst enemy. President Harry Truman justified his asking Congress for civil rights legislation squarely on the world-wide implications of American race relations. Rarely in the next twenty years did a plea for civil rights before the Supreme Court, on the floor of Congress, and emanating from the White House, fail to emphasize that point. In short, fear forced the nation to hasten the redefining of the black status. The more involved in world affairs the United States became, the more imperative grew the task of setting its racial affairs in order.

The rapid growth of nationalistic independence movements among the world's colored peoples had special significance for Afro-Americans. In 1960 alone, sixteen African nations emerged from under white colonial rule. Each proclamation of independence in part shamed blacks in the United States to intensify their struggle for equality and justice, and in part caused a surge of racial pride in Afro-Americans, an affirmation of blackness. The experience of African independence proved the feasibility of change and the vulnerability of white supremacy, while at the same time aiding Afro-Americans to see themselves as members of a world majority rather than as just a hopelessly outnumbered American minority.

The decline in intellectual respectability of ideas used to justify segregation and discrimination similarly provided Afro-Americans with new weapons and shields. The excesses of Nazism and the decline of Western imperialism combined with internal developments in the academic disciplines of anthropology, biology, history, psychology, and sociology to discredit notions of inherent racial differences or predispositions. First in the 1930s, then with accelerating rapidity during World War II and every year thereafter, books and essays attacking racial injustice and inequality rolled off the presses. As early as 1944, Gunnar Myrdal in his monumental *An American Dilemma* termed the pronounced change in scholarship about race "the most important of all social trends in the field of interracial relations." This conclusion overstated the power of the word, but undoubtedly the mountain of new data, theory, and exposition at least helped to erode the pseudo-scientific rationalizations once popularly accepted as the basis for white supremacy.

In such an atmosphere, young blacks could mature without "the mark of oppression." Blacks could safely abandon the "nigger" role. To the extent that textbooks, sermons, declarations by governmental officials, advertising, and movies and TV affirmed the need to transform relationships between the races and to support black demands for full citizenship, blacks could confidently and openly rebel against the inequities they viewed as the sources of their oppression. They could publicly express the rage their parents had been forced to internalize; they could battle for what they deemed their birthright rather than wage war against themselves. Thus, in conjunction with the migration to cities, these new cultural processes helped to produce the "New Negro" hailed by essayists ever since the Montgomery bus boycott in 1956 inaugurated a more aggressive stage in the Afro-American's quest for equality.

In sum, changes in the American economy after 1940 set in motion a host of developments which made possible a transformation in race relations. The increasing income and number of jobs available to blacks and whites, and black migration and social mobility, coalesced with converging trends in politics, foreign affairs, and the mass media to endow those intent on improving race relations with both the resources and consciousness necessary to challenge the status quo. Objective conditions that had little to do with race in a primary sense thus created a context in which organizations and leaders could press successfully for racial changes. This is not to suggest that individuals do not matter in history or that the civil rights movement did not make an indispensable contribution to progress in race relations. It is, however, to emphasize the preconditions for such an endeavor to prevail. Desire and will are not enough. Significant and long-lasting alterations in society flow neither from the barrel of a gun nor from individual conversions. Mass marches, demonstrations, and rhetoric alone cannot modify entrenched behavior and values. Fundamental social change is accomplished only when individuals seize the moment to mobilize the latent power inherent in an institutional structure in flux.

Beginning in the 1930s, blacks, no longer facing a monolithic white power structure solidly arrayed against them, demanded with numbers and a unity that had never existed before the total elimination of racial inequality in American life. For three decades, the tactics and goals of the movement steadily grew more militant as the organization, protests, and power of blacks jumped exponentially. Each small triumph held out the promise of a greater one, heightening expectations and causing blacks to become ever more anxious about the pace of progress.

The first stage centered on securing the enforcement of the Fourteenth and Fifteenth Amendments. Supported mainly by white liberals and upper-middle-class blacks, the civil rights movement in the 1930s and 1940s relied on publicity, agitation, litigation in the courts, and lobbying in the halls of political power to gain the full inclusion of blacks in American life. Advances came in the legal and economic status of blacks, and in the minor social, political, and cultural concessions afforded Afro-Americans in the North, but the all-oppressive system of Jim Crow in the South remained virtually intact.

First in the court system, then in executive actions, and finally in Congress, this unceasing and mounting pressure from the civil rights movement prodded the government consistently in the direction of *real* racial equality. In the 1930s, the black movement failed to secure its two major legislative goals—anti-poll tax and anti-lynching laws—but it did manage to get Franklin D. Roosevelt and other members of his official family to speak on behalf of racial justice, to increase the numbers of blacks in government, to establish a Civil Rights Section in the Justice Department, and to ensure blacks a share of the relief and recovery assistance.

The gains during the New Deal, however, functioned primarily as a prelude to the take-off of the civil rights movement during World War II. The ideological character of the war and the government's need for the loyalty and manpower of all Americans stimulated blacks to expect a better deal from the government; this led to a militancy never before seen in black communities. Membership in the NAACP multiplied nearly ten times; the Congress of Racial Equality, organized in 1942, experimented with various forms of nonviolent direct action confrontations to challenge segregation; and A. Philip Randolph attempted to build his March-on-Washington Committee into an all-black mass protest movement. In 1941, his threat of a march on Washington, combined with the growth of the black vote and the exigencies of a foreign threat to American security, forced Roosevelt to issue Executive Order 8802 (the first such order dealing with race since Reconstruction), establishing the first President's Committee on Fair Employment Practices (FEPC). And, with increasing firmness, liberal politicians pressed for civil rights legislation and emphasized that the practices of white supremacy brought into disrepute America's stated war aims. Minimal gains to be sure, but the expectations they aroused set the stage for the greater advances in the postwar period. By 1945, Afro-Americans had benefited enough from the expansion in jobs and income, service in the armed forces and the massive migration to Northern cities to know better what they now wanted; and they had developed enough political influence, white alliances, and organizational skills to know how to go about getting their civil rights.

Equally vital, the Supreme Court began to dismantle the separate-but-equal doctrine in 1938. That year, the high court ruled that Missouri could not exclude a Negro from its state university law school when its only alternative was a scholarship to an out-of-state institution. Other Supreme Court decisions prior to World War II whittled away at discrimination in interstate travel, in employment, in judicial and police practices, and in the exclusion of blacks from jury service. During the war, the Court outlawed the white primary, holding that the nominating process of a political party constituted "state action." In other decisions handed down during the Truman presidency, the Supreme Court moved vigorously against all forms of segregation in interstate commerce, decided that states and the federal government cannot enforce restrictive racial covenants on housing, and so emphasized the importance of "intangible factors" in quality education that the demise of legally segregated schooling for students at all levels became a near certainty.

Meanwhile, the Truman administration emerged as an ally of the cause of civil rights. Responding to the growth of the black vote, the need to blunt the Soviet Union's exploitation of the race issue, and the firmly organized campaign for the advancement of blacks, Harry Truman acted where Roosevelt had feared to. In late 1946, the President appointed a Committee on Civil Rights to recommend specific measures to safeguard the civil rights of minorities. This was the first such committee in American history, and its 1947 report, *To Secure These Rights*, eloquently pointed out all the inequities of life in Jim Crow America and spelled out the moral, economic, and international reasons for government action. It called for the end of segregation and discrimination in public education, employment, housing, the armed forces, public accommodations, and interstate transportation. Other commissions appointed by Truman stressed the need for racial equality in the armed services and the field of education. Early in 1948, Truman sent the first presidential message on civil rights to Congress. Congress failed to pass any of the measures he proposed, but Truman later issued executive orders ending segregation in the military and barring discrimination in federal employment and in work done under government contract. In addition, his Justice Department prepared *amicus curiae* briefs to gain favorable court decisions in civil rights cases, and Truman's rhetoric in behalf of racial justice helped legitimize goals of the civil rights movement. However small the meaningful accomplishment remained, the identification of the Supreme Court and the Presidency with the cause of racial equality further aroused the expectations of blacks that they would soon share in the American Dream.

No single event did more to quicken black hopes than the coup de grâce to segregated education delivered by a unanimous Supreme Court on May 17, 1954. The *Brown* ruling that separate educational facilities "are inherently unequal" struck at the very heart of white supremacy in the South. A year later, the Court called for compliance "with all deliberate speed," mandating the lower federal courts to require from local school boards "a prompt and reasonable start toward full compliance." The end of legally mandated segregation in education started a chain reaction which led the Supreme Court ever further down the road toward the total elimination of all racial distinctions in the law. For all practical purposes, the legal quest for equality had succeeded: the emphasis on legalism had accomplished its goals. Constitutionally, blacks had become first-class citizens.

But in the decade after the *Brown* decision, the promise of change far outran the reality of it. While individual blacks of talent desegregated most professions, the recessions of the Fifties caused black unemployment to soar and the gap between black and white family income to widen. And despite the rulings of the Supreme Court and the noble gestures and speeches of politicians, massive resistance to desegregation throughout the South proved the rule. This was the context for the second stage of the civil rights movement. When the nation's attempt to forestall integration and racial equality collided with both the Afro-Americans' leaping expectations and their dissatisfaction with the speed of change, blacks took to the streets in a wave of nonviolent, direct-action protests against every aspect of racism still humiliating them.

On the Role of Martin Luther King

August Meier

Catapulted into national prominence by the bus boycott of 1955–56, Martin Luther King, Jr., quickly became the foremost symbol of the direct action phase of the black struggle which produced the Civil Rights Act of 1964 and the Voter Registration Act of 1965. His eloquent articulation of black aspirations impressed the freedom struggle on the American conscience. Like no black leader before or since, King simultaneously energized the black community and reassured white America. As the situation demanded, he was both militant and moderate. Singularly he bridged the differences in the black protest movement and served as the black ambassador to the white establishment. The institution *that was Martin Luther King made the nonviolent direct action movement respectable and successful. So concluded August Meier, Professor of History at Kent State University, in his contemporaneous analysis of the character of King's leadership. What course the black struggle might have followed if King had not been assassinated in 1968 can never be known. It is problematic that this black preacher could have harmonized the cleavages in the Movement or maintained his following among whites in the latter 1960s. Perhaps his debits as a leader had superceded his assets by the time of his death. Still, students ought to note what the Movement lost by the murder of this extraordinary man, and the role that individuals still play in history.*

The phenomenon that is Martin Luther King consists of a number of striking paradoxes. The Nobel Prize winner is accepted by

From "On the Role of Martin Luther King," *New Politics*, Vol. IV (Winter 1965), pp. 52–59. Reprinted by permission of the author.

the outside world as *the* leader of the nonviolent direct action movement, but he is criticized by many activists within the movement. He is criticized for what appears, at times, as indecisiveness, and more often denounced for a tendency to accept compromise. Yet in the eyes of most Americans, both black and white, he remains the symbol of militant direct action. So potent is this symbol of King as direct actionist, that a new myth is arising about his historic role. The real credit for developing and projecting the techniques and philosophy of nonviolent direct action in the civil rights arena must be given to the Congress of Racial Equality which was founded in 1942, more than a dozen years before the Montgomery bus boycott projected King into international fame. And the idea of mass action by Negroes themselves to secure redress of their grievances must, in large part, be ascribed to the vision of A. Philip Randolph, architect of the March on Washington Movement during World War II. Yet, as we were told in Montgomery on March 25, 1965, King and his followers now assert, apparently without serious contradiction, that a new type of civil rights strategy was born at Montgomery in 1955 under King's auspices.

In a movement in which respect is accorded in direct proportion to the number of times one has been arrested, King appears to keep the number of times he goes to jail to a minimum. In a movement in which successful leaders are those who share in the hardships of their followers, in the risks they take, in the beatings they receive, in the length of time they spend in jail, King tends to leave prison for other important engagements, rather than remaining there and suffering with his followers. In a movement in which leadership ordinarily devolves upon persons who mix democratically with their followers, King remains isolated and aloof. In a movement which prides itself on militancy and "no compromise" with racial discrimination or with the white "power structure," King maintains close relationships with, and appears to be influenced by, Democratic Presidents and their emissaries, seems amenable to compromises considered by some half a loaf or less, and often appears willing to postpone or avoid a direct confrontation in the streets.

King's career has been characterized by failures that, in the larger sense, must be accounted triumphs. The buses in Montgomery were desegregated only after lengthy judicial proceedings conducted by the NAACP Legal Defense Fund secured a favorable decision from the U.S. Supreme Court. Nevertheless, the events in Montgomery were a triumph for direct action, and gave this tactic a popularity unknown when identified solely with CORE. King's subsequent major campaigns—in Albany, Georgia; in Danville, Virginia; in Birmingham, Alabama; and in St. Augustine, Florida—ended as failures or with only token accomplishments in those cities. But each of them, chiefly because of his presence, dramatically focused national and international attention on the plight of the Southern Negro, thereby facilitating over-all progress. In Birmingham, in particular, demonstrations which fell short of their local goals were directly responsible for a major Federal Civil Rights Act. Essentially, this pattern of local failure and national victory was recently enacted in Selma, Alabama.

King is ideologically committed to disobeying unjust laws and court orders, in the Gandhian tradition, but generally he follows a policy of not disobeying Federal Court orders. In his recent Montgomery speech, he expressed a crude, neo-Marxist interpretation of history romanticizing the populist movement as a genuine union of black and white common people, ascribing race prejudice to capitalists playing white workers against black. Yet, in practice, he is amenable to compromise with the white bourgeois political and economic Establishment. More important, King enunciates a superficial and eclectic philosophy and by virtue of it he has profoundly awakened the moral conscience of America.

In short, King can be described as a "conservative militant."

In this combination of militancy with conservatism and caution, of righteousness with respectability, lies the secret of King's enormous success.

Certain important civil rights leaders have dismissed King's position as the product of publicity generated by the mass communications media. But this can be said of the success of the civil rights nonviolent action movement generally. Without publicity it is hard to conceive that much progress would have been made. In fact, contrary to the official nonviolent direct action philosophy, demonstrations have secured their results not by changing the hearts of the oppressors through a display of nonviolent love, but through the national and international pressures generated by the publicity arising from mass arrests and incidents of violence. And no one has employed this strategy of securing publicity through mass arrests and precipitating violence from white hoodlums and law enforcement officers more than King himself. King abhors violence; as at Selma, for example, he constantly retreats from situations that might result in the deaths of his followers. But he is precisely most successful when, contrary to his deepest wishes, his demonstrations precipitate violence from Southern whites against Negro and white demonstrators. We need only cite Birmingham and Selma to illustrate this point.

Publicity alone does not explain the durability of King's image, or why he remains for the rank and file, of whites and blacks alike, the symbol of the direct action movement, the nearest thing to a charismatic leader that the civil rights movement has ever had. At the heart of King's continuing influence and popularity are two facts. First, better than anyone else, he articulates the aspirations of Negroes who respond to the cadence of his addresses, his religious phraseology and manner of speaking, and the vision of his dream for them and for America. King has intuitively adopted the style of the old-fashioned Negro Baptist preacher and transformed it into a new art form; he has, indeed, restored oratory to its place among the arts. Second, he communicates Negro aspirations to white America more effectively than anyone else. His religious terminology and manipulation of the Christian symbols of love and nonresistance are partly responsible for his appeal among whites. To talk in terms of Christianity, love, nonviolence is reassuring to the mentality of white America. At the same time, the very superficialities of his philosophy—that rich and eclectic amalgam of Jesus, Hegel, Gandhi, and others as outlined in his *Stride Toward Freedom*—make him appear intellectually profound to the superficially educated middle-class white American. Actually, if he were a truly profound religious thinker, like Tillich or Niebuhr, his influence would of necessity be limited to a select audience. But by uttering moral clichés, the Christian pieties, in a magnificent display of oratory, King becomes enormously effective.

If his success with Negroes is largely due to the style of his utterance, his success with whites is a much more complicated matter. For one thing, he unerringly knows how to exploit to maximum effectiveness their growing feeling of guilt. King, of course, is not unique in attaining fame and popularity among whites through playing upon their guilt feelings. James Baldwin is the most conspicuous example of a man who has achieved success with this formula. The incredible fascination which the Black Muslims have for white people, and the posthumous near-sanctification of Malcolm X by many naïve whites (in addition to many Negroes whose motivations are, of course, very different), must in large part be attributed to the same source. But King goes beyond this. With intuitive, but extraordinary skill, he not only castigates whites for their sins but, in contrast to angry young writers like Baldwin, he explicitly states his belief in their salvation. Not only will direct action bring fulfillment of the "American Dream" to Negroes but the Negroes' use of direct action will help whites to live up to their Christian and democratic values; it will purify, cleanse, and heal the sickness in white society. Whites will benefit as well as Negroes. He has faith that the white man will redeem himself. Negroes must not hate whites, but love them. In this manner, King first arouses the guilt feelings of whites, and then relieves them—though always leaving the lingering feeling in his white listeners that they should support his nonviolent crusade. Like a Greek tragedy, King's performance provides an extraordinary catharsis for the white listener.

King thus gives white men the feeling that he is their good friend, that he poses no threat to them. It is interesting to note that this was the same feeling white men received from Booker T. Washington, the noted early twentieth-century accommodator. Both men stressed their faith in the white man; both expressed the belief that the white man could be brought to accord Negroes their rights. Both stressed the importance of whites recognizing the rights of Negroes for the moral health and well-being of white society. Like King, Washington had an extraordinary following among whites. Like King, Washington symbolized for most whites the whole program of Negro advancement. While there are important similarities in the functioning of both men vis-à-vis the community, needless to say, in most respects, their philosophies are in disagreement.

It is not surprising, therefore, to find that King is the recipient of contributions from organizations and individuals who fail to eradicate evidence of prejudice in their own backyards. For example, certain liberal trade union leaders who are philosophically committed to full racial equality, who feel the need to identify their organizations with the cause of militant civil rights, although they are unable to defeat racist elements in their unions, contribute hundreds of thousands of dollars to King's Southern Christian Leadership Conference. One might attribute this phenomenon to the fact that SCLC works in the South rather than the North, but this is true also for SNCC, which does not benefit similarly from union treasuries. And the fact is that ever since the college students started their sit-ins in 1960, it is SNCC which has been the real spearhead of direct action in most of the South and has performed the lion's share of work in local communities, while SCLC has received most of the publicity and most of the money. However, while King provides a verbal catharsis for whites, leaving them feeling purified and comfortable, SNCC's uncompromising militancy makes whites feel less comfortable and less beneficent. . . .

King's very tendencies toward compromise and caution, his willingness to negotiate and bargain with White House emissaries, his hesitancy to risk the precipitation of mass violence upon demonstrators, further endear him to whites. He appears to them a "responsible" and "moderate" man. To militant activists, King's failure to march past the state police on that famous Tuesday morning outside Selma indicated either a lack of courage, or a desire to advance himself by currying Presidential favor. But King's shrinking from a possible bloodbath, his accession to the entreaties of the political Establishment, his acceptance of face-saving compromise in this, as in other instances, are fundamental to the particular role he is playing, and essential for achieving and sustaining his image as a leader of heroic moral stature in the eyes of white men. His caution and compromise keep open the channels of communication between the activists and the majority of the white community. In brief: King makes the nonviolent direct action movement respectable.

Of course, many, if not most, activists reject the notion that the movement should be made respectable. Yet American history shows that for any reform movement to succeed it must attain respectability. It must attract moderates, even conservatives, to its ranks. The March on Washington made direct action respectable; Selma made it fashionable. More than any other force, it is Martin Luther King who impressed the civil rights revolution on the American conscience and is attracting that great middle body of American public opinion to its support. It is this revolution of conscience that will undoubtedly lead fairly soon to the elimination of all violations of Negroes' constitutional rights, thereby creating the conditions for the economic and social changes that are necessary if we are to achieve full racial equality. This is not to deny the dangers to the civil rights movement in becoming respectable. Respectability, for example, encourages the attempts of political machines to capture civil rights organizations. Respectability can also become an end in itself, thereby dulling the cutting edge of its protest activities. Indeed, the history of the labor movement reveals how attaining respectability can produce loss of original purpose and character. These perils, however, do not contradict the importance of achieving respectability—even a degree of modishness—if racial equality is ever to be realized.

There is another side to the picture: King would be neither respected nor respectable if there were not more militant activists on his left, engaged in more radical forms of direct action. Without CORE and, especially, SNCC, King would appear "radical" and "irresponsible" rather than "moderate" and "respectable."

King occupies a position of strategic importance as the "vital center" within the civil rights movement. Though he has lieutenants who are far more militant and "radical" than he is, SCLC acts, in effect, as the most cautious, deliberate, and "conservative" of the direct action groups because of King's leadership. This permits King and the SCLC to function—almost certainly unintentionally—not only as an organ of communication with the Establishment and majority white public opinion, but as something of a bridge between the activist and more traditionalist or "conservative" civil rights groups, as well. For example, it appears unlikely that the Urban League and NAACP, which supplied most of the funds, would have participated in the 1963 March on Washington if King had not done so. Because King agreed to go along with SNCC and CORE, the NAACP found it mandatory to join if it was to maintain its image as a protest organization. King's identification with the March was also essential for securing the support of large numbers of white clergymen and their moderate followers. The March was the brainchild of the civil rights movement's ablest strategist and tactician, Bayard Rustin, and the call was issued by A. Philip Randolph. But it would have been a minor episode in the history of the civil rights movement without King's support.

Yet curiously enough, despite his charisma and international reputation, King thus far has been more a symbol than a power in the civil rights movement. Indeed his strength in the movement has derived less from an organizational base than from his symbolic role. Seven or eight years ago, one might have expected King to achieve an organizationally dominant position in the civil rights movement, at least in its direct action wing. The fact is that in the period after the Montgomery bus boycott, King developed no program and, it is generally agreed, revealed himself as an ineffective administrator who failed to capitalize upon his popularity among Negroes. In 1957, he founded SCLC to coordinate the work of direct action groups that had sprung up in Southern cities. Composed of autonomous units, usually led by Baptist ministers, SCLC does not appear to have developed an over-all sense of direction or a program of real breadth and scope. Although the leaders of SCLC affiliates became the race leaders in their communities— displacing the established local conservative leadership of teachers, old-time ministers, businessmen—it is hard for an observer (who admittedly has not been close to SCLC) to perceive exactly what SCLC did before the 1960s except to advance the image and personality of King. King appeared not to direct but to float with the tide of militant direct action. For example, King did not supply the initiative for the bus boycott in Montgomery, but was pushed into the leadership by others, as he himself records in *Stride Toward Freedom*. Similarly, in the late fifties and early sixties, he appeared to let events shape his course. In the last two years, this has changed, but until the Birmingham demonstrations of 1963, King epitomized conservative militancy.

SCLC under King's leadership called the Raleigh Conference of April 1960, which gave birth to SNCC. Incredibly, within a year, the SNCC youth had lost their faith in the man they now satirically call "De Lawd," and had struck out on their own independent path. By that time, the spring of 1961, King's power in the Southern direct action movement had been further curtailed by CORE's stunning Freedom Ride to Alabama and Mississippi.

The limited extent of King's actual power in the civil rights movement was illustrated by the efforts made to invest King with the qualities of a Messiah during the recent ceremonies at the State Capitol in Montgomery. Reverend Abernathy's constant iteration of the theme that King is "our Leader," the Moses of the race, chosen by God, and King's claim that he originated the nonviolent direct action movement at Montgomery a decade ago, are all assertions that would have been superfluous if King's power in the movement was very substantial. . . .

It is indeed fortunate that King has not obtained a predominance of power in the movement commensurate with his prestige. For today, as in the past, a diversity of approaches is necessary. Needed in the movement are those who view the struggle chiefly as a conflict situation, in which the power of demonstrations, the power of Negroes, will force recognition of the race's humanity and citizenship rights, and the achievement of equality. Equally needed are those who see the movement's strategy to be chiefly one of capitalizing on the basic consensus of values in American society by awakening the conscience of the white man to the contradiction between his professions and the facts of discrimination. And just as necessary to the movement as both of these are those who operate skillfully, recognizing and yet exploiting the deeply held American belief that compromise among competing interest groups is the best *modus operandi* in public life.

King is unique in that he maintains a delicate balance among all three of these basic strategy assumptions. The traditional approaches of the Urban League (conciliation of the white businessmen) and of the NAACP (most pre-eminently appeals to the courts and appeals to the sense of fair play in the American public) basically attempted to exploit the consensus in American values. It would of course be a gross oversimplification to say that the Urban League and NAACP strategies are based simply on attempting to capitalize on the consensus of values, while SNCC and CORE act simply as if the situation were purely a conflict situation. Implicit in the actions of all civil rights organizations are both sets of assumptions—even where people are not conscious of the theoretical assumptions under which, in effect, they operate. The NAACP especially encompasses a broad spectrum of strategies and types of activities, ranging from time-tested court procedures to militant direct action. Sophisticated CORE activists know very well when a judicious compromise is necessary or valuable. But I hold that King is in the middle, acting in effect as if he were basing his strategy upon all three assumptions described above. He maintains a delicate balance between a purely moral appeal and a militant display of power. He talks of the power of the bodies of Negro demonstrators in the streets, but unlike CORE and SNCC activists, he accepts compromises at times that consist of token improvements, and calls them impressive victories. More than any of the other groups, King and SCLC can, up to this point at least, be described as exploiting all three tactical assumptions to an approximately equal degree. King's continued success, I suspect, will depend to a considerable degree upon the difficult feat of maintaining his position at the "vital center" of the civil rights movement.

Viewed from another angle, King's failure to achieve a position of power on a level with his prestige is fortunate because rivalries between personalities and organizations remain an essential ingredient of the dynamics of the movement and a precondition for its success as each current tries to outdo the others in effectiveness and in maintaining a good public image. Without this competitive stimulus, the civil rights revolution would slow down.

I have already noted that one of King's functions is to serve as a bridge between the militant and conservative wings of the movement. In addition, by gathering support for SCLC, he generates wider support for CORE and SNCC as well. The most striking example is the recent series of demonstrations in Selma where SNCC had been operating for nearly two years with only moderate amounts of publicity before King chose that city as his own target. As usual, it was King's presence that focused world attention on Selma. In the course of subsequent events, the rift between King and SNCC assumed the proportions of a serious conflict. Yet people who otherwise would have been hesitant to support SNCC's efforts, even people who had become disillusioned with certain aspects of SNCC's policies during the Mississippi Summer Project of 1964, were drawn to demonstrate in Selma and Montgomery. Moreover, although King received the major share of credit for the demonstrations, it seems likely that in the controversy between King and SNCC, the latter emerged with more power and influence in the civil rights movement than ever before. . . .

Major dailies like *The New York Times* and the *Washington Post*, basically sympathetic to civil rights and racial equality, though more gradualist than the activist organizations, have congratulated the nation upon its good fortune in having a "responsible and moderate" leader like King at the head of the nonviolent action movement (though they overestimate his power and underestimate the symbolic nature of his role). It would be more appropriate to congratulate the civil rights movement for *its* good fortune in having as its symbolic leader a man like King. The fact that he has more prestige than power; the fact that he not only criticizes whites but explicitly believes in their redemption; his ability to arouse creative tension combined with his inclination to shrink from carrying demonstrations to the point where major bloodshed might result; the intellectual simplicity of his philosophy; his tendency to compromise and exert caution, even his seeming indecisiveness on some occasions; the sparing use he makes of going to or staying in jail himself; his friendship with the man in the White House—all are essential to the role he plays, and invaluable for the success of the movement. It is well, of course, that not all civil rights leaders are cut of the same cloth— that King is unique among them. Like Randolph, who functions very differently, King is really an institution. His most important function, I believe, is that of effectively communicating Negro aspirations to white people, of making nonviolent direct action respectable in the eyes of the white majority. In addition, he functions within the movement by occupying a vital center position between its "conservative" and "radical" wings, by symbolizing direct action and attracting people to participate in it without dominating either the civil rights movement or its activist wing. Viewed in this context, traits that many activists criticize in King actually function not as sources of weakness, but as the foundations of his strength.

Black Power

Stokely Carmichael

Paralleling the rage expressed by Northern blacks in the urban riots, many of the activists in the struggle for racial equality in the South began demanding Black Power in 1966. First used as a slogan by the newly elected head of the Southern Nonviolent Coordinating Committee, Stokely Carmichael, in the Meredith March Against Fear, the Black Power phase of the movement developed out of frustration over the limited pace and scope of racial change and out of bitterness toward unceasing, brutal white opposition to the most minimal black advances. More a slogan than a program, it was an angry reaction against nonviolence as a tactic and integration as a goal. By 1966, the growing white backlash had made King's goal of an integrated society seem even more an impossible dream. Why not, therefore, battle for self-determination rather than pursue an illusionary desegregation? Most of the Southern freedom fighters, moreover, had turned the other cheek too often, with too little to show for it. Why not assert the right of self-defense, or endorse retaliatory violence, or even advocate violence as a legitimate tactic wherever feasible? Virtually every black organization soon adopted some variant of Black Power, each giving it its own congenial connotation. Whatever Black Power meant, it had surely captured the imagination of black America. No other topic was more discussed and debated in the next several years. In the following excerpt from a speech given at the University of California, Berkeley, Carmichael postulates an early explanation and definition of Black Power.

. . . Now we are engaged in a psychological struggle in this country and that struggle is whether or not black people have the right

From a speech by Stokely Carmichael, University of California, Berkeley, November 19, 1966.

to use the words they want to use without white people giving their sanction to it. We maintain, whether they like it or not, we gon' use the word "black power" and let them address themselves to that. We are not gonna wait for white people to sanction black power. We're tired of waiting. Every time black people move in this country, they're forced to defend their position before they move. It's time that the people who're supposed to be defending their position do that. That's white people. They ought to start defending themselves, as to why they have oppressed and exploited us.

It is clear that when this country started to move in terms of slavery, the reason for a man being picked as a slave was one reason: because of the color of his skin. If one was black, one was automatically inferior, inhuman, and therefore fit for slavery. So that the question of whether or not we are individually suppressed is nonsensical and is a downright lie. We are oppressed as a group because we are black, not because we are lazy, not because we're apathetic, not because we're stupid, not because we smell, not because we eat watermelon and have good rhythm. We are oppressed because we are black and in order to get out of that oppression, one must feel the group power that one has. Not the individual power which this country then sets the criteria under which a man may come into it. That is what is called in this country as integration. You do what I tell you to do, and then we'll let you sit at the table with us. And then we are saying that we have to be opposed to that. We must now set a criteria, and that if there's going to be any integration it's going to be a two-way thing. If you believe in integration, you can come live in Watts. You can send your children to the ghetto schools. Let's talk about that. If you believe in integration, then we're going to start adopting us some white people to live in our neighborhood. So it is clear that the question is not one of integration or segregation. Integration is a man's ability to want to move in there by himself. If someone wants to live in a white neighborhood and he is black, that is his choice. It should be his right. It is not because white people will allow him. So vice-versa, if a black man wants to live in the slums, that should be his right. Black people will let him, that is the difference. . . .

The political parties in this country do not meet the needs of the people on a day-to-day basis. The question is, how can we build new political institutions that will become the political expressions of people on a day-to-day basis. The question is, how can you build political institutions that will begin to meet the needs of Oakland, California; and the needs of Oakland, California is not 1,000 policemen with submachine guns. They don't need that. They need that least of all. The question is, how can we build institutions where those people can begin to function on a day-to-day basis, where they can get decent jobs, where they can get decent housing, and where they can begin to participate in the policy and major decisions that affect their lives. That's what they need. Not Gestapo troops. Because this is not 1942. And if you play like Nazis, we're playing back with you this time around. Get hip to that. . . .

We've been saying that we cannot have white people working in the black community and we've based it on psychological grounds. The fact is that all black people often question whether or not they are equal to whites because everytime they start to do something white people are around showing them how to do it. If we are going to eliminate that for the generations that come after us, then black people must be seen in positions of power doing and articulating for themselves. . . .

It is impossible for white and black people to talk about building a relationship based on humanity when the country is the way it is, when the institutions are clearly against us. We have taken all the myths of this country and we've found them to be nothing but downright lies. This country told us that if we worked hard we would succeed, and if that were true we would own this country lock, stock and barrel. It is we who have picked the cotton for nothing; it is we who are the maids in the kitchens of liberal white people; it is we who are the janitors, the porters, the elevator men; it is we who sweep up your college floors; yes, it is we who are the hardest working and the lowest paid. And that it is nonsensical for people to start talking about human relationships until they're willing to build new institutions. Black people are economically insecure. White liberals are economically secure. Can you begin an economic coalition? Are the liberals willing to share their salaries with the economically insecure black people who they so much love? Then if you're not, are you willing to start building new institutions that will provide economic security for black people? That's the question we want to deal with. . . .

We have to raise questions about whether or not we need new

types of political institutions in this country and we in SNCC
maintain that we need them now. We need new political institutions in this country. And any time Lyndon Baines Johnson can
head a party which has in it Bobby Kennedy, Wayne Morse, Eastland, Wallace and all those other supposedly liberal cats, there's
something wrong with the party. They're moving politically, not
morally. And if that party refuses to seat black people from Mississippi and goes ahead and seats racists like Eastland and his
clique, then it is clear to me that they're moving politically and
that one cannot begin to talk morality to people like that. We must
begin to think politically and see if we can have the power to
impose and keep the moral values that we hold high. We must
question the values of this society. And I maintain that black
people are the best people to do that because we have been excluded from that society and the question is, we ought to think
whether or not we want to become a part of that society. That's
what we want. And that is precisely what, it seems to me, the
Student Nonviolent Coordinating Committee is doing. We are
raising questions about this country. I do not want to be a part of
the American pride. The American pride means raping South
Africa, beating Vietnam, beating South America, raping the Phil-
ippines, raping every country you've been in. I don't want any of
your blood money. I don't want it . . . don't want to be part of that
system. And the question is, how do we raise those questions. . . .
How do we raise them as activists?

We have grown up and we are the generation that has found
this country to be a world power, that has found this country to be
the wealthiest country in the world. We must question how she
got her wealth. That's what we're questioning. And whether or
not we want this country to continue being the wealthiest country
in the world at the price of raping everybody across the world.
That's what we must begin to question. And because black people
are saying we do not now want to become a part of you, we are
called reverse racists. Ain't that a gas?

We are never going to get caught up with questions about power.
This country knows what power is and knows it very well. And
knows what black power is because it's deprived black people of it
for 400 years. So it knows what black power is. But the question is,

why do white people in this country associate black power with violence? Because of their own inability to deal with blackness. If we had said Negro power, nobody would get scared. Everybody would support it. And if we said power for colored people, everybody would be for that. But it is the word "black," it is the word "black" that bothers people in this country, and that's their problem, not mine. . . .

So that in conclusion, we want to say that first, it is clear to me that we have to wage a psychological battle on the right for black people to define their own terms, define themselves as they see fit and organize themselves as they see fit. Now, the question is, how is the white community going to begin to allow for that organizing, because once they start to do that, they will also allow for the organizing that they want to do inside their communities. It doesn't make any difference. Because we're going to organize our way anyway. We're going to do it. The question is, how we're going to facilitate those matters. Whether it's going to be done with a thousand policemen with sub-machine guns or whether or not it's going to be done in the context where it's allowed to be done by white people warding off those policemen. That is the question. . . .

And then, in a larger sense, there is the question of black people. We are on the move for our liberation. We have been tired of trying to prove things to white people. We are tired of trying to explain to white people that we're not going to hurt them. We are concerned with getting the things we want, the things that we have to have to be able to function. The question is, can white people allow for that in this country? The question is, will white people overcome their racism and allow for that to happen in this country? If that does not happen, brothers and sisters, we have no choice, but to say very clearly, move on over, or we're going to move on over you.

Black Power after Ten Years

Clayborne Carson

However many things it meant to blacks, "to most whites," as Carmichael observed, Black Power meant that "the Mau Mau are coming to the suburbs at night." It became synonomous with "Burn, Baby, Burn" and "offing the pigs." To that extent, Black Power helped to polarize the races, sanction the cult of violence, fuel the white backlash, and destroy the civil rights movement. Yet it also generated valuable changes. It galvanized many whom the movement had never mobilized. It spawned a vast array of new community organizations. It spurred self-reliance. It focused attention on the needs of the lower classes. It forced the nation to contemplate the plight of powerlessness.

Fundamentally, Black Power made blacks proud to be black, a psychological precondition for equality. It revolutionized the black perspective, proving invaluable in aiding blacks to discard the disabling self-hatred inculcated by white culture. The following retrospective view by a former activist and present historian at Stanford University analyzes some of the positive and negative consequences of Black Power.

In a single decade, an era of Afro-American politics came and went. A legacy remains, but its full meaning is still to be determined, even by blacks who came of age during the 1960s and were transformed by the events of those years. Now we must search our memories to recall the effect on our lives of the evolution from nonviolent desegregation sit-ins to massive marches and

From *The Nation*, August 14, 1976. Reprinted by permission.

rallies to convulsive urban rebellions—the evolution from Martin Luther King to Malcolm X to Stokely Carmichael to Eldridge Cleaver. The 1963 march on Washington is separated from us by thirteen years and three Presidents and the rise and fall of a succession of movements, leaders and dreams.

Just a decade ago, in the midst of the march through Mississippi undertaken after James Meredith was wounded by a shotgun blast, a new form of racial militancy suddenly gained national attention. The cry for "Black Power" arose as a conscious attempt by the young black activists in the Student Non-Violent Coordinating Committee (SNCC) to alter the direction of black politics. Willie Ricks, an Alabama-born SNCC worker who gained his political education in the streets of Chattanooga, Albany and Montgomery and in isolated black-belt regions of Georgia and Alabama, was chosen in June 1966 to test the readiness of blacks for a new militant vocabulary. Nightly venturing away from the main body of marchers, Ricks launched a new phase of Afro-American history in small black Mississippi towns that time seemed to have ignored. He returned each night with reports of enthusiastic receptions for the rhetoric of Black Power.

A year earlier, in similar communities of Lowndes County, Alabama, Ricks and other SNCC workers had organized the Lowndes County Freedom Organization. In that poor, predominantly black county between Selma and Montgomery, SNCC organizers took an important and original political departure simply by doing what they thought necessary. Since their supporters were black and not welcomed by the Democratic Party, they built an independent all-black party. Since blacks in the Deep South understood white power and resented their own powerlessness, they used the slogan, "Black Power for Black People." And since the panther is black and powerful, they called the new party the Black Panther Party. Stokely Carmichael's work as an organizer in Lowndes County became the basis for his successful bid for the chairmanship of SNCC a few weeks before the Mississippi march and by June 1966, the SNCC militants were ready to assert their claim to national black leadership.

Carmichael, who had directed the 1964 voter registration campaign in Mississippi's 2nd Congressional District, when hundreds of Northern whites came South to help, soon concluded that it was time to break loose from the constraints imposed by SNCC's white liberal supporters. Thus, when the march reached Green-wood, the site of his 1964 headquarters, Carmichael told the na-tion's press that there was a new black response to the question, "What do you want?" Black Power.

Carmichael—handsome, articulate, always conscious of the ef-fect of his words on his listeners—was quickly identified as the principal spokesman for Black Power. In most reports, he was described as the firebrand who had sparked the new militancy, when in fact he was the mirror of a new mood among blacks. Carmichael, like nearly all important black leaders since the ante-bellum period, gained a following among blacks not as a prophet of the future but as an interpreter of the past. As was true of Malcolm X, Carmichael was able to surpass other black leaders because he cut through the verbiage of the white oppressors' lan-guage to utter the truths that lay dormant in the experiences of oppressed blacks. Most blacks recognized that their leaders could do little to shape the future, but they were willing to give their support to those who understood their lives. Carmichael became an oracle for the Black Power movement, because he was singu-larly skillful at expressing conclusions, drawn from years of or-ganizing among Southern blacks, in terms that could be under-stood by urban blacks and whites who were closer than poor black sharecroppers to the mainstream of American politics. He not only expressed the desire of rural Southern blacks to gain control over local institutions but also the desire of urban blacks, like himself, to reject the white-controlled institutions in which they were enmeshed. . . .

The celebrated black militants of the past decade gained almost overnight a fame they did not deserve, and gradually they fell into an obscurity they could not have expected. There is little to suggest that they learned enough from their experiences to build a movement capable of achieving fundamental changes in Ameri-can society; at present, few militant black leaders possess even the illusion of revolutionary potential. Ricks and Carmichael were among those blacks who came to identify with Africa during the late 1960s, but their political views are now separated both from the Marxist programs of most African revolutionary movements and from the pragmatism and opportunism that dominate con-temporary Afro-American politics. They have been unable to transform the black discontent expressed by the Black Power slogan into mass support for their present goal of building a power base in a unified Africa.

Other militant spokesmen have similarly found themselves exiled, imprisoned, or simply ignored. Bobby Seale of the Black Panther Party has long since left that moribund organization. Huey Newton, the other co-founder of the party, is now in Cuban exile. Eldridge Cleaver, whose obscenities once helped shape the image of the party, has become a repentant fugitive who expresses support for the American political system and wishes to be allowed to make his singular contribution to men's fashion design. Imamu Amiri Baraka (formerly LeRoi Jones), the poetic ideologue of black separatism, has more recently concluded that Marx was right as well as white and found that his audience has decreased as dialectics replaced theatrical diatribes. James Forman, whose "Black Manifesto," as delivered to white religious organizations, revealed a prevalent confusion of militant tactics and rhetoric with revolutionary strategy, seems now a burned-out firebrand. . . .

The significant changes that did occur during the past decade merely illustrate the paradoxes of the period. The limited nature of those gains has made many blacks more skeptical about the possibility of fundamentally improving their positions in U.S. life through collective action. Racial pride has risen, but it has neither created an effective national black political movement nor measurably increased racial unity. The attempt by blacks to prove themselves "blacker than thou" has proved quite as divisive as earlier efforts to gain acceptance from whites. Blacks who rejected the term Negro did not abandon the term "niggah."

An increase in the number of black politicians holding public office has been accompanied by a decrease in the proportion of blacks who bother to vote and by an increase in factionalism as blacks compete for leadership. Indeed, black political power has grown largely as a result of the inability of blacks to escape from deteriorating conditions in segregated communities. Mass activism among poor and working-class blacks provided the push for the gains of the 1960s, but the poorest segment of the black population has profited least from those gains. Black leaders who claim to speak for "the people" have diverted the black struggle from the effort to wrest economic concessions directly

from the white establishment to the problematic strategy of in-
terposing between the black masses and the white elite a buffer
of black businessmen and bureaucrats who equate their own success with that of the race. Although the overall failure of blacks
to advance economically in recent years can be attributed to the
economic downturn affecting the larger society, it is significant
that the black middle class has expanded during this period—
from 1965 to 1974—the percentage of blacks making more than
$15,000 a year increased by more than 100 percent (to 19 per-
cent of the total black population). Growth of black college enrollment, white-collar employment and entrepreneurship has
gone hand in hand with continued high unemployment. The
rising black bourgeoisie urges self-reliance on the black poor and
working classes, while it as a class has gradually abandoned the
relative independence of self-employment for jobs as hired
hands of government and big business. Black students have
learned to market their blackness as well as to find it. If affirma-
tive-action programs suddenly were to alter their criteria in
order to provide greater opportunities for those who are poor
rather than simply for those who are black, the loudest cries of
protest would doubtless come from middle-class blacks, many of
whom claim that class analysis does not apply to them.

The demand for Black Power was basically a response to the
recognition that blacks were effectively powerless, but the demand
was often tied to the naive notion that power could be achieved by
unifying a black populace whose common concerns and objective
bases for unity were being rapidly eroded by the advances in the
struggle for civil rights. To go on repeating some variant of the
assertion that, no matter how rich or educated, a black man is still
a "nigger," is to obscure the fact that the battle against racism has
widened rather than narrowed the class divisions among blacks.
Those who ignore this trend not only condemn Afro-American
politics to a future of stagnation but also contribute to the erosion
of the racial trust and empathy that made past gains possible.

Despite the remarkable upsurge in political mobilization and
militancy that occurred among blacks during the 1960s, real
power has remained outside their communities. Civil rights laws
were achieved because protests took place when the national political climate was sympathetic to their goals. This climate enabled
the champions of civil rights to prod powerful forces into action

and, to some extent, restrained the Southern repression that could have destroyed the movement in the South. The most perceptive of the black leaders of the 1960s were able to view their own activism in its proper perspective: as a catalyst in the process of social change, but not as a determinant.

A source of the 1960s militancy was Afro-American awareness of the rise of independent Third World leaders who seemed to have broken free of the constraints imposed by the Western political and economic order. There is irony, however, in the fact that, while young black radicals in this country were making their initial contacts with Third World leaders, they were losing the leverage that had been provided by the attempt of the United States to win support in the nonwhite world. During the early 1960s the State Department was directly involved in attempts to end domestic segregation policies that generated negative publicity abroad and to prevent embarrassing incidents involving African diplomats on visits here. By the mid-1960s, however, as the war in Vietnam escalated, it became evident that the future of Africa and Asia would not be decided primarily through propaganda battles but through the use of military and economic power, and American leaders became less concerned about the effect of domestic racial conflicts on the hearts and minds of Africans and Asians. Thus, the indirect relationship between the domestic and foreign policies of the United States during the early 1960s had greater impact on the fortunes of Afro-Americans than did the haphazard efforts of black radicals later in the 1960s to establish direct ties with distant revolutionary movements.

The belief that Afro-Americans were a colonized group analogous to subject peoples elsewhere in the world was widely accepted by the black radical intelligentsia of the late 1960s, but the colonial analogy obscured as much as it clarified. While many blacks identified with the African demand for nationhood, some Third World revolutionary writers were noting that the direction of change in the newly independent African and Asian nations was toward military domination, economic exploitation by native elites, and the continued disruption of internal affairs by the covert and overt agents of Western capitalism. Robert Allen, author of *Black Awakening in Capitalist America,* was among the few blacks in this country who understood by the late 1960s that the crucial lesson to be learned from the recent experiences of Third World nations was that colonization was no longer the principal issue. Allen argued that black nationalism in the United States was being manipulated and co-opted by the white establishment in order to achieve the kind of neo-colonial domination it had already gained in many Third World nations. However, he was no more able than most African and Asian leaders to offer a viable program to end economic exploitation, and the absence of such a program led to cynicism and disillusionment.

Within the United States, blacks gained their equivalent of political independence—that is, nominal control of a few areas where blacks were in the majority—but, as had been the case for African nations, it was a hollow prize. Large corporations were able to retain the benefits of a black market and labor force, while avoiding the problems that arose from the fact that many blacks were not needed by the economic system. Whites were somewhat upset by the growth of black electoral power, but they were also relieved of a burden of guilt and responsibility. As "blackness" became a much desired commodity (there were many rewards for those who could mimic the distinctive forms of black lowerclass behavior) there were some expressions of dismay among whites. But the communications media quickly appropriated the exotic behavior of the black masses as another faddish diversion to attract mass audiences to their clients. As in Africa during the early 1960s, apparent agreement regarding the desirability of black control masked internal divisions that were deep and exploitable. . . .

At present, after an exceptional period of militancy, black leadership is most effectively exercised by those who have traditionally exercised it: black professionals, businessmen, clergymen and elected officials. The Congressional Black Caucus has emerged as the most significant national black political institution, but it has offered neither consistent nor farsighted leadership. The black legislators recognize, perhaps more clearly than most of their constituents, that the period when the issue of racial status took precedence over all others is coming to an end and that the crucial concerns of the future will be economic. Yet they have developed no plans that avoid the drawbacks of previous liberal social welfare programs. Such programs have succeeded only in supplying temporary jobs outside the manufacturing sector and some more permanent jobs for those who study, evaluate, advise and speak for the poor and needy.

For better or worse, the future of Afro-American society will involve a gradual and inexorable movement from the periphery closer to the center of the world economic system. It is this movement that made possible the emergence of viable black social movements during the 1960s, and the same trend will define the character and potential of future black movements. Doubtless, some blacks will remain outside the mainstream of change, but they will also be at the margins of the main currents of Afro-American life. The common experiences that once permeated black racial consciousness are rapidly being displaced as blacks assume new and varied roles in the modern industrial world. Racial unity has become increasingly difficult to achieve as Afro-American society becomes less distinguishable from the pervading mass culture surrounding it. New opportunities exist, however, to develop collective movements among blacks who recognize that important aspirations have remained submerged in order to maintain the illusion that all blacks share the same interests. The persistence of the outworn rhetoric of the past has obscured the continued widening of class divisions among blacks. The present course of Afro-American politics must be reassessed, not only to confront future realities but also to allow all segments of the black populace a share in the valuable legacy from earlier struggles: an awareness of the potential power of people who come to realize their common destiny.

Part Five

THE CHALLENGE TO SEXISM

Together with issues of race and class, the division of society into "masculine" and "feminine" spheres has been one of the major organizing themes of American society. To this day, whether one is born male or female has more to do with shaping one's life possibilities than almost any other factor. It determines the clothes we wear, the emotions we are taught to cultivate, the jobs we are told we should aspire to, the power we exercise—even our sense of who we are and what we are about. Through most of American history, cultural norms prescribed that women should be the tenders of the hearth, keepers of the home, rearers of children, and the moral, spiritual members of the family. Men, by contrast, were to be assertive, dominant, in control, the major source of power, influence, and income. Even though frequently these norms were not implemented in reality, they remained powerful forces in the culture. Particularly for women of the middle and upper class, the norms defined as off-limits any active involvement in the world outside the home. Those women who worked prior to 1940 were primarily single, young, and poor. It was virtually unheard of for a married, middle-class white woman to have a job or pursue a career. For her to do so would be repudiation of her natural role, and a negative reflection of her husband's ability to provide for her. In a culture which defined success for a woman as marriage and homemaking, any deviation from that role marked failure.

As in the case of Afro-Americans, World War II generated significant change. Millions of women took jobs, and under the press of a wartime crisis, old definitions of women's "proper" place were set aside, at least for the moment. On the other hand, discrimination continued. Women were paid less than men, they were barred from executive positions, and despite wartime needs, day care centers were not provided in adequate numbers.

After the war, many of the advances that had occurred were reversed. What Betty Friedan called the "Feminine Mystique" became once again a pervasive cultural force, urging women to return to the home and to aspire to suburban domesticity. On the other hand, employment figures for women continued to increase, with more and more middle-class women taking jobs simply in order to make it possible for a family to aspire to a better life. By the 1960s, a revitalized feminism became a powerful force in the society, exposing the contradiction between traditional definitions of women's place and the new frequency with which women were assuming roles outside the home. Questioning most of the traditional definitions of masculinity and femininity, the women's liberation movement became one of the most significant forces of social change in the 1960s and 1970s.

In the case of the challenge to sexism, as in the black struggle, there are some who focus attention on external and impersonal sources of change, and others who emphasize the role of activists in bringing about social progress. In the following selections, William Chafe writes about some of the aggregate trends in the society that established the framework within which a revitalized feminism developed. Sara Evans discusses the origins of the women's liberation movement in the civil rights struggles of the early 1960s, showing how the experience of fighting for racial equality generated a new commitment to fight for sex equality as well. Robin Morgan gives a first-person account of changes that have taken place in her own life and in the lives of her friends as a consequence of the women's liberation movement.

Among the questions of most interest with regard to the challenge to sexism is why it took until the middle of the 1960s for a women's liberation movement to develop; why more women did not become active feminists during and after World War II; whether the family is dependent upon traditional roles for men and women; and what the implications for the society will be of greater equality for women and men. Perhaps the largest issue is how and whether sex equality can be achieved given the values and the institutions of contemporary American society.

Social Change and the American Woman, 1940–1970

William H. Chafe

In the later years of the 1970s, feminism encountered intense resistance from the anti-ERA movement and the right-to-life groups opposing abortion. More generally, a new conservatism gained force. Many believed that progress had gone too far and that it was time to call a halt to change. Nevertheless, the feminist movement had already succeeded in increasing opportunities for women, in heightening their self-awareness, and in helping to reshape American thinking about such fundamentals as social equality, the family and sexuality.

More difficult to ascertain than the gains of the women's movement, however, were its causes and origins. In the following analysis of the relationship between social change and the contemporary feminist movement, William Chafe focuses on the consequences of increasing female participation in the labor force. He is particularly concerned with the complicated interaction of objective conditions, such as employment patterns and income, and people's perceptions of those conditions, their attitudes and values. His account should provoke a deeper understanding of the sources and nature of women's liberation.

Although historians have largely neglected the role of women in America's past, few groups in the population merit closer study as a barometer of how American society operates. Not only do

Excerpted from William H. Chafe, "The Paradox of Progress: Social Change Since 1930," in James T. Patterson, ed. *Paths to the Present* (Minneapolis: Burgess Publishing Co., 1975). Reprinted by permission of the author.

women comprise a majority of the population, but gender—together with race and class—serves as one of the principal reference points around which American society is organized. The sociologist Peter Berger has observed that "identity is socially bestowed, socially sanctioned and socially transformed," and gender has been one of the enduring foundations on which social identity has rested. It has provided the basis for dividing up the labor of life ("breadwinning" versus "homemaking"), it has been central to the delineation of roles and authority in the family, and it has served as the source for two powerful cultural stereotypes—"masculine" and "feminine." Any change in the nature of male and female roles thus automatically affects the home, the economy, the school, and perhaps above all, the definition of who we are as human beings. . . .

The eruption of World War II made the first significant dent in this pattern. The national emergency caused new industries to develop and new jobs to open up, providing an opportunity for women, like other excluded groups, to improve their economic position. . . . Hardly a job existed which women did not perform.

The statistics of female employment suggest the dimensions of the change. Between 1941 and 1945, 6.5 million women took jobs, increasing the size of the female labor force by 57 percent. At the end of 1940 approximately 25 percent of all women were gainfully employed; four years later the figure had soared to 36 percent—an increase greater than that of the previous forty years combined. Perhaps most important from a social point of view, the largest number of new workers were married and middle-aged. Prior to 1940 young and single women had made up the vast majority of the female labor force. During the war, in contrast, 75 percent of the new workers were married, and within four years the number of wives in the labor force had doubled. Although some of the new labor recruits were newlyweds who might have been expected to work in any event, the majority listed themselves as former housewives and many, including 60 percent of those hired by the War Department, had children of school and preschool age. By the time victory was achieved, it was just as likely that a wife over forty would be employed as a single woman under twenty-five. The urgency of defeating the Axis powers had swept away, temporarily at least, one of America's entrenched customs.

If women took jobs in unprecedented numbers, however, there was little evidence of a parallel shift in attitudes toward equality between the sexes. Women were consistently excluded from top policy-making committees concerned with running the war, and from higher-level management and executive positions. In addition, the war had only a minimal effect on the traditional disparity between men's and women's wages. Although the War Manpower Commission announced a firm policy of equal pay for equal work, enforcement was spotty, and employers continued to pay women less than men simply by changing the description of the job from "heavy" to "light."

The staying power of traditional values received vigorous confirmation in the postwar years. Despite effusive expressions of gratitude for women's contribution to the war effort, many Americans believed that women should return to their rightful place in the home as soon as the war had ended. In one of the most popular treatises of the postwar years, Ferdinand Lundberg and Marynia Farnham argued that female employment was a feminist conspiracy to seduce women into betraying their biological destiny. The independent woman, they claimed, was a "contradiction in terms." Women were born to be soft, nurturant, and dependent on men; motherhood represented the true goal of female life. Sounding the same theme, Agnes Meyer wrote in the *Atlantic* that though women had many careers, "they have only one vocation—motherhood." The task of modern women, she concluded, was to "boldly announce that no job is more exacting, more necessary, or more rewarding than that of housewife and mother." Most Americans seemed to agree. A series of public opinion polls taken in the postwar years showed that a large majority of people continued to subscribe to the idea of a sharp division of labor between the sexes, with husbands making the "big" decisions and wives caring for the home.

In fact, the situation was more complicated than either public opinion polls or magazine rhetoric seemed to indicate. It was one thing to focus renewed attention on traditional values, and quite another to eradicate the impact of four years of experience. As observers noted at the time, women had discovered something new about themselves in the course of the war, and many were unwilling to give up that discovery just because the war had ended. Although most of the women workers viewed their employment as temporary when the war began, a Women's Bureau survey disclosed that by war's end, 75 percent wished to remain in the labor force.

To a surprising extent, these women succeeded in their desire to remain in the job market. Although the number of women workers declined temporarily in the period immediately after the war, female employment figures showed a sharp upturn beginning in 1947, and by 1950 had once again reached wartime peaks. By 1960 the number of women workers was growing at a rate four times faster than that of men, and 40 percent of all women over sixteen were in the labor force compared to 25 percent in 1940. More important, the women who spearheaded the change were from the same groups that had first gone to work in the war. By 1970, 45 percent of the nation's wives were employed (compared to 11.5 percent in 1930 and 15 percent in 1940), and the 1970 figure included 51 percent of all mothers with children aged six to seventeen. In addition, the economic background of the women workers had shifted significantly. During the 1930s employment of married women had been limited almost exclusively to families with poverty level incomes. By 1970, in contrast, 60 percent of all families with an income of more than $10,000 had wives who worked. In short, the whole pattern of female employment had been reversed. Through legitimizing employment for the average wife and making it a matter of patriotic necessity, the war had initiated a dramatic alteration in the behavior of women and had permanently changed the day-to-day content of their lives.

But if the "objective" conditions of female employment changed so much, why did attitudes toward equality not follow suit? Why, if so many wives and mothers were holding jobs, was there so little protest about continued low pay and discrimination? Why, above all, did the woman's movement not revive in the forties or fifties instead of developing only in the late sixties? Such questions have no easy answers, but to the extent that an explanation is possible, it has to do with the context of the times. The prospect for value changes in any period depends on the frame of reference of the participants, their awareness of the possibility or need for action, and the dominant influences at work in shaping the society. When the appropriate conditions are present, change can be explosive. When they are not present, change can take on the character of an underground fire—important in the long run but for the moment beneath the surface. The latter description fits the situation of women in the forties and fifties and a consideration of the context in which their employment increased during these years is crucial to an understanding of the relationship between behavior and attitudes.

To begin with, most women in the forties and fifties lacked the frame of reference from which to challenge prevailing attitudes on sex roles. Although many women worked, the assumptions about male and female spheres of responsibility were so deeply ingrained that to question them amounted to heresy. If social values are to be changed, there must be a critical mass of protestors who can provide an alternative ideology and mobilize opposition toward traditional points of view. In the postwar period, that protest group did not exist. Feminists at the time simply had no popular support and were generally viewed as a group of cranky women who constituted a "lunatic fringe."

In such a situation, it was not surprising that most women workers exhibited little feminist consciousness. Most had taken jobs because of the benefits associated with employment, not out of a desire to compete with men or prove their equality. When a pattern of discrimination is so pervasive that it is viewed as part of the rules of the game, few individuals will have the wherewithal to protest. It takes time and an appropriate set of social conditions before a basis for ideological protest can develop. With their experience in World War II, women had gone through the first stage of a monumental change. But it would be unrealistic to think that they could move immediately into a posture of feminist rebellion without a series of intervening stages. New perceptions had to evolve; new ideas had to gain currency. And both depended to some extent on the dominant influences at work in the immediate environment.

The second reason for the persistence of traditional attitudes was that women's employment expanded under conditions which emphasized women's role as "helpmates." The continued entry of women into the labor force was directly related to skyrocketing inflation and the pent-up desire of millions of families to achieve a higher living standard. In many instances, husbands and wives could not build new homes, buy new appliances, or purchase new cars on one income alone, and the impulse not to be left behind in the race for affluence offered a convenient rationale for women to remain in the labor force. Men who might oppose in theory the idea of married women holding jobs were willing to have their own wives go to work to help the family achieve its middle-class aspirations. But under such circumstances, the wife who held a job was playing a supportive role, not striking out on her own as an "independent" woman. The distinction was crucial. If women had been taking jobs because of a desire to prove their equality with men, their employment would probably have encountered bitter resistance. In contrast, the fact that they were thought to be only "helping out" made it possible for their efforts to receive social sanction as a fulfillment of their traditional family role.

To say that attitudes did not change, however, did not mean that behavior was without important long-range effects. Indeed, the growing employment of women offers an excellent example of the way in which changes in behavior can pave the way for subsequent changes in attitudes. As more and more wives joined the labor force after 1940, the sexual segregation of roles and responsibilities within the family gradually gave way to greater sharing. Sociological surveys showed that wherever wives held jobs, husbands performed more household tasks, especially in the areas of child care, cleaning, and shopping. In addition, power relationships between men and women underwent some change. Women who worked exercised considerably more influence on "major" economic decisions than wives who did not work. In no instance did the changes result in total equality, nor were they ideologically inspired; but sociologists unanimously concluded that women's employment played a key role in modifying the traditional distribution of tasks and authority within the family.

Similarly, the presence of an employed mother exercised a substantial impact on the socialization patterns of children. Young boys and girls who were raised in households where both parents worked grew up with the expectation that women—as well as men—would play active roles in the outside world. A number of surveys of children in elementary and junior high school showed that daughters of working mothers planned to work themselves after marriage, and the same studies suggested that young girls were more likely to name their mother as the person they most admired if she worked than if she did not work. At the same time, it appeared that these daughters developed a revised idea of what it meant to be born female. On a series of personality tests, daughters of working mothers scored lower on scales of traditional femininity and agreed that both men and women should enjoy a variety of work, household, and recreational experiences. Thus if behavioral change did not itself produce a challenge to traditional attitudes, it set in motion a process which prepared a foundation for such a challenge.

All that was required to complete the process was the development of an appropriate context, and in the early 1960s that context began to emerge. After eight years of consolidation and consensus in national politics during the Eisenhower administration, a new mood of criticism and reform started to surface in the nation. Sparked by the demands of black Americans for full equality, public leaders focused new attention on a whole variety of problems which had been festering for years. Poverty, racial injustice, and sex discrimination had a lengthy history in America, but awareness of them crystallized in a climate which emphasized the need for activism to eradicate the nation's ills. Once the process of protest had begun, it generated a momentum of its own, spreading to groups which previously had been quiescent.

Again, the experience of women dramatized the process of change. Just as World War II had served as a catalyst to behavioral change among women, the ferment of the sixties served as a catalyst to ideological change. The first major sign of the impending drive for women's liberation appeared with the publication in 1963 of Betty Friedan's best-selling *The Feminine Mystique*. Writing with eloquence and passion, Friedan traced the origins of women's oppression to a social system which persistently denied women the opportunity to develop their talents as individual human beings. "The core of the problem of women today," she wrote, "is not sexual but a problem of identity—a stunting or evasion of growth. . . ." Friedan pointed out that while men had abundant opportunities to test their mettle, women saw their entire lives circumscribed by the condition of their birth and were told repeatedly "that they could desire no greater destiny than to glory in their own femininity." If a woman had aspirations for a career, she was urged instead to find a full measure of satisfaction in the role of housewife and mother. Magazines insisted that there was no other route to happiness; consumer industries glorified her life as homemaker; and psychologists warned her that if she left her position in the home, the whole society would be endangered. The result was that she was imprisoned in a "comfortable concentration camp," prevented from discovering who she really *was* by a society which told her only what she *could be*. Although Friedan's assessment contained little that had not been said before by other feminists, her book spoke to millions of women in a fresh way, driving home the message that what had previously been perceived as only a personal problem was in fact a *woman* problem, shared by others and rooted in a set of social attitudes that required change if a better life was to be achieved.

A second—and equally important—influence feeding the woman's movement came from the burgeoning drive for civil rights. Although it was true that blacks and women had strikingly different problems, they suffered from modes of oppression which in some ways were similar. For women as well as blacks, the denial of equality occurred through the assignment of separate and unequal roles. Both were taught to "keep their place," and were excluded from social and economic opportunities on the grounds that assertive behavior was deviant. The principal theme of the civil rights movement was the immorality of treating any human being as less equal than another on the basis of a physical characteristic, and that theme spoke as much to the condition of women as to that of blacks. In its tactics, its message, and its moral fervor, the civil rights movement provided inspiration and an organizational model for the activities of women.

Just as significant, the civil rights movement exposed many women to the direct experience of sex discrimination. Younger activists in particular found that they frequently were treated as servants whose chief function was to be sex partners for male leaders. ("The place of women in the movement," Stokely Carmichael said, "is prone.") Instead of having an equal voice in policy making, women were relegated to tasks such as making coffee or sweeping floors. Faced with such discrimination, some female activists concluded that they had to free *themselves* before they could work effectively for the freedom of others. The same women became the principal leaders of the younger, more radical segment of women's liberation, taking the organizing skills and ideological fervor which they had learned in the fight for blacks and applying them to the struggle for women.

Perhaps the most important precondition for the revival of

feminism, however, was the amount of change which had already occurred in women's lives. As long as the overwhelming majority of women remained in the home, there was no frame of reference from which to question the status quo. Woman's "place" was a fact as well as an idea. With the changes which began in World War II, on the other hand, reality ceased to conform to attitudes. The march of events had already delivered a fatal blow to conventional ideas on woman's place, thereby creating a condition which made feminist arguments both timely and relevant. The experience of *some* change gave millions of women the perspective which allowed them to hear the feminists call for more change. Thus if the women who took jobs during the forties did not themselves mount an ideological assault on the status quo, they prepared a foundation which enabled the subsequent generation to take up the battle for a change in attitudes and ideas.

Women's Consciousness and the Southern Black Movement

Sara Evans

"There is no overt anti-feminism in our society in 1964," observed sociologist Alice Rossi, "not because sex equality has been achieved, but because there is practically no feminist spark left among American women." The tinder existed, as Chafe describes in the preceding selection, but an acute awareness of oppression, a fiery consciousness did not. The combustion, however, would soon be provided by the young female participants in the civil rights and New Left movements. These daughters of the middle class ignited a radical critique of sexism and a mass mobilization of American women. In the voter registration campaigns of the South and in the community organizing efforts in Northern ghettos, the female volunteers found the inner strength and self-respect, the new vistas of possibility, and the political skills to pursue their own quest for equality. There they also experienced having their work minimized, even disregarded, by the men they had considered their colleagues. This shattering ordeal spun them out of the male-dominated movements and into a new one for women's liberation. Personal Politics (1979), by Sara Evans, and the following selection provocatively analyze these collective biographical roots of the revitalized challenge to sexism.

Twice in the history of the United States the struggle for racial equality has been midwife to a feminist movement. In the abolition movement of the 1830s and 1840s and again in the civil-rights revolt of the 1960s, women experiencing the contradictory expectations and stresses of changing roles began to move from individual discontents to a social movement in their own behalf. Working for racial justice, they developed both political skills and a belief in human rights which could justify their own claim to equality. . . .

Following the first wave of sit-ins in 1960, the Southern Christian Leadership Conference (SCLC), at the insistence of its assistant director, Ella Baker, called a conference at Shaw University in Raleigh, N.C., on Easter weekend. There black youth founded their own organization, the Student Nonviolent Coordinating Committee (SNCC) to provide a support network for direct action. SNCC set the style and tone of grass-roots organizing in the rural South and led the movement into the black belt. The spirit of adventure and commitment which animated the organization added new vitality to a deeply rooted struggle for racial equality.

In addition to this crucial role within the black movement, SNCC also created the social space within which women began to develop a new sense of their own potential. A critical vanguard of young women accumulated the tools for movement building: a language to describe oppression and justify revolt, experience in the strategy and tactics of organizing, and a beginning sense of themselves collectively as objects of discrimination.

Relative deprivation is an overused and overly clinical term to describe the pain, the anger, and the ambiguity of their experience.

Nevertheless, it was precisely the clash between the heightened sense of self-worth which the movement offered to its participants and the replication of traditional sex roles within it that gave birth to a new feminism. Treated as housewives, sex objects, nurturers, and political auxiliaries, and finally threatened with banishment from the movement, young white Southern women responded with the first articulation of the modern challenge to the sexual status quo. . . .

The movement's vision translated into daily realities of hard work and responsibility which admitted few sexual limitations. Young white women's sense of purpose was reinforced by the knowledge that the work they did and the responsibilities they assumed were central to the movement. In the beginning, black and white alike agreed that whites should work primarily in the white community. They had an appropriate role in urban direct-

action movements where the goal was integration, but their principal job was generating support for civil rights within the white
population. The handful of white women involved in the early
'60s either worked in the SNCC office—gathering news, writing
pamphlets, facilitating communications—or organized campus
support through such agencies as the YWCA.

In direct-action demonstrations, many women discovered un-
tapped reservoirs of courage. Cathy Cade attended Spelman College as an exchange student in the spring of 1962. She had been
there only two days when she joined Howard Zinn in a sit-in in the
black section of the Georgia Legislature. Never before had she so
much as joined a picket line. Years later she testified: "To this day I
am amazed. I just did it." Though she understood the risks involved, she does not remember being afraid. Rather she was exhila-
rated, for with one stroke she undid much of the fear of blacks that
she had developed as a high school student in Tennessee.

Others, like Mimi Feingold, jumped eagerly at the chance to
join the freedom rides but then found the experience more har-
rowing than they had expected. Her group had a bomb scare in
Montgomery and knew that the last freedom bus in Alabama had
been blown up. They never left the bus from Atlanta to Jackson,
Mississippi. The arrest in Jackson was anti-climactic. Then there
was a month in jail where she could hear women screaming as
they were subjected to humiliating vaginal "searches."

When SNCC moved into voter registration projects in the Deep
South, the experiences of white women acquired a new dimen-
sion. The years of enduring the brutality of intransigent racism
finally convinced SNCC to invite several hundred white students
into Mississippi for the 1964 "freedom summer." For the first
time, large numbers of white women would be allowed into "the
field," to work in the rural South.

They had previously been excluded because white women in
rural communities were highly visible; their presence, violating
both racial and sexual taboos, often provoked repression. According to Mary King, "the start of violence in a community was often
tied to the point at which white women appeared to be in the
civil-rights movement." However, the presence of whites also
brought the attention of the national media, and, in the face of
the apparent impotence of the federal law enforcement apparatus, the media became the chief weapon of the movement against

violence and brutality. Thus, with considerable ambivalence, SNCC began to include whites—both men and women—in certain voter registration projects.

The freedom summer brought hundreds of Northern white women into the Southern movement. They taught in freedom schools, ran libraries, canvassed for voter registration, and endured constant harassment from the local whites. Many reached well beyond their previously assumed limits: "I was overwhelmed at the idea of setting up a library all by myself," wrote one woman. "Then can you imagine how I felt when at Oxford, while I was learning how to drop on the ground to protect my face, my ears, and my breasts, I was asked to *coordinate* the libraries in the entire project's community centers? I wanted to cry 'HELP' in a number of ways."

And while they tested themselves and questioned their own courage, they also experienced poverty, oppression and discrimination in raw form. As one volunteer wrote:

> For the first time in my life, I am seeing what it is like to be poor, oppressed, and hated. And what I see here does not apply only to Gulfport or to Mississippi or even to the South. . . . This summer is only the briefest beginning of this experience."

Some women virtually ran the projects they were in. And they learned to live with an intensity of fear that they had never known before. By October, 1964, there had been 15 murders, 4 woundings, 37 churches bombed or burned, and over 1,000 arrests in Mississippi. Every project set up elaborate security precautions— regular communication by two-way radio, rules against going out at night or walking downtown in interracial groups. One woman summed up the experience of hundreds when she explained, "I learned a lot of respect for myself for having gone through all that."

As white women tested themselves in the movement, they were constantly inspired by the examples of black women who shattered cultural images of appropriate "female" behavior. "For the first time," according to one white Southerner, "I had role models I could respect."

Within the movement many of the legendary figures were black women around whom circulated stories of exemplary cour-

age and audacity. Rarely did women expect or receive any special protection in demonstrations or jails. Frequently, direct-
action teams were equally divided between women and men, on
the theory that the presence of women in sit-in demonstrations
might lessen the violent reaction. In 1960, slender Diane Nash
had been transformed overnight from a Fisk University beauty
queen to a principal leader of the direct-action movement in
Nashville, Tennessee. . . .

Perhaps even more important than the daring of younger activists was the towering strength of older black women. There is no
doubt that women were key to organizing the black community.
In 1962, SNCC staff member Charles Sherrod wrote the office
that in every southwest Georgia county "there is always a 'mama.'
She is usually a militant woman in the community, out-spoken,
understanding, and willing to catch hell, having already caught
her share."

Stories of such women abound. For providing housing, food,
and active support to SNCC workers, their homes were fired
upon and bombed. Fannie Lou Hamer, the Sunflower County
sharecropper who forfeited her livelihood to emerge as one of the
most courageous and eloquent leaders of the Mississippi Freedom
Democratic Party, was only the most famous. "Mama Dolly" in
Lee County, Georgia, was a seventy-year-old, grey-haired lady
"who can pick more cotton, slop more pigs, plow more ground,
chop more wood, and do a hundred more things better than the
best farmer in the area." For many white volunteers, they were
also "mamas" in the sense of being mother-figures, new models of
the meaning of womanhood.

Yet new models bumped up against old ones; self-assertion
generated anxiety; new expectations existed alongside traditional
ones; ideas about freedom and equality bent under assumptions
about women as mere houseworkers and sexual objects. These
contradictory forces finally generated a feminist response from
those who could not deny the reality of their new-found strength.

Black and white women took on important administrative roles
in the Atlanta SNCC office, but they also performed virtually all
typing and clerical work. Very few women assumed the public
roles of national leadership. In 1964, black women held a half-
serious, half-joking sit-in to protest these conditions. By 1965, the

situation had changed enough that a quarrel over who would take notes at staff meetings was settled by buying a tape recorder.

In the field, there was a tendency to assume that housework around the freedom house would be performed by women. As early as 1963, Joni Rabinowitz, a white volunteer in the southwest Georgia Project, submitted a stinging series of reports on the "woman's role."

"Monday, 15 April: . . . The attitude around here toward keeping the house neat (as well as the general attitude toward the inferiority and 'proper place' of women) is disgusting and also terribly depressing. I never saw a cooperative enterprize (sic) that was less cooperative."

There were also ambiguities in the position of women who had been in the movement for many years and were perceived by others as important leaders. While women increasingly became a central force in SNCC between 1960 and 1965, white women were always in a somewhat anomalous position. New recruits saw Casey Hayden and Mary King as very powerful. Hayden had been an activist since the late '50s. Her involvement in the YWCA and the Christian Faith and Life Community at the University of Texas led her to join the demonstrations which erupted in Austin in 1959. From that time on she worked full-time against segregation, sometimes through the Y, sometimes through the National Student Association or Students for a Democratic Society, but always most closely with SNCC. Mary King, daughter of a Southern Methodist minister, had visited SNCC on a trip sponsored by the Y at Ohio Wesleyan University in 1962 and soon returned to work full-time.

They and others who had joined the young movement when it included only a handful of whites knew the inner circles of SNCC through years of shared work and risk. They had an easy familiarity with the top leadership which bespoke considerable influence. Yet Hayden and King could virtually run a freedom registration program and at the same time remain outside the basic political decision-making process.

Mary King described herself and Hayden as being in "positions of relative powerlessness." They were powerful because they worked very hard. According to King, "If you were a hard worker and you were good, at least before 1965 . . . you could definitely have an influence on policy."

The key phrase is "at least before 1965," for by 1965 the positions of white women in SNCC, especially Southern women whose goals had been shaped by the vision of the "beloved community," was in steep decline. Ultimately, a growing spirit of black nationalism, fed by the tensions of large numbers of whites, especially women, entering the movement, forced these women out of SNCC and precipitated the articulation of a new feminism.

White women's presence inevitably heightened the sexual tension which runs as a constant current through racist culture. Southern women understood that in the struggle against racial discrimination they were at war with their culture. They reacted to the label "Southern lady" as though it were an obscene epithet, for they had emerged from a society that used the symbol of "Southern white womanhood" to justify an insidious pattern of racial discrimination and brutal repression. They had, of necessity, to forge a new sense of self, a new definition of femininity apart from the one they had inherited. Gradually they came to understand the struggle against racism as "a key to pulling down all the . . . fascist notions and mythologies and institutions in the South," including "notions about white women and repression."

Thus, for Southern women this tension was a key to their incipient feminism, but it also became a disruptive force within the civil-rights movement itself. The entrance of white women in large numbers into the movement could hardly have been anything but explosive. Interracial sex was the most potent social taboo in the South. And the struggle against racism brought together young, naive, sometimes insensitive, rebellious, and idealistic white women with young, angry black men, some of whom had hardly been allowed to speak to white women before. They sat-in together. If they really believed in equality, why shouldn't they sleep together?

In many such relationships there was much warmth and caring. Several marriages resulted. One young woman described how "a whole lot of things got shared around sexuality—like black men with white women—it wasn't just sex, it was also sharing ideas and fears, and emotional support . . . My sexuality for myself was confirmed by black men for the first time ever in my life, see . . . and I needed that very badly . . . It's a positive advantage to be a big woman in the black community."

On the other hand, there remained a dehumanizing quality in

many relationships. According to one woman, it "had a lot to do with the fact that people thought they might die." They lived their lives at an incredible pace and could not be very loving toward anybody. "So [people] would go to a staff meeting and . . . sleep with whoever was there."

Sexual relationships did not become a serious problem, however, until interracial sex became a widespread phenomenon in local communities in the summer of 1964. The same summer that opened new horizons to hundreds of women simultaneously induced serious strains within the movement itself. Accounts of what happened vary according to the perspectives of the observer.

Some paint a picture of hordes of "loose" white women coming to the South and spreading corruption wherever they went. One male black leader recounted that "where I was project director we put white women out of the project within the first three weeks because they tried to screw themselves across the city." He agreed that black neighborhood youth tended to be sexually aggressive. "I mean you are trained to be aggressive in this country, but you are also not expected to get a positive response."

Others saw the initiative coming almost entirely from males. According to historian Staughton Lynd, director of the Freedom Schools, "Every black SNCC worker with perhaps a few exceptions counted it a notch on his gun to have slept with a white woman—as many as possible. And I think that was just very traumatic for the women who encountered that, who hadn't thought that was what going South was about." A white woman who worked in Virginia for several years explained, "It's much harder to say 'No' to the advances of a black guy because of the strong possibility of that being taken as racist."

Clearly the boundary between sexual freedom and sexual exploitation was a thin one. Many women consciously avoided all romantic involvements in intuitive recognition of that fact. Yet the presence of hundreds of young whites from middle- and upper-middle-income families in a movement primarily of poor, rural blacks exacerbated latent racial and sexual tensions beyond the breaking point. The first angry response came not from the surrounding white community (which continually assumed sexual excesses far beyond the reality) but from young black women in the movement.

A black woman pointed out that white women would "do all the shit work and do it in a feminine kind of way while [black women] . . . were out in the streets battling with the cops. So it did something to what [our] femininity was about. We became amazons, less than and more than women at the same time." Another black woman added, "If white women had a problem in SNCC, it was not just a male/woman problem . . . it was also a black woman/white woman problem. It was a race problem rather than a woman's problem." And a white woman, asked whether she experienced any hostility from black women, responded, "Oh tons and tons! I was very, very afraid of black women, very afraid." Though she admired them and was continually awed by their courage and strength, her sexual relationships with black men placed a barrier between herself and black women.

Soon after the 1964 summer project, black women in SNCC sharply confronted male leadership. They charged that they could not develop relationships with black men because the men did not have to be responsible to them as long as they could turn to involvement with white women.

Black women's anger and demands constituted one part of an intricate maze of tensions and struggles that were in the process of transforming the civil-rights movement. SNCC had grown from a small band of sixteen to a swollen staff of 180, of whom 50% were white. The earlier dream of a beloved community was dead. The vision of freedom lay crushed under the weight of intransigent racism, disillusion with electoral politics and nonviolence, and differences of race, class, and culture within the movement itself. Within the rising spirit of black nationalism, the anger of black women toward white women was only one element. . . .

For Southern white women who had devoted several years of their lives to the vision of a beloved community, the rejection of nonviolence and movement toward a more ideological, centralized, and black nationalist movement was bitterly disillusioning. Mary King recalled, "It was very sad to see something that was so creative and so dynamic and so strong [disintegrating] . . . . I was terribly disappointed for a long time. . . . I was most affected by the way that black women turned against me. That hurt more than the guys. But it had been there, you know. You could see it coming."

In the fall of 1965, Mary King and Casey Hayden spent several days of long discussions in the mountains of Virginia. Both of them were on their way out of the movement, though they were not fully conscious of that fact. Finally they decided to write a "kind of memo" addressed to "a number of other women in the peace and freedom movements." In it they argued that women, like blacks, "seem to be caught in a common-law caste system that operates, sometimes subtly, forcing them to work around or outside hierarchical structures of power which may exclude them. Women seem to be placed in the same position of assumed subordination in personal situations too. It is a caste system which, at its worst, uses and exploits women."

Hayden and King set the precedent of contrasting the movement's egalitarian ideas with the replication of sex roles within it. They noted the ways in which women's position in society determined women's roles in the movement—like cleaning houses, doing secretarial work, and refraining from active or public leadership. At the same time, they observed, "having learned from the movement to think radically about the personal worth and abilities of people whose role in society had gone unchallenged before, a lot of women in the movement have begun trying to apply those lessons to their own relationships with men. Each of us probably has her own story of the various results."

They spoke of the pain of trying to put aside "deeply learned fears, needs, and self-perceptions . . . and . . . to replace them with concepts of people and freedom learned from the movement and organizing." In this process many people in the movement had questioned basic institutions, such as marriage and child-rearing. Indeed, such issues had been discussed over and over again, but seriously only among women. The usual male response was laughter, and women were left feeling silly. Hayden and King lamented the "lack of community for discussion: Nobody is writing, or organizing, or talking publicly about women, in any way that reflects the problems that various women in the movement came across." Yet despite their feelings of invisibility, their words also demonstrated the ability to take the considerable risks involved in sharp criticisms. Through the movement they had developed too much self-confidence and self-respect to accept passively subordinate roles.

The memo was addressed principally to black women—long time friends and comrades-in-nonviolent-arms—in the hope that, "perhaps we can start to talk with each other more openly than in the past and create a community of support for each other so we can deal with ourselves and others with integrity and can therefore keep working." In some ways, it was a parting attempt to halt the metamorphosis in the civil-rights movement from nonviolence to nationalism, from beloved community to black power. It expressed Hayden and King's pain and isolation as white women in the movement. The black women who received it were on a different historic trajectory. They would fight some of the same battles as women, but in a different context and in their own way.

This "kind of memo" represented a flowering of women's consciousness that articulated contradictions felt most acutely by middle-class white women. While black women had been gaining strength and power within the movement, white women's position—at the nexus of sexual and racial conflicts—had become increasingly precarious. Their feminist response, then, was precipitated by loss in the immediate situation, but it was a sense of loss against the even deeper background of new strength and self-worth which the movement had allowed them to develop. Like their foremothers in the nineteenth century, they confronted this dilemma with the tools which the movement had given them: a language to name and describe oppression; a deep belief in freedom, equality and community soon to be translated into "sisterhood"; a willingness to question and challenge any social institution which failed to meet human needs; and the ability to organize.

It is not surprising that the issues were defined and confronted first by Southern women whose consciousness developed in a context which inextricably and paradoxically linked the fate of women and black people. These spiritual daughters of Sarah and Angelina Grimke kept their expectations low in November, 1965. "Objectively," Hayden and King wrote, "the chances seem nil that we could start a movement based on anything as distant to general American thought as a sex-caste system." But change was in the air and youth was on the march.

In the North there were hundreds of women who had shared in the Southern experience for a week, a month, a year, and thousands more who participated vicariously or worked to extend the struggle for freedom and equality into Northern communities. These women were ready to hear what their Southern sisters had to say. The debate within Students for a Democratic Society (SDS) which started in response to Hayden and King's ideas led, two years later, to the founding of the women's liberation movement.

Thus, the fullest expression of conscious feminism within the civil-rights movement ricocheted off the fury of black power and landed with explosive force in the Northern, white new left. One month after Hayden and King mailed out their memo, women who had read it staged an angry walkout of a national SDS conference in Champaign-Urbana, Illinois. The only man to defend their action was a black man from SNCC.

Rights of Passage

Robin Morgan

The relationship of women's liberation to the civil rights movement can also be viewed through their analogous stages of protest. Both began with educational campaigns designed to overcome inequities assumed to be largely the result of ignorance or inadvertence. Then, when separate individuals realized that their plight was not unique but actually common to a very large group, they sought a political solution to rectify their powerlessness. Finally, the two movements engaged in a cultural and psychological assault against racism *and* sexism *and the institutions that perpetuate them.*

Because those complex amalgams of attitudes and convictions are the creation of thousands of years of thought and reinforced patterns of behavior so deeply imprinted that they are assumed to be "natural" or "instinctive," their eradication is surely the most difficult aspect of liberation. For individuals, it is often the most painful of passages. Robin Morgan— radical feminist, wife, poet, mother, and director of the New York Women's Law Center—in this excerpt from an autobiographical essay which appeared in Ms. *in 1975 describes her personal odyssey in the women's movement. Students should consider the revolutionary meaning of Morgan's conclusions, and the ways in which the demise of sexism can free both sexes to develop and contribute to their full potential.*

I wanted to write a sort of "personal retrospective" on the Women's Movement: where we've been, where we are, where we

From Robin Morgan, "Rights of Passage," *Ms. Magazine*, November 1975. Reprinted by permission of the publisher.

might be going—all this in a classically theoretical style, preferably obscure, yea, unintelligible, so that people would be unable to understand what in hell I was saying and would label me, therefore, A Brilliant Thinker. But the risk-taking, subjective voice of poetry is more honestly my style, and so, to look at the Women's Movement, I go to the mirror—and gaze at myself. Everywoman? Surely a staggering egotism, that! I hardly believe "Le Mouvement, c'est moi." I *do* still believe, though, that the personal is political, and vice versa (the *politics* of sex, the *politics* of housework, the *politics* of motherhood), and that this insight into the necessary integration of exterior realities and interior imperatives is one of the themes of consciousness that makes the Women's Movement unique, less abstract, and more functionally *possible* than previous movements for social change.

So I must dare to begin with myself, my own experience.

Ten years ago I was a woman who believed in the reality of the vaginal orgasm (and had become adept at faking spiffy ones). I felt legitimized by a successful crown roast and was the fastest hand in the east at emptying ashtrays. I never condemned pornography for fear of seeming unsophisticated and prudish. My teenage rebellion against my mother had atrophied into a permanent standoff. Despite hours of priming myself to reflect the acceptable beauty standards, I was convinced that my body was lumpy, my face was possessed of a caterpillar's bone structure, and my hair was resolutely unyielding to *any* flattering style. And ten years ago my poems quietly began muttering something about my personal pain as a woman—unconnected, of course, to anyone else, since I saw this merely as my own inadequacy, my own battle. . . .

That was the period when I still could fake a convincing orgasm, still wouldn't be caught dead confronting an issue like pornography (for fear, this time, of being "a bad-vibes, uptight, unhip chick"). I could now afford to reject my mother for a new, radical-chic reason: the generation gap. I learned to pretend contempt for monogamy as both my husband and I careened (secretly grieving for each other) through the fake "sexual revolution" of the sixties. Meanwhile, correctly Maoist beancurd and class-conscious rice and beans filled our menus—and I *still* put in hours priming myself to reflect the acceptable "beauty" standards, those of a tough-broad street fighter: uniform jeans, combat boots, long hair, and sunglasses worn even at night (which didn't help one see better when running from rioting cops). And my poems lurched forth guiltily, unevenly, while I developed a chronic case of Leningitis and mostly churned out those "political" essays—although Donne and Dickinson, Kafka, Woolf, and James were still read in secret at our home (dangerous intellectual tendencies), and television was surreptitiously watched (decadent bourgeois privileges).

For years my essays implored, in escalating tones, the "brothers" of the "revolution" to let us women in, to take more-than-lip-service notice of what the women's caucuses were saying, especially since "they" (women) constitute more than half the human species. Then, at a certain point, I began to stop addressing such men as "brothers," and began (O language, thou subtle Richter scale of attitudinal earthquakes!) to use the word "we" when speaking of women. And there was no turning back.

The ensuing years can seem to me a blur of joy, misery, and daily surprise: my first consciousness-raising group and all the "daughter" groups I was in; the guerrilla theater, the marches, meetings, demonstrations, picketings, sit-ins, conferences, workshops, plenaries; the newspaper projects, the child-care collectives, the first anti-rape squads, the earliest seminars (some women now prefer the word "ovulars"—how lovely!) on women's health, women's legal rights, women's sexuality. And all the while, the profound "interior" changes: the transformation of my work—content, language, *and* form—released by this consciousness; the tears and shouts and laughter and despair and growth wrought in the struggle with my husband; the birth of our child (a radicalizing experience, to say the least); the detailed examinations of life experiences, of power, honesty, commitment, bravely explored through so many vulnerable hours with other women— the discovery of a shared suffering and of a shared determination to become whole.

During those years we felt a desparate urgency, arising partly from the barrage of brain-boggling "clicks" our consciousness encountered about our condition as females in a partriarchal world; but also, I must confess, arising from the leftover influence of the male movements, which were given to abstract rhetoric but "ejaculatory tactics." That is, if the revolution as they defined it didn't occur within the next week, month, five years at the minimum—

then the hell with it. We wouldn't be alive, anyway, to see it, so we must die for it (this comfortably settled the necessity for any long-range *planning*).

Today, my just-as-ever-urgent anger is tempered by a patience born of the recognition that the *process,* the *form of change itself, is everything:* the means and the goal justifying *each other.*

There are no easy victories, no pat answers—and anyone who purveys such solutions alarms me now. But when I look back from my still-militantly rocking chair, or sit at my ultimate weapon, the typewriter, I see the transformations spiraling upward so rapidly and so astonishingly that my heart swells with gratitude to have been a part of such changes.

We were an "American phenomenon," they said—an outgrowth of the neurosis and stridency of spoiled American women. ("They" were the patriarchal left, right, and middle, the media, most men, and some women.) They overlooked certain little facts: that women had been oppressed longer than any other group, this subjugation having stood as the model for all subsequent forms of oppression; that women were a *majority* of the world's population; that specific commonalities of biology, attitude, and certainly treatment potentially united us across all the patriarchally imposed barriers of race, age, class, sexual preference, superficial politics, and lifestyles. Now, as I write, this potential is vibrating throughout the globe—among Women's Movements in Senegal and Tanzania, Japan and Australia, China and South America, and all across Europe, New Zealand, Algeria, Canada, Israel, Egypt, and the Indian subcontinent.

We were "a white, middle-class, youth movement," they said. And even as some of us wrung our hands with guilt hand lotion, we knew otherwise. Because there were from the beginning women involved who were of every class and race and age, even if the media did focus on a conveniently stereotyped "feminist image." . . .

They said we were "anti-housewife," though many of us *were* housewives, and it was not us, but society itself, as structured by men, which had contempt for life-sustenance tasks. Today, too many housewives are in open participation in the Women's Movement to be ignored—and many are talking of a housewives' union. (Not to speak of the phenomenon of "runaway wives," as the news media calls them in articles which puzzle over the "motivation" of women who simply have picked up one dirty sock too many from the living-room floor.)

They said we were "a lesbian plot," and the carefully implanted and fostered bigotry of many heterosexual feminists rose eagerly, destructively, to deny that, thereby driving many lesbian women out of the Movement, back into the arms of their gay "brothers," who promptly shoved mimeograph machines at them. What a choice. But the process did continue, and so the pendulum swung into its tactically tragic but expectable position, a reply-in-kind from some lesbian-feminists who created the politics of "dyke separatism," the refusal to work with or sometimes even speak to women who could not prove lesbian credentials. This was sometimes accompanied by the proclamation that lesbians were the only true feminists, or were the feminist "vanguard," and the accusation that all heterosexual women were forever "sold out" to men (leaving lesbian mothers, by the way, in a no-woman's-land). In some parts of the country it was called "the lesbian-straight split"—or even the "lesbian-feminist split"—with a terrifying antagonism on both sides. Yet most serious feminists continued to work together, across sexual-preference labeling, and the process endured (through many, many tears), and we survived. . . .

They said we were "anti-motherhood"—and in the growing pains of certain periods, some of us were. There were times when I was made to feel guilty for having wanted and borne a child—let alone a male one, forgodsake. There were other times when we "collectivized" around children, and I found myself miffed at the temporary loss of that relationship unique to the specific mother and specific child. So much of the transition is understandable now. Since the patriarchy commanded women to be mothers (the thesis), we had to rebel with our own polarity and declare motherhood a reactionary cabal (antithesis). Today, a *new* synthesis is emerging: the concept of mother-right, the affirmation of childbearing and/or child-rearing when it is a woman's *choice*. And while that synthesis itself will in turn become a new thesis (a dialectic, a process, a development), it is refreshing at last to be able to come out of my mother-closet and yell to the world that I love my dear wonderful delicious child—and am not one damned whit less the radical feminist for that.

None of the above-mentioned issues, or even "splits," among us as women is simple. None is "solved." Struggle, experimentation, and examination of each of these differences (and new ones yet to come will continue, must continue, for years.) And we can expect these divisions to be exploited as *diversions* by those who would love to see us fail. But that no longer scares or depresses me, despite the enormity of the job ahead. The only thing that does frighten me is the superficial treatment of any such issue, the simplifying of complexities out of intellectual laziness, fear of the unknown, or rigidified thinking. Yet despite the temptation to fall into such traps of "non-thought," the growth does continue and the motion cannot be stopped. There is no turning back.

I call myself a radical feminist, and that means specific things to me. The etymology of the word "radical" refers to "one who goes to the root." I believe that sexism is the root oppression, the one which, until and unless we *up*root it, will continue to put forth the branches of racism, war, class hatred, ageism, competition, ecological disaster, and economic exploitation. This means, to me, that all the so-called revolutions to date have been *coups d'etat* between men, in a halfhearted attempt to prune the branches but leave the root embedded—for the sake of preserving their own male privileges. Yet this also means that I'm not out for us as women to settle for a "piece of the pie," equality in an unjust society, or for mere "top-down" change which can be corrupted into leaving the basic system unaltered. I think our feminist revolution gains momentum from a "ripple effect"—from each individual woman gaining self-respect and yes, power, over her own body and soul first, then within her family, on her block, in her town, state, and so on out from the center, overlapping with similar changes other women are experiencing, the circles rippling more widely and inclusively as they go. This is a revolution in consciousness, rising expectations, and the actions which reflect that organic process.

In the past decade I have seen just such methods give birth to hundreds of alternate feminist institutions, created and sustained by women's energy—all concrete moves toward self-determination and power. . . .

Whenever I hear certain men sonorously announce that the Women's Movement is dead (a prediction they have been promoting hopefully since 1968), I am moved to an awkwardly unmilitant hilarity. I know, of course, that they mean we seem less sensational: "Where are all those bra-burnings?" (none of which ever took place anyway, to my knowledge). Such death-knell articulations are not only (deliberately?) unaware of multiform alternate institutions that are mushrooming, but unconscious of the more profound and threatening-to-the-status-quo political *attitudes* which underlie that surface. It is, for example, a grave error to see feminists as "retrenching" when the reality is that we have been maturing beyond those aforementioned "ejaculatory tactics" into a long-term, committed attitude toward *winning*. We are digging in, since we know that patriarchy won't be unbuilt in a day, and the revolution we are making is one on *every* front: economic, social, political, cultural, personal, public, sexual, biological, and yes, even metaphysical.

The early ultra-egalitarianism and guilt-ridden "downward mobility" motifs of certain radical feminist groups, for instance, have modulated into a realization that women deserve to have credit for what we accomplish, whether that be the author's name signed to her article (after centuries of being "Anonymous"), or the right to be paid a living wage for her work at a feminist business (instead of falling prey to a new volunteerism—this one "for the revolution's sake"). The early antipathy toward any and all structure has given way to a recognition that we must evolve totally new ways of organizing ourselves, something else than chaotic spontaneity or masculinist hierarchy. The early excesses of collective tyranny have shifted into an understanding that there is a difference between individualism and individuality—and that the latter is precious and to be cherished. The emphases on women's studies reflect the welcome end of anti-intellectual trends (again picked up from male movements—a "line" created by privileged men who already had their college educations along with their charisma points in SDS or the counter-culture). We are daring to demand and explore the delights of hard intellectual work, both as personal challenge and as shared necessity. All the jargon exhorting us to "seize power" won't help if we "seize" the labs, for instance, and stand ignorantly gaping at the test tubes. We are daring to research our own cleverly buried herstorical past, even to develop new radical teaching methods as joint odysseys between teachers and students, without deification—or degradation—of either. . . .

And where, my dear reader may well ask, does this Pollyanna writer see the dangers, the failures, the losses? Or is she so blind, the woman in the mirror, that she thinks we've really come a long way, baby? Hardly.

These arms have held the vomitous shudderings of a sister-prostitute undergoing forced jail-withdrawal from her heroin addiction. These eyes have wept over the suicide of a sister-poet. These shoulders have tightened at the vilifications of men—on the street, in the media, on the lecture platform. These fists have clenched at the reality of backlash against us: the well-financed "friends of the fetus" mobilizing again to retake what small ground we have gained in the area of abortion; the rise in rape statistics (not only because more women are daring to *report* rapes, but also because more rapes are *occurring*); the ghastly mutilation-murders of women rumored to be witches (in the Catskill and Appalachian regions during the past two years) as an ominous message to all women who challenge patriarchal definitions. This stomach has knotted at the anonymous phone calls, the unsigned death threats, the real bombs planted in real auditoriums before a poetry reading or speech, the real bullet fired from a real pistol at the real podium behind which I was standing. (Those who have real power over our lives recognize the threat we pose—even when we ourselves do not.)

And yes, these fingers have knotted *their* versions of "correct lines"—strangling my own neck and the necks of other sisters.

I have watched some of the best minds of *my feminist* generation go mad with impatience and despair. So many other "oldie" radical feminists lost, having themselves lost the vision in all its intricacy, having let themselves be driven into irrelevance: the analytical pioneer whose "premature" brilliance isolated her into solipsism and finally self-signed-in commitment for "mental treatment"; the theorist whose nihilistic fear of "womanly" emotion led her into an obfuscated style and a "negative charisma"—an obsessive "I accuse" acridity corrosive to herself and other women; the fine minds lost to alcohol, or to "personal solutions," or to inertia, or to the comforting central-committeeist neat blueprint of outmoded politics, or to the equally reassuring glaze of "humanism," a word often misused as a bludgeon to convince women that we must put our suffering back at the bottom of the priority list. Some of these women never actually worked on a tangible feminist project—

storefront legal counseling or a nursery or a self-help clinic—or if they did so at one time they have long ago stopped, lost touch with women outside their own "feminist café society" circles. Such alienation from the world of women's genuine daily needs seems to have provoked in some of my sister "oldies" a bizarre new definition of "radical feminist"; that is, one who relentlessly assails any political effectiveness on the part of other feminists, while frequently choosing to do so in terms of personalities and with slashing cruelty. After so many centuries of spending all our compassion on men, could we not spare a little for each other?

I've watched the bloody internecine warfare between groups, between individuals. All that fantastic energy going to fight each other instead of our oppression! (It is, after all, safer to attack "just women.") So much false excitement, self-righteousness and judgmental posturing! Gossip, accusations, counter-accusations, smears—all leapt to, spread, and sometimes believed without the impediments of such things as facts. I've come to think that we need a feminist code of ethics, that we need to create a new *women's* morality, an antidote of honor against this contagion by male supremacist values. . . .

I would say to those few dear "oldies" who are burned out or embittered: you have forgotten that women are not fools, not sheep. We know about the dangers of commercialism and tokenism from the male right, and the dangers of manipulation and cooptation from the male left (the boys' establishment and the boys' movement). We are, frankly, bored by correct lines and vanguards and failurism and particularly by that chronic disease—guilt. Those of us who choose to struggle with men we love, well, we demand respect and support for that, and an end to psychological torture. Those of us who choose to relate solely to other women demand respect and support for *that,* and an end to the legal persecution and attitudinal bigotry that condemns freedom of sexual choice. Those of us who choose to have or choose *not* to have children demand support and respect for *that.* We know that the emerging women's art and women's spirituality are lifeblood for our survival—resilient cultures have kept oppressed groups alive even when economic analyses and revolutionary strategy have fizzled.

We know that serious, lasting change does not come about overnight, or simply, or without enormous pain and diligent examination and tireless, undramatic, everyday-a-bit-more-one-step-at-a-time work. We know that such change seems to move in cycles (thesis, antithesis, and synthesis—which itself in turn becomes a new thesis . . .), and we also know that those cycles are not merely going around in circles. They are, rather, an *upward spiral,* so that each time we reevaluate a position or place we've been before we do so from a new perspective. We are *in process,* continually evolving, and we will no longer be made to feel inferior or ineffectual for knowing and being what we are at any given moment.

Housewives across the nation stage the largest consumer boycott ever known (the meat boycott) and while it may not seem, superficially, a feminist action, *women* are doing this, women who ten years ago, before this feminist movement, might have regarded such an action as unthinkable. The campaign for passage of the Equal Rights Amendment continues to gain supporters (like that fine closet-feminist Betty Ford) despite all the combined right *and* left forces of reaction against it. Consciousness-raising proliferates, in groups, in individuals, in new forms and with new structures. The lines of communication begin to center around content instead of geography, and to stretch from coast to coast, so that women in an anti-rape project, for example, may be more in touch with other anti-rape groups nationally than with every latest development in the Women's Movement in their own backyards. I think this is to the good; it's a widening of vision, an exercising of muscle. It's Thinking Big. . . .

This process has changed my life. Today, my sexuality unfolds in ever more complex, beautiful, and self-satisfying layers. Today, I can affirm my mother and identify with her beyond all my intricate ambivalence. I can confront ersatz "sexual liberation" and its pornographic manifestos for what they are—degrading sexist propaganda. And I can confess my pride at an ongoing committed relationship with the husband I love and have always loved and whose transformation by feminism I have watched over and struggled with and marveled at. This process has given me the tools, as well, to affirm the woman I love, to help raise the child I love in new and freer ways. I have now curled round another spiral, and can admit that I *like* good food and enjoy cooking it (when that's not assumed to be my reason for existing). I have found my own appearance at last. No more "uniforms," but clothes that are comfortable, simple, pleasant, and *me;* hair that I cut or let grow as *I* choose, unconforming to fashion as dictated by *Vogue* or its inverse image, *Rolling Stone.* And this process, most of all, has given me the tools of self-respect as a woman artist, so that I am reclaiming my own shameless singing poet's voice beyond the untenable choices of "ivory tower, uninvolved" fake art or that grim "socialist-realist" polemical pseudo-art.

This ecstatic reclamation of my own art (and my brazen affir-mation, indeed of *all* art) is inseparable from what I have lovingly named "metaphysical feminism"—the refusal to simplify or polar-ize, the insatiable demand for a passionate, intelligent, complex, visionary, and *continuing* process which dares to include in its pat-terns everything from the scientific transformation which stars express as they nova, to the metaphorical use of that expression in a poem; a process which dares to celebrate contradiction and di-versity, dares to see each field-daisy as miraculous, each pebble as profound, each sentient being as holy.

And also, more humbly, this process, this Women's Movement, has given me the chance to travel through it, to witness the splen-dor of women's faces all over America blossoming with hope, to hear women's voices rising in an at-first fragile, then stronger chorus of anger and determination. Pocatello, Idaho, and Esca-naba, Michigan, and Lawrence, Kansas, and Sarasota, Florida, and Sacramento, California, and Portales, New Mexico, and Northampton, Massachusetts—and how many others? It has ex-hausted me, this Women's Movement, and sometimes made me cranky and guilty and gossipy and manipulative and self-pitying and self-righteous and sour. It has exasperated me, frustrated me, and driven me gloriously crazy.

But it is in my blood, and I love it, do you hear? I know in my bones that women's consciousness and our desire for freedom and the power to forge a humane world society will survive even the mistakes the Women's Movement makes—as if feminism were a card-carrying nitsy little sect and not what it *is,* a profoundly radi-cal and perpetually enlarging vision of what can save this planet. . . . There are millions of us now, and the vision is expand-ing its process to include us all.

I trust that process with my life. I have learned to love that Women's Movement, that face in the mirror, wearing its new, wry, patient smile; those eyes that have rained grief but can still see clearly; that body with its unashamed sags and stretch marks; that mind, with all its failings and its cowardices and its courage and its inexhaustible will to try again.

I want to say to that woman: we've only just begun, and there's no stopping us. I want to tell her that she is maturing and stretching and daring and yes, succeeding, in ways undreamt until now. She will survive the naysayers, male *and* female, and she will coalesce in all her wondrously various forms and diverse lifestyles, ages, races, classes, and internationalities into one harmonious blessing on this agonized world. She is so very beautiful, and I love her. The face in the mirror is myself.

And the face in the mirror is you.

Part Six

VIETNAM

The war in Vietnam represents one of the most difficult military and foreign policy experiences in American history. Each step of American involvement seemed merely a modification of past practice, an increment to existing policy, and therefore nothing that required a declaration of war or a full scale reassessment of underlying policies. Through such a process American participation in Vietnam grew from 800 troops in 1960 to 15,000 in 1963 to more than 500,000 in 1968. A civil war between the Vietnamese became an American war; the United States was perceived by most people in the world as a colonialist aggressor; and the American people themselves divided into warring factions over support or opposition to the war.

Ironically, the United States became involved in Vietnam less because of any interest in Southeast Asia itself than in order to achieve other foreign policy goals. Franklin Roosevelt had decided during World War II that colonialism should end in Southeast Asia. But after the war American officials reversed that stance. To mollify France's unhappiness over the rebuilding of Germany, the U.S. countenanced French policy in Southeast Asia. By 1948, the U.S. was providing crucial economic and political sustenance for the French occupation of Indochina.

When the French lost their own Vietnam war in 1954 and the Geneva conference divided Vietnam into two regions, the United States stepped in to provide support for the pro-western government of President Diem. This seemed a moderate enough action at the time, particularly given the fact that President Eisenhower had earlier refused a French request to use atomic weapons against the Vietnamese. But that moderate involvement in support of Diem provided the basis for ever increasing commitments of American money and manpower. When John F. Kennedy became president, Vietnam became a testing point of the battle against communism—again, not so much because of its own intrinsic importance as because of events elsewhere. After the debacle at the Bay of Pigs in April 1961, and Kennedy's confrontation with Khrushchev at Vienna in June 1961, the young American president wanted to find some place where he could take a stand and convey to the Russians his determination to hold firm against communism. Vietnam became such a place, and during the Kennedy years the United States significantly expanded the flow of foreign aid and military equipment to South Vietnam, increased the number of American troops engaged in the conflict to over 15,000, and launched a major effort at counterinsurgency. At the same time, however, the U.S. remained publicly committed to political reform in Vietnam and to the proposition that it was impossible for the United States itself to fight a war that the Vietnamese did not wish to wage.

It was Lyndon Johnson's misfortune to preside over the most massive and disastrous expansion of the war. Deeply committed to maintaining a strong military presence, fearful of abandoning Kennedy's policy, and anxious to put forward an image of strength and power, Johnson never asked the hard questions as to why we were in Vietnam, where our policy would lead, or what would happen as a consequence. As one coup d'état after another brought successive military regimes to power in South Vietnam, Johnson kept pouring more American troops and money into the country, attempting to provide, through external military support, a degree of stability that clearly was not present among the South Vietnamese themselves. The long range results are now history. The Vietnamese countryside was destroyed, millions of lives were lost, search and destroy missions became the hallmark of a senseless effort to accumulate military victories measured by body counts of Vietnamese dead, and the nation entered a downward spiral of divisiveness and mistrust.

There are various ways of interpreting American involvement in Vietnam. Some see the war as simply a logical extension of a Cold War mentality, in which any civil war or nationalist struggle was perceived as part of a communist conspiracy that must be stopped. According to that interpretation, U.S. involvement grew directly from a distorted definition of world events in which all subtleties of internal and cultural politics were lost. A second interpretation views Vietnam as the one exception to a generally successful foreign policy in the postwar world. The Vietnam experience was not the product of erroneous Cold War attitudes, but rather an unrelated mistake in which the United States became too deeply involved before it could make a correct assessment of the situation. A third interpretation is that the war represented a wise policy which went awry. According to this view, U.S. commitment to political reform in South Vietnam was intelligent, and only when America attempted to use military power in place of political persuasion did a good policy turn bad. Finally, there is the view that the policy was wise all along and was prevented from being successful only because the military was hindered by political decisions at home. According to General William Westmoreland, the war was won militarily; it was lost politically.

Whichever interpretation one accepts, there can be little question that the war was a traumatic event for America and the world. The following selections explore some of the explanations for the war, as well as the consequences it brought. John Garry Clifford places the war within the long-term framework of American foreign policy. Leslie Gelb, a State Department official, analyzes the major explanations of the causes of the war and offers his own view of how and why the U.S. became involved so deeply. Richard Hammer describes poignantly and painfully the consequences of American policy for the Vietnamese people as well as for United States soldiers and those at home. His description of My Lai speaks as powerfully as anything to the horror of what occurred as a result of Vietnam.

Some critical questions remain. Was there ever a way that United States involvement could have led to a democratic government in Vietnam? How much racism was involved in U.S. policy? Did an episode such as My Lai represent the natural consequence of a "search and destroy" mentality, or was it a complete aberration? Finally, there is the question of how much American policy in Vietnam represented a fatal flaw in the idea that America has a moral right to tell the rest of the world how to behave.

Vietnam in Historical Perspective

John Garry Clifford

American involvement in Vietnam resulted from a series of assumptions about America's place in the world. John Garry Clifford, a diplomatic historian from the University of Connecticut, has written extensively about postwar American foreign policy. Here, he shows how the war in Vietnam reflected American ideas about the Cold War. Clifford concludes that the Vietnam experience challenged the basic tenets of American policy-makers, forcing a reassessment of how we proceed to achieve our goals. Clifford's essay accurately describes the immediate consequences of the Vietnam war. During the 1970's, Congress limited presidential power to make war without congressional approval, and circumscribed the freedom of action of the CIA. Nevertheless, students may ask whether Clifford's conclusions still hold in the 1980s.

Although it is too early to determine, the Vietnam war may well prove to have been both the logical culmination of American foreign policy since 1945 and a turning point comparable to that of World War II. Certainly on a perceptual level, in the way Americans viewed the world, the war set in motion changes that became obvious by 1970. On an institutional level, in the way government agencies connected with foreign policy defined their goals and procedures, the evidence of change by the early 1970s was less

Excerpted from John Garry Clifford, "Change and Continuity in American Foreign Policy Since 1930," in James T. Patterson, ed. *Paths to the Present* (Minneapolis: Burgess Publishing Co., 1975). Reprinted by permission of the author.

marked. One thing became certain: the options available to American diplomatists were more varied than at any other time since the fall of France in 1940.

Vietnam, which Senator John F. Kennedy described in 1956 as the "cornerstone of the Free World in Southeast Asia, the Keystone to the arch, the finger in the dike," was the logical, if erroneous, culmination of Cold War perceptions. The "lessons" of the past were constantly invoked. "If we don't stop the Reds in South Vietnam," said Lyndon Johnson, "tomorrow they will be in Hawaii, and next week they will be in San Francisco." Former Undersecretary of the Air Force, Townsend Hoopes, described the thinking of Dean Rusk: "In his always articulate, sometimes eloquent, formulations, Asia seemed to be Europe, China was either Stalinist Russia or Hitler Germany, and SEATO was either NATO or the Grand Alliance of World War II." If these analogies seemed somewhat strained, intended more for public persuasion than for internal conviction, the leaders in Washington all subscribed to the belief—unquestioned since Pearl Harbor—that aggression must be deterred. Vietnam became a test of America's will. "I don't need to remind you of what happened in the Civil War," Johnson told a press conference in 1967. "People were here in the White House begging Lincoln to concede and to work out a deal with the Confederacy when word came of his victories. . . . I think you know what Roosevelt went through and President Wilson in World War I. . . . We are going to have this criticism. We are going to have this difference. . . . No one likes war. All people love peace. But you can't have freedom without defending it. . . . We are going to do whatever it is necessary to do to see that the aggressor does not succeed."

But who was the aggressor in Vietnam? The Soviet Union? As the "quagmire" deepened, observers noted that Soviet supplies indeed helped the "enemy," but that Moscow was not masterminding a world-wide Communist conspiracy. The Sino-Soviet split became so evident by the mid-1960s that even the most militant Cold Warriors had to take notice. Perhaps the "enemy" was China, and Dean Rusk conjured up the frightening image of a billion Chinese armed with hydrogen bombs. But even after President Nixon's trips to Moscow and Peking in 1972, the war continued. The suggestion persisted that it was a *civil* war, an internal conflict between two versions of Vietnamese nationality, but this reality did not gibe with Cold War perceptions. Not enough was known in Washington about the fundamental differences in Asian societies, and belief in the Domino Theory came easily, along with visions of armed Communist hordes. Bureaucrats did not want to change their perceptions. James C. Thomson, a White House consultant during the early 1960s, recalls a conversation in March of 1964 with an Assistant Secretary of State. "But in some ways, of course, it *is* a civil war," Thomson said. "Don't play word games with me!" the official snapped.

Bureaucratic style contributed significantly to the tragedy. Part of it derived from technological superiority, which in turn gave rise to a "can do" philosophy. At one extreme, in Walter LaFeber's phrase, was "General Curtis LeMay's notion that Communism could best be handled from a height of 50,000 feet." At a more sophisticated level was the conviction that no matter how resilient the enemy proved, the United States could work its will through "smart" bombs, search and destroy tactics, electronic barriers, superior air power, or sheer economic momentum. A crazy sense of bloodlessness began to emerge. "Every quantitative measurement we have shows we're winning this war," McNamara stated in 1962. Statistics proliferated—infiltration rates, weapons-loss ratios, aircraft sorties rates, expended ammunition tonnages, allied troop contributions, enemy "body counts," friendly casualties. Bureaucratic jargon ("free fire zones," "surgical" air strikes, "threshold of pain," "slow squeeze") obscured the reality of flesh being mangled, villages devastated, ecology ruined. Describing the gradual pressure imposed by the "Rolling Thunder" bombing campaign, one State Department official said: "Our orchestration should be mainly violins, but with periodic touches of brass."

This armchair atmosphere could not be dispelled by battle reports or occasional trips to Saigon. A process of self-hypnosis seemed at work. David Halberstam has told the story of Daniel Ellsberg's return from a tour of duty in Vietnam and his attempts to tell presidential adviser Walt Rostow how badly the war was going. "No, you don't understand," said Rostow. "Victory is very near. I'll show you the charts. The charts are very good." "I don't want to see any charts," Ellsberg replied. "But, Dan, the charts are very good," Rostow insisted. Similarly, James Thomson has described his shock on returning to Harvard after several years in the State Department. He suddenly realized that "the young men, the flesh and blood I taught and saw on these university streets, were potentially some of the numbers on the charts of those far-away planners. In a curious sense, Cambridge is closer to this war than Washington."

The imperviousness of official Washington from external dissent contributed to the debacle. The smugness that came with access to classified information was partly responsible. The experts knew the facts, the critics did not. Internal dissenters were rarer and somehow safer to government leaders. President Johnson used to greet Bill Moyers rather affectionately: "Well, here comes Mr. Stop-the-Bombing." And when the war protest became especially shrill in 1966 and 1967, Johnson, who had followed the experts into the morass, displayed his furious temper. Dissenters, he said, were "nervous Nellies," "chickenshit." "I'm the only President you have," he would say. "Why don't you get on the team?" When hawks like Bundy and McNamara began to waver, Johnson sarcastically called the former "George McBundy" and unceremoniously nominated the latter to head the World Bank. This presidential temperament reinforced the natural bureaucratic tendency to remain silent so as not to lose one's effectiveness. Townsend Hoopes has described Vice-President Hubert Humphrey's abortive dissent in 1965: "His views were received at the White House with particular coldness, and he was banished from the inner councils for some months thereafter, until he decided to 'get back on the team.' " Not until the Tet offensive of early 1968 did effective criticism penetrate the Oval Office, and then it took someone of the stature of Dean Acheson to shake Lyndon Johnson. "With all due respect, Mr. President," said the mustachioed Dean of Middletown, "the Joint Chiefs of Staff don't know what they are talking about." When the Senior Advisory Group on Vietnam corroborated Acheson's estimates a few weeks later, the President's plaintive reaction underlined the extent to which policy had been made in a vacuum. "What did you tell them that you didn't tell me?" he asked his staff. "You must have given them a different briefing."

Momentum was another reason for escalation. The men in Washington may have thought they controlled events, but in actuality the genii of war were beyond control. For all their sophisticated technology, for all their favorable statistics, for all their "can do" spirit, American leaders never understood the extent to which decisions closed options previously available, making other decisions almost inevitable. Moreover, policy decisions often resulted from compromise, as in the case of the Kennedy administration sending military advisers to South Vietnam in 1961, notwithstanding the Taylor-Rostow report which recommended 8,000 troops. These compromises represented the usual adjustment of differences between the various agencies involved: the Saigon embassy, CIA, the State Department, the White House Staff, and the Joint Chiefs. Once advisers were committed, however, pressure rose for increasing their numbers.

Similarly, in the winter of 1964–65, certain "dovish" planners in the State Department who were strongly opposed to bombing the North urged instead that ground forces be sent to the South. They thought such a move would increase bargaining leverage against the North and be a prod for negotiations. At the same time, military men determined not to fight another "land war" in Asia were calling for the air-strike option. Still other civilians seeking peace wanted to bomb Hanoi into early peace talks. Within eight months all factions were disappointed: there was a costly and ineffective air campaign against the North, a mushrooming ground commitment in the South, and negotiations farther away than before. Each step also added greater weight to the military's demands. As soon as the Army's mission had changed from advising to saving Saigon, it was inevitable that the Joint Chiefs should press for escalation. Each service had its special panaceas, and under a tacit agreement the Joint Chiefs usually spoke in unison. McNamara then scaled down their demands. The result: escalation. Even after Nixon began withdrawing ground forces in 1969, military pressure to "protect" these troops resulted in decisions to invade Cambodian sanctuaries, to mine the harbors of Haiphong and Hanoi, and to resume aerial bombardment of the North at ever-increasing rates.

Vietnam brought about an "agonizing reappraisal" in American foreign policy far more searching than anything John Foster Dulles had envisaged in the 1950s. Dissent in American wars was not a new phenomenon. New England Federalists had opposed the War of 1812, abolitionists had protested the Mexican War, and Mugwumps and anti-imperialists had been vocal in 1898. Generally these dissenters were relatively small in number, well educated, respectable (usually upper class WASP), and quite orthodox in the way they protested—pamphlets, petitions, rallies, letter writing campaigns, efforts in behalf of anti-war candidates. The Vietnam war protest was different. The movement had enough diversity to include such heterogeneous spokesmen as Norman Mailer, Muhammed Ali, Abby Hoffman, John Kenneth Galbraith, George Kennan, Jane Fonda, Joan Baez, Jeannette Rankin, Martin Luther King, Robert Kennedy, Timothy Leary, Dick Gregory, and Noam Chomsky. Protest went from genteel teach-ins, to Senator Eugene McCarthy's brash campaign for the Democratic nomination in 1968, to marches on Washington, moratoria, and violent attempts by revolutionary groups to bring the war "home" to America. Protest literature ranged from the witty to the obscene.

People opposed the war for different reasons. Some still clung to the Cold War arguments for containment, but denied that the doctrine applied to Asia, or particularly to Vietnam. Others saw the war as killing reform at home, diverting attention from desperate conditions in the cities and in race relations. A less articulate group protested the deaths of American soldiers in Asian jungles, but seemed willing to permit American aircraft to drop billions of tons of bombs on yellow peoples. Others blamed President Johnson. "We've got a wild man in the White House," said Senator McCarthy. "A desperate man who was likely to get us into war with China," warned Senator Albert Gore of Tennessee.

More and more, protest occurred because of a moral revulsion to the war. Reaction to napalm bombing and "defoliation," horror at the destruction of the city of Hue in order to "save" it, incredulity at the My Lai massacre and the shootings of students at Kent State and Jackson State in 1970—all these events called into question the ethical standards of American policy. Confused about the identity of the aggressor in Vietnam—the Viet Cong? Hanoi? China?—more and more Americans came to agree with Walt Kelly's possum, Pogo: "We have met the enemy and they are us."

By the late 1960s this moral revulsion, fueled by the obvious *practical* failure of the American effort, had prompted a reassessment of long-held assumptions. One State Department official complained in 1966: "There is a considerable sort of feeling of unhappiness here that elements in the population that used to be thought of as our 'natural constituency' are not doing yeoman service for the Department now. We do have a constituency of sorts—the Foreign Policy Association, the Council on Foreign Relations, and all the other groups like that. These people have helped us all along for years, with the United Nations, the Marshall Plan, NATO, Korea, and all the others. But they are not helping us with the American public on the Vietnam issue. When they come to town to be briefed on Vietnam, they do not leave with marching orders, as they used to." When Dean Acheson told President Johnson that the generals did not know what they were talking about, he was also serving notice that the foreign policy consensus in existence since World War II had shattered. Another symbolic confrontation occurred in the spring of 1970 following the Cambodia invasion, when a group of prominent academicians, headed by Richard Neustadt, visited Henry Kissinger and recanted their support for executive predominance in foreign policy. These defections did not mean that Nixon could not count on continued support from the "silent majority," that Congress suddenly cut off military appropriations, or that the Navy decided to convert its aircraft carriers into hospital ships. What did emerge was an eventual repudiation of the Vietnam war by a majority of the so-called "foreign policy public." "What the hell is an Establishment for, if it's not to support the President," Kissinger complained. The reaction was especially strong among academicians. The political scientist Bruce Russett wrote: "Vietnam has been to social scientists what Alamogordo was to the physicists. Few of those who have observed it can easily return to their comfortable presumptions about America's duty, or right, to fight in distant lands." . . .

Historians cannot predict the future. To suggest, however, that changes in American assumptions about the world began in the 1960s and that Watergate and Vietnam accelerated these changes, is not presumptuous. The "lower profile" of American involvement abroad, as proclaimed by the Nixon Doctrine, will result in "lower" perceptions about American power and responsibilities. The intellectual capital that financed the Marshall Plan, NATO, and Korea was expended in Southeast Asia in the 1960s. The Nixon-Kissinger policies of détente toward the Soviet Union and the People's Republic of China have in themselves altered Cold War patterns. Do these changes signal a return to the isolationism of the 1930s, as defenders of the Vietnam war sometimes suggested? In the sense that domestic needs will not automatically take second place to foreign policy, or that Congress will not rubber-stamp executive initiatives, these changes do reflect some of the concerns of the Stimson-Hoover era. Nevertheless, the huge foreign policy bureaucracy spawned by World War II and the Cold War will remain, and it will take time for new perceptions to become embedded. Public opinion, decidedly noninterventionist in Asia because of the failure of the ground war in Vietnam, may well permit intervention by means of naval and aerial bombardment in future crises. The renewal of war between Israel and the Arab states in the fall of 1973, combined with the Arab embargo of oil, raised the prospect of American intervention in the Middle East, and with it the possibility of a Soviet-American confrontation. Like all previous empires in decline, the United States will retreat reluctantly.

Nevertheless, Vietnam and Watergate have left an ambivalence which allows room for cautious optimism. As the political scientist Robert W. Tucker has observed, Pearl Harbor and the Berlin Blockade will not be automatic reference points for the coming generation of "foreign policy elites." Rather, memories of My Lai and the Cuban Missile Crisis will be much sharper. "Never again," a slogan which the Army brought out of the Korean War, ought to remain a convenient watchword. The waning of anti-Communism as a political issue, as well as the need to combat industrial pollution, to conserve energy, to revitalize public transportation, and to obtain public health insurance, should tend to "lower" profiles and "cool" American foreign policy. Gradually, one may predict, the traditional American mission of erecting a "city on the hill" and solving domestic problems will take precedence over building "democratic" governments in remote areas of the world.

John Quincy Adams said it well more than 150 years earlier:

> Wherever the standard of freedom and Independence has been or shall be unfurled, there will her [America's] heart, her benediction and her prayers be. But she goes not abroad in search of monsters to destroy. . . . She well knows that by once enlisting under other banners than her own, were they even the banners of foreign independence, she would involve herself beyond the power of extrication. . . . The fundamental maxims of her policy would change from *liberty* to *force*.

Causes of the War

Leslie Gelb

Those who know most about the decision-making process in American foreign policy frequently can say least about it. Officials at the State Department and the Pentagon see a myriad of classified information everyday. While lacking the independence and detachment of external observers, they have a unique vantage point on how and why particular policies are pursued. Leslie Gelb, a State Department official during the Vietnam war years, reflects this "insider's" familiarity with all the currents and cross currents of advice shaping American foreign policy decisions on Vietnam. In this selection from testimony given before Congress, Gelb assesses the relative influence of the various forces acting upon the presidential decision-making process. Although Gelb does not cite chapter and verse of secret memoranda supporting various positions on the war, his is one of the most informed studies of how and why the United States became so deeply involved in Vietnam. His conclusion that pervasive anti-communist attitudes provide the key to our involvement in Southeast Asia supports the argument that the Vietnam war, far from being a deviation from postwar foreign policy, was in fact a logical extension of the Cold War.

Wars are supposed to tell us about ourselves. Are we a wise and just nation? Or are we foolish and aggressive? Merciless or humane? Well led or misled? Vital or decadent? Hopeful or hope-

From Leslie H. Gelb statement to Hearings before the Committee on Foreign Relations, United States Senate, 82 Congress, 2nd Session, May 1972.

less? Nations in war and after war, win or lose, try to scratch away at the paste or glue or traditions or values that held their societies together and see of what they are made. It is arguable whether a society should indulge in such self-scrutiny. Societies are, as Edmund Burke wrote, "delicate, intricate wholes" that are more easily damaged than improved when subjected to the glare of Grand Inquisitors.

But in the case of our society and the war in Vietnam, too many people are seeking answers and are entitled to them, and many are only too eager to fill in the blanks. The families and friends of those who were killed and wounded will want to know whether it was worth it after all? Intellectuals will want to know "why Vietnam"? Men seeking and holding political office will demand to know who was responsible? The answers to these questions will themselves become political facts and forces, shaping the United States' role in the world and our lives at home for years to come.

CAUSES OF THE WAR: THE RANGE OF EXPLANATIONS

Central to this inquiry is the issue of causes of U.S. involvement in Vietnam. I have found eight discernible explanations advanced in the Vietnam literature. Different authors combine these explanations in various ways, but I will keep them separate for the purpose of analysis. I will, then, sketch my own position.

The Arrogance of Power

This view holds that a driving force in American involvement in Vietnam was the fact that we were a nation of enormous power and like comparable nations in history, we would seek to use this power at every opportunity. To have power is to want to employ it, is to be corrupted by it. The arrogance derives from the belief that to have power, is to be able to do anything. Power invokes right and justifies itself. Vietnam was there, a challenge to this power and an opportunity for its exercise, and no task was beyond accomplishment.

There can be no doubt about this strain in the behavior of other great powers and in the American character. But this is not a universal law. Great powers, and especially the United States have demonstrated self-restraint. The arrogance of power, I think, had more to do with our persisting in the war than with our initial involvement. It always was difficult for our leaders back in Washington and for operatives in the field to believe that American resources and ingenuity could not devise some way to overcome the adversary.

Bureaucratic Politics

There are two, not mutually exclusive, approaches within this view. One has it that national security bureaucrats (the professionals who make up the military services, civilian Defense, AID, State and the CIA) are afflicted with the curse of machismo, the need to assert and prove manhood and toughness. Career advancement and acceptability within the bureaucracy depended on showing that you were not afraid to propose the use of force. The other approach has it that bureaucrats purposefully misled their superiors about the situation in Vietnam and carefully constructed policy alternatives so as to circumscribe their superiors, thus forcing further involvement in Vietnam.

The machismo phenomenon is not unknown in the bureaucracy. It was difficult, if not damaging, to careers to appear conciliatory or "soft." Similarly, the constriction of options is a well-known bureaucratic device. But, I think, these approaches unduly emphasize the degree to which the President and his immediate advisers were trapped by the bureaucrats. The President was always in a position to ask for new options or to exclude certain others. The role of the bureaucracy was much more central to shaping the programs or the means used to fight the war than the key decisions to make the commitments in the first place.

Domestic Politics

This view is quite complicated, and authors argue their case on serveral different levels. The variants are if you were responsible for losing Vietnam to communism, you would: (a) lose the next election and lose the White House in particular; (b) jeopardize your domestic legislative program, your influence in general, by having to defend yourself constantly against political attack; (c) invite the return of a McCarthyite right-wing reaction; and (d) risk undermining domestic support for a continuing U.S. role abroad, in turn, risking dangerous probes by Russia and China.

There can be no doubt, despite the lack of supporting evidence in the Pentagon Papers, about the importance of domestic political considerations in both the initial commitment to and the subsequent increase in our Vietnam involvement. Officials are reluctant, for obvious reasons, to put these considerations down in writing, and scholars therefore learn too little about them. It should also be noted that domestic political factors played a key part in shaping the manner in which the war was fought—no reserve call-ups, certain limitations on bombing targeting, paying for the war, and the like.

Imperialism

This explanation is a variant of the domestic politics explanation. Proponents of this view argue that special interest groups maneuvered the United States into the war. Their goal was to capture export markets and natural resources at public expense for private economic gain.

The evidence put forward to support this "devil theory" has not been persuasive. Certain groups do gain economically from wars, but their power to drive our political system into war tends to be exaggerated and over-dramatized.

Men Making Hard Choices Pragmatically

This is the view that our leaders over the years were not men who were inspired by any particular ideology, but were pragmatists weighing the evidence and looking at each problem on its merits. According to this perspective, our leaders knew they were facing tough choices, and their decisions always were close ones. But having decided 51 to 49 to go ahead, they tried to sell and implement their policies one hundred percent.

This view cannot be dismissed out-of-hand. Most of our leaders, and especially our Presidents, occupied centrist political positions. But Vietnam is a case, I believe, where practical politicians allowed an anti-communist world view to get the best of them.

Balance of Power Politics

Intimately related to the pragmatic explanations is the conception which often accompanies pragmatism—the desire to maintain some perceived balance-of-power among nations. The principal considerations in pursuing this goal were: seeing that "the illegal use of force" is not allowed to succeed, honoring commitments, and keeping credibility with allies and potential adversaries. The underlying judgment was that failure to stop aggression in one place would tempt others to aggress in ever more dangerous places.

These represent the words and arguments most commonly and persuasively used in the executive branch, the Congress, and elsewhere. They seemed commonsensical and prudential. Most Americans were prepared to stretch their meaning to Vietnam. No doubt many believed these arguments on their own merits, but in most cases, I think, the broader tenet of anti-communism made them convincing.

The Slippery Slope

Tied to the pragmatic approach, the conception of balance of power, and the arrogance of power, is the explanation which holds that United States involvement in Vietnam is the story of the slippery slope. According to this view, Vietnam was not always critical to U.S. national security; it became so over the years as each succeeding administration piled commitment on commitment. Each administration sort of slid further into the Vietnam quagmire, not really understanding the depth of the problems in Vietnam and convinced that it could win. The catchwords of this view are optimism and inadvertence.

While this explanation undoubtedly fits certain individuals and certain periods of time, it is, by itself, a fundamental distortion of the Vietnam experience. From the Korean War, stated American objectives for Vietnam were continuously high and absolute. U.S. involvement, not U.S. objectives, increased over time. Moreover, to scrutinize the range of official public statements and the private memos as revealed in the Pentagon Papers makes it difficult to argue that our leaders were deceived by the enormity of the Vietnam task before them. It was not necessary for our leaders to believe they were going to win. It was sufficient for them to believe that they could not afford to lose Vietnam to communism.

Anti-Communism

The analysts who offer this explanation hold that anti-communism was the central and all-pervasive fact of U.S. foreign policy from at least 1947 until the end of the sixties. After World War II, an ideology whose very existence seemed to threaten basic American values had combined with the national force of first Russia and then China. This combination of ideology and power brought our leaders to see the world in "we-they" terms and to insist that peace was indivisible. Going well beyond balance of power considerations, every piece of territory became critical, and every besieged nation, a potential domino. Communism came to be seen as an infection to be quarantined rather than a force to be judiciously and appropriately balanced. Vietnam, in particular, became the cockpit of confrontation between the "Free World" and Totalitarianism; it was where the action was for 20 years.

In my opinion, simple anti-communism was the principal reason for United States involvement in Vietnam. It is not the whole story, but it is the biggest part.

As of this point in my own research, I advance three propositions to explain why, how, and with what expectations the United States became involved in the Vietnam war.

First, U.S. involvement in Vietnam is not mainly or mostly a story of step by step, inadvertent descent into unforeseen quicksand. It is primarily a story of why U.S. leaders considered that it was vital not to lose Vietnam by force to Communism. Our leaders believed Vietnam to be vital not for itself, but for what they thought its "loss" would mean internationally and domestically. Previous involvement made further involvement more unavoidable, and, to this extent, commitments were inherited. But judgments of Vietnam's "vitalness"—beginning with the Korean War—were sufficient in themselves to set the course for escalation.

Second, our Presidents were never actually seeking a military victory in Vietnam. They were doing only what they thought was minimally necessary at each stage to keep Indochina, and later South Vietnam, out of Communist hands. This forced our Presidents to be brakemen, to do less than those who were urging military victory and to reject proposals for disengagement. It also meant that our Presidents wanted a negotiated settlement without fully realizing (though realizing more than their critics) that a civil war cannot be ended by political compromise.

Third, our Presidents and most of their lieutenants were not deluded by optimistic reports of progress and did not proceed on the basis of wishful thinking about winning a military victory in South Vietnam. They recognized that the steps they were taking were not adequate to win the war and that unless Hanoi relented, they would have to do more and more. Their strategy was to persevere in hope that their will to continue—if not the practical effects of their actions—would cause the Communists to relent.

One Morning in the War

Richard Hammer

More than any other single group in the population, journalists were responsible for bringing to public attention the shortcomings and contradictions of American policy in Vietnam. As early as 1963, David Halberstam, The New York Times *correspondent in Vietnam, pointed out that conventional military tactics had no place in a guerrilla war, and that a civil struggle between competing Vietnamese political factions could not be resolved by external military intervention. The contradiction between journalistic accounts of the war and official reports sent to the Pentagon and the White House continued throughout the years of American involvement in Southeast Asia.*

During the last half of the 1960s, television and newspaper reporters played a major role in turning American public opinion against the war as people saw American soldiers igniting Vietnamese thatched huts and heard an Army major say that "we had to destroy the village in order to save it." It was a journalist who first made public the atrocities committed at My Lai. In the following selection, Richard Hammer describes in searing detail one "search and destroy" mission of the war. To some, the My Laï episode represented a total abberation, with a single company going insane for one day. To others, the episode typified—in extreme form—a practice that was all too frequent. Almost everyone agrees that the My Lai tragedy dramatized the impossibility of attempting to use external military force to fight a civil war where one could not tell who was a friend and who was an enemy.

In these early days of combat, the men began to solidify their previously formed and now lasting impressions of their officers and sergeants. Medina, for one, seemed totally impervious to danger. In fact, he seemed almost to be searching for it, to test the courage of his men and of himself. At the same time, he seemed totally dedicated to the welfare of his own men, concerned about them, grieving when one of them was wounded, concerned that they be fed well, have shelter and ammunition. It was, one of the men remembers, "like he was some kind of hen taking care of her brood, if you know what I mean. If we was out in the field, one platoon going one way and another going a different way and there was some shots, then Medina'd be on the field phone right away, wanting to know what the shooting was about, if anybody was hurt, if reinforcements were needed, that kind of thing. He had to know everything that was happening everywhere in the company."

But if Medina was concerned about his own men, those who served under him noticed that he seemed utterly oblivious to the Vietnamese. On occasions when the company entered a hamlet and all was peaceful, Medina seemed bored, anxious to get moving after he had posed a few questions to the village chiefs through his interpreter, and there would be a look of weary impatience when his soldiers passed out cigarettes and canned fruit to the villagers. "I mean," one of his soldiers says, "he didn't ever talk about the gooks. He didn't call them any names, just didn't seem to care one way or another about them. . . . Except, of course, when some guy got hit, then Medina'd get real angry and talk about how we'd get ours back at them. . . ."

Calley was something different. About the best that anyone had to say for him was the summation by one corporal in his platoon: "He wasn't the best officer in the world, but then he wasn't the worst one, either."

There were others, however, who weren't quite so sure of that. . . . "It was like he was all wound up tight, just waiting to bust loose. And when he busted, everyone around him was going to be hit by the pieces. . . . Like he was a little guy, see, all puffed up, trying to make himself bigger and taller than anybody else. I guess maybe you can only do that for so long and then look out, man."

There were a number of men who pointed to an episode early

in February when they were looking for some concrete evidence to back their then-vague feelings about Calley. According to James Bergthold, for one, one afternoon Calley deliberately murdered a Vietnamese civilian without any provocation. The platoon was on a routine patrol when Bergthold brought in a Vietnamese civilian, about sixty years old, whom he had just discovered in a paddy. "I brought the guy in," he said. "He was standing in a field all by himself. I brought him in, and the lieutenant asked him questions and then threw him in a well and shot him in the head. He never said why he did it." . . .

More and more as these daily patrols went on without end, the men in Task Force Barker grew to hate the dirty war they were part of, a war where everything and nothing was the enemy and fair game, where trouble could come from anyone or anything. And they began to take casualties now and again, here and there. Moving down a trail one afternoon somewhere in their district (no one is sure exactly where, as most of the men were never really sure where they were except that they were somewhere in Vietnam), a mine suddenly exploded. Three men went down, one of them dead. Just off the trail, hidden in the brush, was a fifteen year old girl, her hand still on the detonator of the mine. Simultaneously, four or five soldiers fired. The girl fell over the detonator, riddled with bullets, dead.

Another hamlet. Some of the men see a young Vietnamese girl. They grab her and pull her inside the nearest hootch. There are screams and cries from inside and then silence. Soon the men come walking out, satisfied.

The people have gathered in the center of another hamlet, smiling and greeting the Americans, milling around them while cigarettes, gum, canned fruits are passed out. A couple of the men wander casually about the settlement. They go into one hootch and emerge carrying a number of trinkets, relics and family heirlooms and start to rejoin the rest of the platoon. An old man breaks away from the group and trots after them. He bows his head, folds his hands and with a humble, obsequious smile murmurs words in Vietnamese to them and points with anguish at the souvenirs they are carrying away. It was his hootch and he would like his possessions returned. He grows tiresome and one of the soldiers turns and without a thought shoots him.

Day after day the dirty incidents of this kind, in this kind of war, mount. . . .

There was no way to tell when a fire fight might break out. The morning would start as usual, with a routine search-and-destroy mission scheduled. But sometime during the day, the VC would be waiting, the blood would be spilled on the land. Day after day it was the same thing. There was no relief. It was days out on patrol, many nights bivouacked in some field or in some hamlet, the men sleeping only from fatigue, the sentries constantly on the alert. Then it would be back to the fire base, back to LZ Dottie, back to the bunkers with no amusements, no nights off for a drink or a girl. Just the grinding fear and hate and frustration of war.

Then word came that the opportunity to strike back at the enemy in what might well be a major engagement had arrived.

At dusk that evening, Medina gathered his company together at the fire base to brief them on the operation for the next day. "I told them," he says, "that the intelligence reports indicated that the 48th VC Battalion was in the village and the intelligence reports indicated that there would be no women and children in the village, that they would have gone to market." . . .

Others, however, remember the briefing in a different way. Richard Pendleton says, "He told us there were Viet Cong in the village and we should kill them before they kill us."

It was just about seven in the morning when the first shells began to rain on Xom Lang that March 16th. Those who were still at home—most of the people in the sub-hamlet, for it was still early and many of them were just beginning breakfast—quickly sought shelter in their family bunkers. Almost every house had its bunker dug into the ground nearby. The VC when they had arrived had forced the people to build them, and from friends in other hamlets they had heard enough tales to know that in case of a bombardment, a bunker was one of the few hopes of survival. So each family dug its own.

The shells continued to thud into the ground and explode, destroying houses and gouging deep craters for about twenty minutes. The artillery barrage marched up and down the hamlet and the area around it, preparing the landing zone for the troop-carrying helicopters. Overhead, helicopter gunships hovered without any opposition, pounding the hamlet and the ground around it with rockets and machine gun fire. . . .

Captain Ernest Medina was in the lead chopper, watching the artillery and the gunships level Xom Lang. He "could see the smoke and flash of artillery" as the settlement was ripped apart. Then his helicopter settled into a paddy about a hundred and fifty meters west. Immediately the door gunners strafed the surrounding countryside with machine gun fire in case there happened to be VC waiting among the growing rice and brush.

As far as Medina could tell there was no return fire. "My instant impression," he says, "was that I didn't hear the familiar crackle of rifle bullets zinging over my head."

Accompanied by his radio operator and other company aides, Medina clambered down from the helicopter and rushed across the paddy to the edge of a small graveyard just at the edge of Xom Lang. Still there was no return fire, and all around him the other choppers were settling to the ground and the men of Company C were pouring through the doors, firing toward the houses as they emerged. It seemed to have occurred to no one at that moment that the lack of return fire might mean that this was not the hamlet where the VC was centered, that this was not "Pinkville." . . .

"When the attack started," Sergeant Charles West recalls, "it couldn't have been stopped by anyone. We were mad and we had been told that the enemy was there and we were going in there to give them a fight for what they had done to our dead buddies."

Approaching Xom Lang, "we went in shooting," West says. "We'd shoot into the hootches and there were people running around. There were big craters in the village from the bombing. When I got there I saw some of the people, some of the women and kids all torn up."

"I was just coming to the first row of houses, with five or six other guys," says another member of the platoon, "when we heard this noise behind us. Everybody was scared and on edge, and keyed up, too, to kill, and somebody turned quick and snapped off a shot. We all turned and shot. And there was this big old water buffalo, I guess that's what it was, standing in the middle of this field behind us. Everybody was shooting at it and you could

see little puffs jumping out where the bullets hit. It was like something in slow motion, and finally that cow just slumped down and
collapsed." His face contorted by the remembrance, he adds,
"Now it seems kind of funny, but it didn't then. And once the
shooting started, I guess it affected everyone. From then on it was
like nobody could stop. Everyone was just shooting at everything
and anything, like the ammo wouldn't ever give out."

The contagion of slaughter was spreading throughout the
platoon.

Combat photographer Ronald Haeberle and Army Correspondent Jay Roberts had requested permission to accompany a combat mission in order to get both pictures and a story of American
soldiers in action. They had been assigned to Charley Company
and to Calley's platoon. Leaving their helicopter with about ten or
fifteen other soldiers, they came upon a cow being slaughtered,
and then the picture turned sickenly grisly. "Off to the right,"
Haeberle said, "a woman's form, a head appeared from some
brush. All the other GI's started firing at her, aiming at her, firing
at her over and over again."

The bullets riddled the woman's body. She slumped against a
well pump in the middle of the rice paddy, her head caught
between two of its poles. She was obviously already dead, but the
infection, the hysteria was now ascendant. The men were oblivious to everything but slaughter. "They just kept shooting at her.
You could see the bones flying in the air, chip by chip."

There were the sounds: the shots running into and over each
other from inside the hamlet; it sounded as though everyone had
his rifle on automatic, no one bothering to save ammunition by
switching to single shot. And not drowned by the sharp bark of
the rifles and duller thuds of grenades were screams; they
sounded like women and children, but how can anyone tell in that
kind of moment from a distance who is screaming?

Four or five Americans were outside the hamlet, moving along
its perimeter. The job of their platoon was to seal it off and so
prevent the VC inside from fleeing from Calley's men, to catch
them in a pincer and slaughter them. Vernardo Simpson and
these other soldiers were probing the bushes on the outskirts,
delicately, searching for mines and booby traps. As they neared
the first group of houses, a man dressed in black pajamas—the
dress convinced Simpson that he must be a VC even though black

pajamas were traditional peasant dress—suddenly appeared from nowhere, from some bushes and began running toward the hamlet. A woman and child popped up from the same underbrush and started "running away from us toward some huts."

"Dong lai! Dong lai!" The Americans shouted after the Vietnamese. But they kept on running. Lieutenant Brooks, the leader of this second platoon, gave the orders to shoot. If these people did not stop on command, then they must necessarily be VC. "This is what I did," Simpson says. "I shot them, the lady and the little boy. He was about two years old."

A woman and a child? Why?

"I was reluctant, but I was following a direct order. If I didn't do this I could stand court martial for not following a direct order."

Before the day was over, Simpson says, he would have killed at least ten Vietnamese in Xom Lang.

With the number killed there, his total was about the average for each soldier.

When the shelling stopped, Pham Phon crept from the bunker near his hootch. About fifty meters away, he saw a small group of American soldiers. Poking his head back into the bunker, he told his wife and three children—two sons aged nine and four, and a seven year old daughter—to come up and walk slowly toward the Americans.

Like almost all Vietnamese in the hamlets around the country, Phon and his family had learned from the three previous American vists and from the tales told by refugees who had come to Xom Lang to seek shelter after their hamlets had been turned into battlegrounds and from tales carried by others from far away, just how to act when American troops arrived.

It was imperative not to run, either toward the Americans or away from them. If you ran, the Americans would think that you were VC, running away from them or running toward them with a grenade, and they would shoot.

It was imperative not to stay inside the house or the bunker. If you did, then the Americans would think you were VC hiding in ambush, and they would shoot or throw grenades into the house or bunker.

It was imperative to walk slowly toward the Americans, with hands in plain view, or to gather in small groups in some central spot and wait for the Americans to arrive—but never to gather in large groups, for then the Americans would think the group was VC waiting to fire. It was absolutely imperative to show only servility so that the Americans would know that you were not VC and had only peaceful intent.

So Phon and his family walked slowly toward the soldiers. The three children smiled and shouted, "Hello! Hello! Okay! Okay!"

Only this time, unlike the three previous American visitations, there were no answering grins, no gifts of candy and rations. The Americans pointed their rifles at the family and sternly ordered them to walk to the canal about a hundred meters away.

Inside the hamlet, the men of the first platoon were racing from house to house. They planted dynamite and explosive to the brick ones and blew them into dust. They set fires with their lighters to the thatched roofs and to the hootches, watched them flare into a ritual bonfire and then raced on to the next hootch. Some soldiers were pulling people from bunkers and out of the houses and herding them into groups. Some of the Vietnamese tried to run and were immediately shot. Others didn't seem to know what was happening, didn't understand what the Americans were doing or why. But most of them behaved as they had learned they must behave. Meekly they followed any order given.

Some of the groups were marched away in the direction of the canal, and those who straggled behind, could not keep up, were promptly shot.

There were soldiers standing outside the hootches, watching them burn, and as Vietnamese suddenly emerged from the pyres, would shoot them.

And through everything, through the sound of gunfire and through the crackling of flames, through the smoke that had begun to cover everything like a pall, came high pitched screams of pain and terror, bewildered cries, pleading cries. All were ignored.

Michael Bernhardt remembers coming into the hamlet and seeing his fellow soldiers "doing a whole lot of shooting up. But none of it was incoming. I'd been around enough to tell that. I figured we were advancing on the village with fire power."

Inside the hamlet, Bernhardt "saw these guys doing strange

things. They were doing it in three ways. They were setting fire to the hootches and huts and waiting for the people to come out and then shooting them. They were going into the hootches and shooting them up. They were gathering people in groups and shooting them."

The raging fever in the other members of his platoon stunned and shocked Bernhardt. He watched one soldier shooting at everything he saw, blazing away indiscriminately and laughing hysterically as he kept pulling the trigger, kept his finger on the trigger until all the bullets in a clip were gone, then throwing away the clip and reloading and starting again. And laughing all the time. "He just couldn't stop. He thought it was funny, funny, funny." . . .

For Private Herbert Carter it was too much, a nightmare from which there seemed no awakening. "People began coming out of their hootches and the guys shot them and burned the hootches— or burned the hootches and then shot the people when they came out. Sometimes they would round up a bunch and shoot them together. It went on like that for what seemed like all day. Some of the guys seemed to be having a lot of fun. They were wise-cracking and yelling, 'Chalk that one up for me.' "

When he could stand the sight no longer, Carter turned and stumbled out of the hamlet. He sat down under a tree and shot himself in the foot.

He was Charley Company's only casualty that morning.

When the first shells hurled their way into Xom Lang, Nguyen Thi Nien and her family took shelter in their bunker adjacent to their house. In the bunker with her were her eighty-year-old father-in-law, her sister and her sister's seven-year-old daughter, her own husband and their three children. They cowered in the bunker for a considerable length of time. Finally they heard steady rifle fire around them and American voices yelling: "VC di ra! VC di ra!"—VC, get out! VC, get out!

The family crawled slowly and carefully out of the bunker, making every effort to display no hostility. But once they were out they noticed that the Americans were still some distance away. Taking her youngest child, still a baby, in one arm and holding her second youngest by the hand, Nguyen Thi Nien started away, toward the rice paddies. She did not run, but walked on steadily. Her husband and the oldest child started to follow her. But her sister and her sister's daughter hung back, then started in another direction. And her father-in-law turned and started back to the house.

"I am too old," she remembers him calling after her. "I cannot keep up. You get out and I will stay here to keep the house."

There was almost no argument. "We told him," Nguyen Thi Nien says, "all right, you are too old. So you stay here and if the GI's arrive you ask them not to shoot you and not to burn the house."

The old man called that that was exactly what he intended to do. He would stand guard over the family house. But then Nguyen Thi Nien's husband decided that he could not leave his father alone in the house. He turned, sending the oldest child after his wife and the other children, and went back to his father. They stood outside the house for a brief moment arguing. The son trying to convince the old man to get out of the house and go with them to the paddies before the Americans arrived. The Americans were approaching and they could hear the clatter of shots, they could see the flames licking around other houses, and the smoke.

But the old man remained adamant. He was too old, he kept insisting. He could not make it to the paddy. He refused to leave, turning from his son and starting into the house.

The Americans were almost on them; the firing was all around them now. Nien realized that he could wait no longer. If he were to escape the approaching Americans—he realized by then that this was not a friendly visit, that the Americans were hostile this time and were shooting at everything—he would have to flee immediately.

About four hundred meters away, he saw his wife and three children just ducking into the rice paddies, safe. He started after them. Ahead of him, just a few feet, was an old woman, a nearby neighbor. "But suddenly," he says, "five GI's were in front of me, about a hundred meters or so from me. The GI's saw us and started to shoot and the lady was killed. I was hit and so I lay down. Then I saw blood coming from my stomach and so I took a handkerchief and put it over my wound. I lay on the ground there for a little while and then I tried to get back to my house, to my old father and my sister-in-law and her child who must still be there. I could not walk very well and so I was crawling. On the way back to my house I saw five children and one father lying dead on the ground. When I reached my house, I saw it was on fire. Through the fire I could see the bodies of my old father, my sister-in-law and her child inside the house. Then I lost consciousness and I do not know anything more of what happened." . . .

"I was just coming into the middle of that ville," remembers one soldier, refusing to look around or to meet his questioner's eyes as he talks, "and I saw this guy. He was one of my best friends in the company. But honest to Christ, at first I didn't even recognize him. He was kneeling on the ground, this absolutely incredible . . . I don't know what you'd call it, a smile or a snarl or something, but anyway, his whole face was distorted. He was covered with smoke, his face streaked with it, and it looked like there was blood on him, too. You couldn't tell, but there was blood everywhere. Anyway, he was kneeling there holding this grenade launcher, and he was launching grenades at the hootches. A couple of times he launched grenades at groups of people. The grenades would explode, you know, KAPLOW, and then you'd see pieces of bodies flying around. Some of the groups were just piles of bodies. But I remember there was this one group a little distance away. Maybe there was ten people, most of them women and little kids, huddled all together and you could see they were really scared, they just couldn't seem to move. Anyway, he turns around toward them and lets fly with a grenade. It landed right in the middle of them. You could hear the screams and then the sound and then see the pieces of bodies scatter out, and the whole area just suddenly turned red like somebody had turned on a faucet."

Did you do anything to try to stop him?

"You got rocks or something? All you had to do was take one look at him, at his face and you knew the best thing was to leave him alone. I think if I had even said a word to him at all, he would have turned and killed me and not thought a damn thing about it." . . .

Jay Roberts and Ronald Haeberle moved about the havoc taking pictures. They came upon one group of Americans surrounding a small group of women, children and a teen-age girl. She was perhaps twelve or thirteen and was wearing the traditional peasant black pajamas. One of the Americans grabbed her by the shoulders while another began to try to strip the pajamas off her, pulling at the top of the blouse to undo it.

"Let's see what she's made of," one of the soldiers laughed.

Another moved close to her, laughing and pointing at her. "VC, boom-boom," he said. He was telling her in the GI patois that she was a whore for the VC, and indicating that if she did it for them why not for the Americans.

A third soldier examined her carefully and then turned to the others. "Jesus," he said, "I'm horny."

All around there were burning buildings and bodies and the sounds of firing and screams. But the Americans seemed totally oblivious to anything but the girl. They had almost stripped her when her mother rushed over and tried to help her escape. She clutched at the American soldiers, scratched them, clawed at their faces, screaming invectives at them. They pushed her off. One soldier slapped her across the face; another hit her in the stomach with his fist; a third kicked her in the behind, knocking her sprawling to the ground.

But the mother's actions had given the girl a chance to escape a little. She took shelter behind some of the other women in the group and tried to button the top of her blouse. Haeberle stepped in, knelt and took a picture of the scene.

Roberts remembers that at that moment, "when they noticed Ron, they left off and turned away as if everything was normal. Then a soldier asked, 'Well, what'll we do with 'em?'

" 'Kill 'em,' another answered.

"I heard an M-60 go off, a light machine gun, and when we turned all of them and the kids with them were dead." . . .

Another soldier says he saw a teen-age girl running across a rice paddy, trying to hide from an American who was chasing her. As he watched, he saw this American soldier aim with his rifle and shoot. The girl gave a cry and fell down. The soldier went after her and vanished into the paddy. A few minutes later there was another shot from the area and then the soldier walked back from the field into the hamlet. . . .

A small boy, three or four, suddenly appears from nowhere on the trail in front of a group of Americans. He is wounded in the arm. Michael Terry sees "the boy clutching his wounded arm with his other hand while the blood trickled between his fingers. He was staring around himself in shock and disbelief at what he saw. He just stood there with big eyes staring around like he didn't understand what was happening. Then the captain's radio operator put a burst of 16 into him."

When Paul Meadlo came into Xom Lang, Lieutenant Calley set him and some of the other men to work gathering the people together in groups in a central location. "There was about forty, forty-five people that we gathered in the center of the village," Meadlo told an interviewer. "And we placed them in there, and it was like a little island, right there in the center of the village."

The soldiers forced the people in the group to squat on the ground. "Lieutenant Calley came over and said, 'You know what to do with them, don't you?' And I said, 'Yes.' So I took it for granted he just wanted us to watch them. And he left and came back about ten or fifteen minutes later, and said, 'How come you ain't killed them yet?' And I told him that I didn't think he wanted us to kill them, that you just wanted us to guard them. He said, 'No, I want them dead.' "

At first Meadlo was surprised by the order—not shocked or horrified, but surprised. "But three, four guys heard it and then he stepped back about ten, fifteen feet, and he started shooting them. And he told me to start shooting. I poured about four clips into the group."

A clip is seventeen rounds. Meadlo fired sixty-eight rounds into this group of people. "I fired them on automatic," he said, "so you can't . . . you just spray the area on them and so you can't know how many you killed 'cause they were going fast. So I might have killed ten or fifteen of them."

One slaughter was over, but there was more to come, and the thirst for blood had become so contagious that no one thought anything about what he was doing. "We started to gather them up, more people, " Meadlo says, "and we had about seven or eight people that we was gonna put into a hootch and we dropped a hand grenade in there with them."

Then Meadlo and several other soldiers took a group of civilians—almost exclusively women and children, some of the children still too young to walk—toward one of the two canals on the outskirts of Xom Lang. "They had about seventy, seventy-five people all gathered up. So we threw ours in with them and Lieutenant Calley told me, he said, 'Meadlo, we got another job to do.' And so he walked over to the people and started pushing them off and started shooting."

Taking his cue from Calley, Meadlo and then the other members of this squad "started pushing them off and we started shooting them. So altogether we just pushed them all off and just started using automatics on them. And somebody told us to switch off to single shot so that we could save ammo. So we switched off to single shot and shot a few more rounds.''

In the heat and the passion of that morning, it is almost impossible to know who is telling the real truth about any of the events or any of the people, or if there is even any real truth. And perhaps it is less than the major quest in the story of what happened and why it happened that morning in March to discover and decide just who killed whom, where and when. Many hundreds of people, most of them children, women and old men, were slaughtered at Xom Lang and Binh Dong. A mass hysteria swept over a large number of American soldiers who became executioners, indiscriminate butchers. And in the horror of it all, is there really sense and meaning in saying that one did such and such and this one did this and that? In a senseless slaughter, the attempt to fix blame for specific killings on specific people is an attempt to find sense and logic where it does not and cannot exist. The responsibility for what happened at Xom Lang lies not just with the man or the men who pulled the triggers and threw the grenades. The responsibility goes further and higher.

As darkness fell that night over Xom Lang, over Son My, over all of Vietnam, it was morning half a world away, in Washington, D.C. If the repercussions of what had happened that morning in this one corner of Vietnam had not yet reached the American capital, repercussions of Vietnam itself, of all that had led up to that morning in the war, had reached the center of government of the United States.

Senator Eugene McCarthy and his young idealists, the advocates of the "New Politics," were celebrating the victory earlier in the week over Lyndon Johnson in the New Hampshire Democratic primary. Eugene McCarthy, until then not a well-known national politician, had upset the incumbent President, the leader of his own party. The issue which he had raised to win that victory was that of the war in Vietnam.

In the caucus room of the United States Senate, Robert Francis Kennedy was about to declare that he was a candidate for his party's presidential nomination, that he, too, would take on the

President, his brother's Vice President. And the quarrel which had led to this break was the war in Vietnam, what the United States under Lyndon Johnson had done to Vietnam and what it had done to itself.

In the White House, the President was in an anguished personal struggle. As a result of the war in Vietnam, the people had turned against him, had lost confidence in his ability to lead the nation. Less than four years after he had won the greatest political victory in American history as a candidate of peace, even the voters of his own party had rejected him, now identified as the candidate of war. Within two weeks, he would make his fateful decision. He would stop the bombing of North Vietnam. He would seek a beginning of peace negotiations. And he would not seek re-nomination or re-election as President of the United States. He, too, had been destroyed by the war in Vietnam.

But on that March 16, 1968, Xom Lang and Binh Dong and My Hoi, My Lai and Son My and Pinkville were names that these political leaders had never heard. They were names that most of the military in Vietnam had never heard.

There had been a minor engagement there that day. On the next day and in the days to follow, it would be hailed as a victory.

But the target of the day, the Viet Cong soldiers, had been untouched. From their camp at My Khe sub-hamlet they had heard, early in the morning, the sound of planes and guns to the west; they had heard the sounds moving across the village as the day progressed. And before the Americans came near to My Khe—My Lai (1) or Pinkville—the VC had faded from the scene, moving silently out of the hamlet and north to the sanctuary of Batangan. They would be back.

Part Seven

YEARS OF POLARIZATION

During the late 1960s American society was more profoundly divided than at any time since the Civil War. As the peaceful petitions of the nonviolent civil rights movement were replaced by black power slogans, white support for blacks plummeted. The emergence of feminism created profound divisions over traditional family roles and definitions of masculinity and femininity. The student movement began as a request for moderate changes, but with the growing crisis over Vietnam became a major challenge to the very structure of the university and government. As the protest over Vietnam grew, many cities and university campuses became domestic battlefields, with police barricades confronting student demonstrators.

The civil rights movement was crucial to the development of political activism on America's campuses. As white students and black students joined together in civil rights protests, they came face to face with the duplicity and brutality of law enforcement officials in the South. When, as frequently happened, the federal government failed to provide corrective assistance, demonstrators began to suspect that even those authorities they thought they could trust were part of the problem. What had begun as a specific protest against Southern racism gradually developed into a more critical challenge to established authority generally.

When Mario Savio and others came back to campus from summer civil rights demonstrations in Mississippi in 1964, they carried their newfound criticism to university life itself. After officials at the University of California at Berkeley attempted to control distribution of political materials on a campus plaza, the Berkeley free speech movement began. Significantly, the issues were not specific, but involved protest against the "university machine" it-self as a manifestation of corporate control of America. Students protested the depersonalization of the multiversity with its computerized systems, its huge classrooms, and its insensitivity to issues of human community.

By 1967 and 1968, the spirit of Berkeley had spread across the country, fueled by the fires of anti-war demonstrations. Universities were denounced for being instruments of the military-industrial complex. Students demanded the cancellation of university contracts to conduct research on weapons development. Army and Navy ROTC courses came under attack for providing a bond between the university and U.S. policy in Vietnam. When weapons manufacturers came to campus to recruit, students protested their presence, insisting that the university had no right to support the war effort—even indirectly—by making its facilities available to those who profited from the war.

Culture and politics became intermixed as long hair, mari-juana, more casual attitudes toward sex, and rejection of middle-class values became associated with the anti-war movement. When students took over university buildings to protest the war, they boasted of their communal lifestyle, their hostility to monogamy, and their freedom to carve out a different lifestyle than that of their parents or elders. The so-called generation gap involved not only political disagreements, but also fundamental personal conflicts over how one would dress, what kind of language one would use, and who one would sleep with. By the end of the 1960s the moderate reformism of the Students for a Democratic Society in 1962 had given way to the militant and violent rhetoric of the Weathermen. In the meantime, reaction against youthful protest and the counterculture had spread. Commentators developed a new phrase—"Middle America"—to describe those who rejected totally the assault on middle-class values by young people of the left.

The following selections highlight some of the tensions of that era. The Port Huron statement of SDS in 1962 offers a vivid contrast to the Weatherman SDS statement of the late 1960s, illustrating how the moderation of the early years was transformed into a posture that justified the trashing of university buildings and the use of terrorism. The selection by Jerry Avorn and others on the Columbia "Revolution" of 1968 shows how, on one campus, protest over the war and racism evolved, and how university response to that protest helped to radicalize the majority of "moderate" students.

William O'Neill's acerbic assessment of the Counterculture portrays some of the parallel shifts taking place in lifestyle, music, and attitudes toward sex and drugs. Although the counterculture was in some senses different from political activism, it also represented a vehicle through which the young felt they could contribute toward changing the values of the society. Finally, the article on Joe Kelly describes vividly the clash between cultural perspectives and generations in the 1960s.

Some of the key questions that remain are why the earlier, more moderate protests of the 1960s met with such little success. Did the intransigence of those in power necessitate the shift toward a more radical position? How basic were the issues raised by political activists and supporters of the counterculture? Did they call into serious question the structures and values of the larger society? Was there a way in which young and old could have talked to each other with less hostility and intolerance? Finally, have we lost some of the valuable perspectives which that era brought, as well as its coercive divisiveness?

The Port Huron Statement

Students for a Democratic Society

To young Americans in the early 1960s, everything seemed possible. A youthful, activist President had come into office promising that "we can do better." Black students throughout the South had demonstrated through sit-ins and kneel-ins that people willing to act on their convictions could help to turn society around. Inspired by these examples and given hope by the new leadership in Washington, young white reformers came together to draw up a manifesto for social change. Those who formed Students for a Democratic Society (SDS) were deeply critical of the complacency and indifference of their society. They hoped to marshall the resources of technology, the university, corporations, and government to eliminate poverty and racism. Hence, their agenda of reform. What remains most impressive from the Port Huron Statement, however, is its moderation, its faith that change can take place within the system, its conviction that social democracy could be achieved quickly and effectively, without revolution. The Port Huron Statement speaks eloquently to the idealism of a generation of student activists. Just as eloquently, it testifies to their innocence.

INTRODUCTION: AGENDA FOR A GENERATION

We are people of this generation, bred in at least modest comfort, housed now in universities, looking uncomfortably to the world we inherit.

Excerpted from Tom Hayden et al., Port Huron Statement, mimeographed (n.p., Students for a Democratic Society, 1962)

When we were kids the United States was the wealthiest and strongest country in the world; the only one with the atom bomb, the least scarred by modern war, an initiator of the United Nations that we thought would distribute Western influence throughout the world. Freedom and equality for each individual, government of, by, and for the people—these American values we found good, principles by which we could live as men. Many of us began maturing in complacency.

As we grew, however, our comfort was penetrated by events too troubling to dismiss. First, the permeating and victimizing fact of human degradation, symbolized by the Southern struggle against racial bigotry, compelled most of us from silence to activism. Second, the enclosing fact of the Cold War, symbolized by the presence of the Bomb, brought awareness that we ourselves, and our friends, and millions of abstract "others" we knew more directly because of our common peril, might die at any time. We might deliberately ignore, or avoid, or fail to feel all other human problems, but not these two, for these were too immediate and crushing in their impact, too challenging in the demand that we as individuals take the responsibility for encounter and resolution.

While these and other problems either directly oppressed us or rankled our consciences and became our own subjective concerns, we began to see complicated and disturbing paradoxes in our surrounding America. The declaration "all men are created equal . . ." rang hollow before the facts of Negro life in the South and the big cities of the North. The proclaimed peaceful intentions of the United States contradicted its economic and military investments in the Cold War status quo. . . .

Our work is guided by the sense that we may be the last generation in the experiment with living. But we are a minority—the vast majority of our people regard the temporary equilibriums of our society and world as eternally-functional parts. In this is perhaps the outstanding paradox: we ourselves are imbued with urgency, yet the message of our society is that there is no viable alternative to the present. Beneath the reassuring tones of the politicians, beneath the common opinion that America will "muddle through," beneath the stagnation of those who have closed their minds to the future, is the pervading feeling that there simply are no alternatives, that our times have witnessed the exhaustion not only of Utopias, but of any new departures as well. . . .

Some would have us believe that Americans feel contentment

amidst prosperity—but might it not be better be called a glaze above deeply-felt anxieties about their role in the new world? And if these anxieties produce a developed indifference to human affairs, do they not as well produce a yearning to believe there *is* an alternative to the present, that something *can* be done to change circumstances in the school, the workplaces, the bureaucracies, the government? It is to this latter yearning, at once the spark and engine of change, that we direct our present appeal. The search for truly democratic alternatives to the present, and a commitment to social experimentation with them, is a worthy and fulfilling human enterprise, one which moves us and, we hope, others today. On such a basis do we offer this document of our convictions and analysis: as an effort in understanding and changing the conditions of humanity in the late twentieth century, an effort rooted in the ancient, still unfulfilled conception of man attaining determining influence over his circumstances of life. . . .

THE STUDENTS

If student movements for change are still rareties on the campus scene, what is commonplace there? The real campus, the familiar campus, is a place of private people, engaged in their notorious "inner emigration." It is a place of commitment to business-as-usual, getting ahead, playing it cool. It is a place of mass affirmation of the Twist, but mass reluctance toward the controversial public stance. Rules are accepted as "inevitable," bureaucracy as "just circumstances," irrelevance as "scholarship," selflessness as "martyrdom," politics as "just another way to make people, and an unprofitable one, too." . . .

Tragically, the university could serve as a significant source of social criticism and an initiator of new modes and molders of attitudes. But the actual intellectual effect of the college experience is hardly distinguishable from that of any other communications channel—say, a television set—passing on the stock truths of the day. Students leave college somewhat more "tolerant" than when they arrived, but basically unchallenged in their values and political orientations. With administrators ordering the institution, and faculty the curriculum, the student learns by his isolation to accept elite rule within the university, which prepares him to accept later forms of minority control. The real function of the educational system—as opposed to its more rhetorical function of "searching for truth"—is to impart the key information and styles that will help the student get by, modestly but comfortably, in the big society beyond.

THE SOCIETY BEYOND

Look beyond the campus, to America itself. That student life is more intellectual, and perhaps more comfortable, does not obscure the fact that the fundamental qualities of life on the campus reflect the habits of society at large. The fraternity president is seen at the junior manager levels; the sorority queen has gone to Grosse Pointe; the serious poet burns for a place, any place, to work; the once-serious and never-serious poets work at the advertising agencies. The desperation of people threatened by forces about which they know little and of which they can say less; the cheerful emptiness of people "giving up" all hope of changing things; the faceless ones polled by Gallup who listed "international affairs" fourteenth on their list of "problems" but who also expected thermonuclear war in the next few years; in these and other forms, Americans are in withdrawal from public life, from any collective effort at directing their own affairs.

The very isolation of the individual—from power and community and ability to aspire—means the rise of a democracy without publics. With the great mass of people structurally remote and psychologically hesitant with respect to democratic institutions, those institutions themselves attenuate and become, in the fashion of the vicious circle, progressively less accessible to those few who aspire to serious participation in social affairs. The vital democratic connection between community and leadership, between the mass and the several elites, has been so wrenched and perverted that disastrous policies go unchallenged time and again.

POLITICS WITHOUT PUBLICS

The American political system is not the democratic model of which its glorifiers speak. In actuality it frustrates democracy by confusing the individual citizen, paralyzing policy discussion, and consolidating the irresponsible power of military and business interests.

A most alarming fact is that few, if any, politicians are calling for changes in these conditions. Only a handful even are calling on the President to "live up to" platform pledges; no one is demanding structural changes, such as the shuttling of Southern Democrats out of the Democratic Party. Rather than protesting the state of politics, most politicians are reinforcing and aggravating that state. . . .

THE ECONOMY

We live amidst a national celebration of economic prosperity while poverty and deprivation remain an unbreakable way of life for millions in the "affluent society," including many of our own generation. We hear glib references to the "welfare state," "free enterprise," and "shareholder's democracy" while military defense is the main item of "public" spending and obvious oligopoly and other forms of minority rule defy real individual initiative or popular control. Work, too, is often unfulfilling and victimizing, accepted as a channel to status or plenty, if not a way to pay the bills, rarely as a means of understanding and controlling self and events. In work and leisure the individual is regulated as part of the system, a consuming unit, bombarded by hard-sell, soft-sell, lies and semi-true appeals to his basest drives. He is always told that he is a "free" man because of "free enterprise." . . .

The Military-Industrial Complex

The most spectacular and important creation of the authoritarian and oligopolistic structure of economic decision-making in America is the institution called "the military-industrial complex" by former President Eisenhower—the powerful congruence of interest and structure among military and business elites which affects so much of our development and destiny. Not only is ours the first generation to live with the possibility of world-wide cataclysm—it is the first to experience the actual social preparation for cataclysm, the general militarization of American society. . . .

Since our childhood these two trends—the rise of the military and the installation of a defense-based economy—have grown fantastically. The Department of Defense, ironically the world's largest single organization, is worth $160 billion, owns 32 million acres of America and employs half the 7.5 million persons directly dependent on the military for subsistence, has an $11 billion payroll which is larger than the net annual income of all American corporations. Defense spending in the Eisenhower era totaled $350 billions and President Kennedy entered office pledged to go even beyond the present defense allocation of 60 cents from every public dollar spent. Except for a war-induced boom immediately after "our side" bombed Hiroshima. American economic prosperity has coincided with a growing dependence on military outlay—from 1911 to 1959 America's Gross National Product of $5.25 trillion included $700 billion in goods and services purchased for the defense effort, about one-seventh of the accumulated GNP. . . .

TOWARDS AMERICAN DEMOCRACY

Every effort to end the Cold War and expand the process of world industrialization is an effort hostile to people and institutions whose interests lie in perpetuation of the East-West military threat and the postponement of change in the "have not" nations of the world. Every such effort, too, is bound to establish greater democracy in America. The major goals of a domestic effort would be:

1. America must abolish its political party stalemate.
2. Mechanisms of voluntary association must be created through which political information can be imparted and political participation encouraged.
3. Institutions and practices which stifle dissent should be abolished, and the promotion of peaceful dissent should be actively promoted.
4. Corporations must be made publicly responsible.
5. The allocation of resources must be based on social needs. A truly "public sector" must be established, and its nature debated and planned.
6. America should concentrate on its genuine social priorities: abolish squalor, terminate neglect, and establish an environment for people to live in with dignity and creativeness.

You Don't Need a Weatherman To Know Which Way the Wind Blows

(Submitted by Karin Ashley, Bill Ayers, Bernardine Dourn, John Jacobs, Jeff Jones, Gerry Long, Howie Machtinger, Jim Mellen, Terry Robbins, Mark Rudd and Steve Tappis)

Just seven years after the Port Huron Statement, SDS met again in national convention. In the intervening years the war in Vietnam had expanded dramatically, the integrationist petitions of the early civil rights movement had turned into demands for Black Power, and a movement for student autonomy had generated massive protests on university campuses. For at least some, the primary lesson of the sixties had been the impossibility of securing change peacefully. Teach-ins at universities had not changed the government's Vietnam policy; campaigns on behalf of anti-war candidates seemed an exercise in futility; for those who were most bitter and radicalized, revolution seemed the only answer. With young people as an advance party, these activists demanded that SDS support a world-wide revolution against capitalism and imperialism. The following selection from the Weatherman Manifesto—"you don't need a weatherman to tell which way the wind is blowing"—appears, in retrospect, a hopelessly doctrinaire plea. Just one year later, three of those who endorsed it blew themselves to pieces making bombs in Greenwich Village. Yet the statement also reflects just how corrosive the 1960s had been in destroying the idealism of seven years earlier.

INTERNATIONAL REVOLUTION

The contradiction between the revolutionary peoples of Asia, Africa and Latin America and the imperialists headed by the United States is the principal contradiction in the contemporary world. The development of this con-

Excerpted from Karin Ashley et al. "You Don't Need A Weatherman To Know Which Way The Wind Blows," mimeographed statement, 1969.

tradition is promoting the struggle of the people of the whole world against US imperialism and its lackeys.

Lin Piao
Long Live the Victory of People's War!

People ask, what is the nature of the revolution that we talk about? Who will it be made by, and for, and what are its goals and strategy,

The overriding consideration in answering these questions is that the main struggle going on in the world today is between US imperialism and the national liberation struggles against it. . . .

So the very first question people in this country must ask in considering the question of revolution is where they stand in relation to the United States as an oppressor nation, and where they stand in relation to the masses of people throughout the world whom US imperialism is oppressing. . . .

It is in this context that we must examine the revolutionary struggles in the United States. We are within the heartland of a world-wide monster, a country so rich from its world-wide plunder that even the crumbs doled out to the enslaved masses within its borders provide for material existence very much above the conditions of the masses of people of the world. The US empire, as world-wide system, channels wealth, based upon the labor and resources of the rest of the world, into the United States. The relative affluence existing in the United States is directly dependent upon the labor and natural resources of the Vietnamese, the Angolans, the Bolivians and the rest of the peoples of the Third World. All of the United Airlines Astrojets, all of the Holiday Inns, all of Hertz's automobiles, your television set, car and wardrobe already belong, to a large degree, to the people of the rest of the world. . . .

The goal is the destruction of US imperialism and the achievement of a classless world: world communism. Winning state power in the US will occur as a result of the military forces of the US overextending themselves around the world and being defeated piecemeal; struggle within the US will be a vital part of this process, but when the revolution triumphs in the US it will have been made by the people of the whole world. For socialism to be defined in national terms within so extreme and historical an oppressor nation as this is only imperialist national chauvinism on the part of the "movement."

In this context, why an emphasis on youth? Why should young people be willing to fight on the side of Third World peoples? . . .

As imperialism struggles to hold together this decaying, social fabric, it inevitably resorts to brute force and authoritarian ideology. People, especially young people, more and more find themselves in the iron grip of authoritarian institutions. Reaction against the pigs or teachers in the schools, welfare pigs or the army is generalizable and extends beyond the particular repressive institution to the society and the State as a whole. The legitimacy of the State is called into question for the first time in at least 20 years, and the anti-authoritarianism which characterizes the youth rebellion turns into rejection of the State, a refusal to be socialized into American society. Kids used to try to beat the system from inside the army or from inside the schools; now they desert from the army and burn down the schools.

The crisis in imperialism has brought about a breakdown in bourgeois social forms, culture and ideology. The family falls apart, kids leave home, women begin to break out of traditional "female" and "mother" roles. There develops a "generation gap" and a "youth problem." Our heroes are no longer struggling businessmen, and we also begin to reject the ideal career of the professional and look to Mao, Che, the Panthers, the Third World, for our models, for motion. We reject the elitist, technocratic bullshit that tells us only experts can rule, and look instead to leadership from the people's war of the Vietnamese. Chuck Berry, Elvis, the Temptations brought us closer to the "people's culture" of Black America. The racist response to the civil rights movement revealed the depth of racism in America, as well as the impossibility of real change through American institutions. And the war against Vietnam is not "the heroic war against the Nazis"; it's the big lie, with napalm, burning through everything we had heard this country stood for. Kids begin to ask questions: Where is the Free World? And who do the pigs protect at home?

THE RYM AND THE PIGS

A major focus in our neighborhood and citywide work is the pigs, because they tie together the various struggles around the state as the enemy, and thus point to the need for a movement oriented toward power to defeat it.

The pigs are the capitalist state, and as such define the limits of all political struggles; to the extent that a revolutionary struggle shows signs of success, they come in and mark the point it can't go beyond. . . . Our job is not to avoid the issue of the pigs as "diverting" from anti-imperialist struggle, but to emphasize that they are our real enemy if we fight that struggle to win.

The most important task for us toward making the revolution, and the work our collectives should engage in, is the creation of a mass revolutionary movement, without which a clandestine revolutionary party will be impossible. A revolutionary mass movement is different from the traditional revisionist mass base of "sympathizers." Rather it is akin to the Red Guard in China, based on the full participation and involvement of masses of people in the practice of making revolution; a movement with a full willingness to participate in the violent and illegal struggle. It is a movement diametrically opposed to the elitist idea that only leaders are smart enough or interested enough to accept full revolutionary conclusions. It is a movement built on the basis of faith in the masses of people.

The task of collectives is to create this kind of movement. (The party is not a substitute for it, and in fact is totally dependent on it.) This will be done at this stage principally among youth, through implementing the Revolutionary Youth Movement strategy discussed in this paper. It is practice at this, and not political "teachings" in the abstract, which will determine the relevance of the political collectives which are formed.

The strategy of the RYM for developing an active mass base, tying the city-wide fights to community and city-wide anti-pig movement, and for building a party eventually out of this motion, fits with the world strategy for winning the revolution, builds a movement oriented toward the power, and will become one division of the International Liberation Army, while its battlefields are added to the many Vietnams which will dismember and dispose of US imperialism. Long Live the Victory of People's War!

Up Against the Ivy Wall

Jerry Avorn, Robert Freedman, and Members of the Staff of the Columbia Daily Spectator

No campus experienced greater upheaval than Columbia University in 1968. A Hollywood producer could hardly have created a scenario more replete with typecast characters and issues. On one side stood a rigid, conservative university president, tied through board membership to corporate America and through university contracts to government policy in Vietnam, refusing consistently to make any concessions to student protestors. On the other stood an assortment of radicals frustrated by the intransigence of the university and committed to finding any available issue as a basis for confrontation. Add to the picture a black student body intent upon acting independently of white movements, and a faculty desperately searching for some middle ground to avoid a campus tragedy.

The immediate issues were simple. Columbia sought to construct a university gymnasium in a public park overlooking Harlem, with a separate entrance at the back of the gym for community people who wished to use the facility. A second issue involved the university's ties to the Defense Department through research contracts that, at least indirectly, helped to support the war. Compounding each of these was a failure of communication between students and administration. All these strands came together in the spring of 1968. The following selection, written by the editors of the student newspaper, highlights how a combination of university stubbornness, student rebellion, and the overuse of police force resulted in the radicalization of a significant portion of the university student body. The Columbia story became a microcosm of what was to happen on other campuses throughout the country, helping to create a widespread sense that everything was coming apart, and that no institution—no matter how venerated—was safe from radical challenge.

"What is the singular of 'swine'?" asked Warren Goodell, vice president for administration of Columbia University, as he walked into the offices of the *Columbia Daily Spectator.*

"It must be 'pig,' " one of the editors suggested. "Why?"

"They called me one yesterday," the vice president said with a nervous smile. "They marched over to my office, and one of them yelled, 'There's another one of these swine around here,' and they came looking for me. But I wasn't in."

The incident had occurred on March 27, 1968, during a demonstration in which over one hundred members of the Columbia chapter of Students for a Democratic Society marched into Low Memorial Library, the domed-and-columned edifice that houses the offices of Columbia's top administrators. Officially the demonstration had been called to protest Columbia's affiliation with the Institute for Defense Analyses, an organization that does military research for the federal government. But beyond this it had another goal: to flout an edict, issued at the start of the academic year by Columbia President Grayson Kirk, banning all protests inside University buildings. SDS claimed that the rule was an attempt at political repression and wanted to draw the administration into a confrontation over the regulation. Inside Low, chanting "IDA Must Go!", the mass of students burst into several offices, including that of one administrator who admitted he was against the war but said he had more pressing problems. The students presented him with a petition calling for Columbia's disaffiliation from IDA, signed by more than 1,500 students and faculty. They then coursed through the building for the next fifteen minutes, chanting anti-war slogans and distracting secretaries.

Now, as Goodell spoke of the event, he grew agitated. "Take over," he murmured, "the word has gone out from national SDS—take over the universities. . . . Those students have no respect for property," the vice president said. "You should have seen the things they were doing in Low yesterday—writing on the wall, everything. I have a Picasso hanging in my office, you know. Those kids probably won't even know it's a Picasso. If they touch my Picasso they're going to the state penitentiary! . . .

In the midst of a rapidly changing University climate, Grayson Kirk, sixty-four years old, imposing, President of Columbia University, meticulously clad in gray vest and suit, sat in his large Low Library office surrounded by his familiar mementos and objets d'art. He leaned forward in a leather chair and lit his pipe. It was five days before the uprising. His ample jowls swelling red as he puffed, Kirk explained to a small group of student editors why he had refused for eight months to make public the contents of a report he had commissioned on student life at Columbia. The report had been submitted in late August by a committee of students, faculty and administrators who had worked for nearly two years on the project. It contained an extensive set of proposals for student involvement in University decision-making, as well as rules governing student rights and protest. Kirk had finally released the report only after the student council threatened to make its copy public, and now declined to comment on any of the proposals it contained.

"For me to comment on the Student Life Report would foreclose discussion about it on campus," the President remarked with the stammer that mars much of his speech. "I would not want to say at this time in what spheres of University life the students should have a voice, because there hasn't been time to read the report carefully enough."

Discussion turned to the March 27 political demonstration inside Low Library and the disciplining of students that might follow. "The University is free to expel anyone for any reason it deems equitable," Kirk stated, "and that is as it should be. Of course, I have—under the Trustees—the final disciplinary authority." . . .

April 22, the day before it all began at Columbia, a student sent an open letter to President Kirk. It began with a quotation:

> *Our young people, in disturbing numbers, appear to reject all forms of authority, from whatever source derived, and they have taken refuge in a turbulent and inchoate nihilism whose sole objectives are destruction. I know of no time in our history when the gap between the generations has been wider or more potentially dangerous.*
>
> Grayson Kirk, April 12, 1968
> Charlottesville, Va.

DEAR GRAYSON,

Your charge of nihilism is indeed ominous; for if it were true, our nihilism would bring the whole civilized world, from Columbia to Rockefeller Center, crashing down upon all our heads.

Though it is not true, your charge does represent something: you call it the generation gap. I see it as a real conflict between those who run things now—you, Grayson Kirk—and those who feel oppressed by, and disgusted with, the society you rule—we, the young people.

You might want to know what is wrong with this society, since, after all, you live in a very tight self-created dream world. We can point to the war in Vietnam as an example of the unimaginable wars of aggression you are prepared to fight to maintain your control over your empire (now you've been beaten by the Vietnamese, so you call for a tactical retreat). We can point to your using us as cannon fodder to fight your war. We can point out your mansion window to the ghetto below you've helped to create through your racist University expansion policies, through your unfair labor practices, through your city government and your police. We can point to this University, your University, which train us to be lawyers and engineers, and managers for your IBM, your Socony Mobil, your IDA, your Con Edison (or else to be scholars and teachers in more universities like this one). We can point, in short, to our own meaningless studies, our identity crises, and our revulsion with being cogs in your corporate machines as a product of and reaction to a basically sick society. . . .

You are quite right in feeling that the situation is "potentially dangerous." For if we win, we will take control of your world, your corporation, your University and attempt to mold a world in which we and other people can live as human beings. Your power is directly threatened, since we will have to destroy that power before we take over. We begin by fighting you about your support of the war in Vietnam and American imperialism—IDA and the School of International Affairs. We will fight you about your control of black people in Morningside Heights, Harlem, and the campus itself. And we will fight you about the type of mis-education you are trying to channel us through. We will have to destroy at times, even violently, in order to end your power and your system—but that is a far cry from nihilism.

Grayson, I doubt if you will understand any of this, since your fantasies have shut out the world as it really is from your thinking. Vice President Truman says the society is basically sound; you say the war in Vietnam was a well-intentioned accident. We, the young people, who you so rightly fear, say that the society is sick and you and your capitalism are the sickness.

You call for order and respect for authority; we call for justice, freedom and socialism.

There is only one thing left to say. It may sound nihilistic to you, since it is the opening shot in a war of liberation. I'll use the words of LeRoi Jones, whom I'm sure you don't like a whole lot: "Up against the wall, motherfucker, this is a stick-up."

> Yours for freedom,
> Mark [Rudd]

... By the time of the IDA demonstration a new sub-group had come to dominate SDS. It became known as the "action faction," and advocated a new tactical approach—confrontation politics—to replace the dramatization-politicization style of the "praxis axis." The superficial dynamic of the tactic was simple: a physical confrontation—a sit-in, a blockade, the takeover of a building—is set up to discomfit the adversary who holds the power, in this case the University administration. He can respond by giving in to the substantive demands of the radicals or by crushing them with coercion of his own. If he is unusually perceptive, he may be able to trace a third course, resorting to neither capitulation nor repression, but making small concessions to "co-opt" the dissidents and seduce them to coöperate with the power structure. But, in the coming days, such political sophistication was to prove beyond the resources of the men who ran Columbia.

The tactical elegance of confrontation politics lay in the fact that the radicals had a good chance of winning whether the administration gave in to their substantive demands or overcame them by repression. The use of coercive force on the part of the adversary—whether it came in the form of the University discipline or police violence—could be a powerful force to "radicalize" liberal or moderate students. For the crucial part of the SDS view is that while escalated tactics are necessary to bring pressure for change on substantive issues, the "radicalization" of large segments of the population is far more important. As Rudd said later:

> Confrontation politics puts the enemy up against the wall and forces him to define himself. In addition, it puts the individual up against the wall. He has to make a choice. Radicalization of the individual means that he must commit himself to the struggle to

change society as well as share the radical view of what is wrong
with society.

Shortly after the March 27 demonstration in Low the administration formulated its response to the confrontation. . . . Six students were singled out—Rudd, four other members of the SDS
steering committee and the chairman of a campus draft-resistance
organization—and summoned to the office of a dean to discuss
their participation in the protest. . . . On April 22 the students—
who came to be known as the "IDA Six"—finally agreed to meet
with the dean but declined to discuss their participation in the
IDA demonstration. They were summarily placed on disciplinary
probation.

That evening SDS called an emergency general assembly meeting in a classroom in Fayerweather Hall. . . .

The "ideal" course for SDS to take was suggested in a rather
remarkable proposal presented by sophomore Steve Komm, who
several weeks before had lost to Rudd in the race for the chairmanship. His manifesto was entitled, "PROPOSAL FOR A SPRING OFFENSIVE
AGAINST COLUMBIA RACISM" and was marked in heavy letters, "For
internal circulation." It stated the problem in the following way:

> [The administration's action] comes at a time when SDS is vocif-
> erous but isolated from a mass student and faculty base of sup-
> port. . . . Moderation would give credence to and ratify the admin-
> istration's conduct regulations, which amount to a political castra-
> tion of SDS. Our reply to the administration's attack must be a
> political offensive against the University on the substantive issues
> which maximize the opportunities for student and faculty support.

Komm went on to outline immediate and longer-range tactics.
The former were fairly conventional for SDS. The demonstrators
would first stage a rally at the Sundial. Following the rally the
demonstration would flow inside Low Library where Rudd would
present President Kirk with a written demand for open hearings
for the "IDA Six" on Monday April 29.

The reminder of Komm's proposal—in which concrete plans
gave way to less "realistic" but strangely prophetic suggestions—
was offered lightly, even whimsically, with the understanding that

the actual plans for longer-range tactics would be developed at a steering committee meeting the next night. It read:

> CONTINGENCY A: Fistfights, police violence, similar excitement. Steering Comm. Tues. night plans large demo. Wed., perhaps with campus ant-racism coalition [black students]. We all pull out quotations from M. L. King. Dorm canvassing late into night. If Wed. all right, see "Escalate," below (d). (Two scenarios: one, ever-bigger demonstrations effectively shutting down afternoon classes until they give in; two, Thurs. 500 or more people sit in [take over] Kirk's/Platt's office until demands granted; Fri. morning they call a sympathy strike.) . . .

As ex-chairman Ted Kaptchuk commented after the disturbances:

> All SDS tactics are based on the assumption that you use the sit-in, takeover and strike when you can. That much is taken for granted. We knew that day that we would try to get into Low to demonstrate, because that was the natural consequence of our politics. When someone gets busted for breaking a rule, like demonstrating inside a building, the thing to do is for everyone to break the rule *en masse;* it flows from our egalitarian ideology. After all, these assumptions are common to all SDS chapters' tactics. They are the unwritten standard radical student tactics. . . .

The sun broke through a gray cloud cover shortly before noon Tuesday, April 23, 1968. Nearly one thousand Columbia students and faculty milled on Low Plaza waiting for the featured event of the afternoon—a march into Low Library sponsored by Students for a Democratic Society.

Cicero Wilson, newly elected president of the Students' Afro-American Society, stepped onto the Sundial. In a sense, Wilson's presence at the SDS rally was as significant as his speech. SDS had never been able to unite with black militants on campus and, until now, the white radicals had been unable even to get a representative of the blacks to speak at an SDS function.

"This is Harlem Heights, not Morningside Heights," Wilson told the crowd that had now grown to five hundred. Waving his fists in the air, he attacked the University's plans to build a gymnasium in Morningside Park. "What would you do if somebody came and took your property? Took your property as they're doing over at Morningside with this gym?" Wilson asked. "Would you sit still? No, you'd use every means possible to get your property back—and this is what the black people are engaged in right now." . . .

After conferring again with his fellows, Rudd mounted the Sundial. . . . Rudd looked up toward Low and saw his runner signal that the huge front door was indeed locked. "The doors are locked at Low," Rudd yelled. "We won't get in the fucking office. Maybe—"

Suddenly, before Rudd could complete his sentence, Tom Hurwitz, a radical junior sporting a revolutionary red bandana around his forehead, leapt onto the Sundial and shouted, "Did we come here to talk or did we come here to go to Low?"

Raising his right arm to the sky, Hurwitz started toward Low. The six leftist leaders who had been disciplined the day before linked arms and pushed to the front of the crowd that was following Hurwitz across the plaza. As the demonstrators strode swiftly up the steps to Low, chanting "IDA Must Go! IDA Must Go!" several administrators frantically tried to stop the surging crowd. . . .

Rudd jumped on top of a trash can just outside the security entrance and asked for quiet so he could address the crowd. Jeff Sokolow, a sophomore member of SDS, tugged at Rudd and said, "Tell 'em we could have gotten in, but someone would have gotten hurt." Rudd told the crowd just that and then once again outlined the alternatives open to them. In the middle of Rudd's speech, however, someone in the front of the crowd shouted, "To the gym, to the gym site!" and nearly three hundred of the demonstrators streamed away from Low toward a gate at Amsterdam Avenue and 117th Street. The students moved off the campus led by Cicero Wilson and several other SAS members.

By 12:30 P.M., just one-half hour after the protest had begun at the Sundial, students had pulled down nearly forty feet of fence at the gym site. As protesters continued to rush down the hill toward the open gate fifteen more policemen converged on the demonstrators and started pulling people away from the fallen fence.

Several scuffles broke out between students and police. An officer from the 24th Precinct grabbed Fred Wilson, a white student, and tried to arrest him. A large circle of students gathered around the pair as they struggled. The crowd began shouting, "Let him go, let him go! Take all of us!" and pushed in around the policeman and his prisoner. The officer slipped in the loose dirt and fell to the ground, dragging Wilson down on top of him. The circle of demonstrators piled onto the policeman, kicking at his hands and body, trying to free Wilson.

Robbie Roth, a thin Columbia sophomore from Queens, suggested that the entire crowd regroup at the Sundial. "We're going to have to go back and get together," he said, "with the crowd building, we can still salvage it." The group filed out of the gym site, walking slowly back through the park toward the campus.

Rudd stepped onto the Sundial again. "We don't have an incoherent mob; it just looks that way. I'll tell you what we want to do. We want the people under discipline to get off of discipline. We want this guy who got busted today to get the charges dropped against him; to get unbusted—I guess that's how you say it. We want them to *stop* the fucking gym over there. So I think there's really one thing we have to do and we're all together here; we're all ready to go—now. We'll start by holding a hostage."

"Where are we going to get one?" one student asked.

"We're going to hold whoever we can," Rudd said, "in return for them letting go of the six people under discipline, letting go of IDA and letting go of the fucking gym. We can't get into Low Library. We can't hold the administrators in Low hostage because we can't get in that place and, also, it's too big a place. *But*—there is one part of this administration that's responsible for what's happened today—and that's the administration of Columbia College."

Someone in front of the Sundial boomed, "SEIZE HAMILTON!" and Rudd shouted, "Hamilton Hall is right over there. Let's go!" The crowd surged along the narrow path leading to the classroom building. Within minutes the lobby of the building was overflowing with four hundred students chanting thunderously. "IDA MUST GO! IDA MUST GO!"

"Now we've got the Man where we want him," Rudd told the crowd. "He can't leave unless he gives into some of our demands." A roar rose from the demonstrators.

"Now, let me tell Dean Coleman why we're here; We're here because of the University's bullshit with IDA. After we demand an end to affiliation in IDA, they keep doing research to kill people in Vietnam and in Harlem. That's one of the reasons why we're here. We're here because the University steals land from black people, because we want them to stop building that gym. We're here because the University busts people for political stuff, as it tried to bust six of us, including myself and five other leaders of SDS for leading a demonstration against IDA. We're not going to leave until that demand, no discipline for us, is met." After sustained applause, Rudd continued, "Another demand is that our brother who got busted today—he got some sort of assault charge—that brother is released, and all the other people who have been busted for demonstrating over there. So it's clear that we can't leave this place until most of our demands are met." . . .

When it became apparent late Tuesday night that there would be no new developments at least until dawn, the Hamilton Hall demonstration turned from a sit-in to a sleep-in. As the tired speakers said their last words, the last of the tired demonstrators left the lobby for the upper floors of the building where they made temporary lodgings on corridor and classroom floors. Scattered on blankets, informal groups on each floor held bedtime parties with peanut butter and jelly sandwiches, beer, and guitars. The main classroom building of the all-male College had been transformed for one night into a coed hostel. But, though sexually integrated, the demonstration was becoming racially strained. The fragile alliance between SAS and SDS, born on the Sundial in the afternoon, was dying with the night. The blacks had segregated themselves on the third floor, leaving the remainder of the building to the whites. But the sleeping arrangements were only a sign. Though the integrated steering committee still hung together, a split over tactics was becoming more pronounced. . . .

SDS had always been concerned with mass support. "Alienating the faculty would also be dangerous," Rudd warned, "because they could approve some of our demands." The blacks, however, were not at this point concerned with the psychological impact that barricading buildings would have on the rest of the University community. They did not share the ideology of the New Left and were not obsessed with visions of mass support from the white world. While the whites wanted to radicalize the rest of the campus and use the political pressure of popular support to win their demands, the blacks preferred to rely only on the more military advantage of holding buildings, regardless of whether the campus liked it or not.

When the three white delegates to the steering committee reached the first-floor room where the blacks had been meeting, they were told, "We want to make our stand here. It would be better if you left and took your own building." Although the whites had expected all night that the break would eventually come, many were nevertheless shaken by what amounted to an order. They were even more upset when the blacks told them that there were guns in the building. Rumors had been circulating all night, but now it seemed that many blacks were prepared to make a violent stand. The prospect scared the white radicals who were becoming brazen about taking buildings but remained timid about actual violence. The blacks tried to ease the bitterness by telling the white leaders that, by leaving the building, they could act as a diversion when the police came and possibly start a second front. . . .

In an attempt to keep the demoralized group together, Rudd proposed further action. "The blacks have chosen to make *their* stand," he said; "we should—not in support, but in attack of our common enemy, the administration—go and find our own building to make a stand in."

The large center doors to Hamilton Hall were opened and the whites filed out, dazed, into the dawn. Behind them the blacks hurriedly piled desks, chairs, file cabinets and anything else that could be used to block the doors. By 6 A.M. the white exodus was over, the building barricaded and locked. . . .

Out of the confusion, a band of about two hundred students shuffled slowly across a deserted College Walk and, as if drawn by a compulsion to repeat an earlier part of their scenario, they marched to the southeast security entrance of Low Library.

Three or four students at the front of the contingent charged the security door, trying unsuccessfully to force it with their shoulders. One student spotted a board lying on a nearby bench. It was picked up and positioned in front of the large plate glass window of the door. Twice, on the verge of launching the plank through the window, the students hesitated and dropped it. On the third attempt they brought the thick board back slowly and then, in one even motion, smashed the pane. The tinkling of the glass was the only sound to crack the clammy quiet of a gray sunrise. The crowd shuddered—some because of the temperature, others because of the act. The protest had crossed another line. . . .

The students toyed with office equipment, sipped Kirk's sherry and puffed his White Owl "President" cigars. There was the President's huge mahogany desk, his sofa, his telephones, his private bathroom, his $450,000 Rembrandt "Portrait of a Dutch Admiral," his sculptured ebony lion statuette. Everything was there just as Grayson Kirk had left it. . . .

More students from the groups at the Sundial and Hamilton had entered Low, and a plan of action became necessary. The meeting of almost two hundred students was shifted from the hallway to the center of the rotunda, a place normally reserved for formal receptions and lectures by distinguished speakers. Rudd stood before the crowd and in the well-established SDS tradition, outlined the alternative actions available to the demonstrators. Suggestions to leave Low or barricade the entire building were summarily dismissed. A proposed sit-in in the rotunda was rejected for tactical reasons, after Rudd pointed out that the administration could simply lock the huge iron gates that surround the rotunda and leave them sitting there forever. At this point a runner brought news that the New York City police had arrived on campus, were stationed in the basement of Low and would probably be ordered to clear the building. Rudd suggested that the group return to Kirk's office and barricade the doors. The plan was accepted, and the students reëntered the suite, moved into both Kirk's and Truman's private offices and placed desks, chairs and file cabinets against the three doors that lead to the hallway. They filled wastepaper baskets with water from the President's sink to be used as protection against tear gas, and they waited.

Meanwhile, as the demonstrators inside Low were deciding whether to occupy his office, Vice President Truman arrived on campus. Wearing a trench coat, his hat pulled down over his forehead, Truman paced worriedly back and forth on College Walk. The vice president, who normally smokes a pipe, chain-smoked cigarettes as he walked. Several students attempted to speak to him, but he brushed by them. . . .

At 6:50 A.M. Truman called Kirk to brief him and to ask him to come to the campus. Though Truman had argued against bringing in the police on Tuesday afternoon, with the breaking and entering into Low he changed his mind. Over the phone Kirk and Truman now agreed that it was time for the police to clear out Low.

At 7:15 A.M. a delegate from the administration was sent up to the President's office with an offer. He spoke to Rudd through the broken pane in Kirk's door and told him that if the students walked out now and turned in their identification cards they would face only University discipline and no criminal trespass charges. Rudd rejected the proposal, explaining later that it would have been foolish to accept the deal when they knew they had another way out—through the windows. . . .

Meanwhile, Truman was having trouble with the police officials. Kirk had arrived on campus, and the two were trying to arrange for the arrest of any students who remained in the President's office. As firm as they were in their decision that police should be used to clear out Low, they were also set against using the police in Hamilton, for fear of large-scale violence. . . .

The police, however, balked at this selectivity, Truman reported later, telling him that it would be impossible for them to clear out one building and not the other.[4] It was to be all or nothing, and the dangers that could arise in Hamilton Hall convinced the administrators to do nothing. That the police were not brought in proved critical. Had they been used to clear Low, the demonstration probably would have been contained, and the administration would have had to deal only with the blacks in Hamilton. . . .

Surrounded by statues of Buddha and bodhisattvas in the Faculty Room of Low Library, Kirk told reporters:

> The University is committed to maintaining order on the campus. We insist that there be respect for the rules and conditions that make University life possible. We have exercised great restraint in the use of police and security forces, because at almost all costs, we wish to avoid physical confrontation. We have constantly tried to communicate with those students who have seized the buildings, and as late as this morning, contact was made with all of the protesting groups, but with no success. We are prepared to talk with the protesting groups, but disciplinary action will have to be taken

against those students who flagrantly violated University rules. The students have had ample opportunity to leave the buildings and to engage in *lawful* protest if they so desire.

"We cannot give in on amnesty," Truman said. "This goes far beyond this University." Asked about the gym Kirk replied, "Contract obliges us to continue construction."

Professor Westin was disturbed by the hard-line approach he heard. "It was a disconcerting press conference," he said later, "because the President and vice president took a very strong position—a 'We have no alternative but to turn to law and order' type of presentation." At the close of the conference Westin turned to Vice President Goodell and asked whether it would be possible for Truman to meet with a group of faculty in Philosophy Hall. Westin wanted Truman to discuss the administration's policy with them and, as Westin later phrased it, "to share with us why he felt there was no possibility of give on these issues, and why he seemed to be heading toward such a climax." Goodell said he would try to arrange the meeting, and Westin left Low to gather together as many professors as possible.

When Truman arrived in Philosophy more than one hundred faculty members were there to hear him. He recapitulated the development of the crisis, adding at the end in an unsteady voice, "I just don't know how much longer this situation can go on." He maintained that the gym was not a real issue and that the University could not afford to stop construction because it would cost six million dollars to break the contracts. Westin told the vice president that as a lawyer, he could not believe that the contracts could not be severed for less. Truman insisted that this would be impossible.

"Is there anything the faculty can do?" Professor Rothman asked.

"Nothing," Truman answered.

After twenty minutes Truman cut off discussion, saying he was already late for another meeting in Low and that the faculty would have to excuse him. He left the group, probably without realizing that he had greatly alienated many former colleagues, some of whom later said that he had appeared "uncommunicative," "uncompromising," and unable to meet the crisis. Robert Belknap, a professor of Russian who was present during Truman's appearance, later said:

It was what he didn't say that bothered us. He hadn't said that negotiations were proceeding. He hadn't drawn up a statement saying what could or could not be done. He hadn't appointed a faculty group to advise him. . . . He lost his cool."

By Friday some of the strikers' demands seemed well on their way to realization. But victories on matters such as gym construction were not the developments in which the strike leaders took most satisfaction. More significant was the change that had come over the life-style of the students who occupied the buildings. This transformation of the quality of life and the existential involvement of the individual were the ends toward which all of the SDS ideology pointed. The radicals saw the routinized patterns of society as repressive, manipulative and dehumanizing. The "respectable" lives of businessmen, bureaucrats and professionals to which many of them had once aspired were seen as drab, confining, cardboard existences. Now, insulated from the norms and forms of American culture by several feet of office furniture and barricades, the students inside the "liberated" buildings were able to create social patterns of their own. The takeover of the buildings had begun as a political tactic designed to bring about the goal of social reconstruction. It quickly evolved into the realization, on a small scale, of that very goal. The process of personal liberation was founded in a common existential credential—all the students in the buildings had placed their careers at Columbia in some jeopardy by joining the protest; a common tactic—confrontation; a common enemy—the administration; and a common set of immediate goals—the six demands. In addition, in the day-to-day conduct of the demonstrations each student could feel that he was in direct touch with the sources of power and decision-making within the strike apparatus. This was accomplished through participatory democracy, a central element of SDS ideology as has been noted. Students could, within the strike context, *make the decisions that affected their lives.*

Shortly before noon Saturday hopes for a peaceful mediation of the crisis suffered another setback. Members of the board of Trustees, normally distant from campus affairs, were slowly being drawn into the crisis. On Friday morning, William Petersen, president of the Irving Trust Company, who serves as chairman of the Colum-

bia Trustees, made his first major attempt to bring peace to the
Morningside campus. He phoned the Mayor of New York City.
Lindsay aide Barry Gottehrer later described the conversation:

> Petersen wanted the Mayor to come up to Columbia and settle
> the situation. Lindsay was willing, but asked what leverage he
> would be given in mediating. Petersen said they would give him no
> leverage. He just asked the Mayor to come onto campus and walk
> around, talking to people, as he does in Harlem. He expected a
> miracle.

Lindsay never came, but Petersen continued his search for a solution. Friday evening the Trustees were called together for an
informal meeting downtown to discuss what was happening to
their University.

Chairman Petersen took it upon himself to issue a public statement Saturday morning stating his interpretation of the opinions
expressed by the quorum of Trustees present. The Petersen
statement was read to the Ad Hoc Faculty Group late Saturday
morning:

> The Trustees and the University met and conferred yesterday
> (Friday) regarding the situation on the Morningside Heights cam-
> pus. They expressed approval of the course which had been fol-
> lowed by the University administration. . . . In common with the
> administration the Trustees deplore the complete disruption of
> normal University operations and the illegal seizure and occupation
> of University buildings, perpetrated by a *small minority of students,
> aided and abetted by outsiders* who have injected themselves into the
> situation. . . .
> The Trustees have advised the President that they wholeheart-
> edly support the administration position that there shall be no am-
> nesty accorded to those who have engaged in this illegal conduct.
> Moreover, they not only support the President's stand, but *affirma-
> tively direct, that he shall maintain the ultimate disciplinary power* over the
> conduct of students of the University as required by the Charter
> and Statutes of the University.
> Insofar as the gymnasium is concerned, the Trustees feel that
> the attempt to depict the construction of the building as a matter
> involving a racial issue or discrimination is an attempt to create an
> *entirely false issue* by individuals who are either not conversant with,
> or who disregard, the facts. However, the Trustees have approved

the action taken by the administration *at the request of the Mayor* of New York City, on Thursday, April 25, to halt construction activities *temporarily*. This action represented an appropriate response, and *a courtesy to the chief executive of the City* at a time of tension. . . .

The Petersen statement was received with hostility in nearly every quarter of the campus and was seen as written proof that the Trustees were as out of touch with University life as everyone had imagined. Herbert Deane said later that the Petersen statement "almost blew us out of the water." The administration had announced on Thursday night that gym construction had been suspended, a partial concession to one of the Six Demands. Now on Saturday, when the gym had all but dropped out of the picture, the Trustees proclaimed that the gym was "an entirely false issue" and that construction had only been halted temporarily as a courtesy to the Mayor. Before the Petersen statement the administration had seemed ready to modify its stand on discipline by delegating some authority to the tripartite commission proposed by the Galanter committee. Now the Trustees ordered the President to "maintain the ultimate disciplinary power." . . .

If Mark Rudd had drafted the statement for the Trustees instead of Petersen it could not have made the situation more critical or the University look worse. . . . To the demonstrators a statement like Petersen's was tactically welcome, for in clearly defining the "enemy" position it further polarized the campus. And when sides were chosen few opted to be on the same team as Petersen.

The paradox of negotiations was now clear: the students had been listening to offers they would never consider; the faculty had been promising them things the administration would refuse to accept; and the administration had been making concessions which the Trustees now rejected out of hand. . . .

Inside Low Library the administrators were settling into routinized crisis operations. Kirk and Truman had inched as far as they would go in modifying their position. Faculty members who spoke to the two men over the weekend later said that it was clear then that the administration had no more to offer, especially regarding amnesty. Whatever timid departures they had begun to make from their old stand had been frozen by the Petersen statement, and they now stood rigid and immobile at a point somewhere between partial concession and no concession at all.

In the occupied buildings a similar sort of diplomatic rigor mortis prevailed among the strike leaders and negotiators, if not among their constituents. The strikers had not won their six demands. They had offered and would offer no compromise on any of those demands, especially amnesty. Over the weekend it became clear that the crisis was quickly heading for one of only two possible ends—amnesty or bust.

Rumors had been circulating all Monday night that the police would arrive within hours. But the same rumors had circulated Sunday night and throughout the rest of the occupation, and few students paid much attention to them. For hours busloads of police had been unloading at five precinct centers in different parts of Manhattan. Because the Columbia operation would be on such a massive scale the men had been drawn from precincts in all boroughs of the city—Manhattan, Brooklyn, Queens, Staten Island and the Bronx. Shortly after midnight the police began gathering on the periphery of the campus. Word of the mobilization was carried on radio news broadcasts, as breathless students ran among the occupied buildings to report that at the 100th Street precinct house police buses and paddy wagons were lined up for blocks along the street.

Since the middle of the occupation the black students in Hamilton had communicated with hardly anyone, except through an occasional press release. Their secrecy had reinforced the growing image of militancy hinted at by their official statements and the conclusions of observers. With the expected police attack, most people on campus expected a small-scale Armageddon. Now, with tension higher than it had been at any other time since the crisis began, the occupants of Hamilton were addressing a rally of Harlem residents from windows overlooking Amsterdam Avenue.

More than 150 demonstrators were marching peacefully on the sidewalk carrying crudely lettered anti-Columbia placards and chanting, "Columbia goes from jerk to jerk—Eisenhower to racist Kirk." As white students joined the demonstration and the rally grew, a window opened on the fourth floor of Hamilton and Cicero Wilson leaned out over the street to deliver his first public address since April 23.

"I'd like to thank you brothers for coming out here tonight," Wilson said. "We're here to stop the gym and to get amnesty for the black students in Hamilton Hall." Teddy Kaptchuk ap-

proached a reporter standing near him in the crowd and nervously commented, "You know what he just said really doesn't
matter. They're still with us. It's just a tactical thing." But, despite
their protestations of unity, the white strike leaders had come to
realize that Hamilton was indeed a separate decision-making unit
whose actions in the next hours would be completely unpredict-
able. . . .

Near Low, professors and their teaching assistants pushed their
way through the dense crowd that continued to accumulate outside Kirk's offices. "Please don't stand here," they yelled, "it will
be very bad if you are standing here when the police come. Go
down to the Sundial where there is a rally taking place." Few
students moved—most wanted to see the action firsthand. One
young girl in tears, a teaching assistant in the English department,
began frantically tugging at the sleeves of people she recognized,
urging, "Please, go away from here. You will be badly hurt. Go to
the Sundial." . . .

All the occupied buildings were now being sealed off from the
inside. . . .

Tuesday, 2:10 A.M., April 30: a girl taking a drink of water in
Fayerweather noticed that the fountain trickled to a stop. The
water supply to the other occupied buildings was also shut off. At
Strike Central a student was speaking by phone with occupied
Low when the receiver went dead. Two minutes later the phones
in the *Spectator* office in Ferris Booth Hall were cut off. The bust
was beginning.

Mark Rudd left Strike Central with Lew Cole, Juan Gonzalez and
several other strike leaders. Almost running, he crossed the Sundial and headed for Low. As he arrived a student messenger
dashed to his side "They're—leaving—Hamilton—Mark," he
panted. Rudd sent another runner to Hamilton to get details.

The runner sent to Hamilton now returned. "The blacks are
letting themselves be taken out, Mark," the student said incredu-
lously. No shots rang out in the air over Hamilton. No angry
masses swarmed across Morningside Park from Harlem. . . .

In contrast with SDS the blacks had decided that there was
nothing to gain from a bloody arrest episode. . . .

A crowd of about 250 students and faculty was standing in

front of the security entrance to Low chanting, "No Violence!"
and "Cops Must Go!" They tried to sing Columbia's alma mater,
"Sans Souci," but after several false starts gave up because hardly
anybody remembered the words. The shouting changed to cries
of "STRIKE! STRIKE! STRIKE!" as a column of thirty-five Tactical
Patrol Force squared of directly in front of the crowd. . . .

While the captain talked Frederick Courtney, an instructor in
the Spanish department who was standing at the top of the steps,
remarked to students alongside him that he had left his motorcycle helmet and camera under a hedge by St. Paul's Chapel and
that he thought the helmet might be a good thing to have. He
stepped down and started walking across the grassy plot between
Low and the chapel. Suddenly six men leapt out of the hedges
and seized him. Courtney was knocked to the ground and, as the
demonstrators on the steps watched in amazement, he was
punched, kicked and blackjacked. The men were plainclothesmen; some were wearing dark slacks and blue nylon wind-
breakers, which resembled Columbia jackets, and had looked like
students in the dark. Courtney was dragged away, an officer holding each arm and leg.

As administration officials watched from a window above,
another column of TPF moved into position behind the first.

The TPF captain in charge announced to the crowd, "You are
obstructing police in the performance of their duty. Please move."
His order was met with more cries of "No Violence!" and "No
Cops!" A few athletes standing on a nearby ledge urged the police
to go in and smash the demonstrators, yelling Columbia's football
slogan, "Let's go, Lions!" Others yelled, "Beautiful!" and cheered
as they spotted more light blue police helmets. Again the captain
made his announcement: "You are blocking our progress here."
Again no one moved. The captain's jovial face hardened. Suddenly the police pulled out blackjacks and flashlights and charged,
ramming them into the nearest faces. Most students were merely
grabbed and thrown over the low hedges onto the brick pathways
out of the way of the police. Some were clubbed as they fell. The
front row of resisters was hurled back and to the sides and the
police now began plowing through the remaining five rows in a
similar manner, throwing people onto the grass or bricks. Dean
Platt, standing nearby to observe, was punched in the chest by a
badgeless plainclothesman. Screaming, the crowd split; some ran

north toward Avery and Fayerweather, others south to College Walk. "Is there a physician in the crowd?" someone yelled, helping a limping girl down the steps of Low Memorial Library, "we need a doctor." "Call Dr. Kirk!" an angry student shouted. The name was greeted with cries of "Butcher, Butcher!" One girl who had been in the security entrance rush now stood crying at the Sundial. "They knock you down but that's not enough, they don't let you up again. They just keep hitting. . . ." "They were pros," another student said, "those TPF guys don't even use clubs." Students returning from the confrontation reported, trembling, that girls were smashed against the stone walks when the police came in. "One guy, in uniform, grabbed me by the hair," said one student bleeding from a gash in his lips, "and said, okay, buddy, you're next. Then wham wham wham wham four times in the face." A Barnard girl who had been in the midst of the attack, nearly hysterical, kept screaming over and over, "Cops suck!" until she broke down into fits of sobbing. "This had to happen," quietly observed one student standing near her in the crowd, "it can't be a thinking process when you come to a stalemate." . . .

As each new crowd of prisoners was loaded into a van, the students lining the edge of College Walk cheered in support of the arrested strikers. Television lights blinked on, revealing about two hundred students, most of them from Math, many of them bleeding, holding their fingers aloft in the "V" symbol. The crowd, which included many students who until now had taken no sides in the demonstration responded by raising its hands in a "V" and chanting, "STRIKE! STRIKE!" and "KIRK MUST GO!" In the crowd of observers someone was listening to a professor on WKCR saying, "We had hoped for a breakthrough. . . ."

Melvin Morgulis, who had been filming the entire bust, went up to one of the police facing the College Walk crowd and earnestly began telling him that what was happening was a tragedy in American history. The policeman turned his back, but Melvin continued talking to him. The long-haired student went on, trying to communicate the misery he felt to another policeman on the line who just kept staring back at him with a blank, bored expression. Melvin began to break down. "Why won't you listen to me?" he cried, "Can't you see what you're doing to my buddies out there?" The rest of his words became unintelligible as he lapsed into tears, winding his movie camera convulsively.

As Melvin screamed at the policeman a tall student staggered toward the College Walk crowd from the area of the police vans. Blood dripped from his left eye and covered most of his face. He was controlled, but on the verge of delirium. "Anyone want to take a picture of me?" he asked calmly, dragging on a cigarette; "Are you going to stay in a University like this? Look what the men who run this University have done to me." Another student approached an officer standing on College Walk. He asked him whether he felt the slightest bit of guilt for what was going on behind him. "I'm a compartmentalized man," the lieutenant answered, smiling. "I do what I'm told, and I do it where I'm told."

As the arrested students were piled into police vans on College Walk, they began chanting and shouting furiously. Choruses of "We Shall Overcome" and "Up against the wall, motherfuckers!" resounded from the metallic innards of the paddy wagons. One group of prisoners began banging rhythmically on the inside of their van, and soon the occupants of each wagon took up the new protest.

The crowd of observers on the south side of College Walk had been chanting anti-cop slogans for some time when they noticed hundreds of police marching in drill formation and regrouping on Low Plaza. Through a series of right- and left-faces and advances the policemen, mostly TPF, maneuvered to within several yards of the crowd and ordered them to move back. The group retreated grudgingly and continued to taunt the police. A group of athletes stood on the Sundial chanting "TPF! TPF!" and shouting insults at the pro-demonstration students around them. A moment later, without warning, the line of uniformed officers and plainclothesmen charged into the crowd. The paddy wagons parked on College Walk swung around, their headlights spotlighting South Field and temporarily blinding the students staring up at the plaza. Flailing their clubs the police chased several hundred students onto the lawn, the glare of the bright lights at their backs as they charged. The athletes on the Sundial were overrun with the rest, their pro-police chants disregarded. The students who ran slowest in the stampede were struck with clubs, tripped or kicked. In the darker recesses of the field plainclothesmen stationed themselves near hedges and pummelled demonstrators who tried to run past them. The students who moved faster found, as they reached the south side of the campus, that all of the gates had been closed and locked. With the police sweeping across South Field, they had no place to go but inside the lobbies of the dormitories which were now filling up with the limping, the bruised and the frightened. One student running for Ferris Booth Hall was clubbed and kicked just outside the building. He lay bleeding near the door, jerking spasmodically, until he was carried away on a stretcher by volunteer medical aides.

For the next hour the police crisscrossed again and again over South Field and its environs, "clearing the campus" by chasing or clubbing the students they found. "It was the only way to disperse the crowd quickly," police spokesman Jacques Nevard explained later, "It is folly for people to stand around and watch when there is trouble. . . . Once you start using force, the chances of excessive force increase greatly."

As most police left Columbia with the coming of daylight a new armband appeared on campus. Students stood at the gates and on College Walk handing out strips of black crepe paper, signs of mourning for the death of a University. That morning *Spectator* carried a blank editorial surrounded by a black border. A new SDS flyer was hastily produced and distributed:

At 2:30 this morning, Columbia University died. . . . WE WILL AVENGE THE 139 WOUNDED MEMBERS OF THE LIBERATION. . . . DOWN WITH THE UNIVERSITY, UP WITH THE STUDENTS, UP WITH THE COM- MUNITY, LONG LIVE THE FORCES OF LIBERATION AT COLUMBIA. . . .

The black armbands were also a sign of outrage. Though the liberals had previously refused to identify themselves completely with the students in the buildings, they were now forced to take sides, and it was unlikely that they would move behind the forces of "legitimate violence." Most Columbia students and faculty had never come closer to mass violence than TV news broadcasts, and the new first-hand experience of police confrontation shook them—at least temporarily—out of middle-of-the-road politics. With many students and faculty members walking around campus wearing head bandages and slings as badges of brutalization, it was hard to remain placidly uncommitted.

The protest that had been born during the occupations grew enormously in scope and support as the newly activated liberals joined its ranks. The crisis developed into its next phase: a full-scale strike against the University. The same phenomenon had occurred at Berkeley in 1964, when a widespread student-faculty strike followed police clearance of a sit-in in Sproul Hall. Now at Columbia the pattern was being repeated. At 7:15 A.M. Mike Nichols, executive vice president of the Columbia University Student Council, stood on Low Plaza amid reporters and shouting students and announced that the student council would support a general strike against the administration. One year ago Nichols had appeared at a campus debate to condemn SDS and the New Left. Now he was joining forces with them against Kirk and Truman. Within hours hundreds of students joined the Strike Coördinating Committee in endorsing the strike.

The Counter–Culture

William L. O'Neill

To at least some young Americans, the difficulty of changing the "system" from within led to a determination to create an alternative way of life. Like the utopian reformers of the 1840s and the Greenwich Village Bohemians of the 1920s, these young people attempted to build a new society with different values, institutions, and priorities from the old. Characterized in the popular mind by communes, drugs, religious sects, free love, and long hair, the counterculture was perceived as an open defiance of traditional standards of respectability.

Although the pursuit of an alternative lifestyle was not a movement in any classical sense, it did represent a diffuse shedding of the images and symbols of middle-class identity. Social life consisted of getting stoned on a communal "joint," "being" was more important than "becoming," living now more valuable than the drive to get ahead. The difficulty was that drugs had the potential of destroying the mind, and that the spell of a religious "guru" frequently faded, leaving disillusionment and despair in its wake. In the following selection William O'Neill chronicles some of the manifestations of the counterculture, focusing on the contradictions, as well as the idealism, of those who participated in it.

No group contributed more to the counter-culture than the Beatles, though, like folk music and the twist, their future significance was not at first apparent. Beatlemania began on October 13, 1963, when the quartet played at the London Palladium. The police, caught unawares, were hardly able to control the maddened throngs. On February 9, 1964, they appeared on U.S. television. The show received fifty thousand ticket requests for a theater that seated eight hundred. They were mobbed at the airport, besieged in their hotel, and adored everywhere. Even their soiled bed linen found a market. Their next recording, "Can't Buy Me Love," sold three million copies in advance of release, a new world's record. Their first movie, *A Hard Day's Night* (1964), was both a critical and a popular success. Some reviewers compared them with the Marx brothers. They became millionaires overnight. The Queen decorated them for helping ease the balance-of-payments deficit. By 1966 they were so rich that they could afford to give up live performance. . . .

The Beatles did not fade away as they were supposed to. Beatlemania continued for three years. Then the group went through several transformations that narrowed its audience to a smaller but intensely loyal cult following in the Dylan manner. The group became more self-consciously artistic. Their first long-playing record took one day to make and cost £400. "Sergeant Pepper's Lonely Hearts Club Band" took four months and cost £25,000. They were among the first to take advantage of new recording techniques that enabled multiple sound tracks to be played simultaneously. The Beatles learned new instruments and idioms too. The result was a complex music that attracted serious inquiry. Critics debated their contributions to musicology and argued over whether they were pathfinders or merely gifted entrepreneurs. In either case, they had come a long way aesthetically from their humble beginnings. Their music had a great effect on the young, so did their styles of life. They led the march of fashion away from mod and into the hairy, mustached, bearded, beaded, fringed, and embroidered costumes of the late sixties. For a time they followed the Maharishi, an Indian guru of some note. They married and divorced in progressively more striking ways. Some were arrested for smoking marijuana. In this too they were faithful to their clientele. . . .

Beatlemania coincided with a more ominous development in the emerging counter-culture—the rise of the drug prophet Timothy

Leary. He and Richard Alpert were scientific researchers at Harvard University who studied the effects of hallucinogenic drugs, notably a compound called LSD. As early as 1960 it was known that the two were propagandists as well as scientists. In 1961 the University Health Service made them promise not to use undergraduates in their experiments. Their violation of this pledge was the technical ground for firing them. A better one was that they had founded a drug cult. Earlier studies of LSD had failed, they said, because the researchers had not themselves taken the drug. In order to end this "authoritarian" practice, they "turned on" themselves. Their work was conducted in quarters designed to look like a bohemian residence instead of a laboratory. This was defended as a reconstruction of the natural environment in which social "acid-dropping" took place. They and many of their subjects became habitual users, not only of LSD but of marijuana and other drugs. They constructed an ideology of sorts around this practice. After they were fired the *Harvard Review* published an aritcle of theirs praising the drug life: "Remember, man, a natural state is ecstatic wonder, ecstatic intuition, ecstatic accurate movement. Don't settle for less."

With some friends Leary and Alpert created the International Foundation for Internal Freedom (IF-IF) which published the *Psychedelic Review*. To advertise it a flyer was circulated that began, "Mescaline! Experimental Mysticism! Mushrooms! Ecstasy! LSD-25! Expansion of Consciousness! Phantastica! Transcendence! Hashish! Visionary Botany! Ololiuqui! Physiology of Religion! Internal Freedom! Morning Glory! Politics of the Nervous System!" Later the drug culture would generate a vast literature, but this was its essential message. The truth that made Western man free was only obtainable through hallucinogenic drugs. Truth was in the man, not the drug, yet the drug was necessary to uncover it. The natural state of man thus revealed was visionary, mystical, ecstatic. The heightened awareness stimulated by "consciousness-expanding" drugs brought undreamed-of sensual pleasures, according to Leary. Even better, drugs promoted peace, wisdom, and unity with the universe. . . .

At advanced universities social smoking of marijuana was as acceptable as social drinking. More so, in a way, for it was better suited to the new ethic. One did not clutch one's solitary glass but shared one's "joint" with others. "Grass" made one gentle and pacific, not surly and hostile. As a forbidden pleasure it was all the more attractive to the thrill-seeking and the rebellious. And it helped further distinguish between the old world of grasping, combative, alcoholic adults and the turned-on, cooperative culture of the young. . . .

To "turn on and drop out" did not weaken the state. Quite the contrary, it drained off potentially subversive energies. The need for drugs gave society a lever should it ever decide to manipulate rather than repress users. Pharmacology and nervous strain had already combined to make many adult Americans dependent on drugs like alcohol and tranquilizers. Now the young were doing the same thing, if for different reasons. In a free country this meant only that individual problems increased. But should democracy fail, drug abuse among both the young and old was an instrument for control such as no dictator ever enjoyed. The young drug-takers thought to show contempt for a grasping, unfeeling society. In doing so they opened the door to a worse one. They scorned their elders for drinking and pill-taking, yet to outsiders their habits seemed little different, though ethically more pretentious. In both cases users were vulnerable and ineffective to the extent of their addiction. Of such ironies was the counter-culture built.

Another sign of things to come was the rise and fall of Ken Kesey and his Merry Pranksters. . . . Kesey found work in a mental hospital, which was the subject of his first published novel, *One Flew over the Cuckoo's Nest*. It enjoyed a great success in 1962. He also figured in medical experiments conducted at the hospital. One of the drugs tested on him was LSD. Soon he was moving in psychedelic drug circles. In 1963, with the profits from his book, he bought a log house and some land near La Honda, about fifteen miles from Palo Alto.

Among the restless types who joined him was Neal Cassidy, a legendary figure who had been the model for Dean Moriarty in Jack Kerouac's famous beat-generation novel *On the Road*. The Merry Pranksters, as they became known, developed a unique life style. Sex played a part in it (a lean-to called the Screw Shack was added to the cabin for this purpose), but music and drugs more so. Everyone was also involved in The Movie—a continuing film record of their experiences. In the spring of 1964 the Pranksters bought a school bus, fitted it out with camping facilities, loaded the refrigerator with orange juice and acid, painted it in psyche-delic colors, wired it for sound, and set off for the World's Fair in New York. . . .

What really put Kesey at the center of the new culture, however, were the "acid tests." These were big public gatherings with light shows, rock music, mad dancing, and, of course, acid-dropping. "Can you pass the acid test?" was their motto. These were the first important multi-media happenings, combining light shows, tapes, live rock bands, movie and slide projectors, strobe lights, and other technical gimmicks. Their climax was reached at the San Francisco Tripps Festival in January 1966. It was meant to release all the new forms of expression in the cultural underground. Bill Graham, who had managed the San Francisco Mime Troupe, was its organizer. Kesey and the Pranksters gave the acid test. The Tripps Festival was a great success. Several rock groups (The Grateful Dead and Big Brother and the Holding Company) pro-claimed the emergence of a new musical genre—acid rock. Gra-ham began staging such affairs regularly in the Fillmore Audito-rium in San Francisco. Out of this came the "San Francisco Sound," which made the city a provincial capital in the music industry. Hippie culture, with its drugs, rock groups, psychedelic folk art, and other apparatus, was well and truly launched. . . .

Rock as an idiom was more concerned with social and sexual freedom than politics. The Rolling Stones' subversive appeal was more formalistic than not. The group's real power derived from its sexuality. Mick Jagger hopped about, whacking the stage with a leather belt. Jim Morrison of the Doors was arrested twice for indecent exposure. More articulate than most rock stars, Morrison described his group's function this way: "A Doors' concert is a public meeting called by us for a special kind of dramatic discus-sion and entertainment." And, further, "We make concerts sexual politics. The sex starts with me, then moves out to include the charmed circle of musicians on stage. The music we make goes out to the audience and interacts with them: they go home and interact with the rest of reality, then I get it all back by interacting with that reality, so the whole sex thing works out to be one big ball of fire." Their listeners took the message perfectly. Morrison was famous in the rock underground for supposedly being able to hold an erection through a two-hour performance. . . .

The counter-culture's influence on fashion was nearly as great as on rock. Fashions began to change radically even before the hippies and other such groups appeared. An early sign of this was Rudi Gernreich's topless bathing suit for women in 1964. Designed more in fun than avarice, this curious garment (knitted trunks suspended from a cord around the neck) actually sold. Only a few gallant models really bared their breasts in public, yet it was clearly an idea whose time had come. Discothèques (night clubs featuring recorded music) were starting up, and they inspired customers with writhing "go-go" girls who demonstrated the new dance routines. Some of these went topless, and before long, in California at least, others followed. The first thing one saw on leaving the Los Angeles airport was a sign reading "Topless Bowling." This did not mean that customers went half-nude but that cocktail waitresses did. Later bottomlessness was added, even in such unlikely places as Madison, Wisconsin. Although only performers went this far, as a rule, a new exposure prevailed. Rudi Gernreich raised his skirts three inches above the knee and introduced the no-bra bra, a wispy creation appropriate to the new designs.

In London things had already gone further. Skirts were so short that some were calling them "mini-skirts." Young designers like Mary Quant were making Carnaby Street synonymous with fashion. The "mod" look would soon reach New York. Bikinis were now seen on American beaches in sizable numbers. Less abbreviated than the European models, they still astonished people accustomed to the reinforced swimsuits of the fifties. Before long they would be standard among girls and young women. The most striking thing about these changes was that they came from below. Fashion had always been dictated from above, by Parisian couturiers and other authorities. It was a monopoly of the rich. But in the sixties it was the young, and relatively unknown designers like Quant and Gernreich who catered to them, who set the pace. Young people did the twist first, shortened their skirts first, and made being "kicky" and "switched on" desirable. More expensive versions of their styles were then designed for the modish rich. Not since the 1920's had women's clothing changed so radically. No one could remember when the flow of fashion had been reversed on such a scale. . . .

No doubt older people would have resented the new styles in any case, but the way they emerged made them doubly offensive. They were introduced by young bohemians, mainly in New York and San Francisco, whose deviant attributes were highly publicized. New York hippies were concentrated in a section called the East Village. . . .

The mainstream of East Village cultural life was more formally political and artistic. The many activities of Ed Sanders suggest the range of enterprises generated there. He was editor and publisher of *Fuck You: A Magazine of the Arts.* A typical editorial in it began: "Time is NOW for TOTAL ASSAULT ON THE MARIJUANA LAWS. It is CLEAR to us that the cockroach theory of grass smoking has to be abandoned. IN THE OPEN! ALL THOSE WHO SUCK UP THE BENEVOLENT NARCOTIC CANNABIS, TEENSHUN!! FORWARD, WITH MIND DIALS POINTED: ASSAULT! We have the facts! Cannabis is a nonaddictive gentle peace drug! The marijuana legislations were pushed through in the 1930's by the agents and goonsquads of the jansensisto-manichean fuckhaters' conspiracy. Certainly after 30 years of the blight, it is time to rise up for a bleep blop bleep assault on the social screen. . . . But we can't wait forever you grass cadets to pull the takeover: grass-freak senators, labor leaders, presidents, etc.! The Goon Squads are few and we are many. We must spray our message into the million lobed American brain IMMEDIATELY!"

As these few examples suggest, the East Village gained from its proximity to the New York avant garde. The mature counter-culture owed a lot to this relationship, but even in its early stages the East Village suffered from the influx of teenie-boppers and runaways who were to spoil both it and the Haight-Ashbury for serious cultural radicals. The people who were soon to be called hippies meant to build alternatives to the straight world. Against the hostile competitive, capitalistic values of bourgeois America they posed their own faith in nonviolence, love, and community. Drugs were important both as means to truth and advancers of the pleasure principle. The early hippies created institutions of sorts. Rock bands like the Jefferson Airplane, the Grateful Dead, Country Joe and the Fish flourished, as did communal societies, notably the Diggers. They were inspired by the seventeenth-century communists whose name they took. In practice they were a hip version of the Salvation Army.

Hippies lived together, in "tribes" or "families." Their golden rule was "Be nice to others, even when provoked, and they will be nice to you." In San Francisco their reservation was the Haight-Ashbury district near Golden Gate Park. They were much resented in the East Village by the natives, poor ethnics for the most part. In the Hashbury, on the other hand, they were welcome at first. Though peculiar, they were an improvement over the petty criminals they displaced. Even when freaked-out in public from drugs, a certain tolerance prevailed. After all, stepping over a drooling flower child on the street was better than getting mugged. Civic authorities were less open-minded. The drug traffic bothered them especially, and the Hashbury was loaded with "narks" (narcotics agents). Hunter S. Thompson wrote that "love is the password in the Haight-Ashbury, but paranoia is the style. Nobody wants to go to jail."

The fun-and-games era did not last long, perhaps only from 1965 to 1966. The hippie ethic was too fragile to withstand the combination of police surveillance and media exposure that soon afflicted it. The first hippies had a certain earnestness. But they were joined by masses of teen-age runaways. Nicholas von Hoffman observed that the Hashbury economy that began as a fraternal barter system quickly succumbed to the cash nexus. It became the first community in the world to revolve entirely around the buying and selling and taking of drugs. Marijuana and LSD were universal; less popular, but also commonplace, were LSD's more powerful relative STP, and amphetamines. "Speed kills" said the buttons and posters; speed freaks multiplied anyhow. To support themselves some hippies worked at casual labor or devised elaborate, usually unsuccessful schemes to make money out of hippie enterprises. Panhandling was popular, so was theft, disguised usually as communism. . . .

The publicity given the summer of love attracted nameless thousands of disturbed youngsters to the Hashbury and the East Village in 1967. San Francisco was not burdened with the vast numbers originally expected. But many did come, bringing in their train drug peddlers, and all sorts of criminals. Drug poisoning, hepititis (from infected needles), and various diseases resulting from malnutrition and exposure thinned their ranks. Rapes, muggings, and assaults became commonplace. Hippies had little money, but they were incredibly easy marks. Hippie girls were safe to assault. They reacted passively, and as many were drug users and runaways they could not go to the police.

So the violence mounted. On the West Coast one drug peddler was stabbed to death and his right forearm removed. Superspade's body was found hanging from a cliff top. He had been stabbed, shot, and trussed to a sleeping bag. On October 8 the nude bodies of Linda Rea Fitzgerald, eighteen, and James Leroy "Groovy" Hutchinson, twenty-one, were discovered in an East Village boiler room. They had been murdered while high on LSD. Though pregnant, Miss Fitzpatrick had also been raped: That was how the summer of love ended. . . .

While the attempt to build parallel cultures on a large scale in places like the Hashbury failed, the hippies survived in many locales. Isolated farms, especially in New England and the Southwest, were particularly favored. And they thrived also on the fringes of colleges and universities, where the line between avantgarde student and alienated dropout was hard to draw. In tribes, families, and communes the hippies lived on, despite considerable local harassment wherever they went.

Though few in number, hippies had a great effect on middleclass youth. Besides their sartorial influence, hippies made religion socially acceptable. Their interest in the supernatural was contagious. Some of the communes which sprang up in the late sixties were actually religious fellowships practicing a contemporary monasticism. One in western Massachusetts was called the Cathedral of the Spirit. Its forty members were led by a nineteen-year-old mystic who helped them prepare for the Second Coming and the new Aquarian Age when all men would be brothers. The Cathedral had rigid rules against alcohol, "sex without love," and, less typically, drugs. Members helped out neighboring farmers without pay, but the commune was essentially contemplative. Its sacred book was a fifty-seven-page typewritten manuscript composed by a middle-aged bus driver from Northfield, Massachusetts, which was thought to be divinely inspired. Another commune in Boston, called the Fort Hill Community, was more outward looking. Its sixty members hoped to spread their holy word through the mass media.

Some of the communes or brotherhoods sprang from tradi-

tional roots. In New York City a band of young Jews formed a
Havurah (fellowship) to blend Jewish traditions with contemporary inspirations. They wanted to study subjects like "the prophetic mind; new forms of spirituality in the contemporary world;
and readings from the Jewish mystical tradition." At the University of Massachusetts a hundred students celebrated Rosh Hasha-
nah not in a synagogue but in a field where they danced and sang
all night. Courses in religion multiplied. At Smith College the
number of students taking them grew from 692 in 1954 to nearly
1,400 in 1969, though the student body remained constant at
about 1,000. Columbia University had two hundred applicants for
a graduate program in religion with only twenty openings.

Students saw traditional religion as a point of departure rather
than a place for answers. Comparatively few joined the new fellowships, but large numbers were attracted to the concepts they
embodied. Oriental theologies and the like grew more attractive,
so did magic. At one Catholic university a coven of warlocks was
discovered. They were given psychiatric attention (thereby miss-
ing a great chance. If only they had been exorcised instead, the
Establishment would have shown its relevance). When a Canadian
university gave the studentry a chance to recommend new courses
they overwhelmingly asked for subjects like Zen, sorcery, and
witchcraft. A work of classic Oriental magic, *I Ching* or the *Book of
Changes*, became popular. The best edition, a scholarly product of
the Princeton University Press, used to sell a thousand copies a
year. In 1968 fifty thousand copies were snapped up. . . .

The most surprising man to protest this new turn was Paul
Goodman. Goodman's life and work were more nearly of a piece
than most people's. He was a secular anarchist, but while hoping
to wreck the old order, he believed that the old tools—reason,
expertise, science—would still be needed. Hence, though he was
one of the chief intellectual mentors of the counter-culture, its
growing spiritualism, indeed anti-intellectualism, disturbed him.

Late in 1969 he wrote that this first became clear to him while
giving a graduate seminar on "professionalism." He hoped to
teach the difference between careerism and fidelity to a professional calling. To his astonishment the class rejected the notion
that there was such a thing as a true profession. All decisions were
made by the power structure. Professionals were merely peer
groups formed to delude the public and make money. "Didn't

every society, however just, require experts?" he asked. No, they insisted; it was only important to be human, and all else would follow.

> Suddenly I realized that they did not really believe that there was a nature of things. Somehow all functions could be reduced to interpersonal relations and power. There was no knowledge, but only the sociology of knowledge. They had so well learned that physical and sociological research is subsidized and conducted for the benefit of the ruling class that they did not believe there was such a thing as the simple truth. To be required to learn something was a trap by which the young were put down and co-opted. Then I knew that I could not get through to them. I had imagined that the world-wide student protest had to do with changing political and moral institutions, to which I was sympathetic, but I now saw that we had to do with a religious crisis of the magnitude of the Reformation in the fifteen hundreds, when not only all institutions but all learning had been corrupted by the Whore of Babylon.

The young knew nothing of society's institutions, how they worked, where they came from, what had made them what they were. For many, history began in 1968. "I am often hectored to my face," Goodman said, "with formulations that I myself put in their mouths, that have become part of the oral tradition two years old, author prehistoric." They didn't trust people over thirty because they didn't understand them and were too conceited to try. "Having grown up in a world too meaningless to learn any-thing, they know very little and are quick to resent it." The most important thing to the young was being together, en masse if possible. At the rock festivals they found the meaning of life which, as they explained it, consisted of people being nice to each other. A group of them passing a stick of marijuana behaved like "a Quaker meeting waiting for the spirit." And, Goodman con-cluded, "in the end it is religion that constitutes the strength of this generation, and not, as I used to think, their morality, politi-cal will, and common sense." Neither moral courage nor honesty was their salient trait, but rather "metaphysical vitality." . . .

The greatest event in counter-cultural history was the Wood-stock Festival in Bethel, New York. It was organized on the pat-tern of other large rock festivals. Big-name groups were invited for several days of continuous entertaining in the open. A large crowd was expected, but nothing like the 300,000 or 400,000 youngsters who actually showed up on August 15, 1969. Everything fell apart in consequence. Tickets could not be collected nor services provided. There wasn't enough food or water. The roads were blocked with abandoned autos, and no one could get in or out for hours at a time. Surprisingly, there were no riots or disasters. The promoters chartered a fleet of helicopters to evacuate casualties (mostly from bad drug trips) and bring in essential supplies. Despite the rain and congestion, a good time was had by all (except the boy killed when a tractor accidentally drove over his sleeping bag). No one had ever seen so large and ruly a gathering before. People stripped down, smoked pot, and turned on with nary a discouraging word, so legend has it. Afterward the young generally agreed that it was a beautiful experience proving their superior morality. People were nicer to each other than ever before. Even the police were impressed by the public's order (a result of their wisely deciding not to enforce the drug laws).

But the counter-culture had its bad moments in 1969 also. Haight-Ashbury continued to decay. It was now mainly a slum where criminals preyed on helpless drug freaks. Worse still was the Battle of Berkeley, which put both the straight culture and the counter-culture in the worst possible light, especially the former. The University of California owned a number of vacant lots south of the campus. The land had been cleared in anticipation of buildings it was unable to construct. One block lay vacant for so long that the street people—hippies, students, dropouts and others—transformed it into a People's Park. Pressure was brought on the University by the local power structure to block its use, which was done. On May 15 some six thousand students and street people held a rally on campus, then advanced on the park. County sheriffs, highway patrolmen, and the Berkeley police met them with a hail of gunfire. One person died of buckshot wounds, another was blinded. Many more were shot though few arrested. Those who were arrested were handled so brutally that the circuit court enjoined the sheriff to have his men stop beating and abusing them. Disorders continued. Governor Reagan declared a state of emergency and brought in the National Guard. Five days later one of its helicopters sprayed gas over the campus, thus making the educational process at Berkeley even more trying than usual. . . .

The rock festival at Altamont that winter was another disaster. It was a free concert that climaxed the Rolling Stones' whirlwind tour of the U.S. They called it their gift to the fans. Actually it was a clever promotion. The Stones had been impressed with the moneymaking potential of Woodstock. While Woodstock cost the promoters a fortune, they stood to recoup their losses with a film of the event. This inspired the Stones to do a Woodstock themselves. At the last minute they secured the use of Dick Carter's Altamont Raceway. It had been doing poorly and the owner thought the publicity would help business. Little was done to prepare the site. The police didn't have enough notice to bring in reserves, so the Stones hired a band of Hell's Angels as security guards (for $500 worth of beer). The Stones did their thing and the Angels did theirs. . . .

The violence was quite bad enough, but what especially bothered *Rolling Stone* was the commercial cynicism behind it. That huge gathering was assembled by the Stones to make a lucrative film on the cheap. They could have hired legitimate security guards, but it cost less to use the Angels. (At Woodstock unarmed civilians trained by the Hog Farm commune kept order.) They were too rushed for the careful planning that went into Woodstock, too callous (and greedy) to pour in the emergency resources that had saved the day there. And, appropriately, they faked the moviemaking too so as to have a documentary of the event they intended, not the one they got. *Rolling Stone* said that a cameraman was recording a fat, naked girl freaking out backstage when the director stopped him. "Don't shoot that. That's ugly. We only want beautiful things." The cameraman made the obvious response. "How can you possibly say that? Everything here is so ugly."

Though much in the counter-culture was attractive and valuable, it was dangerous in three ways. First, self-indulgence led frequently to self-destruction. Second, the counter-culture increased social hostility. The generation gap was one example, but the class gap another. Working-class youngsters resented the counter-culture. They accepted adult values for the most part. They had to work whether they liked it or not. Beating up the long-haired and voting for George Wallace were only two ways they expressed these feelings. The counter-culture was geographical too. It flourished in cities and on campuses. Elsewhere, in Middle America especially, it was hated and feared. The result was a national division between the counter-culture and those adults who admired or tolerated it—upper-middle-class professionals and intellectuals in the Northeast particularly—and the silent majority of workers and Middle Americans who didn't. The tensions between these groups made solving social and political problems all the more difficult, and were, indeed, part of the problem. . . .

The counter-cultural ethic remained as beguiling as ever in theory. In practice, like most utopian dreams, human nature tended to defeat it. At the decade's end, young believers looked forward to the Age of Aquarius. Sensible men knew there would be no Aquarian age.

Joe Kelly Has Reached His Boiling Point

Richard Rogin

Inevitably, the social protests of the 1960s provoked a counter-response. By the end of the decade a group, dubbed by the media as "middle-Americans," had rallied to the defense of the flag, traditional authority, and good manners. One definition of "middle-Americans" was primarily economic. Earning between $5,000 and $15,000 a year, they made up 55 percent of the population. The majority were blue-collar workers, lower-echelon bureaucrats, school teachers, and white-collar employees. As they saw the federal government pour money into impoverished areas, they developed a sense of neglect and resentment, believing that they were being ignored while vocal protestors received all the attention. Just as important, however, was a sense of crisis in cultural values, a belief that the rules were being changed in midstream. As Newsweek's Karl Fleming observed, middle Americans felt "threatened by a terrifying array of enemies: hippies, Black Panthers, drugs, the sexually liberated, those who questioned the sanctity of marriage and the morality of work." Anti-war protests galvanized these "middle Americans" into action. From their perspective, it was blasphemy to wear the American flag on the seat of one's pants, burn one's draft card, or shout obscenities at authorities. In the following selection, Richard Rogin provides a first-hand account of how millions of Americans reacted to demonstrators who challenged their most deeply cherished values. In the process, he illuminates just how profound the polarization of the 1960s was.

"When you were still up on Broadway you could hear the ruckus, the hollering. The peace demonstrators trying to outshout the construction workers. The construction workers hollering, 'U.S.A., all the way' and 'We're Number One.' And the peace demonstrators screaming up there that the war was unjust and everything else, right by the Treasury Building on Broad Street there.

"There was just a lot of hollering and screaming going back and forth until whoever the individual was—oh, he was no spring chicken, he was forty, forty-five years old—that spit on the flag. I was maybe four or five rows back in with the construction workers. I saw him make a gesture, you know, a forward motion. That was it. That was the spark that ignited the flame. It came out in the roar of the crowd. 'He spit on the flag! He spit on the flag!' And of course the construction worker got up there on top of the monument and he gave him a good whack and off came the guy's glasses and I guess he followed his glasses off the pedestal there.

"And then there just seemed to be a rush, a mob scene. The chant then was, 'Get the flags up on the steps where they belong. It's a government building.' And they can say what they want about the New York Police Department, they coulda had the National Guard there with fixed bayonets and they would not have held the construction workers back then.

"When we first went up on the steps and the flags went up there, the whole group started singing 'God Bless America' and it damn near put a lump in your throat. It was really something. I could never say I was sorry I was there. You just had a very proud feeling. If I live to be a hundred, I don't think I'll ever see anything quite like that again."

Joe Kelly's big chin and right hand tremble as he is caught in the deep, remembered passions of that noontime on Friday, May 8. He is thirty-one years old, a brawny 6 feet 4 inches, 210 pounds, blue eyes and receding red hair under his yellow plastic construction helmet decorated with U.S. flag decals and "FOR GOD AND COUNTRY."

It is now late afternoon, nearly two weeks later, and we are sitting in a gray wooden construction shanty on the sprawling World Trade Center site in lower Manhattan where he works. Joe is a well-liked, skillful mechanic in an intricate and demanding trade, elevator construction—installing the elevators and the heavy complex machinery to make the cars run.

On that violent day, soon after he came down for his half-hour lunch break from the forty-second floor of the soaring red steel skeleton of Tower A—another high, seemingly timeless, world which will rise 110 stories overlooking New York and the indus-trial hinterlands of New Jersey, where men walk almost casually on springy planks laid over open steel now seventy flights up—Joe Kelly reached his "boiling point." He found he could not "sit back" any longer, and he became a demonstrator for the first time in his life. Though "not much of a shouter," and a strong believer that violence solves nothing, he also shouted and threw his first punch in more than ten years.

During that long menacing midday several hundred construc-tion workers, accused by reporters of using metal tools as weap-ons, were joined by office workers on a rampage through lower Manhattan. They beat up and injured seventy antiwar protesters and bystanders, including four policemen. With cries of "Kill the Commie bastards," "Lindsay's a Red," and "Love it or leave it," they surged up to City Hall. There they forced the flag, which had been lowered to half-staff in mourning for the four dead Kent State students, to be raised again. Then, provoked by peace banners, they stormed through Pace College across the street. It was a day that left New York shaken.

His face taut with fury, Mayor John V. Lindsay went on televi-sion to call the workers' attacks "tough and organized" though the unions promptly denied any influence. But he lashed out even more strongly at the outnumbered police whom many witnesses had accused of inadequate preparations and of standing by toler-antly during the assaults on the peaceful rally. Only six arrests were reported. He charged the police with failing as "the barrier between [the public] and wanton violence."

Others called the workers bullies or Nazi brownshirts. "We have no control over what they want to call us," says Joe Kelly. "But I think that the large majority of people, going as high as 85 to 90 percent, are more than happy. Not so much for the violence but for the stand that we took. And now they're standing up. the construction worker is only an image that's being used. The hard-hat is being used to represent all of the silent majority."

It was the wild start of two weeks of almost daily noon-hour, flag-waving, bellicose, damn-Lindsay (the most common signs called him a Communist or a faggot) and praise-Nixon counter-

marches through downtown New York, which Joe Kelly enthusi-
astically joined. Some of his fellow workers even happily lost an
hour's pay for marching too long after lunch. Despite the fact that
many of the men returned late following Friday's slugfest, none
were docked. "I was going to dock one man who came back an
hour and a half late," says Frank Pike, general elevator construction foreman, "but he said, 'I saw these kids spit on the flag. What
could I do?' How could I dock the man?"

The union word had come down: "Demonstrate all you want
but be careful, no violence." Others say that the union tried to
stop the men from all informal demonstrations. In any event,
there was no more major violence; thousands of helmeted police
patrolled the streets.

The construction workers loaded their unfinished skyscrapers
with huge U.S. flags and their hardhats became a national symbol
of fervent support for the Nixon Administration and its Indochina war policy. President Nixon was even presented with a
hardhat at a White House ceremony. The climax came on May 20
when an estimated one hundred thousand construction workers
and longshoremen sang and chanted from City Hall to Battery
Park in a massive display of jingoistic sentiment probably unparal-
leled during the uncertain years of the Vietnam conflict.

That day Joe Kelly was given the honor of carrying the gold-
fringed American flag with the gold eagle, its wings outspread,
on the top of the pole, leading a contingent of hundreds of his
fellow workers from Local No. 1, International Union of Elevator Constructors. With his yellow helmet on, he marched, resolutely serious-faced, rarely showing a thin smile, ignoring the
pretty secretaries leaning over the police barriers. He displayed
the training he received when he was an M.P. with an Army
honor guard stationed in Heidelberg, West Germany. Around
him Broadway boomed with the chants: "We're Number One,"
"U.S.A., all the way," "Good-by Lindsay, we hate to see you go."
The marchers sang "God Bless America" and "You're a Grand
Old Flag." "Yankee Doodle" and "Over There" blared forth.
The workers cheered and whistled through the applause from
spectators and the shower of ticker tape and computer cards
from high office windows.

They marched to the green lawns of Battery Park, with the
breeze coming off the upper bay cooling a hot blue day. Joe

Kelly's friends came up to him and shook his hand, saying: "Beautiful." "Like a champ, Joe." Joe clenched and unclenched the fingers of his right hand, which had held the flagpole for two hours. "I feel fine," he said. "This is terrific. It'll wake a few people up. This will happen not only down here but in the rest of New York and across the country now." The first thing to happen, though, was that Frank Pike docked himself and all the elevator constructors an hour's pay for parading instead of working. A few men never made it back to the job that afternoon.

Within the next few weeks in belligerent defense of Nixon's Southeast Asia policies, nearly twenty thousand construction workers paraded (and pummeled antiwar spectators) in St. Louis, and several hundred workers scuffled with students holding a peace rally at Arizona State University in Tempe.

Joe Kelly is proud, confident, and outspoken in the old American style. He is almost mystically proud of his flag, his country, the Establishment, and eager to end the Indochina war by striking more aggressively, though the deaths of young soldiers and innocent civilians sadden him. He is determined to be on guard against Communism and to crush it wherever it threatens his nation. Joe is convinced that a subversive conspiracy of teachers, influenced by foreign powers, is brainwashing the students to Communist beliefs. Distressed by the hippie lifestyle of so many youths, he is also furious at student radicals who burn and shut down schools which his taxes pay for and which most of his fellow workers cherish because they never had a chance to go to them. He is a stalwart charter member of Richard Nixon's silent majority, a devout Roman Catholic and fiercely loyal to his President, whose office he regards with almost holy respect.

"The Pope to the Catholic Church is the same as the President to the American people," he says. "He's the one who decides. He's infallible when he speaks of religion as far as the Catholic Church goes. I'm not saying Nixon is infallible. But he's Commander in Chief of the Armed Forces. He's in charge."

Vietnam: "I just hope that these people give Nixon the play to go in there in Cambodia and knock the living hell out of their supply lines. If this is what it takes to stop the loss of American lives, well, let's go the hell in there and get it over with."

My Lai massacre: "I don't believe anybody in the United States, nice and cozy, has a right to judge them [the accused] until every-thing comes out in the trial."

Kent State: "They [the National Guardsmen] must have felt their lives were threatened; that's why they shot."

Inflation: "I have faith in Nixon. I think he'll curb inflation, given the chance."

High taxes: "If this is what it takes to run this country, I don't mind paying them. You couldn't live anyplace else like you do here."

The flag: "I think of all the people that died for that flag. And somebody's gonna spit on it, it's like spitting on their grave. So they better not spit on it in front of me. You think you could get it better someplace else—well, then, don't hang around, go there."

Unemployment: "I don't know where they're getting these fig-ures from [up to a five-year high for all jobs and 11.9 percent in construction] because here in New York you got a [construction] boom going on."

Joe Kelly has what used to be faithfully accepted as the old-fashioned, authentic American credentials: he is hard-working, conscientious, obedient and trusting in authority, an adherent of law and order, patriotic, sentimental, gentle and affectionate with his loved ones, angry and determined to right wrongs as he sees them, moderately compassionate, a believer in the virtues of his way of life.

To the antiwar protesters and others grieving and critical over America's present course in Indochina and what they perceive as unfeeling repressive policies at home, he probably appears as an anachronism. To them, he is Joe Kelly, yesterday's comic-book hero, a relic from the somehow simpler, self-righteous days of the old world wars when, with a grin and a wave and a song, Americans marched off to solve the world's problems. "The Jack Armstrong of Tower A," one of his fellow workers called him approvingly.

Joe Kelly and millions of Americans like him would not share the gloomy conclusion of John W. Gardner, a Republican and chairman of the National Urban Coalition, that the country is disintegrating. They see a country in momentary disarray, under stress, but they retain a sturdy optimism. They know but do not suffer the dark fear that a complex and subtle civil war is wasting the land with hate and with overt and invisible violence: white against black, conservatives against liberals, workers against students, old against young, fathers against sons. Even the old hawks of organized labor now face opposition within their own ranks over the Indochina war.

America heaves against the old grain. The kids are on the loose trying to shake off the crusty habits of the country the way a snake sheds its skin. The antis feel depressed by their own Government, if not worse, and sense mendacity everywhere.

The kids, Joe Kelly thinks, ought to feel lucky to be in America where they have the legitimate right to dissent and stage peaceful demonstrations. If they did the equivalent of burning draft cards or desecrating the flag in Russia or China, they would, he says, be shot down in the street.

"These kids," he says, "they can do as they feel like. I mean burn, loot, steal, do anything they feel like in the name of social reform. But can the average Joe Blow citizen go out and do this?" A crime is a crime, he says, even if it's for social reform, and he argues that there is a double standard of justice for students, especially in New York.

What about the kids' mockery of the Puritan ethic? "If they don't want to educate themselves or go out and work hard for a living and make a few dollars, spend a few dollars, and save a few dollars for a rainy day, that's their prerogative. But in general, again, this has been bred into them somewhere. This is not the American way."

Joe Kelly never thought the picture presented by his hardworking life would need any defense. There is his pretty blonde wife, Karen; two strawberry-blonde daughters, Robin Lynn, four, and Kerry Ann, one and a half, and now a newborn son, James Patrick. "I had two cheerleaders," he says, "now I got a ballplayer." There is also a collie named Missy and a newly bought brick-and-shingle, two-story, $40,000 house on an irregular 50 by 100 foot lot, tastefully furnished, with a modern kitchen ("All you can get for two arms"), and a freshly sodded lawn on one of those breezy Staten Island streets with the gulls overhead, children pedaling red tricycles, the hum of an electric mower, and a man hosing down a gleaming red Dodge Challenger, all the residents of the neighborhood blue-collar whites, doing well.

Joe Kelly and his neighbors, the steamfitter, the bus driver, the policeman, the TV color processor, have worked too hard to get to that street to give it all up. They have had too many peace protests,

too many moratoriums, too many harsh laments and shouted obscenities against their country, too many rock-throwings and strikes
and fires on campuses where they want their children to make it,
too many bombings and too many Vietcong flags waving down the
streets of their city, too many long-haired youths and naked boys
and girls, too many drugs, too much un-Americanism, not to feel
angry and resentful.

Joe Kelly sits on his plastic-covered orange couch in front of his
new Motorola Quasar color TV console and seethes as he watches
the six o'clock news day after day. What really galls him, he says,
is what he considers small groups of radical students closing down
schools. "In California," he says, "they burned a bank to the
ground. You just watch and boil. Who do these university presidents, responsible people, think they have an obligation to? The
students are burning something every day. They're taking over
something in the chancellor's office every day."

And then that Friday morning, Joe Kelly mounted his tur-
quoise Triumph 500-cc. motorcycle, rode down to the ferry slip,
read *The Daily News* and had a coffee as the ferry crossed to
Manhattan, then rode his motorcycle again to his job. When he
walked into the shanty on the building site, he heard that a shov-
ing incident the previous day between peace demonstrators and
construction workers elsewhere in the downtown area had trig-
gered the men from a number of skyscrapers to action. For the
workers, "it was the straw that broke the camel's back," he recalls.
Spontaneously, Joe says, perhaps a quarter of the World Trade
Center's 212 elevator constructors decided to go down the seven
blocks and "see what this peace demonstration was all about."

"My partner, Tommy, he climbed up on top of the light stanchion
down on Wall Street and planted the flag up there, right in front of
the Treasury Building, to a great round of applause. The flags
were up on the top steps. The construction workers and the Wall
Street workers, they had the steps of the Treasury Building filled
and the demonstrators were now down in the street.

"And they started to chant in unison '—, no, we won't go,' and
they just kept it up. And all of a sudden, just the same as the
movement had started up onto the steps, the movement started
back down off the steps. This chant that they kept up, it just raised
the anger to a degree that it just seemed that everybody would just
want to get down there and disperse them. When I say, 'disperse,' I

don't mean physically take these kids and manhandle them, but just to break them up, break up the group and break up this chant because it just seemed so un-American.

"I guess the average construction worker is what you would call a flag-waver. You can call me a flag-waver any day of the week. I think that's something to be proud of, to be a flag-waver, to be proud of your country. And these kids just kept it up and kept it up.

"As the movement started down off the steps, again there was a certain amount of them [protesters] that wanted to stand their ground, and they're dealing with men that work with iron and steel every day of the week and do manual labor every day of the week, and they just made a mistake. They just never heard about that discretion business. I will say this: there was as many of these anti-war demonstrators whacked by Wall Street and Broadway office workers as there were by construction workers. The feeling seemed to be that the white-collar-and-tie-man, he was actually getting in there and taking as much play on this thing as the construction worker was.

"This was something. Listen. I'm thirty-one years old. I'd never witnessed anything like this is my life before, and it kinda caught me in awe that you had to stop and see what was going on around you. It was almost unbelievable. This was the financial district of New York City, probably the financial district of the world, and here was this mass clash of opposite factions, right on Wall Street and Broad, and you could hardly move, there were so many people talking part in this aside from the five hundred construction workers. It was just something that you had to stand back and blink your eyes and actually look a second and third time, and you couldn't believe that this was actually taking place in that particular area.

"There was one kid came after me, I don't know why. He just came flying out of the crowd. I don't claim to be a violent person. I couldn't possibly remember the last time I ever struck anybody. It had to be at least ten years ago, maybe twelve years ago. And for some reason this guy picked out somebody and it just happened to be me. He came running at me with arms flailing and I gave him a whack and back he went. He went down, I know that, and I just figured he wouldn't be back for more."

. . . Joe attends noon Mass on Sundays and he also coaches basket-ball and baseball teams in a boy's league in Blessed Sacrament

parish. (After the Army, he spent three years as a weekend coun-
selor at an orphanage on Staten Island.) His reading consists of
The Daily News, the *Advance,* the sports section of *The New York Post*
and *Popular Mechanics* magazine. The Kellys go out to the movies
perhaps every six weeks and may stop in afterward for "a couple
of drinks in a nice, quiet, respectable place." Once a week his wife
leaves him at home when she goes to play bingo. There is usually
a Christmas party for the men on the job, and Otis [Elevator Co.]
throws a picnic in the summer. Recently, the elevator constructors
and their wives had a $20-a-couple dinner dance at the Com-
muter's Cafe on Cortlandt Street, across from the Trade Center
site. . . .

On television, Joe enjoys Johnny Cash and Jackie Gleason and
sometimes Dean Martin. He likes to be in bed by 11 P.M. Before
he was married, Joe played basketball four nights a week in a
community-center league. With family responsibilities, his heavy
work schedule, and his relative slowness of foot today, he has cut
it out completely. "I go down once in a while to watch and eat my
heart out," he says.

Joe gets his extravocational workouts now around the house,
putting in sod, helping to grade the backyard for a large aboveground plastic swimming pool for the children, planting two blue
spruces and yews and rhododendrons in the front.

The Kellys haven't been able to take any vacations, though Joe
has had two weeks off yearly and will get three weeks under the
new contract starting this summer (there was either a strike, or
they were saving for the house, or the children were too small).
Perhaps twice a summer they drive down to the New Jersey shore
around Belmar in their 1967 English Ford station wagon and go
swimming.

Why does he work so hard? "A lot of people ask me that," he
says. "I wanted the house. Right? I wanted something nice for the
wife and the kids, someplace where the kids could grow up and
have their own backyard. They wouldn't have to be running out
in the street. And now I have the house and I want it fixed up
nice. And maybe when it is fixed up nice, I'll relax a bit." Meanwhile, he is at the "boiling point."

"My belief is, physical violence doesn't solve a damn thing. One
party has to sway the other party to his belief and then the argu-

ment is settled. I honestly don't believe that there will be any more physical violence in New York City. I think that one Friday and it's over with. I don't like to see anybody get bounced. I saw some of those kids go down and I didn't think they were gonna get up. I certainly don't agree with them. I would much rather prefer grabbing them by the head of the hair and taking a scissors and cutting their hair off, something that was much less violent but you still would have gotten your message across.

"Up at City Hall it became obvious that they had better get that flag back up to the top of the mast. Within a few minutes the flag went back up and everybody seemed nice and happy and again they started singing, 'God Bless America' and the national anthem and again it made you feel good. Not that I like seeing those four kids out in wherever it was, Kent, get killed. I don't like to see anybody get beat up, never mind lose their life.

"I don't think Mayor Lindsay has the right to put that flag at half-staff. That flag represents this country, so the leading representative of the country, who is President Nixon to me, is the only one that has the power or the right to raise or lower a flag."

Joe Kelly says he never even asked what his father's politics were, believing it to be a man's private affair. How did he arrive as a militant member of the no-longer-silent majority? What brought him to believe that Communism was undermining America from within?

"Two people stand out in my mind," Joe says, "why I'm taking part. Joe McCarthy often said, beware of this school system; they're going to infiltrate, brainwash the kids. And Khrushchev in 1960 banging on the UN table. He said they wouldn't have to take over this country physically, they'd do it from within." Though he was only a youngster during McCarthy's heyday, Kelly says: "It's something I've read somewhere along the line." He feels that the students are only dupes in the hands of subversive teachers who, Joe hints, are under the control of foreign powers. In some way, the bad teachers have to be weeded out, he says.

Joe Kelly first voted in 1960, when he chose John F. Kennedy over Nixon for President because he was impressed with Kennedy's performance in the TV debates. Though he still reveres President Kennedy, he wouldn't vote that way again. By 1964 he had swung to the right and voted for Goldwater over Johnson. In the 1965 and 1969 New York mayoral races, he voted the Conservative party line for William F. Buckley, Jr., and John Marchi. He cast his ballot for Nixon for President in 1968.

It was the Goldwater campaign that crystallized Joe's feeling about the war in Vietnam. "I think that it all goes back again, like history repeating itself, to Hitler," he says. "When Hitler kept marching into these countries and, instead of just fighting Hitler's country, you were fighting all these countries after a while. You just can't let Communism take over everything around you because when they got everything around you, they're gonna come after you."

Three men who command his admiration now are John Wayne, Vice-President Agnew, and Chicago Mayor Richard Daley. In fact, Joe wishes New York could borrow Daley for six months to give the city a stiff dose of law and order. He has complete disdain for Mayor Lindsay. He believes Lindsay has turned New York into "welfare city" and is trying to be the champion of welfare recipients and the young antiwar generation in a bid for the Presidency. "Do what you want in Lindsay's city—" he says caustically, "burn the schools. He's got to raise the budget this year to pay for what they burned down."

Of the recent influx of minority workers into his once closely bound union, he says: "They're here to stay, entitled to. But if they're going to work with us, if we go up on the iron and risk our lives walking it, by God, they have to go along with us. There've been several instances in the city where they've refused because they didn't have to."

As for a black family living on his street, he is adamantly against it, feeling that panic-selling would drive down the value of his property. "I had to bust my backside for five years to get that down payment for that house," he says. "I am not interested in seeing all that go down the drain."

It is on this precious ground—his home and his family—that he takes a defiant, mildly worried stand. He would like his daughters to go to college or nursing school and his son to get as much schooling as possible, to become a doctor or a lawyer—"something where he can use his head to make a living, not his back like his old man does."

While his wife hopes and prays that her daughters will never wear their hair straight and long like the hippies and that her children's minds will be protected in parochial schools despite the danger of lay teachers, Joe Kelly tells a story about a neighbor's friend's son, a boy of sixteen.

"This boy," he says, "came home from school one day and told his father he was a bum, that he was part of the Establishment. And this fellow was a World War II veteran, decorated several times and wounded twice. And he just turned around and he gave the kid a good whack and I guess he broke his jaw or broke his nose and the father was in a turmoil. This is his own flesh and blood talking to him.

"I cannot imagine having my kids come home and tell me I'm a bum because I believe in the Establishment—and there is nobody that believes in the Establishment more than I do. The more I see of this stuff, the closer I try to become to my kids. I believe that my way is correct, the Establishment way, law and order first, and this is what I'm gonna do my damndest to breed into them so that they don't get some other off-the-wall ideas."

Joe says that if his children ever called him a bum because he believes in the flag, they'd better leave his house. "I would do everything to control myself not to hit them. I mean, this is what I brought into the world. But it's awful hard. I certainly can see that man flying off the handle and whacking the kid. Oh, yeah, he certainly did regret it. But his big question is, Where did his kid get this trend of thinking?"

Joe Kelly doesn't believe that melees such as the memorable one at noon on May 8 are any solution. So his answer, he says reflectively, is to arm himself with education, engage in dialogue.

"When they throw a point at you," he says, "be able to talk to them on their theories on socialism, Communism. This is the best way—to talk them out of the stuff instead of just saying it's un-American or using your fists."

Ironically, Mayor Lindsay has said much the same thing: "Perhaps their [the construction workers'] demonstrations, in the end, will help us break through to a new dialogue in which we not only talk, but listen."

Part Eight

POLITICS OF THE 1970s AND 1980s

The 1970s represented the end of an era. Throughout the thirty years after World War II American politics had functioned on the premise that nothing was impossible if America wished to achieve it. We would be guardians of freedom, send a man to the moon, conquer social injustice, eliminate poverty, develop impressive technology—in short, control the universe. That sense of confidence and of power had been a hallmark of all political factions in the country, even young radicals who thought that by their own endeavors they could change the world. In the 1970s, however, a new sense of limits struck home. The United States had suffered its first loss in war. Richard Nixon became the first president forced to resign in disgrace, in large part because he himself had no sense of limits as to how far he could abuse presidential power. The oil producing countries of OPEC quickly made Americans conscious of their dependence on the rest of the world during the oil boycott of 1973–74, and the sporadic shortages thereafter. When Iranian revolutionaries held American diplomats hostage for more than a year, the sense of being subject to powers beyond one's control became a reality reinforced by every newscast. The American tendency toward what the Greeks call *hubris*—the arrogant confidence that one can do anything—had come face to face with the realities of human frailty, mortality, and interdependency.

If tragedy is the working out of a fatal flaw that eventually destroys one's hopes, the Nixon administration represents perhaps the purest example of American political tragedy. Nixon's own political life covered the entire span of the postwar period. First elected to Congress in 1946, he came to power through his active participation in the anti-communist campaign of the postwar era, and particularly his inquisition of Alger Hiss. As Vice-President under Dwight Eisenhower, Nixon led the attack on liberals, accusing Democratic presidential-nominee Adlai Stevenson of being soft on communism. It seemed to many that Nixon's career was over after he lost the presidential election to John Kennedy in 1960 and then two years later was defeated for the governorship of California. But Nixon's most fundamental characteristic was his tenacity. One of a series of "new" Nixons emerged in the middle 1960s, and in 1968, a supposedly more mature, relaxed, and flexible Nixon offered himself to the American people with a plan to end the war in Vietnam, and to "bring us together again."

Nixon's presidency was a series of contradictions. On the one hand, he scored major triumphs in foreign policy. As only an inveterate anti-communist could do, Nixon opened the door to China, reversing three decades of anti-Chinese policy in a period of weeks. Nixon also pressed hard for a relaxation of tensions with the Soviet Union, seeking to build a world order where Europe, China, the Soviet Union, and the United States could operate in a relative balance of power. He made major strides toward stability in the Middle East, using Presidential Advisor and Secretary of State Henry Kissinger to promote exchanges between Arab countries and Israel that might provide a basis for lasting peace in that area.

But these major achievements in foreign policy were dwarfed by the excesses of Nixon's abuse of power domestically, and his almost inherent refusal to speak candidly of his goals. He promised to end the war in Vietnam, then expanded the war by the massive secret bombing of Cambodia. He pledged to speak the truth at all times and to run an open administration, then lied repeatedly to the American people and placed wiretaps on reporters and administration officials. The underlying problem was one of duplicity and pettiness. In order to disguise the illegal bombing of Cambodia, orders were given that military reports should be falsified. When former Pentagon official Daniel Ellsberg released the Pentagon Papers, an internal study of how the Vietnam war had come about, Nixon sought to discredit Ellsberg by having a secret unit of investigators—called the "plumbers"—break into Ellsberg's psychiatrist's office to get harmful information about him. Angry at anti-war demonstrators and those

Democrats who supported them, the President encouraged a series of efforts, official and unofficial, to dig up information that would injure his opponents. The operation came to a head during the 1972 re-election campaign, when CREEP, the Committee to Re-elect the President, sponsored break-ins and wiretaps as well as false letters and rumors to subvert the Democratic opposition. When some of CREEP'S "plumbers," attempting to break in at the Democratic National Headquarters at the Watergate building, were caught, the entire web began to unravel.

The story of Watergate, like the story of Vietnam, embodies the ultimate destruction that occurs when tactics and weapons are used that go too far and stretch limits of tolerance beyond their capacity. Americans did not want to believe that My Lai had occured, that their president had lied about the bombing of Cambodia, or that the White House had been involved in the kind of "dirty tricks" that subverted basic American freedoms and violated the law of the land. But as newspaper and congressional investigations eventually demonstrated, there was no end to the Nixon administration's abuse of trust. America's basic faith in her political system was called into question. The country had been betrayed.

Jimmy Carter spoke directly to that sense of betrayal when in 1976 he told the American people that they deserved a government as good as they were, one based upon faith, honesty, integrity, dignity, and respect for traditional American values. Gerald Ford, Nixon's vice president, had done a superb job of healing the immediate wounds left by Watergate, but Carter offered an almost religious salve designed to reverse the damage. Running on the platform of an outsider who would bring a fresh perspective to Washington, Carter seemed to represent the simplicity and decency that would restore the faith of Americans in their political process.

The problem was that Carter knew very little about getting along in Washington. Arrogant and insensitive toward Congress, self-righteous about his own positions, he entered into a permanent deadlock with the major institutions of the society. Although he accomplished some positive goals in foreign policy, particularly with the Camp David accords in the Middle East, he was never able to deliver on his pledge of turning the government around. While he diagnosed and articulated the crisis of confidence that existed in the American political process in the post-Nixon years, he brought little in the way of constructive solutions to that crisis. The intractable problems of energy and Iran accurately symbolized the sense of powerlessness that he conveyed.

The election of Ronald Reagan represented still another effort to recover what had been lost, this time by going back to a rhetoric and program that reminded the United States of its former power and moral leadership. Reagan possessed the genius to make people believe in simple verities. America should be strong. Communism represented a false God. Free enterprise worked. And every individual should be responsible for himself. With remarkable skill, the new President pushed through legislation to cut taxes, eliminate social welfare benefits, increase military expenditures, and restore conservative values. In some ways, it seemed that the country had emerged from the malaise of the 1970s.

Yet, Reagan had been elected by less than 27 percent of those Americans eligible to vote. Almost half of the electorate had failed to go to the polls, dramatizing the alienation and sense of distance that millions felt toward the political process. Many of those same people who had not voted became the primary victims of Reagan's social policies, as food stamps were cut, housing subsidies reduced, and basic levels of social support eliminated. Even as Reagan talked about restoring America's greatness, larger and larger segments of the population seemed to have no stake whatsoever in the government that ruled them.

The following selections chronicle this story of America in the 1970s and 1980s. Johnathan Schell explores the intricacies of Watergate, giving us some flavor of the bizarre quality of the Nixon White House. Alan Baron and William E. Leuchtenburg analyze the election of 1980, pointing out what has and has not changed within the American political process, and who is—or is not—voting for the new politics. Jimmy Carter's 1978 energy speech poignantly presents his ability to articulate the "malaise of the American spirit" even as it reveals his inability to come forward with effective answers.

Some of the questions that remain are whether it is possible for a democracy to function for long when half of its people fail to vote (as opposed to voting rates of over 80 percent in most western European democracies); how successful the American political system was in dealing with the poison of Watergate; and whether it is good or bad to accept a sense of limits on America's national power. Such questions are crucial not only for understanding the 1970s and 1980s, but also for assessing what policies are appropriate for the 1990s, and the 21st Century.

Watergate

Jonathan Schell

If the decade of the 1960s is remembered for the war in Vietnam and civil rights, the decade of the 1970s will inevitably be associated with Watergate. Through a bizarre series of events, the Nixon administration found itself in a situation where, in order to cover up high-level involvement in a burglary, it created a set of circumstances that brought down the entire administration. The ironies of the situation were endless. Nixon had such a commanding lead over his opponents that virtually no one could challenge him, yet in order to gain a still greater edge, he, or his associates, authorized a break-in at Democratic national headquarters. Even with the evidence turned up by journalists and congressional hearings, Nixon would probably have remained in office, yet the taping system he himself had installed in order to preserve history tripped him up. Perhaps appropriately, the man who sought office in order to "bring us together again" ended up accomplishing his purpose by uniting the country in revulsion against his unconstitutional actions. Jonathan Schell presents here a vivid portrait of how and why the Watergate episode occurred, revealing in the process the dangers inherent in what Arthur Schlesinger, Jr., has called "the imperial presidency."

At some point back at the beginning of the Vietnam war, long before Richard Nixon became President, American history had split into two streams. One flowed aboveground, the other underground. At first, the underground stream was only a trickle of

Excerpted from Jonathan Schell, *A Time of Illusion* (New York: Alfred A. Knopf, 1975). Reprinted by permission of Random House.

events. But during the nineteen sixties—the period mainly described in the Pentagon Papers—the trickle grew to a torrent, and
a significant part of the record of foreign affairs disappeared
from public view. In the Nixon years, the torrent flowing underground began to include events in the domestic sphere, and soon
a large part of the domestic record, too, had plunged out of sight.
By 1972, an elaborate preelection strategy—the Administration
strategy of dividing the Democrats—was unfolding in deep secrecy. And this strategy of dividing the Democrats governed not
only a program of secret sabotage and espionage but the formation of Administration policy on the most important issues facing
the nation. Indeed, hidden strategies for consolidating Presidential authority had been governing expanding areas of Administration policy since 1969, when it first occurred to the President to
frame policy not to solve what one aide called "real problems" but
to satisfy the needs of public relations. As more and more events
occurred out of sight, the aboveground, public record of the period became impoverished and misleading. It became a carefully
smoothed surface beneath which many of the most significant
events of the period were being concealed. In fact, the split between the Administration's real actions and policies was largely
responsible for the new form of government that had arisen in
the Nixon White House—a form in which images consistently
took precedence over substance, and affairs of state were ruled by
what the occupants of the White House called scenarios. The
methods of secrecy and the techniques of public relations were
necessary to one another, for the people, lacking access to the
truth, had to be told something, and it was the public-relations
experts who decided what that something would be.

When the President made his trip to Russia, some students of
government who had been worried about the crisis of the American Constitutional system allowed themselves to hope that the
relaxation of tensions in the international sphere would spread to
the domestic sphere. Since the tensions at home had grown out of
events in the international sphere in the first place, it seemed
reasonable to assume that an improvement in the mood abroad
would give some relief in the United States, too. These hopes
were soon disappointed. In fact, the President's drive to expand
his authority at home was accelerated; although the nation didn't
know it, this was the period in which White House operatives

advanced from crimes whose purpose was the discovery of national-security leaks to crimes against the domestic political opposition. The Presidential Offensive had not been called off; it had merely been routed underground. The President spoke incessantly of peace, and had arranged for his public-relations men to portray him as a man of peace, but there was to be no peace— not in Indo-China, and not with a constantly growing list of people he saw as his domestic "enemies." Detente, far from relaxing tensions at home, was seen in the White House as one more justification for its campaign to crush the opposition and seize absolute power.

On Sunday, June 18, 1972, readers of the front page of the *Times* learned, among other things, that heavy American air strikes were continuing over North Vietnam, that the chairman of President Nixon's Council of Economic Advisers, Herbert Stein, had attacked the economic proposals of Senator George McGovern, who in less than a month was to become the Presidential nominee of the Democratic Party, and that the musical "Fiddler on the Roof" had just had its three-thousand-two-hundred-and-twenty-fifth performance on Broadway. Readers of page 30 learned, in a story not listed in the "News Summary and Index," that five men had been arrested in the headquarters of the Democratic National Committee, in the Watergate office building, with burglary tools, cameras, and equipment for electronic surveillance in their possession. In rooms that the men had rented, under aliases, in the adjacent Watergate Hotel, thirty-two hundred-dollar bills were found, along with a notebook containing the notation "E. Hunt" (for E. Howard Hunt, as it turned out) and, next to that, the notation "W. H." (for the White House). The men were members of the Gemstone team, a White House undercover group, which had been attempting to install bugging devices in the telephones of Democrats.

Most of the high command of the Nixon Administration and the Nixon reelection committee were out of town when the arrests were made. The President and his chief of staff, H. R. Halderman, were on the President's estate in Key Biscayne, Florida. The President's counsel, John Dean, was in Manila, giving a lecture on drug abuse. John Mitchell, the former Attorney General, who was then director of the Committee for the Re-Election of the President, and Jeb Magruder, a former White House aide, who had become the committee's assistant director, were in California. In the hours and days immediately following the arrests, there was a flurry of activity at the headquarters of the committee, in a Washington office building; in California; and at the White House. Magruder called his assistant in Washington and had him remove certain papers—what later came to be publicly known as Gemstone materials—from his files. Gordon Liddy, by then the chief counsel of the Finance Committee to Re-Elect the President, went into the headquarters himself, removed from his files other materials having to do with the break-in, including other hundred-dollar bills, and shredded them. At the White House, Gordon Strachan, an aide to Haldeman, shredded a number of papers having to do with the setting up of the reelection committee's undercover operation, of which the break-in at the headquarters of the Democratic National Committee was an important part. Liddy, having destroyed all the evidence in his possession, offered up another piece of potential evidence for destruction: himself. He informed Dean that if the White House wished to have him assassinated he would stand at a given street corner at an appointed time to make things easy. E. Howard Hunt went to his office in the Executive Office Building, took from a safe ten thousand dollars in cash he had there for emergencies, and used it to hire an attorney for the burglars. In the days following, Hunt's name was expunged from the White House telephone directory. On orders from John Ehrlichman, the President's chief domestic-affairs adviser, his safe was opened and his papers were removed. At one point, Dean— also said to have been acting under instructions from Ehrlichman—gave an order for Hunt to leave the country, but then the order was rescinded. Hunt's payment to an attorney for the burglars was the first of many. The President's personal attorney, Herbert Kalmbach, was instructed by Dean and, later, by Ehrlichman, Haldeman, and Mitchell to keep on making payments, and he, in turn, delegated the task to Anthony Ulasewicz, a retired New York City policeman who had been hired to conduct covert political investigations for the White House. Theirs was a hastily improvised operation. Kalmbach and Ulasewicz spoke to each other from phone booths. (Phone booths apparently had a strong attraction for Ulasewicz. He attached a change-maker to his belt to be sure to have enough coins for his calls, and he chose to make several of his "drops" of the payoff money in them.) He and

Kalmbach used aliases and code language in their conversations. Kalmbach became Mr. Novak and Ulasewicz became Mr. Rivers— names that seem to have been chosen for no specific reason. Hunt, who had some forty mystery stories published, was referred to as "the writer," and Haldeman, who wore a crewcut, as "the brush." The payoff money became "the laundry," because when Ulasewicz arrived at Kalmbach's hotel room to pick up the first installment he put it in a laundry bag. The burglars were "the players," and the payoff scheme was "the script." Apparently, the reason the White House conspirators spoke to one another from phone booths was that they thought the Democrats might be wire-tapping them, just as they had wiretapped the Democrats. In late June, the President himself said to Haldeman, of the Democrats, "When they start bugging us, which they have, our little boys will not know how to handle it. I hope they will, though." Considerations like these led Kalmbach, Ulasewicz, and others working for the White House to spend many unnecessary hours in phone booths that summer.

All these actions were of the sort that any powerful group of conspirators might take upon the arrest of some of their number. Soon, however, the White House was taking actions that were possible only because the conspirators occupied high positions in the government, including the highest position of all—the Presidency. For almost four years, the President had been "reorganizing" the executive branch of the government with a view to getting the Cabinet departments and the agencies under his personal control, and now he undertook to use several of these agencies to cover up crimes committed by his subordinates. In the early stages of the coverup, his efforts were directed toward removing a single evidentiary link: the fact that the Watergate burglars had been paid with funds from his campaign committee. There was a vast amount of other information that needed to be concealed—information concerning not just the Watergate break-in but the whole four-year record of the improper and illegal activities of the White House undercover operators, which stretched from mid-1969, when the warrantless wiretaps were placed, to the months in 1972 when the secret program for dividing the Democrats was being carried out—but if this one fact could somehow be suppressed, then the chain of evidence would be broken, and the rest of it might go undetected. On June 23rd, the President met with

Haldeman and ordered him to have the C.I.A. request that the F.B.I. halt its investigation into the origin of the Watergate burglars' funds, on the pretext that C.I.A. secrets might come to light if the investigation went forward. The problem, Haldeman told the President, was that "the F.B.I. is not under control, because Gray doesn't exactly know how to control it." Patrick Gray was Acting Director of the F.B.I. "The way to handle this now," he went on, "is for us to have Walters call Pat Gray and just say, 'Stay to hell out of this.' " The reference was to Vernon Walters, Deputy Director of the C.I.A. A moment later, Haldeman asked the President, concerning the F.B.I., "And you seem to think the thing to do is get them to stop?" "Right, fine," the President answered. But he wanted Haldeman to issue the instructions. "I'm not going to get that involved," he said. About two hours later, Haldeman and Ehrlichman met with C.I.A. Director Richard Helms and Deputy Director Walters, and issued the order.

The maneuver gave the White House only a temporary advantage. Six days later, on June 29th, Gray did cancel interviews with two people who could shed light on the origin of the burglars' funds. (On the twenty-eighth, Ehrlichman and Dean had handed him all the materials taken from Hunt's safe, and Dean had told him that they were never to "see the light of day." Gray had taken them home, and later he burned them.) But soon a small rebellion broke out among officials of the F.B.I. and the C.I.A. Meetings were held, and at one point Gray and Walters told each other they would rather resign than submit to the White House pressure and compromise their agencies. Several weeks after the request was made, the F.B.I. held the interviews after all. The rebellion in the ranks of the federal bureaucracy was not the first to break out against the Nixon White House. As early as 1969, some members of the Justice Department had fought Administration attempts to thwart the civil-rights laws. In 1970, members of the State Department and members of the Office of Education, in the Department of Health, Education, and Welfare, had protested the invasion of Cambodia. In 1970, too, J. Edgar Hoover had refused to go along with a White House scheme devised by a young lawyer named Tom Huston for illegal intelligence-gathering. The executive bureaucracy was one source of the President's great power, but it was also acting as a check on his power. In some ways, it served this function more effectively than the checks provided by the

Constitution, for, unlike the other institutions of government, it at least had some idea of what was going on. But ultimately it was no replacement for the Constitutional checks. A President who hired and fired enough people could in time bring the bureaucracy to heel. And although a Gray, a Walters, or a Helms might offer some resistance to becoming deeply involved in White House crimes, they would do nothing to expose the crimes. Moreover, the bureaucracy had no public voice, and was therefore powerless to sway public opinion. Politicians of all persuasions could—and did—heap abuse on "faceless," "briefcase-toting" bureaucrats and their "red tape," and the bureaucracy had no way to reply to this abuse. It had only its silent rebellions, waged with the passive weapons of obfuscation, concealment, and general foot-dragging. Decisive opposition, if there was to be any, had to come from without.

With respect to the prosecutorial arm of the Justice Department, the White House had aims that were less ambitious than its aims with respect to the F.B.I. and the C.I.A., but it was more successful in achieving them. Here, on the whole, the White House men wished merely to keep abreast of developments in the grand-jury room of the U.S. District Court, where officials of the Committee for the Re-Election of the President were testifying on Watergate, and this they accomplished through the obliging cooperation of Henry Petersen, the chief of the Criminal Division, who reported regularly to John Dean and later to the President himself. Dean subsequently described the cooperation to the President by saying, "Petersen is a soldier. He played—he kept me informed. He told me when we had problems, where we had problems, and the like. Uh, he believes in, in, in you. He believes in this Administration. This Administration had made him." What happened in the grand-jury room was further controlled by the coordinating of perjured testimony from White House aides and men working for the campaign committee. As for the prosecutors, a sort of dim-wittedness—a failure to draw obvious conclusions, a failure to follow up leads, a seeming willingness to construe the Watergate case narrowly—appeared to be enough to keep them from running afoul of the White House.

While all these moves were being made, the public was treated to a steady stream of categorical denials that the White House or the President's campaign committee had had anything to do with the break-in or with efforts to cover up the origins of the crime. The day after the break-in, Mitchell, in California, described James McCord, one of the burglars, as "the proprietor of a private security agency who was employed by our Committee months ago to assist with the installation of our security system." Actually, McCord was the committee's chief of security at the moment when he was arrested. Mitchell added, "We want to emphasize that this man and the other people involved were not operating either in our behalf or with our consent. . . . There is no place in our campaign or in the electoral process for this type of activity, and we will not permit nor condone it." On June 19th, two days after the break-in, Ronald Ziegler, the President's press secretary, contemptuously dismissed press reports of White House involvement. "I'm not going to comment from the White House on a third-rate burglary attempt," he said. On June 20th, when Lawrence O'Brien, the chairman of the Democratic Party, revealed that the Party had brought a one-million-dollar civil-damages suit against the Committee for the Re-Election of the President and the five burglary suspects, charging invasion of privacy and violation of the civil rights of the Democrats, Mitchell stated that the action represented "another example of sheer demagoguery on the part of Mr. O'Brien." Mitchell said, "I reiterate that this committee did not authorize and does not condone the alleged actions of the five men apprehended there."

Among the nation's major newspapers, only one, the Washington *Post,* consistently gave the Watergate story prominent headlines on the front page. Most papers, when they dealt with the story at all, tended to treat it as something of a joke. All in all, the tone of the coverage was not unlike the coverage of the Clifford Irving affair the previous winter, and the volume of the coverage was, if anything, less. "Caper" was the word that most of the press settled upon to describe the incident. A week after the break-in, for instance, the *Times* headlined its Watergate story "WATERGATE CAPER." When another week had passed, and Howard Hunt's connection with the break-in had been made known, *Time* stated that the story was "fast stretching into the most provocative caper of 1972, an extraordinary bit of bungling of great potential advantage to the Democrats and damage to the Republicans in this election year." In early August, the *Times* was still running headlines like "THE PLOT THICKENS IN WATERGATE WHODUNIT" over accounts of the repercussions of the burglary. "Above all, the purpose of the break-in seemed obscure," the *Times* said. "But these details are never explained until the last chapter." The President held a news conference six weeks after the break-in, and by then the story was of such small interest to newsmen that not one question was asked concerning it.

Disavowals such as those made by Mitchell and Ziegler carried great weight in the absence of incontrovertible evidence refuting them. The public had grown accustomed to deception and evasion in high places, but not yet to repeated, consistent, barefaced lying at all levels. The very boldness of the lies raised the cost of contradicting them, for to do so would be to call high officials outright liars. Another effective White House technique was to induce semi-informed or wholly uninformed spokesmen to deny charges. One of these spokemen was Clark MacGregor, a former member of Congress from Minnesota, who became reelection-campaign director early in July, when John Mitchell resigned, pleading family difficulties. A few weeks later, when Senator McGovern described the break-ins as "the kind of thing you expect under a person like Hitler," MacGregor called McGovern's remark "character assassination." The practice of using as spokesmen officials who were more or less innocent of the facts was one more refinement of the technique of dissociating "what we say" from "what we do." In this manner, honest men could be made to lend the weight of their integrity to untruths. They spoke words without knowing whether the words were true or false. Such spokesmen lent their vocal cords to the campaign but left their brains behind, and confused the public with words spoken by nobody.

On September 15th, the five men who had been caught in the Democratic National Committee headquarters were indicted—together with E. Howard Hunt and G. Gordon Liddy, who were elsewhere in the Watergate complex at the time of the break-in—for the felonies of burglary, conspiracy, and wiretapping. A few days later, the seven defendants pleaded not guilty. As the case stood at that moment, their crimes were officially motiveless. The prosecutors had not been able to suggest who might have asked employees of the Committee for the Re-Election of the President to wiretap the Democratic headquarters, or why a check belonging to that committee should have found its way into the bank

account of Bernard Barker. That afternoon, the President met
with Haldeman and Dean, and congratulated Dean on his work.
"Well," he said, "the whole thing is a can of worms. . . . But the,
but the way you, you've handled it, it seems to me, has been very
skillful, because you—putting your fingers in the dikes every time
that leaks have sprung here and sprung there." Representative
Wright Patman, the chairman of the House Banking and Currency Committee, was planning to hold hearings on the Watergate break-in, and the President, Dean, and Haldeman went on to
discuss ways of "turning that off," as Dean put it. Dean reported
to the two others that he was studying the possibility of blackmail-
ing members of the Patman committee with damaging information about their own campaigns, and then the President suggested
that Gerald Ford, the minority leader of the House, would be the
man to pressure Patman into dropping the hearings. Ford should
be told that "he's got to get at this and screw this thing up while
he can," the President said. Two and a half weeks later, a majority
of the members of the committee voted to deny Patman the
power to subpoena witnesses. But Patman made the gesture of
carrying on anyway for a while, and asked questions of an empty
chair.

At the end of September—more than a month before the election—the Washington *Post* reported that John Mitchell had had
control of a secret fund for spying on the Democrats. Throughout
October, denials continued to pour out from the Administration.
As before, some were outright lies by men who knew the facts,
and others were untruths spoken by men who were simply repeating what they had been told. On October 2nd, Acting Director
Gray of the F.B.I. said that it was unreasonable to believe that the
President had deceived the nation about Watergate. "Even if some
of us [in federal law enforcement agencies] are crooked, there
aren't that many that are. I don't believe everyone is a Sir Gala-
had, but there's not been one single bit of pressure put on me or
any of my special agents." In reality, of course, Gray had once
considered resigning because the pressure from the White House
to help with the coverup had been so intense, and even as he
spoke he was keeping the contents of E. Howard Hunt's safe in a
drawer of a dresser at his home in Connecticut. Gray went on to
say, "It strains the credulity that the President of the United
States—if he had a mind to—could have done a con job on the

whole American people." Gray added, "He would have to control the United States."

In the months since the election, the issue of Watergate had faded, and the papers had devoted their front pages to other news. Shortly after the trial began, however, the front-page news was that all the defendants but two had pleaded guilty. In the courtroom, Judge John Sirica, who presided, found himself dissatisfied with the questioning of witnesses by the government prosecutors. The prosecutors now had a suggestion as to the burglars' motive. They suggested that it might be blackmail. They did not say of whom or over what. At the trial, the key prosecution witness, the former F.B.I. agent Alfred Baldwin, related that on one occasion he had taken the logs of the Watergate wiretaps to the headquarters of the Committee for the Re-Election of the President. But this suggested nothing to the Justice Department, one of whose spokesmen had maintained when the indictment was handed up in September that there was "no evidence" showing that anyone except the defendants was involved. Sirica demurred. "I want to know where the money comes from," he said to the defendant Bernard Barker. "There were hundred-dollar bills floating around like coupons." When Barker replied that he had simply received the money in the mail in a blank envelope and had no idea who might have sent it, Sirica commented, "I'm sorry, but I don't believe you." When the defense lawyers protested Sirica's questioning, he said, "I don't think we should sit up here like nincompoops. The function of a trial is to search for the truth."

All the Watergate defendants but one were following the White House scenario to the letter. The exception was James McCord. He was seething with scenarios of his own. He hoped to have the charges against him dismissed, and, besides, he had been angered by what he understood as a suggestion from one of his lawyers that the blame for the Watergate break-in be assigned to the C.I.A., his old outfit, to which he retained an intense loyalty. There was some irony in the fact that McCord's anger had been aroused by an Administration plan to involve the C.I.A. in its crimes. McCord believed that Nixon's removal of C.I.A. director Richard Helms, in December of 1972—at the very time that McCord himself was being urged to lay the blame for Watergate at the door of the C.I.A.—was designed to pave the way for an

attempt by the Administration itself to blame the break-in on the
agency and for a takeover of the agency by the White House. He
had worked for the White House, but he did not see the reorgani-
zational wars from the White House point of view. He saw them
from the bureaucrats' point of view; in his opinion, President
Nixon was attempting to take over the C.I.A. in a manner reminiscent of attempts by Hitler to take control of German intelligence
agencies before the Second World War. The White House, that is,
belatedly discovered that it had a disgruntled "holdover" on its
hands. And this particular holdover really was prepared to perform sabotage; he was prepared, indeed, to sabotage not just the
President's policies but the President himself, and, what was more,
he had the means to do it. McCord was putting together a scenario that could destroy the Nixon Administration. In a letter
delivered to his White House contact, the undercover operative
John Caulfield, McCord pronounced a dread warning: If the
White House continued to try to have the C.I.A. take responsibility for the Watergate burglary, "every tree in the forest will fall,"
and "it will be a scorched desert." Piling on yet another metaphor
of catastrophe, he wrote, "Pass the message that if they want it to
blow, they are on exactly the right course. I am sorry that you will
get hurt in the fallout." McCord was the first person in the Watergate conspiracy to put in writing exactly what the magnitude of
the Watergate scandal was. Many observers had been amazed at
the extreme hard line that the President had taken since his landslide reelection—the firings in the bureaucracies, the incompre-
hensible continuation of the attacks on Senator McGovern, the
renewed attacks on the press, the attacks on Congress's power of
the purse, the bombing of Hanoi. They could not know that at the
exact moment when President Nixon was wreaking devastation on
North Vietnam, James McCord was threatening to wreak devastation on him.

On February 7th, the Senate, by a vote of seventy-seven to
none, established a Select Committee on Presidential Campaign
Activities, to look into abuses in the Presidential campaign of
1972, including the Watergate break-in; and the Democratic
leadership appointed Senator Sam Ervin, of North Carolina, the
author of the resolution to establish the Select Committee, to be
its chairman. Three days later, the Administration secretly con-
vened a Watergate committee of its own, in California—at the La

Costa Resort Hotel and Spa, not far from the President's estate in San Clemente, with John Dean, H. R. Haldeman, John Ehrlichman, and Richard Moore, a White House aide, in attendance. The meeting lasted for two days. Its work was to devise ways of hampering, discrediting, and ultimately blocking the Ervin committee's investigation.

The President's drive to take over the federal government was going well. By the end of March those legislators who were worried about the possibility of a collapse of the Constitutional system were in a state of near-hopelessness. It seemed that the President would have his will, and Congress could not stop him; as for the public, it was uninterested in Constitutional matters. Senator Muskie had now joined Senator McGovern in warning against the dangers of "one-man rule," and he said that the Administration's proposal for preventing the release of "classified" information, no matter how arbitrarily the "classified" designation had been applied, could impose "the silence of democracy's graveyard." Senator William Fulbright, of Arkansas, had expressed fear that the United States might "pass on, as most of the world had passed on, to a totalitarian system." In the press, a new feeling seemed to be crystallizing that Congress had had its day as an institution of American life. Commentators of all political persuasions were talking about Congress as though it were moribund. Kevin Phillips, a political writer who had played an important role in formulating "the Southern strategy," and who had once worked in John Mitchell's Justice Department, wrote, in an article in *Newsweek* called "Our Obsolete System," that "Congress's separate power is an obstacle to modern policy-making." He proposed a "fusion of powers" to replace the Constitution's separation of powers. "In sum," he wrote, "we may have reached a point where separation of powers is doing more harm than good by distorting the logical evolution of technology-era government." In *The New Republic*, the columnist TRB, who, like Senator McGovern and Senator Muskie, was worried that "one-man rule" was in prospect, wrote, "President Nixon treats Congress with contempt which, it has to be admitted, is richly deserved. We have a lot of problems—the economy, inflation, the unfinished war, Watergate—but in the long run the biggest problem is whether Congress can be salvaged, because if it can't our peculiar 18th-century form of government, with separation of powers, can't be salvaged," And he wrote, "A vacuum has to be filled. The authority of Congress has decayed till it is overripe and rotten. Mr. Nixon has merely proclaimed it." At the Justice Department, Donald Santarelli, who was shortly to become head of the Law Enforcement Assistance Administration, told a reporter, "Today, the whole Constitution is up for grabs." These observers took the undeniable fact that the Congress was impotent as a sign that the Congress was obsolete. And the executive branch, having helped reduce the Congress to helplessness, could now point to that helplessness as proof that the Congress was of no value.

The coverup and the takeover had merged into a single project. For four years, the President's anger at his "enemies" had been growing. As his anger had grown, so had that clandestine repressive apparatus in the White House whose purpose was to punish and destroy his enemies. And as this apparatus had grown, so had the need to control the Cabinet departments and the agencies; and the other branches of government, because they might find out about it—until, finally, the coverup had come to exceed in importance every other matter facing the Administration. For almost a year now, the coverup had been the motor of American politics. It had safeguarded the President's reelection, and it had determined the substance and the mood of the Administration's second term so far. In 1969, when President Nixon launched his Presidential Offensive, he had probably not foreseen that the tools he was developing then would one day serve him in a mortal struggle between his Administration and the other powers of the Republic; but now his assault on the press, the television networks, the Congress, the federal bureaucracy, and the courts had coalesced into a single, coordinated assault on the American Constitutional democracy. Either the Nixon Administration would survive in power and the democracy would die or the Administration would be driven from power and the democracy would have another chance to live. If the newly reelected President should be able to thwart investigations by the news media, the agencies of federal law enforcement, the courts, and Congress, he would be clear of all accountability, and would be above the law; on the other hand, if the rival institutions of the Republic should succeed in laying bare the crimes of his Administration and in bringing the criminals to justice, the Administration would be destroyed.

In the latter part of March, the pace of events in this area of the coverup quickened. Under the pressure of the pending sentences, two of the conspirators were breaking ranks: James McCord and Howard Hunt. McCord, who had been threatening the White House with exposure since December, now wrote a letter to Judge Sirica telling what he knew of the coverup. Hunt, for his part, was angry because he and the other defendants and their lawyers had not been paid as much money as they wanted in return for their silence. In November, 1972, he called Charles Colson to remind him that the continuation of the coverup was a "two-way street," and shortly after the middle of March he told Paul O'Brien, an attorney for the reelection committee, that if more funds weren't forthcoming immediately he might reveal some of the "many things" he had done for John Haldeman—an apparent reference to the break-in at the office of Daniel Ellsberg's psychiatrist. Shortly thereafter, O'Brien informed Dean of Hunt's demand. These events on one edge of the coverup had an immediate influence on the chemistry of the whole enterprise. On March 21st, John Dean, convinced now that the coverup could not be maintained, met with the President and told him the story of it as he knew it from beginning to end. The President's response was to recommend that the blackmail money be paid to Hunt. "I think you should handle that one pretty fast," he said. And later he said, "But at the moment don't you agree that you'd better get the Hunt thing? I mean, that's worth it, at the moment." And he said, "That's why, John, for your immediate thing you've got no choice with Hunt but the hundred and twenty or whatever it is. Right?" The President was willing to consider plans for limited disclosure, and the meeting ended with a suggestion from Haldeman, who had joined the two other men: "We've got to figure out where to turn it off at the lowest cost we can, but at whatever cost it takes."

The defection of Hunt and McCord had upset the delicate balance of roles demanded by the coverup. Information that had to be kept secret began to flow in a wide loop through the coverup's various departments. Not only Hunt and McCord but Dean and Magruder began to tell their stories to the prosecutors. The prosecutors, in turn, relayed the information to Attorney General Kleindienst and Assistant Attorney General Petersen, who then relayed it to the President, who then relayed it to Haldeman and

Ehrlichman, who in this period were desperately attempting to avoid prosecution, and were therefore eager to know what was happening in the Grand Jury room. Any defections placed the remaining conspirators in an awkward position. In order to get clear of the collapsing coverup, they had to become public inquisitors of their former subordinates and collaborators. Such a transformation, however, was not likely to sit well with the defectors, who were far from eager to shoulder the blame for the crimes of others, and who, furthermore, were in possession of damaging information with which to retaliate.

Notwithstanding these new tensions, the President sought to continue the coverup. In the weeks following his meeting with Dean on March 21st, his consistent strategy was what might be called the hors d'oeuvre strategy. The President described the strategy to Haldeman and Ehrlichman after a conversation with Dean on April 14th by saying, "Give 'em an hors d'oeuvre and maybe they won't come back for the main course." His hope was that by making certain public revelations and by offering a certain number of victims to the prosecutors he could satisfy the public's appetite, so that it would seek no more revelations and no more victims. (This technique, which Ehrlichman, on another occasion, called a "modified limited hang-out," was also what Haldeman had had in mind when he suggested that they should "turn it off at the lowest cost" they could.) Hors d'oeuvres of many kinds came under consideration. Some were in the form of scapegoats to be turned over to the prosecutors, and others were in the form of incomplete or false reports to be issued to the public. By now, the country's appetite for revelations was well developed, and in the White House it was decided that no less a man than Mitchell was needed to satisfy it.

As Ehrlichman explained the new plan to the President, Mitchell would be induced to make a statement saying, "I am both morally and legally responsible."

"How does it redound to our advantage?" the President asked.

"That you have a report from me based on three weeks' work," Ehrlichman replied, "that when you got it, you immediately acted to call Mitchell in as the provable wrongdoer, and you say, 'My God, I've got a report here. And it's clear from this report that you are guilty as hell. Now John . . . go on in there and do what you should.' "

That way, the President could pose as the man who had cracked the conspiracy.

Shortly thereafter, Mitchell was called down to the White House, and Ehrlichman proposed the plan. Mitchell did not care for it. He not only maintained his innocence but suggested that the guilt lay elsewhere; namely, in the White House. Ehrlichman told the President when Mitchell had left that Mitchell had "lobbed, uh, mud balls at the White House at every opportunity." Faced with Mitchell's refusal to play the scapegoat, the President, Haldeman, and Ehrlichman next invited Dean to step into the role. Soon after Ehrlichman's unsatisfactory experience with Mitchell, the President met with Dean and attempted to induce him to sign a letter of resignation because of his implication in the scandal.

The President approached the subject in an offhand manner. "You know, I was thinking we ought to get the odds and ends, uh . . . we talked, and, uh, it was confirmed that—you remember we talked about resignations and so forth," he said.

"Uh huh," Dean replied.

"But I should have in hand something, or otherwise they'll say, 'What the hell did you—after Mr. Dean told you all of this, what did you do?' " the President went on.

Again Dean answered "Uh huh."

The President then related that even Henry Petersen had been concerned about "this situation on Dean," and Dean once more answered with an "uh huh."

"See what I mean?" the President asked the uncommunicative Dean.

"Are we talking Dean, or are we talking Dean, Ehrlichman, and Haldeman?" Dean finally asked.

"Well, I'm talking Dean," the President answered.

But Dean, like Mitchell before him, was talking Ehrlichman and Haldeman, too, and would not resign unless they also resigned. He did not want to be an hors d'oeuvre any more than Mitchell did. And since Dean was in possession of highly detailed information that implicated not only Haldeman and Ehrlichman but the President as well, the President was unable to "bite the Dean bullet," as he put it, until he also was willing to let Haldeman and Ehrlichman go. Their turn came quickly. By now the President was under intense pressure to act soon. If he did not, he could hardly pose as the man who had cracked the case. On April 17th, the day after the unproductive conversation with Dean, the President said to Haldeman and Ehrlichman. "Let me say this. . . . It's a hell of a lot different [from] John Dean. I know that as far as you're concerned, you'll go out and throw yourselves on a damned sword. I'm aware of that. . . . The problem we got here is this. I do not want to be in a position where the damned public clamor makes, as it did with Eisenhower, with Adams, makes it necessary or calls—to have Bob come in one day and say, 'Well, Mr. President, the public—blah, blah, blah—I'm going to leave.' " But Ehrlichman was not willing to throw himself on a sword. The person he was willing to throw on a sword was Dean. "Let me make a suggestion," he responded. It was that the President give Dean a leave of absence and then defer any decision on Ehrlichman and Haldeman until the case had developed further. However, the President pursued the point, seeming at times to favor Haldeman's and Ehrlichman's resignation, and finally Ehrlichman did what McCord, Hunt, Mitchell, and Dean had done before him. He lobbed mud balls at the White House—which in this case meant the President.

If he and Haldeman should resign, Ehrlichman observed, "we are put in a position of defending ourselves." And he went on, "The things that I am going to have to say about Dean are: basically that Dean was the sole proprietor of this project, that he reported to the President, he reported to me only incidentally."

" 'Reported to the President'?" the President inquired.

A moment later, speaking in his own defense, the President said, "You see the problem you've got there is that Dean does have a point there which you've got to realize. He didn't see me when he came out to California. He didn't see me until the day you said, 'I think you ought to talk to John Dean.' "

At this point, Ehrlichman retreated into ambiguity, and said, "But you see I get into a very funny defensive position then vis-à-vis you and vis-à-vis him, and it's very damned awkward. And I haven't thought it clear through. I don't know where we come out."

On April 17th, the President made a short statement saying simply that there had been "major developments in the case concerning which it would be improper to be more specific now." He was unable to offer any diversionary reports or propitiatory victims to deflect the public's wrath at the forthcoming disclosures. He and his aides had talked over countless schemes, but all of them had foundered on the unwillingness of any of the aides to sacrifice themselves for him—or for "the Presidency," as he had asked them to do. The coverup was all one piece, and it cohered in exposure just as it had cohered in concealment.

The President had become adept at recollecting whatever was needed at a particular moment. By April of 1973, he and his aides were spending most of their time making up history out of whole cloth to suit the needs of each moment. Unfortunately for them, the history they were making up was self-serving history, and by April their individual interests had grown apart. Each of them had begun to "recollect" things to his own advantage and to the detriment of the others. As their community of interests dissolved under the pressure of the investigation, each of them was retreating into his own private, self-interested reality. The capacity for deception which had once divided them from the country but united them with one another now divided them from one another as well.

In the White House, the fabric of reality had disintegrated altogether. What had got the President into trouble from the start had been his remarkable capacity for fantasy. He had begun by imagining a host of domestic foes. In retaliating against them, he had broken the law. Then he had compounded his lawbreaking by concealing it. And, finally, in the same way that he had broken the law although breaking it was against his best interests, he was bringing himself to justice even as he thought he was evading justice. For, as though in anticipation of the deterioration of his memory, he had installed another memory in the Oval Office, which was more nearly perfect than his own, or anyone else's merely human equipment: he had installed the taping system. The Watergate coverup had cast him in the double role of conspirator and investigator. Though the conspirator in him worked hard to escape the law, it was the investigator in him that gained the upper hand in the end. While he was attempting to evade the truth, his machines were preserving it forever.

At the moment when the President announced "major developments" in the Watergate case, the national process that was the investigation overwhelmed the national process that was the coverup. The events that followed were all the more astounding to the nation because, at just the moment when the coverup began to explode, the President, in the view of many observers, had been on the point of strangling the "obsolete" Constitutional system and replacing it with a Presidential dictatorship. One moment, he was triumphant and his power was apparently irresistible; the next moment, he was at bay. For in the instant the President made his announcement, the coverup cracked—not just the Watergate coverup but the broader coverup, which concealed the underground history of the last five years—and the nation suffered an inundation of news. The newspaper headlines now came faster and thicker than ever before in American history. The stories ran backward in time, and each day's newspaper told of some event a little further in the past as reporters traced the underground history to the early days of the Administration, and even into the terms of former Administrations. With the history of half a decade pouring out all at once, the papers were stuffed with more news than even the most diligent reader could absorb, Moreover, along with the facts, non-facts proliferated as the desperate men in the White House put out one false or distorted statement after another, so that each true fragment of the story was all but lost in a maze of deceptions, and each event, true or false, came up dozens of times, in dozens of versions, until the reader's mind was swamped. And, as if what was in the newspapers were not already too much, television soon started up, and, in coverage that was itself a full-time job to watch, presented first the proceedings of the Ervin committee and then the proceedings of the House Judiciary Committee, when it began to weigh the impeachment of the President. And, finally, in a burst of disclosure without anything close to a precedent in history, the tapes were revealed—and not just once but twice. The first set of transcripts was released by the White House and was doctored, and only the second set, which was released by the Judiciary Committee, gave an accurate account of the President's conversations.

As the flood of information flowed into the public realm, overturning the accepted history of recent years, the present scene was also transformed. The Vice-President was swept from office when his bribe-taking became known, but so rapid was the pace of events that his departure was hardly noticed. Each of the institutions of the democracy that had been menaced by the President—and all had been menaced—was galvanized into action in its turn:

the press, the television networks, the Senate, the House of Representatives, and, finally, in a dispute over release of the tapes, the Supreme Court. The public, too, was at last awakened, when the President fired the Special Prosecutor whom he had appointed to look into the White House crimes. In an outpouring of public sentiment that, like so much else that happened at the time, had no precedent in the nation's history, millions of letters and telegrams poured in to Congress protesting the President's action. The time of letters sent by the President to himself was over, and the time of real letters from real people had come. No one of the democracy's institutions was powerful enough by itself to remove the President; the efforts of all were required—and only when those efforts were combined was he forced from office.

America's Crisis of Confidence

Jimmy Carter

Very early in his campaign for the presidency, Jimmy Carter established a new and successful mode of relating to the American people. Speaking partly as a moralist, partly a preacher, partly a friend, he communicated a sense of caring deeply about the underlying values of the American people. When Carter came to Washington, he discovered that the same style did not work with government bureaucrats or Congressional leaders. Frustrated by his failure to win support for his plans to solve the energy crisis, Carter returned to the style of his campaign and reached over the heads of Congress to the American people. Retreating to Camp David in the Maryland mountains, Carter asked religious leaders, historians, poets, and psychiatrists to journey to Camp David and tell him what was wrong with America. The result was the speech that follows. Significantly, it traces all of America's problems to an underlying "crisis of confidence," a disease of the soul. The speech reveals both Carter's greatest strength and his greatest weakness. He successfully identifies a pervasive feeling of uncertainty and unease in the population. Yet, he failed to translate his insight into effective policy. Carter the preacher and therapist was a success. Carter, the politician, was a failure.

This is a special night for me. Exactly three years ago on July 15, 1976, I accepted the nomination of my party to run for President of the United States. I promised to you a President who is not isolated from the people, who feels your pain and shares your dreams and who draws his strength and his wisdom from you.

Excerpted from *The New York Times*, July 16, 1979.

During the past three years, I've spoken to you on many occasions about national concerns: the energy crisis, reorganizing the Government, our nation's economy and issues of war, and especially peace. But over those years the subjects of the speeches, the talks and the press conferences have become increasingly narrow, focused more and more on what the isolated world of Washington thinks is important.

Ten days ago I had plans to speak to you again about a very important subject—energy. For the fifth time I would have described the urgency of the problem and laid out a series of legislative recommendations to the Congress, but as I was preparing to speak I began to ask myself the same question that I now know has been troubling many of you: Why have we not been able to get together as a nation to resolve our serious energy problem?

It's clear that the true problems of our nation are much deeper—deeper than gasoline lines or energy shortages. Deeper, even, than inflation or recession. And I realize more than ever that as President I need your help, so I decided to reach out and to listen to the voices of America. I invited to Camp David people from almost every segment of our society: business and labor; teachers and preachers; governors, mayors and private citizens.

And then I left Camp David to listen to other Americans. Men and women like you. It has been an extraordinary 10 days and I want to share with you what I heard.

ADVICE FROM THE PEOPLE

First of all, I got a lot of personal advice. Let me quote a few of the typical comments that I wrote down.

This from a Southern Governor: "Mr. President, you're not leading this nation, you're just managing the Government."

"You don't see the people enough anymore."

"Some of your Cabinet members don't seem loyal. There's not enough discipline among your disciples."

Many people talked about themselves and about the condition of our nation. This from a young woman in Pennsylvania: "I feel so far from government. I feel like ordinary people are excluded from political power." And this from a young Chicano: "Some of us have suffered from recession all our lives. Some people have wasted energy but others haven't had anything to waste." And this from a religious leader: "No material shortage can touch the important things like God's love for us or our love for one another."

Several of our discussions were on energy, and I have a notebook full of comments and advice. I'll read just a few.

"We can't go on consuming 40 percent more energy than we produce. When we import oil, we are also importing inflation plus unemployment. We've got to use what we have. The Middle East has only 5 percent of the world's energy, but the United States has 24 percent."

And this is one of the most vivid statements: "Our neck is stretched over the fence and OPEC has the knife."

These 10 days confirmed my belief in the decency and the strength and the wisdom of the American people, but it also bore out some of my long-standing concerns about out nation's underlying problems. I know, of course, being President, that Government actions and legislation can be very important.

That's why I've worked hard to put my campaign promises into law, and I have to admit with just mixed success. But after listening to the American people I have been reminded again that all the legislatures in the world can't fix what's wrong with America.

A FUNDAMENTAL THREAT

So I want to speak to you tonight about a subject even more serious than energy or inflation. I want to talk to you right now about a fundamental threat to American democracy.

I do not mean our political and civil liberties. They will endure. And I do not refer to the outward strength of America—the nation that is at peace tonight everywhere in the world with unmatched economic power and military might. The threat is nearly invisible in ordinary ways. It is a crisis of confidence. It is a crisis that strikes at the very heart and soul and spirit of our national will.

We can see this crisis in the growing doubt about the meaning of our own lives and in the loss of a unity of purpose for our nation.

The erosion of our confidence in the future is threatening to destroy the social and the political fabric of America. The confidence that we have always had as a people is not simply some romantic dream or a proverb in a dusty book that we read just on the Fourth of July. It is the idea which founded our nation and which has guided our development as a people. Confidence in the future has supported everything else—public institutions and private enterprise, our own families and the very Constitution of the United States. Confidence has defined our course and has served as a link between generations.

We've always believed in something called progress. We've always had a faith that the days of our children would be better than our own.

CLOSING THE DOOR ON OUR PAST

Our people are losing that faith. Not only in Government itself, but in their ability as citizens to serve as the ultimate rulers and shapers of our democracy. As a people, we know our past and we are proud of it. Our progress has been part of the living history of America, even the world. We always believed that we were part of a great movement of humanity itself called democracy, involved in the search for freedom. And that belief has always strengthened us in our purpose. But just as we are losing our confidence in the future, we are also beginning to close the door on our past.

In a nation that was proud of hard work, strong families, close-knit communities and our faith in God, too many of us now tend to worship self-indulgence and consumption. Human identity is no longer defined by what one does but by what one owns.

But we've discovered that owning things and consuming things does not satisfy our longing for meaning.

We have learned that piling up material goods cannot fill the emptiness of lives which have no confidence or purpose. The symptoms of this crisis of the American spirit are all around us. For the first time in the history of our country a majority of our people believe that the next five years will be worse than that past five years. Two-thirds of our people do not even vote. The productivity of American workers is actually dropping and the willingness of Americans to save for the future has fallen below that of all other people in the Western world.

As you know there is a growing disrespect for Government and for churches and for schools, the news media and other institutions. This is not a message of happiness or reassurance but it is the truth. And it is a warning. These changes did not happen overnight. They've come upon us gradually over the last generation. Years that were filled with shocks and tragedy.

We were sure that ours was a nation of the ballot, not of the bullet, until the murders of John Kennedy and Robert Kennedy and Martin Luther King, Jr. We were taught that our armies were always invincible and our causes were always just only to suffer the agony of Vietnam. We respected the Presidency as a place of honor until the shock of Watergate. We remember when the phrase "sound as a dollar" was an expression of absolute dependability until 10 years of inflation began to shrink our dollar and our savings. We believed that our nation's resources were limitless until 1973, when we had to face a growing dependence on foreign oil.

These wounds are still very deep. They have never been healed.

ISOLATION OF GOVERNMENT

Looking for a way out of this crisis, our people have turned to the Federal Government and found it isolated from the mainstream of our nation's life. Washington, D.C., has become an island. The gap between our citizens and our Government has never been so wide. The people are looking for honest answers, not easy answers, clear leadership, not false claims and evasiveness and politics as usual. What you see too often in Washington and elsewhere around the country is a system of government that seems incapable of action.

You see a Congress twisted and pulled in every direction by hundreds of well-financed and powerful special interests. You see every extreme position defended to the last vote, almost to the last breath, by one unyielding group or another.

Often you see paralysis and stagnation and drift. You don't like it.

And neither do I.

What can we do? First of all, we must face the truth and then we can change our course. We simply must have faith in each other. Faith in our ability to govern ourselves and faith in the future of this nation. Restoring that faith and that confidence to America is now the most important task we face.

TURNING POINT IN HISTORY

Our fathers and mothers were strong men and women who shaped the new society during the Great Depression, who fought world wars and who carved out a new charter of peace for the world. We ourselves are the same Americans who just 10 years ago put a man on the moon. We are the generation that dedicated our society to the pursuit of human rights and equality.

And we are the generation that will win the war on the energy problem, and in that process rebuild the unity and confidence of America. We are at a turning point in our history. There are two paths to choose. One is the path I've warned about tonight—the path that leads to fragmentation and self-interest. Down that road lies a mistaken idea of freedom.

All the traditions of our past, all the lessons of our heritage, all the promises of our future point to another path: the path of common purpose and the restoration of American values. That path leads to true freedom for our nation and ourselves. We can take the first steps down that path as we begin to solve our energy problem. Energy will be the immediate test of our ability to unite this nation.

You know we can do it. We have the natural resources. We have more oil in our shale alone than several Saudi Arabias. We have more coal than any nation on earth. We have the world's highest level of technology. We have the most skilled work force, with innovative genius.

And I firmly believe we have the national will to win this war.

What Conservative Landslide?

William E. Leuchtenburg

In FDR and the New Deal, *William E. Leuchtenburg showed how the Roosevelt coalition of farmers, labor, blacks, white ethnics, and city dwellers came into being. Ever since the 1930s, the Roosevelt coalition has provided the foundation for every Democratic victory. Its essential health almost made it possible for Hubert Humphrey to overcome anti-war sentiment and defeat Richard Nixon in 1968. The resilience of the coalition helped Jimmy Carter to triumph over Gerald Ford in 1976. Yet when Ronald Reagan defeated Carter in 1980, it became a cliché to say that the Roosevelt coalition was shattered, that a new conservative ideology had taken root among the electorate.*

In the following selection, Leuchtenburg disputes that contention, using voting statistics and electoral analysis to suggest that Reagan's victory was more personal than ideological. If Leuchtenburg is correct and the New Deal coalition remains a significant factor in American politics, it bodes ill for the future of Reaganism in American politics. For, whatever his personal popularity, Reagan's legislative program represents the most systematic attack upon New Deal premises that has taken place since the Roosevelt coalition first came into being.

Rarely have political analysts found themselves in such agreement as they are today about the meaning of the 1980 election. From every quarter we hear that Reagan won by a "landslide," a word that is in peril of dying from overuse. Furthermore, it is said that

From William E. Leuchtenburg, "*What Conservative Landslide?*" Reprinted by permission of the author.

the returns are a harbinger of a new age of Republican dominance comparable to the Democratic reign that began in 1932. Lastly, a chorus of commentary sings out in unison that the country has shifted sharply to the Right and that Reagan has a conservative mandate. In truth, every one of these generalizations is open to serious objection.

Reagan did not come close to winning by a "landslide." By common usage among political scientists and historians, the term refers to a popular vote of at least 55 percent. Reagan barely won a majority. His 51 percent does not begin to compare to the 61 percent registered by Johnson in 1964 and again by Nixon in 1972. (In each of these instances, it might be noted, the humiliated party triumphed in the very next presidential election.) The impression that Reagan scored a landslide victory owes much to the shock produced by the confounding of our expectation of a close contest, but the tribulations of the pollsters do not add a single digit to Reagan's percentage. The erroneous conception of a landslide derives, too, from the lopsided electoral margin, but that is merely a testament to the nationalizing forces that make it possible for an advantage in the popular vote to be spread through a larger segment of the electorate than in an earlier era.

Nor do the configurations of Reagan's totals bear any resemblance to the kind of coalition that historically has inaugurated a new political age. It is not merely that Reagan's 51 percent falls far short of the share polled by a winning candidate in a realigning election. Even more indicative is the failure of the Republicans to capture the House of Representatives, something they have been able to do only twice in the last half-century. Until the GOP is able to win both houses of Congress as well as the presidency, and until a more substantial proportion of the electorate identifies itself as Republican, any talk about a new Republican epoch is decidedly premature.

The widely accepted claim that the elections demonstrate the demise of New Deal liberalism and the ascendancy of conservatism is also suspect. Whatever else the Reagan-Carter duel may have been, it surely was not a referendum on the New Deal. In nearly four years in office, Carter was almost never able to bring himself even to mention Franklin Roosevelt's name. Both his policies and his rhetoric have departed from the New Deal tradition again and again. Indeed, much of Carter's difficulty on Election

Day came not from being too liberal but from being so little in the image of FDR that millions in the Roosevelt coalition did not go to the polls and many others were so uninspired that they did nothing in the campaign save cast a dutiful vote.

Those who see a conservative tide running have more to sustain their argument in the Senate races, where many liberal Democrats went down to defeat, but even here there were crosscurrents. Christopher Dodd rolled over the archconservative Republican, James Buckley, in Connecticut; voters returned liberal Democrat Patrick Leahy in Vermont, long a Republican bastion; and in Reagan's home state of California, Alan Cranston crushed his Republican challenger, despite the fact that *Christian Voice* assigned him a vote of zero. In Colorado, conservatives took dead aim on Gary Hart, but they could not unseat him in a state where Reagan outdistanced Carter, 55–31. One should recognize, too, that this was a particularly vulnerable Democratic class, which had last encountered the electorate in 1974 in the artificial atmosphere created by revulsion over Watergate.

A good part of the Senate debacle may be attributed to the handicap imposed on liberal Democrats by a lackluster president. In Wisconsin, Gaylord Nelson's 49 percent was nearly good enough, but the Senator could not overcome the burden of Carter's 43 percent. Similarly, Birch Bayh in Indiana and John Culver in Iowa each polled a respectable 46 percent, testaments to the strength of liberalism in states where Carter was getting no more than 39 percent, a miserable showing. Even more striking is the situation in Idaho where Frank Church, with 49 percent, almost made it, though he carried the albatross of Carter's dismal 25 percent. What is remarkable about the Idaho election, which has been seen as irrefutable proof of the country's conservative disposition, is how many Reagan supporters crossed over to return to office a liberal internationalist.

This demurrer has even more force if we look at the House returns. So much attention has been focused on isolated events like the defeat of John Brademas that the real story has been missed—that, to an overwhelming extent, liberal Democrats were re-elected. In a time of putative rightwing revolution, voters in every section of the country walked into polling booths and pulled down the levers that sent Richard Bolling of Missouri, Stephen Solarz and Richard Ottinger of New York, Paul Simon of Illinois,

Claude Pepper of Florida, Mo Udall of Arizona, and Don Edwards of California back to Washington.

Consider what happened in the Eighth Virginia. Here conservatives are chortling because they targeted the liberal Democrat Herbert Harris, and he lost. But a closer look at the returns reveals that his Republican opponent polled only 49 percent, less than a majority. Despite the handicap of running on a ticket headed by Carter, who got only 34 percent (barely one-third) in his district, Harris ran up a respectable 48 percent, almost enough. He lost by an eyelash only because an independent candidate who agreed with his liberal outlook cut into his following with 3 percent of the vote, sufficient to provide the margin of difference. In the Eighth Virginia, 51 percent of the ballots went to a liberal Democrat and to a woman who wanted to legalize marijuana. Yet the results in this district are now cited as evidence of a firestorm of reaction.

Undeterred by all of the contrary evidence, election analysts have deduced from the returns that America wants the government to get off its back, another commonplace that deserves more careful examination. No one can gainsay the fact that millions of people are fed up with mindless bureaucratic regulation. That is not at all the same thing, though, as saying that the country has wearied of the progressive State. It is singular that only one out of every ten Reagan voters said that they were for him because he was a conservative. Much of the dissatisfaction of the voters does not appear to be ideological but is centered rather at irritation over Carter's inadequacy as a leader or the failure to resolve particular dilemmas. The New York Times–CBS poll concluded that though the electorate seemed more conservative, "it had hardly made a clear move to the right. The polls showed strong public support for a substantial government role in economic matters and for a variety of government programs in health care and education." Not even the Far Right wants to dispense with the State. Far from desiring an end to government intrusion in every area, the Moral Majority, in sponsoring a constitutional amendment on abortion, wants to meddle in the most intimate of personal relations at the same time that it proposes to expand the walls of the Pentagon until they buckle.

This is not the first time that conservatives and Republicans have thought that they saw the dawning of a new era, but the others have turned out to be false dawns. In 1946, for example, the GOP Old Guard won a far bigger victory than in 1980. That was the year that it gained control of both houses of Congress, with men like Joe McCarthy coming to the Senate for the first time and Richard Nixon making his debut in the House. New Deal liberalism, everyone agreed, was dead. Confident that the electorate had provided a mandate for conservative policies, the Eightieth Congress put the axe to New Deal programs with a vengeance. In fact, it turned out that the nation was expressing not disapproval of liberalism but a momentary exasperation with inflation, which may also account for much of the behavior this time. Just two years later, the voters returned Congress to the Democrats in an election that began the Senate or gubernatorial careers of men like Adlai Stevenson, Chester Bowles, Lyndon Johnson, and Hubert Humphrey.

Again in 1952 when Eisenhower swept Republicans into control of Congress for the last time in the modern era, the wise men all agreed that the New Deal was dead and an age of GOP suprem- acy had been ushered in. But the Eisenhower coalition proved as brittle as Reagan's may turn out to be. For Reagan will find, as Eisenhower did, that if he adheres to a rightward course, he will lose those Democratic voters who defected to him this year not out of a change in their ideology but in search of solutions. On the other hand, if he does not veer to the right, he will disappoint the conservative ideologues just as Eisenhower evoked the wrath of Joe McCarthy. There are already signs that some of Reagan's supporters are sick and tired of the scolds in the Moral Majority. In 1954, only two years after the Eisenhower landslide, the Demo- crats took over both houses of Congress, and there is every reason to suppose that in 1982 history will repeat, if for no better reason than that the party in power almost always loses seats in a mid- term election.

All of these considerations send a message to the Congressional Democrats, for the real meaning of the 1980 election will be de- termined neither by historians nor by journalists but by the policy makers in Washington. If liberal Democrats interpret the results as a repudiation of liberalism, then that is what the 1980 election will mean, irrespective of what the voters intended. It is under- standable that they will be inclined to do so, for whatever the motivations the citizenry may have had, there is no denying that the impact on Senate liberals has been devastating.

Yet there is nothing in what we now know of the contours of the election to suggest that a long Republican reign and a conservative resurgence, though both are conceivable, are foreordained. There is no warrant for Senator Tsonga's statement, "Basically, the New Deal died yesterday." And it was foolish for the Democratic chairman in Ohio to say, "The election tells me one thing. That is that any public figure who is a liberal Democrat has two chances: find another job or change his philosophy." Reagan did not win in a landslide. The Republicans do not hold letters patent on the future. The assertion that the attitudes of the country have moved sharply to the right is contradicted both by many of the election returns and the poll data. But if each of these conclusions and prognoses continues to go unchallenged, they may well determine the direction of American politics for the rest of this century.

The 1980 Election

Alan Baron

Looking at the 1980 election from another perspective, journalist and editor Alan Baron poses the question of where American party politics will go in the aftermath of Ronald Reagan's election. Baron, like Leuchtenburg, doubts whether the 1980 returns signify a massive swing to the right. On the other hand, he also questions the continued vitality of the liberal/New Deal coalition. The problem with the New Deal, he says, is that it succeeded. But what next? Do Democrats have a new agenda of programs? Are they ready to move toward a platform similar to that of European Social Democrats? By implication, at least, Baron suggests that those who most accurately assess the underlying changes in the body politic will have the best chance for success in the last half of the 1980s. by permission.

Analyses of election results generally focus on one of two areas: either on the candidates, their strategies and campaigns, or on the electorate itself. These differing perspectives were exemplified in the two major post-election books of the 1960s: the first in Theodore White's *The Making of the President, 1960*, following John Kennedy's election; and the second in Kevin Phillips's *The Emerging Republican Majority*, following Richard Nixon's 1968 victory. Both books pinpointed fundamental changes in American politics. White provided the first major insight into the decline of the parties as viable institutions and their replacement by indepen-

Excerpted from Alan Baron, "How To Read an Election, *New Republic*, December 30, 1981. Reprinted by permission.

dent candidate organizations and the media. Phillips presented one of the earliest analyses of the dissolution of the New Deal coalition.

But both books also shared a fault common to nearly all post-election studies: their tones reflected the fact that the authors knew the results of the elections. Had some 15,000 voters in two states (out of more than 68 million voters) switched from John Kennedy to Richard Nixon in 1960, Nixon would have been elected and White's book would have had a very different focus. Had some 118,000 voters in four states (out of some 73 million) voted for Hubert Humphrey instead of Nixon in 1968, Humphrey would have been elected and Phillips's book would have been scrapped, or at least retitled, by his publishers.

Following the 1980 elections, the two parties joined election analysts in dividing into those who focused on candidates and those who looked to the electorate in analyzing the outcome. Liberal Democrats said, and nervously hoped, that the key to the result was the candidates, their campaigns and their strategies—that Jimmy Carter had alienated his Democratic base, mismanaged the presidency, poorly handled the politics of reelection, and given the election to Ronald Reagan. Conservative Republicans, on the other hand, wanted the focus placed on the voters; they said, and nervously hoped, that the Reagan victory reflected a fundamental shift to the right in public opinion, a basic realignment in the electorate, and the emergence, delayed by Watergate, of a conservative Republican majority.

Public opinion polls did little to resolve the matter. One Sunday morning a few weeks after the election, the *New York Times* and the *Washington Star* both reported on national post-election polls. The *Times* story found little ideological shift and viewed the election as a referendum on the Carter presidency; the *Star* saw a clearer move to the right ideologically. In fact the two stories were based on the same poll—simply written by different reporters.

My own reading of the 1980 election—after reviewing the events and the polls—does not fit neatly into either the candidate/campaign-oriented explanation of the liberals or the ideological/electorate-oriented analysis of the conservatives.

I begin with the view that an American presidential election is, fundamentally, a referendum on the status quo, rather than a choice betwen competing ideologies or issue positions. Carter "lost" this referendum early in 1980. He was the only Democratic President in history to seek reelection during a year of increasing unemployment and was perceived to be a weak and ineffective leader. The people wanted change. The real campaign, therefore, was Reagan versus Reagan. The real issue was whether Reagan's election posed too great a risk—either to peace or to social security benefits—to take in order to get rid of an unacceptable incumbent.

The ball was in Reagan's court and there was little Carter could do about it by the time of the general election. What he could do was (1) appear presidential; (2) unite the Democratic Party's base constituencies in fear of Reagan; and (3) avoid debating Reagan and giving him the opportunity to appear "equal" in stature to the President and a "safe" choice. Carter displayed some lack of skill in all three areas—but that was what brought him the trouble in the beginning.

Reagan's managers, from the inception of the campaign, understood the problem. They worked as much as they could (1) to emphasize economic issues, rather than social and cultural ones, which divide the Republicans; (2) to stress Reagan's record as governor and his ability to get "good people" under him; and (3) to limit, as much as possible, Reagan's ability and opportunity to make spontaneous remarks. They generally succeeded in these goals.

Reagan was also helped in his effort by two other people in addition to his managers. First, John Anderson: he had credibility with millions of independent moderates who were too pragmatic to vote for him, but were swayed by his pronouncement that Carter and Reagan were equally bad and concluded that choosing Reagan posed no greater risk than maintaining the status quo. Second, Ronald Reagan: his age and affable personality made it tough to portray him as a dangerous radical.

The fact that these "personal" factors shaped the results should not, however, reassure liberals that more fundamental problems are not facing them. One reason for the failure of the Carter presidency—and for the despondency in liberal ranks following his defeat—was the fact that liberals had no clearcut, identifiable agenda for the nation. The main items on their agenda were enacted (civil rights, environmental safeguards, nutritional programs, etc.) and there was little consensus on why one should support Carter, other than to stop Reagan. As recently as several weeks ago, a leading liberal trade unionist told a group of liberal Democrats in Washington that they were lucky *not* to be in power. "Assume Mondale was in the White House," he asked, "just what the hell would he do about these problems?"

Nor can liberals and Democrats afford to ignore the fact that conservatives are correct, to a large extent, when they talk about the dissolution of the New Deal coalition. That gradual dissolution has been taking place since the coalition elected FDR in 1932. The New Deal Majority consisted of a group of minorities—Catholics, Jews, first-generation Americans, Southerners, blacks, union members, urban dwellers—each of which considered itself outside the power structure and alienated from an American majority, which was perceived to be Northern, white, Protestant, native-born, middle-class, and Republican. The goal of the New Deal coalition was to broaden the American mainstream to include its minorities and, with the notable exception of blacks, it succeeded.

Take Southerners. When FDR took office, the per capita income in the poorest state (South Carolina) was 25 percent that of the richest (Connecticut); now the figure is about 75 percent. Since FDR, one border-state politician with Confederate roots (Truman) and two Southerners (Johnson and Carter) have entered the White House. Civil rights reforms have encouraged industry and individuals to move to the South. Being Southern is no longer the basis for voting Democratic. The United States Senate tells the story: in 1954, the last time the Republican Party controlled the Senate, the 22 Southern senators were all Democrats (Northerners were Republican, 49–25); today the 22 Southern senators are evenly divided (Northerners are narrowly Republican, 42–36).

Or take Catholics. When I grew up in Iowa, the state was about 75 percent Protestant and 25 percent Catholic. Usually, the Protestants voted 2 to 1 Republican, and the Catholics 3 to 1 Democratic. When former Senator Dick Clark lost to Senator Roger Jepsen in 1978, Clark drew some 45 percent of the Protestant vote, far higher than normal for Democrats in the past. But he dropped to only 55 percent of the Catholic vote. The level of Democratic support among Catholic voters over that of support among Protestant voters had fallen from 40 percent to 10 percent. Why? Polls showed that "Catholic issues" like abortion and tuition tax credits had some limited impact, but far more important was the fact that Catholics no longer perceived themselves to be members of a minority outside the American mainstream.

To be a Catholic or a Southerner no longer makes one an outsider—and no longer automatically classifies one as a Democrat. (Such voters do remain generally Democratic in elections with no meaningful issue differences. Most people vote the party of their parents, and change is gradual.) Indeed, if FDR and Herbert Hoover were to return to America today, they would be greatly surprised to find that Alabama and Oklahoma are represented by Catholic Republicans in the U.S. Senate. Differences based on class and ethnicity are also declining. Race remains a clear indicator, since blacks remain outside the mainstream, but Democrats cannot count on blind loyalty from blacks either. Such Republican Senators as Thad Cochram (Mississippi), Mack Mattingly (Georgia), and Charles Percy (Illinois) received significant black support.

The New Deal's problem? Basically, it is that it worked. But the dissolution of the New Deal coalition does not portend its replacement by another majority coalition. There will not necessarily be a realignment along clear class, religious, regional, or other lines.

And the evidence of a realignment along ideological lines is just as slim. The fact is that Ronald Reagan's basic campaign strategy was to focus the election on valence, or nonideological issues, on which both candidates take the same position (against hostages, against inflation, against unemployment, against waste and inefficiency in government, against crime, for honesty, for competence). The contest thus becomes which candidate can best handle them. On most of the ideological issues dividing the candidates (national health insurance, abortion, gun control, ERA, SALT, etc.) the public was closer to Carter's position than to Reagan's. President Reagan's claims that the election provided him with an ideological mandate were made after the campaign, not during it, when, for example, he asserted that the differences between him and Carter on ERA simply involved methodology for achieving equality.

What then can be concluded from the 1980 election?

First, that the New Deal coalition—and, to some extent, political coalitions based on regional, religious, ethnic, and, to a lesser extent, class lines—is losing its coherence and power. The issues and campaigns in American politics have been nationalized; at the same time, the media has had an opposite, individualizing effect on politics, by making the relationship between the voter and the candidate more direct than it has ever been. Groups are no longer the important intermediaries they once were.

Second, that the liberal agenda of the 1960s (voting rights, Medicare for the elderly, Medicaid for the poor, school lunches, environmental regulations, etc.) has not been replaced by any new liberal program. The aim now is simply to preserve the old gains from assault by the New Right.

Third, that the American voter is pragmatic rather than ideological. Support for basic New Deal programs and the major social advances of the 1960s has not lessened. Antipathy to government programs and spending has increased, but that antipathy is less ideological than pragmatic. It is based on concerns about the programs, impracticality, and their failure to meet the goals for which they were created, along with worry about increasing government deficits and inflation.

Fourth, the problems of the country are severe enough, the public alienated enough, and the presidency demystified enough, that people are probably more inclined to risk change—on the grounds that things can't get worse—than they have been during much of the past. (Polls shortly before the election showed that 30 percent of the voters would have supported Anderson if they had thought he had a chance to win.)

In the current political period, the danger for conservative Republicans is to attempt to read more than this conclusion from the 1980 results. The danger for liberal Democrats is to attempt to read less than this conclusion.

Part Nine

WHERE DO WE GO FROM HERE?

As America approaches the last decade of this century, issues that developed as an outgrowth of World War II continue to dominate our national agenda. In foreign policy we need to work out stable relationships with other superpowers as well as to cooperate effectively with developing nations. The world cannot afford a nuclear war. Yet as the capacity to make nuclear weapons proliferates, it becomes more and more difficult to prevent that possibility from becoming a reality. If the United States and the Soviet Union are not able to reduce their own armaments and prevent the development of nuclear weapons in countries like Libya and South Africa, it may be impossible to hold back the threat of a world-wide nuclear holocaust.

Within our own society, major problems continue in the areas of race and sex discrimination, economic productivity, and maldistribution of wealth and resources. It is difficult for the United States to be a place of equal opportunity unless people from different races and backgrounds begin from relatively the same place. Yet that cannot happen as long as the top 5 percent of the population controls nearly 53 percent of the wealth, and the bottom 20 percent of the population has less than half of 1 percent of the wealth. Many people believe that each American must be treated as an individual, equal before the law, if we are to hold on to our traditional values. Others, however, insist that we need to recognize the importance of group differences in setting social policy. If women and black Americans have suffered through most of our history because they have belonged to a specific gender or racial group, is it not necessary to use these same categories in order to overcome past oppression and bring members of these groups into the mainstream of American society?

Domestic problems and international issues come together around such problems as energy. The rich industrial societies of the world have only a small portion of the world's population, yet use the vast majority of energy resources. At least some observers believe that the only way to prevent a north-south world civil war is to redistribute the world's wealth to the poverty-stricken areas of the south. But can we embark on such policies without their having a significant impact on the way we organize our lives at home?

The following selections deal with these issues. McGeorge Bundy offers an analysis of why affirmative action may be necessary for the next generation if America is to come to grips with its legacy of racial oppression. According to Bundy, fairness requires that those who have borne the brunt of injustice in the past now be given aid toward achieving a position of equality. Kevin Phillips, by contrast, insists that such encouragement of group identification will eventually tear apart the society and destroy its possibility for homogeneity. Robert Heilbroner discusses the problems of America within a world framework, and asks whether the crises of energy, a world-wide population explosion, and the threat to our environment of technological and military change can ever be contained in a peaceful and democratic way. Are we destined to move toward totalitarianism? Is development of a more equitable distribution of resources possible within a democratic framework? Finally, George Kennan—one of those most involved in defining the rationale for our opposition to Communism in the Cold War—presents a moving argument for retreating from the brink of nuclear destruction. His assessment of where we are and what we need to do in order to prevent annihilation of the universe is a powerful and fitting place for this book to end.

The Issue before the Court: Who Gets Ahead in America?

McGeorge Bundy

There are few domestic issues that have been more perplexing than affirmative action. After the 1964 Civil Rights Act prohibited discrimination on the basis of race or sex, the Johnson administration ordered executive agencies to take "affirmative action" to guarantee civil rights. Initially, the words were interpreted simply to mean recruiting minority candidates for job openings. Over time, however, more explicit rules were established, designed to correct past injustices. In one Southern state, for example, only 3.6 percent of the employees in a state agency were black, all of them janitors. Although it was likely that more blacks would be hired for a variety of jobs after the 1964 Act, it was improbable that an equitable proportion would be employed as long as hiring took place on an individual basis. Hence the need for affirmative action plans which mandated preferential employment to overcome past injustices.

To some people, such practices seemed like "reverse discrimination"—denying equal protection before the law to white individuals. The controversy over affirmative action came to a head with the Bakke case in 1978. There, the issue was whether a percentage of places at the University of California Medical School at Davis should be set aside for minorities. Although nearly everyone agreed that this particular case was not totally representative of the problem (the Davis Medical School, for example, was new and so had no historical record of discrimination against minorities), it became the focal point for Supreme Court action. The following article by McGeorge Bundy, then president of the Ford Foundation, argues the case for affirmative action.

Bundy, a former Dean at Harvard and National Security Advisor to Presidents Kennedy and Johnson, became an active proponent of social reform during his tenure as president of the Ford Foundation. Here, he places the question of affirmative action in an historical context, contend-

ing that only through such programs will it be possible for the United States to achieve in practice, as well as in theory, the principle of racial equality.

The struggle for racial equality is old, but the constitutional questions presented by special admissions to colleges and graduate schools are new. Through the 1930s and 1940s the cases that rose to the Supreme Court were concerned with the exclusion of blacks from segregated professional schools. In the 1950s and 1960s the Court was occupied first with its great decision in *Brown,* declaring segregation in the public schools unconstitutional, and then with a long series of cases in which it was presented with one effort after another to evade the import of that decision. It did not confront problems like those of Allan Bakke because programs like the one to which he objects did not exist. In the early 1970s, a quite similar case, that of Marco DeFunis against the Law School of the University of Washington, was never decided because DeFunis was eventually admitted to the Law School and had almost finished by the time the Supreme Court was ready. The DeFunis case had great consequences in arousing feelings and stirring reflection, but it did nothing to clarify the constitutional standing of special admissions.

Large-scale attempts to increase the numbers of minorities in selective colleges and professional schools have a short history. In medical schools, for example, the effort became general less than ten years ago. These initial actions were compelled neither by government nor by courts. They were the product rather of the recognition, by whites as well as blacks, that the barriers to educational opportunity did not tumble in a day after the civil rights victories of the 1950s and early 1960s. Black demand, white awareness, riots in the cities, and the death of Martin Luther King, Jr. were all a part of what brought the change, but its deeper and more durable cause was the growing conviction that there was a fundamental contradiction between an asserted opposition to racism and the maintenance, by whatever process of selection, of essentially all-white col-

Excerpted from McGeorge Bundy, "The Issue Before the Court: Who Gets Ahead in America?" *The Atlantic Monthly,* November 1978. Reprinted by permission of the author.

leges and professional schools. Law schools, medical schools, graduate schools, and selective colleges all across the country began to recognize a direct responsibility to find and make room for larger numbers of qualified nonwhites.

Many legitimate purposes have animated those engaged in this effort, but the deepest and most general objective—toward which any one school or college can do only a little—has been to ensure full and fair access to all parts of our social, economic, and professional life for nonwhite Americans. Of course *all* kinds of Americans deserve such access, and it is right to remember from the outset that no past injustice permits us to set any one group above any other. But there can be no blinking the enormous and unique set of handicaps which our whole history, right up to the present, has imposed on those who are not white. It is not the fault of today's laws or of the present Supreme Court that racism should be our most destructive inheritance. But that reality makes the effort to overcome it a matter of the most compelling interest.

The essence of this new enterprise, whether at the college or the graduate level, has been the making of special attempts to find, attract, enroll, and support students who are members of disadvantaged racial minorities. So far this has meant mainly blacks, and in this discussion I shall often refer to them alone, simply to shorten matters. But the programs are directed also at Hispanic students and native Americans, and often at Americans of Asian origin. They include one or all of the following elements: active recruitment, targets or goals or even quotas for numbers enrolled, high levels of financial aid, and special courses or other academic arrangements when they are needed to help the student succeed. In all these programs attention to race, indeed special attention *because* of race, has been essential.

These new programs, in medical schools and elsewhere, have not yet been comprehensively and comparatively studied, and even if we knew more about them than we do, we could not know enough for confident judgment of their effects. The first medical students to enter by special admissions have not yet had time to prove themselves as practicing physicians, and in any case the programs of the medical schools have changed in shape while the number of minority students admitted has been growing, from less than 300 in 1968 to 1400 in 1976. Such evidence as we have—much of it oral and informal—suggests that most medical schools have had a great deal to learn in this short time about judging minority candidates, about helping them to come to terms with their own environment, and about treading the narrow and necessary path between sympathetic recognition of difficulties and cynical or condescending acceptance of unsatisfactory performance. Many minority students have had much to learn about these same matters. . . .

Racial mistrust and misunderstanding have not been exorcised by these programs, and sensitive observers know that all concerned, white and nonwhite alike, have a long way to go. But there is a clear and positive relation between effort and success in these programs, and much evidence that they are working better now than when they began. . . .

The moral and intellectual standing of those who complain against special admissions is not in doubt. When we find on the same side men as different as Justice Douglas and the late Alexander Bickel of Yale, and when a Court that has earned respect and even criticism for its liberalism comes down as hard as has the Supreme Court of California, we must understand what troubles them so much.

The first and strongest of their contentions is simply that both in the law and in common feeling there has developed a heavy suspicion of any program, whatever its motive, which gives members of one race any advantage over members of another on account of race alone. Ironically but understandably, the most sweeping and eloquent expressions of this sentiment may have come from the leaders in the battle for black civil rights.

In 1947 Thurgood Marshall himself, then the director of the Legal Defense and Educational Fund of the NAACP, denounced the classification by race under which the laws of Texas deprived Herman Sweatt of admission to law school: "There is no understandable factual basis for classfication by race, and under a long line of decisions by the Supreme Court, not on the question of Negroes, but on the Fourteenth Amendment, all courts agree that if there is no rational basis for the classification, it is flat in the teeth of the Fourteenth Amendment." As we shall see, the defenders of special admissions programs argue strongly today that the use of racial classifications in those programs is not only rational but necessary for compelling purposes; but what deserves emphasis first is that it is easy to relate both the logic and the feeling of Thurgood Marshall's outburst in Texas to the reaction of those who feel that when it comes to choosing who shall be a doctor, there is no rational basis for using color as a test.

A closely related objection to special admissions is that they seem to many to require the use of racial quotas. There has been much haggling about the difference between goals and quotas, and I shall argue that the distinction is not trivial, but when in fact a fixed number of places is reserved for qualified minorities (the situation at Davis), it becomes hard to deny that some spaces that would otherwise be open to all are now closed off to whites. One cannot miss the fervor in the opinion of Justice Mosk for the California court: "No college admission policy in history has been as thoroughly discredited in contemporary times as the use of racial percentages. Originated as a means of exclusion of racial and religious minorities from higher education, a quota becomes no less offensive when it seems to exclude a racial majority." The fervor is underlined, if anything, by the rhetorical excess of the suggestion that a majority that has a full and open chance at 84 percent of the places available is "excluded."

Not surprisingly, it is Professor Bickel who is most eloquent of all. Nothing in the briefs supporting Mr. Bakke's claim is as strong as the argument Bickel put forth in *DeFunis*. He tells us flatly that it is quite simply wrong

> to require the employment or the admission to a school or to any other position of unqualified or less qualified persons solely on the basis of their race. When this is done, a cost is paid in loss of efficiency and in injustice . . . [I]n a society in which men and women expect to succeed by hard work and to better themselves by making themselves better, it is no trivial moral wrong to proceed systematically to defeat this expectation; the more so as for some groups that do not now benefit from affirmative action programs prejudice has only recently been overcome, and the expectation that members of such groups might rise by merit has just begun to be fully met . . . [T]o reject an applicant who meets established, realistic, and unchanged qualifications in favor of a less qualified candidate is morally wrong, and in the aggregate, practically disastrous.

Driven by convictions like these, Justice Douglas (in a separate opinion on the merits in *DeFunis*) reached the conclusion that any admissions program must fail unless it is handled in a "*racially neutral way*" (his italics). Sharing this judgment, and quoting liberally from the Douglas opinion, the California Supreme Court reached the same conclusion: Whatever the processes of admission, they must be racially neutral. Whatever methods and standards are used, they must be "applied without regard to race."

To the average reader, all this may seem fair enough. Why then is it so shocking to the institutions that would be principally affected? The reason is simple, if also painful: the gaps in social, economic, educational, and cultural advantage between racial minorities and the white majority are still so wide that *there is no racially neutral process of choice that will produce more than a handful of minority students in our competitive colleges and professional schools.*

Let us stay with medical schools and blacks alone and look back at 1967–1968, the last year before special admissions began to be significant. In that year there were 735 blacks in medical schools, but 71 percent of them had been admitted by ways that were far from racially neutral: they were at Howard and Meharry, then and now the country's two predominantly black medical schools. Out in the broad white world of a hundred other medical schools, the 211 blacks enrolled in all four classes were only 0.6 percent of the total, though blacks are about 12 percent of the total population. Today, as a consequence of a nation-wide ten-year effort, there are some 3000 blacks, 5 percent of the total, in the mainly white medical schools. It is an extraordinary transformation. And what most close observers believe is that if these same mainly white medical schools were driven back to "racially neutral" admissions, the number of blacks would slide back close to where it was in 1968. A parallel impact would be felt in other professional schools and in selective colleges. The consequences of such a backsliding, both to the aspirations of racial minorities and to the honorable efforts of whites, are mildly described by the word catastrophic. The message would go out, to something like one sixth of our nation, that all the words of a generation since *Brown* are hollow—that the educational doors are to be neutrally open, but only to an overcrowded staircase on which nearly all of those with a head start will be white.

The reasons for this conclusion are both multiple and simple. First, we must agree that selective colleges and professional schools do want entering students who are not merely qualified but highly qualified. They have learned that when other things are equal, the applicant with the better academic record and the better test scores is more likely to succeed. Records and scores must be handled with care, and it is easy to make too much or too little of them. It is much less easy to deny the reality they tend to reflect: that developed capacity for certain kinds of analysis, familiarity with certain kinds of knowledge, successful experience of certain kinds of mental effort, and natural exposure to a social environment in which those things are encouraged are all strongly relevant to a person's promise. In America today disadvantaged racial minorities are still greatly underrepresented among those best qualified on these criteria alone. The burden of centuries has not been lifted in the short and stressful decades since *Brown*. Selective colleges and professional schools admitting students as they admitted them fifteen years ago would soon be nearly lily-white again. . . .

Among those who have worked hardest and longest on this matter the agreement is overwhelming. If you want to enlarge the numbers of minority students in selective colleges and professional schools you simply *must* make race a factor in your work. You must target blacks and Hispanics and others in your recruiting; you must assess their promise in the light of the specific disadvantage that their race itself still carries. If you wish to attract well-qualified candidates you must earn a reputation for real accessibility; you must become known as a place that accepts minorities in more than token numbers. You must then spend time and money well beyond your normal standards in helping them survive and succeed. Precisely because it is not yet "racially neutral" to be black in America, a racially neutral standard will not lead to equal opportunity for blacks. . . .

So far we may have established the importance of action to increase minority enrollment, and we may even have made good our claim that this simply cannot be done in a racially neutral way. But the two hurdles we recognized at the outset remain: Is it not somehow wrong to admit "less qualified" people because of race, and is it not doubly wrong to reserve space for them at the inescapable expense of others in the competition? . . .

The weight of the evidence available suggests that a steadily growing percentage of the men and women of minority origin who are admitted to selective colleges, law schools, medical schools, and graduate schools are "making it." Schools are choosing with more skill and giving better support to those who enroll. Some fail or drop out, as some (but relatively fewer) whites do. But the rates of minority attrition are now reported to be roughly comparable to the failure and dropout rate of white males some thirty or forty years ago. Middle-aged men who received their own professional training at about that time can fairly be asked to consider whether a class with records as good as their own should be considered as underqualified.

I labor this point because both logic and sentiment suggest that it may be central to the thinking of a great many Americans, however little it may appear in records and arguments. *No one is arguing for the admission of the unqualified, and there is no finding in* Bakke *that such admissions have occurred.* Indeed, there is not in *Bakke* any serious legal challenge to the generally accepted proposition that the elemental decision on whether a candidate is qualified for medical school must be left to the professional judgment of faculties and their agents. . . .

We are near the center of the matter. Let us recognize the reality: in affirmative action to admit more members of racial minorities, there are and will be measurable differences, among those admitted, between the average test scores and academic records of minorities and those of whites. The scores and records of blacks and other minorities are such that this result is inescapable, at least for the present. A similar relative weakness in test scores has existed in other groups in the past and has been gradually overcome. There is also a clear relation between low scores and low socioeconomic status, which hits racial minorities with particular force. Of course not all members of racial minorities have low scores or poor records, just as not all are culturally or economically disadvantaged. There is indeed a growing pool of applicants who are black or brown and bright by any test. Nonetheless, the average scores for most racial minorities are lower than the comparable scores for whites.

But does it follow, as Professor Bickel seems to have thought, that to admit such lower-scoring minority applicants is "morally wrong" and "practically disastrous"? Does a difference in such "established, realistic, and unchanged qualifications" mean that those who fall short on these measurements are "less qualified"? Or does it mean only that when one prefers a candidate who is weaker in such relatively measurable qualifications, one must have some good and solid reason? Race for a moment aside, the latter standard is clearly the right one. Sensitive admissions officers agree that while scores and records can tell you a lot at the upper and lower margins, they give little guidance in the hard cases of choice among those who are academically qualified but not extraordinary. . . .

Even where records and tests have been used most mechanically it has been only because of their *relative* advantage; among thoughtful admissions officers it has always been agreed that when time permitted and educational need required, it was right to look at other things. I put the point most gently. Especially at the undergraduate level, most admissions officers will say that mechanical reliance on any such measurement is what would be "morally wrong" and "practically disastrous." Recognizing their fallibility, knowing they will make mistakes and commit unfairness, they nonetheless reach out to try to identify promise and quality of all sorts. They look at other things, not only for help at the margins, but because they think these other things are critical to the quality of the student body as a whole.

Now we are right at the heart of it. Is race itself permissibly such another thing to look at? If I am a qualified black (in the basic sense already discussed), may not my blackness perhaps make me *more* qualified? Have I had something extra to go through? If I score 550 where a middle-class white scores 650, have I shown as much or more of what is so critical to success in learning—a *determination* to learn? Can I bring a different and needed perspective? Is there a special need for people like me in courts and hospitals and on college faculties? May the profession itself be better if more people of my race are in it? Can my presence and participation as a student enlarge the educational experience of others? Does the whole society somehow have a need for me in this profession that it simply does not have, today, for one more white? If the answer to these questions, or some of them, is yes, are not my qualifications by that much improved, and improved precisely by my blackness? If so, at some point it becomes right that I should be admitted; I am not "less qualified" when all things are considered.

I put this case by questions because I wish to emphasize that it is not necessary here to be dogmatic in response to dogma. It is quite enough to argue that it would be a dangerous and sweeping business, in the present state of our knowledge and experience, to answer all these questions in the negative. Yet that is precisely what Professor Bickel's argument and the opinion of the California court would require. . . .

But what about quotas, or even goals? Are they not arbitrary and discriminatory? Certainly they could be, if unqualified candidates were admitted or if their numbers went beyond the compelling needs of the profession or the state. There is no such claim in *Bakke;* at Davis about one sixth of the places were held for qualified members of minorities, who make up about a quarter of the state's population. Even if it really was the minority entrants who beat Bakke out, and even though his scores were better than theirs, still, as long as one grants that to be black or Chicano can be in itself a qualification, the program does not seem excessive. Indeed, it is not the sixteen places that are denounced by Bakke and his supporters—it is the award of any admission *at all* on grounds even partly related to race. It is not the size of the space reserved, or even its existence, that is the ultimate basis of the invocation of "equal protection." What Bakke and his friends assert is that race must play *no* part in selective admissions, and they may feel themselves forced to this argument because no other will justify their appeal for constitutional protection.

Thus Bakke and the California court are asserting an absolute claim when what we really face here is conflicting values which have to be compared in weight. There can be no doubt at all that if the number of nonwhites goes up in selective schools and colleges, the number of whites will go down. Some will be rejected who would otherwise have been accepted. But what needs attention is the magnitude of this consequence.

Set Bakke himself to one side for a moment and consider the net damage to disappointed white applicants, as a group, arising from the nationwide admission of racial minorities to medical schools. (This is a reasonable course even in considering Bakke as an individual, because he applied not only to Davis, with its relatively large and rigid goal for minorities, but to a number of other medical schools with other kinds of programs. He wants to be a doctor, not a Davis graduate.) In 1975–1976, there were just under 35,000 white applicants for medical school, and 22,000 of them were not accepted. In the same year the total number of minority candidates accepted and enrolled was 1400. If not one minority candidate had been accepted, the entering classes throughout the country could have accommodated less than 7 percent of the disappointed whites. In this raw statistical sense, at least 93 percent of the majority's problem lies in something else.

The most important "something else" is a simple excess of demand over supply. More people of all sorts want to be doctors than ever before, and for powerful reasons. In the last ten years the number of formal applicants has increased by 130 percent, while the number of places available has increased by only 66 percent. . . .

Most of the competition the white males face comes from other white males, but it is interesting that even if one persists in pitting white males against others, their most dangerous rivals, quantitatively, are not specially admitted black or Hispanic males, but women of all races. Since 1968 the number of women entering medical schools has risen from 8 percent to 25 percent of the total. . . . The 4000 young women who have entered medical school this year have a lot more to do with the rejection of men like Bakke than any special admissions program for minorities.

But let us return to Bakke: it is not statistics alone that suggest the fault assignable to minority admissions programs in his case is small. It is evident in the history of his effort, if not in the appellate arguments, that his central trouble was his age. He was ten years older than the ordinary candidate for admission. Medical education is a prolonged affair at best, and the profession has been troubled for years by the fact that even if a student proceeds promptly along all the usual tracks—college, medical school, internship, and often specialty boards—he or she can be well in the thirties before being fully prepared for practice. Bakke would have been over forty at best, and rightly or wrongly this fact was a considerable handicap to him.

Conversely, what is most impressive about Bakke is not his scores but his determination. It seems at least possible, from the admittedly fragmentary evidence, that the authorities at Davis would have made a better judgment to admit Allan Bakke precisely because he so clearly cared so much; moreover, his health

and energy levels appear to be high enough to justify some flexi-
bility in considering his age. And it can be argued today that
whether he wins or loses his legal case, he has made sacrifices in
fighting it which somehow ought to win for him even now what
he has wanted most in life—a chance to be a doctor.

Both Bakke's age and his determination are largely absent from
the legal arguments. Constitutionally they do not seem to count.
But they are what really mattered in his case. Together they are a
powerful concrete demonstration of the difficulty of the art of
choice among those qualified.

Thus both general and specific evidence, not reached by the
legal arguments, combine to suggest that any hurt sustained by
whites in general or Bakke in particular is only doubtfully and
marginally related to special admission of minorities. Moreover,
there is no way of avoiding some such displacement if in fact
there are to be more nonwhites in medical schools. Since everyone
except perhaps Bakke himself appears to agree that more qualified nonwhites are in fact needed, there is a flavor of Catch-22
about the arguments of his friends and the California court. They
want more blacks, and that means fewer whites, but any program
that produces more blacks by considering blackness in any way is
by that very fact unconstitutionally unfair! Can this kind of thinking lead to sound constitutional law? . . .

Through most of [our] history, most institutions of higher
learning, like the rest of America, have been blatantly racist; the
exceptions have been as few as they have been honorable. For
only about ten years out of our two centuries as a nation has there
been a serious nationwide attempt to make room in the higher
reaches of this world for those who have been held back so long.
The results so far are uncertain, but the achievement is real, while
the asserted dangers are hypothetical. If the process is not yet as
open and skillful as it should be, it is much more open and skillful
than it was. Faculties still insist on their responsibilities, but they
are more and more aware that there are constituencies all around
them that have a right to an accounting. Their efforts to meet
competing claims do not proceed in a vacuum. The whole process
is incomparably broader than the narrow chains of legal reasoning which are offered to the Court, and members of the white
majority are hardly powerless in that process. Whatever is selective will always be imperfectly equitable, but in the absence of a

persuasive showing of any grave or general damage to basic constitutional rights, it would seem genuinely tragic to block this
great new effort at racial fairness just as it begins. . . .

I repeat that this effort is young, difficult, and hopeful. What
most needs emphasis is its youth. In the lives of the races, the
professions, and the universities, ten years are but a moment.
Some of those who defend affirmative action sometimes speak as
if it could be a relatively short matter. If we measure in generations, they may be right. It seems fair to hope that we can have
decisive progress by the time the children of today's children are
of college age. But that single generation takes us well beyond the
year 2000. For the rest of the working lives of those who are now
concerned with these matters, persistence will be the name of the
game.

No one can deny that special admissions programs, even at
their best, have costs and dangers; the grievances of Allan Bakke
and others may be overstated and even misdirected, but they are
deeply felt. Racial preference can arouse racial antagonism, and
the general rule that judgment should be based on personal merit
alone has its high claims. Still, it seems clear that to take race into
account today is better than to let the doors swing almost shut
because of the head start of others. We must hope and believe
that in the long run our effort for equal opportunity will put the
need for special programs behind us. In that deep sense there is
no conflict between special admissions and every other form of
action to help the disadvantaged, white and nonwhite alike. But
what special admissions, and only special admissions, can do today
is to make access to the learned professions a reality for nonwhites. To get past racism, we must here take account of race.
There is no other present way. In the words of Alexander Heard
of Vanderbilt, "To treat our black students equally, we have to
treat them differently.". . .

My own last thought is this: It is right to ask of the Court in this
case that it should find its way to a result which somehow respects
the reality that the world of American higher learning is at last
embarked upon a long-delayed and indispensable effort to do its
part to deal with our most deeply rooted social evil, one which was
the proximate cause of the Fourteenth Amendment itself. To
read the words of that amendment in ways that would cripple that
effort would seem a cruel irony. What is worse, it would be to

assert that in the learned professions the equal protection clause somehow requires the perpetuation of de facto white supremacy. Worst of all, it would place the great moral authority of the Court on the wrong side of a fundamental issue, on which it has a hard-won right to speak for the national conscience.

In asking whether the equal protection clause really requires all this, I have found myself rereading two of the most famous of all judicial comments on the Constitution—what it is and what it permits. They both came from the pen of John Marshall in 1819.

> In considering this question, then, we must never forget, that it is *a constitution* we are expounding.

And later in the same opinion:

> Let the end be legitimate, let it be within the scope of the constitution, and all means which are appropriate, which are plainly adapted to the end, but consist with the letter and spirit of the constitution, are constitutional.

If the Constitution is read in this grand manner, can it truly be *unconstitutional* to make room for qualified members of racial minorities on the staircase to the professions?

The Balkanization of America

Kevin Phillips

Many Americans have seen affirmative action as but one example of a growing tendency toward disintegration in American society, posing one group over against another, and destroying any sense of our common identity as Americans. In the following selection, Kevin Phillips—a political consultant, writer, and former government official—contends that traditional American values of individualism are profoundly threatened by this revitalization of group assertiveness. Thus, instead of America being seen as a melting pot, various ethnic, regional, religious, and racial groups are pitted against each other, with no consensus on shared values.

Ironically, Phillips himself was the architect in the 1960s of the so-called Southern strategy, arguing that the Republican Party could win significant gains by appealing to regional political and economic interests. Phillips also helped to popularize the notion of the Sun Belt as a political and geographic entity. Here, he contends that whatever the short-term benefits derived from such identification, the long-range interests of American society require a higher allegiance to common values which de-emphasize class, racial, or sectional differences.

They are wrong, or too superficial, these people who calibrate the alleged decline of the United States by the decreasing relative hitting power stored in North American missile silos or by the second-place number of ship miles logged by the U.S. Navy in the

Indian Ocean. Would that our national problem were such a simple matter of matériel and logistics. Unhappily for us all, the larger crisis of spirit engaging the United States has relatively little to do with the too-few and too-old destroyers in the Persian Gulf or the too-old and too-few heavy bombers expected to reach Novosibirsk in a Maximum Alert. One can argue—and I will—that the Union of the United States (both as an idea and as a matter of domestic political geography) is unraveling in more fundamental ways. This is no small irony: that even as modern American technology has learned to package instant steel-bonding cyanoacrylate in a dimestore tube, the bonds of American society itself should be weakening or dissolving.

All too many examples suggest themselves: the congealing of the melting pot and the re-emergence of ethnicity; the proliferation of sexual preferences and religious cults; the new political geography of localism and neighborhoods; the substitution of causes for political parties; the narrowing of loyalties; the fragmentation of government; the twilight of authority. Some months back, Energy Secretary James Schlesinger, who had not yet ascended to that dismal eminence, suggested that the well-known and much-dreaded energy crisis might bring about the "Balkanization" of America. Fair enough: The parochial politics of energy *do* smack enough of Bulgarian or Serbian bickering circa 1911 to make the term "Balkanization" reasonably appropriate. In a larger perspective, however, the trend that Schlesinger feared *already* has established itself as a fact of national life. As the politics of natural-gas pipelines resemble the plots and counterplots of Zagreb and Sofia, so also one can find just as much social Balkanization in the rise of feminism or "gay rights," or in the "Red Power" demands of American Indians—for tribal sovereignty and the return of former Indian lands—from Maine to California. For the past several years the symptoms of decomposition have appeared throughout the body politic—in the economic, geographic, ethnic, religious, cultural, biological sectors of society. Small loyalties are replacing larger ones. Small outlooks are also replacing larger ones. . . .

In such a context, then, the Balkanization of America is closely related to what Andrew Hacker has called "the end of the American era." Can it be coincidental that U.S. political and social decomposition has accelerated in tandem with Vietnam and the end of Pax Americana, the concurrent failure of the Great Society, the end of energy abundance, the downfall of cultural optimism, and—of course—Watergate and public loss of confidence in the U.S. political system? On the contrary, the breakdown of these unities, hopes, and glories has been enough to send Americans, too, scrambling after a variety of lesser combinations and self-identifications: ethnicities, regions, selfish economic interests, sects, and neighborhoods.

At this point, let me admit that regionalism, separatism, fragmentation, and rampant ethnicity are hardly new in the United States. On the contrary, they are as old as Jamestown, New Amsterdam, and Plymouth. But the critical historical distinction must lie in the tidal flow and ebb: From George Washington's day through the Trajan-like imperial high-water mark of the early 1960s, Americans retrospectively can see ethnicity, regionalism, and states' rights yield before growing concepts of global optimism, the melting pot, equality, homogeneity, and centralization of (benign federal) power. Since that time, however, the reemergence of ethnicity, regionalism, states' rights, and political splintering has occurred in a very different psychological climate—amidst the *end* of optimism, the *collapse* of Manifest Destiny, the *failure* of the Great Society, the *failure* of the melting pot, and of all the other hopes and slogans of America's national rise. Credit this distinction, and today's social Balkanization process takes on a significance little rebutted by invocations of ethnicity circa 1880, regionalism circa 1896, feminism circa 1912, or states' rights circa 1948. Only the pre-Civil War period raises some parallel.

SUN BELT VERSUS FROST BELT

Let's begin with the most frequently discussed example of the phenomenon, which in many ways is also the pivot: Sun Belt versus Frost Belt. To be sure, regional conflict has been a staple of American history—as late as 1948, Harry Truman was declaiming that the Northeast treated the South and the West like colonies. What *is* new is the first regional attempt in over a century to remove national leadership from the Northeast. Ten years ago, when I coined the term "Sun Belt," it seemed like a good phrase for a boom region owing its ascendance to the shining of the sun—tourism, retirement, irrigated agribusiness, year-round military facilities. But over the past decade, the term has come to represent a phenomenon of much greater importance.

Competition for natural and energy resources is one major factor in the increasingly high-voltage regional rivalries. By and large, the Sun Belt states, which contain most of the country's oil and natural gas, favor energy deregulation and progrowth economic development. The most intense demand for energy regulation, allocation, and conservation, meanwhile, is centered in the North. Mutual suspicion characterizes the attitudes of both factions. The Washington lobbyist for the state of Louisiana told an interviewer last year that "the attitudes today are the same as those preceding the Civil War. The North wants everything its own way. This time, it won't get it."

The point hardly need be dwelt upon for anyone who has seen Texas's bumper stickers ("Drive fast, freeze a Yankee") or who has noticed hostile alignments of Sun Belt and Frost Belt political organizations and lobby groups. Less well known is the extent of squabbles over water and energy at the state level. Virginia and North Carolina are fighting over water from the Roanoke and Chowan rivers; Arizona and California are fighting over the Colorado River. . . .

Economic and geographic Balkanization is at once confirmed and, if anything, surpassed by the biological fragmentation overtaking the United States. Five biological denominators currently lend themselves to civil-rights campaigns and the assertion of group identities: sex, sexual preference, age, race, and ethnic origin. Rising egocentrism is a related development.

Fragmentation of American society by sex and sexual-preference group need not be greatly elaborated here, given the (excessive) extent to which it has been dwelt upon elsewhere. Escalating definitions of "rights" produce at least two unfortunate results: group categorization and militance. Feminism has gone far beyond Susan B. Anthony. Certainly the organization, cohesion, and civil-rights militance of homosexuals is a new phenomenon in American society—"Gay Power" has as much political weight in San Francisco (and maybe Manhattan) as does the steel caucus in Ohio's Mahoning Valley.

Age is yet another denominator. The group awareness of senior citizens—"Gray Power"—is a considerable phenomenon in Florida, Arizona, and California. At the other end of the age chart, more and more legal rights are being defined for children. Even second- and third-trimester fetuses have had their own bio-political Balkan army marshalled for them in the right-to-life movement.

The concept of racial Balkanization is open to argument. On one hand, pre-1960s segregation resulted in what was in effect two nations—one white, one black. Against *that* backdrop, desegregation has increased racial unity. Yet in another sense, the last few years have seen a definite resegregation in many cities, coupled with a growth of black sentiment to go it alone. Today's trend toward predominantly nonwhite central cities raises critical questions, as does official fondness for the racial-quota system. Indeed, the use of either quotas or "affirmative action" programs verging on quotas is tantamount to an official recognition of Balkanization—acceptance of the notion that equality can be pursued only by racial and ethnic group categorization.

Therein lies the problem. The consequence of the attempt to *proscribe* discrimination may be to *prescribe* opportunity by various biological categories. Officially mandated quotas and preferences for nonwhites have already produced a variety of unfortunate practices. In Queens County, New York, parents claiming a certain racial background in order to get their children assigned to a local school must present themselves at a Board of Education racial-inspection office. Under the signature of the Honorable Bert Lance, the federal Office of Management and Budget last May promulgated guidelines for collecting uniform racial and ethnic data. Central or South American antecedents put you in a minority group; Middle East antecedents do not. The classification is elaborate and likely to become more so. Daniel P. Moynihan (Dem.-N.Y.) has invoked the specter of Germany's Nuremberg race laws.

There will be those who say, quite correctly, that such criteria are nothing new to America, that through the 1960s many state statutes included definitions of Negroes as persons of one-eighth or even one-thirty-second Negro ancestry. Such classifications were indisputably the stuff of cultural apartheid. The point is that we had seemed to be getting away from such racial measurements for a decade or so, but now they are reemerging, together with official prescriptions for housing, education, and employment eligibility. . . .

Meanwhile, ethnic consciousness certainly is resurgent. Rev. Jesse Jackson, currently a black favorite of the white media, preaches a gospel of self-determination—"for us, by us, of us." In Joliet, Illinois, black parents have set up their own school rather than let their children be bused to predominantly white schools. From Eastport and Nantucket to Palm Springs, Indians are asserting Red Power and seeking tribal sovereignty. What's more, the melting pot is rehardening for northwestern Europeans—even for the basic "Anglo-Saxon American" H.L. Mencken loathed so much. Dozens of Midwestern German towns have begun celebrating *Oktoberfest* again, and Pan American World Airways has been running commercials reminding white Anglo-Saxons of their British-American heritage to get them to fly back to *their* "old country" the way Italians and Norwegians do.

All in all, there's virtually no facet of human biology—sex, color, age, ethnic heritage—that isn't currently gaining strength as a denominator of social fragmentation. That phenomenon may not be without precedent, but I don't know of one. . . .

FURTHER SPLINTERING

If biological and cultural Balkanization illustrates the breadth of our impetus for national fragmentation, potentially more important symptoms are visible in the decomposition of the American polity. Only ten to fifteen years ago, it seemed that states' rights would be stripped away by a benign centralism, that the flow of public opinion was toward federal authority, with less and less of a role for local government, education, and customs. On a more exalted plane, the Presidency was gaining ground, its imperial promise accredited by no less a prophet than Prof. Arthur Schlesinger, Jr. If anything, the expectation was for further universality—for the onset of metropolitan government in our cities, for racial integration, for the withering away of state lines, and even for the possible loss of national identity to a new world order.

Instead, over the past few years, the tide has begun running strongly in the other direction. Far from becoming an effective world federation, the United Nations is being made less and less useful by the rise (and U.N. admission) of dozens of small states and mini-states. . . . Resurgent parochialism is the theme. Scotland flies its Red Lion once again, and Wales its Dragon. Belgium is dissolving into Flemings and Walloons. Brittany and Corsica would like to detach themselves from France. Nearer home, Quebec threatens to secede from Canada.

Too few Americans realize the extent to which we have similar problems. As Rep. Lloyd Meeds (Dem.-Wash.) has put it, the growing demand of American Indian tribes for "sovereignty" over their reservation lands presents the prospect of *two hundred and sixty* Quebecs. . . .

Demographers also have begun to draw attention to the huge and fast-growing U.S. Hispanic minority. In a generation, Hispanics will outnumber blacks. Each year, the Southwestern states increase their percentage of Spanish-speaking residents. Many are legal residents; many are not. In Texas and California the gathering of huge Hispanic populations (and the prospect that Mexico's poverty and birthrate can only spur more emigration) has prompted regional talk of a *reconquista*—literally a Spanish reconquest of the once-Spanish Southwest. . . .

Turning from the geographical to the institutional aspect of U.S. political Balkanization, one best begins in Washington, D.C. Over the past fifteen years, the executive and legislative branches of the federal government have staffed-up in a new kind of rivalry. Congressional staffs have multiplied to enable Representatives and Senators to entrench themselves institutionally as well as electorally. If the White House has a Budget Office (or a National Security Council or a Science/Technology Office), well then, so must the Congress. For years, much of this intellectual-political arms race was attributed to the 1969–76 desire of a Democratic Congress to match the resources of the GOP White House. But now, with Democrat Jimmy Carter in the Presidency, it's clear that the institutional Balkanization of Washington has a life of its own.

The phenomenon is a long way from being harmless or quaint. Richard Nixon was infuriated by his inability to control the government from the White House, and his frustration brought him much of the way to Watergate. In his book *The Ends of Power*, H.R. Haldeman, former White House chief of staff, explains how, as of 1972–73, the "four major power blocs in Washington"—the press, the bureaucracy, the Congress, the intelligence community—were "under threat" by a President who hoped to use various reorganization techniques to break the independent, unresponsive authority of the bureaucracy and the Cental Intelligence Agency. Likewise, Haldeman sees the critical Watergate events of the spring of 1973 not as the unfolding of justice but as a coup d'état by the threatened interests. To be sure, most Americans will disagree with Haldeman's effort to transform Watergate into a multi-institutional power play. It's an interesting analysis, however; one at least touched with truth (if not permeated by it), and worth pondering with regard to a larger question: How can any President deal with these same power blocs? . . .

Further evidence of Balkanization can be found *within* the several branches of government. If the Executive has rival bureaucracies, Congress, for its part, has been divided by new subgroups and special-interest mechanisms. A recent article in *Roll Call,* the weekly newspaper of Capitol Hill, mentioned an almost feudal arrangement: "Subcommittee staffs have grown which no longer feel responsible to the committee chairman, central authority and discipline have eroded, and lobbyists have learned how to take advantage of this situation by playing one committee against another, or as one veteran put it, 'playing one Balkan prince against another Balkan prince.' " From yet another perspective, the early ideological subgroupings that took shape in Congress during the 1960s paralleled and respected party divisions—the Democratic Study Group for party liberals, the Republican Study Group for GOP conservatives, the Wednesday Club for GOP liberals. Over the past few years, a new set of caucuses is growing up to promote special interests across party lines. And Sun Belt and Frost Belt forces are already marching up and down the aisles of Congress, turning debate after debate into a display of comparative and combative economic geography.

Arguably, these nonparty mechanisms have come into being in part because the 120-year-old Republican-Democratic party system is no longer an effective arbiter of regional, cultural, and economic differences (just as its predecessor during the 1850s wasn't). Indeed, talk of a breakdown in the two-party system and/ or the need for new parties is a recurrent staple of political discussion. There is nothing unusual about this; we have had splinter movements before, usually absorbed by one of the major parties in periodic realignments. What *is* unusual is the way the party mechanisms thus far have been unable or unwilling to respond to public desires. Many Americans have either loosened their affiliation, begun to put ideology ahead of party, or simply decided not to vote. Issues like abortion, gun control, the right to work, taxes, busing, feminism, and "gay" liberation appear to be superseding parties as the basis of political mobilization. The obvious description is: *ideological* Balkanization. . . .

A NATION DIVIDED

The United States has been divided and fragmented before, but—save for the Civil War—with the underlying trend pointing in the direction of unity, fraternity, and increasing federal authority. Now American society seems determined to pursue smaller loyalties—regional, economic, political, ethnic, and even sexual—rather than larger ones. Unless the trend reverses in the next few years, and no such prospect is apparent, it bespeaks a fundamental reversal in the American experience. The heterogeneity of America will become a burden, the constitutional separation of powers crippling, the economy threatened, the cohesion of society further diminished. Which brings us to the unhappy question: is American Balkanization a sign of national decline?

I think it is such a sign, despite the optimism and relevance of counterarguments perceiving strength, not weakness, in the renewed closeness of Americans to neighborhood, ethnic, and regional roots. The overall hypothesis of decline is too well supported by the great theories of biological, psychological, and historical-cultural evolution. Progress has always flowed in a movement from the limited, the parochial, to the more general and universal. This is true whether one cites Charles Darwin on the evolution of species, Sigmund Freud's analyses of personality, or Arnold Toynbee's theories of history. A species, a personality, or an empire—they all grow or rise from the parochial to the general and then, as their hour or role passes, *reparochialize*. Progress flows toward the universal, but when that impetus expires, the particularisms and subdivisions—of function, personality, culture, or politics—reassert themselves. "Parochial" and "clannish" may be negative concepts, but we recognize basic human nature much less pejoratively with terms like "grass roots," "homeland," "kinfolk," and even "bedrock."

Given the imperial, political, and societal nature of my discourse on the Balkanization of America, Toynbee's analysis is perhaps the most relevant, linking the advent of a great nation to its *élan vital* and the leadership of a creative minority able to define national values and goals. But that growth period does not last forever. Sooner or later, there comes a failure of creativity and an end to mass inspiration. At this point, in Toynbee's words,

> the loss of harmony between elements which had formerly coexisted in a society as an integral whole leads inevitably to an outbreak of social discord. The broken-down society is rent in two different dimensions simultaneously by the social schisms in which this discord is expressed. There are "vertical" schisms between geographically segregated communities and "horizontal" schisms between geographically intermingled but socially segregated classes.

Overschematized, perhaps, but true. The "articulation of society into a number of parochial states" that Toynbee posited describes all too well the process overtaking the contemporary United States. Different kinds of vertical and horizontal schisms are apparent all around us. Less apparent to most upper-middle-income Americans, however, is the deepening socioeconomic disillusionment of the poorer third of the American population. Consumer-confidence surveys illustrate a marked attitudinal disparity. Upper-middle-income professionals may be buying imported cheese at $4.50 a pound, but low-income and lower-middle-income Americans are losing economic hope. The American Dream is slipping away. A few pollsters such as Louis Harris play down such attitudes, saying that people are developing a new nonmaterialist outlook. Perhaps. If Harris isn't correct, though, economically and socially disillusioned "Middle America" may represent the "internal proletariat" that Toynbee found characteristic of every disintegrating major civilization.

As for another of Toynbee's measurements—unproductive elite leadership by a "dominant minority" that has lost its earlier creativity—we have to look at our current national leadership elites. The "Eastern Establishment" that imposed Pax Americana on the post-World War II world has now given way to a "Parody Establishment," wearing the same tailored suits and bench-made shoes but lacking the élan of their predecessors in the 1940s, 1950s, and even in the 1960s. The national media elite is no better. Indeed, today's American Balkanization in large measure represents the failure of these leadership elites to understand the simple facts of race, ethnicity, territory, greed, and inequality.

Approached from yet another direction, the failures of the Sixties and Seventies have helped bring on what conservative sociologist Robert Nisbet has called "the twilight of authority." Nisbet's thesis: The United States has lost its sense of authority and common purpose—more or less what Toynbee called élan vital and the Romans call civitas. The crumbling of authority is certainly clear enough, not just in polls measuring popular attitudes toward leading institutions but in the events of the past decade and a half. Yesterday's "Eastern Establishment" has been partially displaced by provincial centers of power—regional, cultural, and institutional—but none of these has had the energy to assume effective national command. . . .

From a different perspective, the sexual and religious Balkanization of America offers another glum thought. In an interview, Will Durant, coauthor with his wife Ariel of the eleven-volume Story of Civilization, expressed concern that

we're in the stage in which Greece was when the gods ceased to be gods and became mere poetry, and therefore exercised no element of order or command upon human behavior. There was the development of city life, of science and philosophy, and the result was a period of pagan license—say around 200 B.C. to 100 A.D.—in which morals floundered in an ocean of competing religions, just as you have a flotsam and jetsam of religions today. By the time of Caesar, you had a permissive society and a pagan society in the sense of sexual enjoyment with a minimal moral restraint. Now . . . we shall have to wait for a new religion, the way the Greeks and Romans did, because . . . what happened was the old civilization decayed to a point where it cried out for a new religion, for something to worship and obey.

Of course, Balkanization is not all bad. No doubt cheerful things can be said about the new commitment to neighborhood, the new individual fulfillment of accepting (even trumpeting) ethnicity rather than cowering before the melting pot, the resurging attention to states' rights, the renewed concern with family and church. Yet much of the new localism seems essentially romantic—the obverse of the last decade's romantic universalism. Too many of the same naive people who were for global unity a decade or two ago are now saying "Small is beautiful," ecstasizing over self-governing Vermont communes and renovated central-city blocks of brownstones. The trouble is that these regional, ethnic, and local forces now seem to be recurring in a U.S. context of societal fragmentation and decomposition, rather than (as in 1800 or 1900) as grass-roots evidence of cultural vigor and functioning political federalism. *Decomposition is just not the same thing as revitalized diversity.* Moreover, in the present-day context of U.S. and world affairs, small-is-beautiful is likely to be overshadowed by small-is-divisive or even small-is-dangerous. An ineffective 1978 U.S. political system is not like a loose, immature 1878 U.S. political system. Under current circumstances, a Balkanized United States is likely to lose headway externally, in the world of nuclear missiles and global oil supplies, as well as internally, in the minds of the American people.

And the future? Just as nature abhors a vacuum, history abhors fragmentation. Some sort of new, sweeping force—a charismatic politics or a religious revival—could emerge out of America's contemporary muddle. A new universalism may yet unite our political, geographic, religious, biological, and economic factions. In the meantime, policies that do not recognize U.S. Balkanization are probably doomed to further promote it.

Reflections on the Human Prospect

Robert Heilbroner

Under the immediate pressure of local, national and immediate crises, too few people step back and look at long term historical currents, or the relationship between what transpires in one nation and what occurs in the rest of the world. Robert Heilbroner exemplifies an alternative to such parochialism. A philosopher, economist, and historian, he has devoted much of his writing to themes and issues that involve the entire world. In the following selection, Heilbroner poses the critical question of whether we will survive as a civilization. Examining the world-wide energy shortage, population growth, and nuclear proliferation, he attempts to outline the larger vision that should inform national leaders. In an age when unlimited economic growth is no longer possible, and where resources will inevitably shrink, Heilbroner asks whether we can achieve stability and security, and at the same time maintain our traditional freedoms. Clearly, no universal agreement is likely on how to solve these underlying problems. Yet unless the questions are confronted, the human race may run out of time to shape its own destiny.

There is a question in the air, more sensed than seen, like the invisible approach of a distant storm, a question that I would hesitate to ask aloud did I not believe it existed unvoiced in the minds of many: "Is there hope for man?"

In another era such a question might have raised thoughts of man's ultimate salvation or damnation. But today the brooding

Excerpted from Robert C. Heilbroner, *An Inquiry into the Human Prospect* (New York: W.W. Norton, 1974). Reprinted by permission.

doubts that it arouses have to do with life on earth, now, and in the relatively few generations that constitute the limit of our capacity to imagine the future. For the question asks whether we can imagine that future other than as a continuation of the darkness, cruelty, and disorder of the past; worse, whether we do not foresee in the human prospect a deterioration of things, even an impending catastrophe of fearful dimensions. . . .

Today [our] sense of assurance and control has vanished, or is vanishing rapidly. We have become aware that rationality has its limit with regard to the engineering of social change, and that these limits are much narrower than we had thought; that many economic and social problems lie outside the scope of our accustomed instrumentalities of social change; that growth does not bring about certain desired ends or arrest certain undesired trends. One of these unmanageable events is the apparently unstoppable inflation that we witness in every industrialized capitalist nation. Another is the seemingly uncontrollable force of racial hatred, evident not only at home but in the relations of Hindus and Moslems, Jews and Arabs, Africans and Africans. Yet another is the stubborn resistance of world poverty to the ministrations of foreign aid, a phenomenon that we may perhaps understand better when we reflect on our inability to prevent the decline of some American cities into wastelands.

Hence, in place of the brave talk of the Kennedy generation of managerialists—not to mention the prophets of progress or of a benign dialectical logic of events—there is now a recrudescence of an intellectual conservatism that looks askance at the possibilities for large-scale social engineering, stressing the innumerable cases—for example, the institutionalization of poverty through the welfare system, or the exacerbation of racial friction through efforts to promote racial equality—in which the consequences of well-intentioned acts have only given rise to other, sometimes more formidable problems than those they had set out to cure. . . .

The advent of an energy "crisis" alerts us to the prospect of a ceiling on industrial production, imposed by an inability to overcome the rapidly diminishing returns of a natural world that is being mined more voraciously each year. Such a prospect brings the troubling consideration of how we would manage the direction of events if economic growth—the central pillar of support for the sanguine views of Victorians, traditional Marxists, and managerialists alike—were forced to come to an early end.

But this prospect, though it may be the more immediate cause of our new-found concern with growth, is fundamentally less troubling than another recently recognized state of affairs. This is the stunning discovery that economic growth carries previously unsuspected side effects whose cumulative impact may be more deleterious than the undoubted benefits that growth also brings. In the last few years we have become apprised of these side effects in a visible decline in the quality of the air and water, in a series of man-made disasters of ecological imbalance, in a mounting general alarm as to the environmental collapse that unrestricted growth could inflict. Thus, even more disturbing than the possibility of a serious deterioration in the quality of life if growth comes to an end is the awareness of a possibly disastrous decline in the material conditions of existence if growth does not come to an end. . . .

The values of an industrial civilization, which has for two centuries given us not only material advance but also a sense of élan and purpose, now seem to be losing their self-evident justification. As yet, the doubts and disillusions as to that civilization are only faint breezes that stir the leaves of the tree and will certainly not uproot a way of life anchored deeply in the earth of our beings. But the breezes blow and the stirrings they cause must be added to the sense of sometimes indefinable unease that is so much a part of our age.

It must be clear from these introductory remarks that I do not pose the question at the outset of this book—"Is there hope for man?"—as a mere rhetorical flourish, a straw figure to be dismantled as we proceed into more "serious" matters. The outlook for man, I believe, is painful, difficult, perhaps desperate, and the hope that can be held out for his future prospect seems to be very slim indeed. . . .

The external challenges can be succinctly reviewed. We are entering a period in which rapid population growth, the presence of obliterative weapons, and dwindling resources will bring international tensions to dangerous levels for an extended period. Indeed, there seems no reason for these levels of danger to subside unless population equilibrium is achieved and some rough measure of equity reached in the distribution of wealth among nations, either by great increases in the output of the underdeveloped world or by a massive redistribution of wealth from the richer to the poorer lands.

Whether such an equitable arrangement can be reached—at least within the next several generations—is open to serious doubt. Transfers of adequate magnitude imply a willingness to redistribute income internationally on a more generous scale than the advanced nations have evidenced within their own domains. The required increases in output in the backward regions would necessitate gargantuan applications of energy merely to extract the needed resources. It is uncertain whether the requisite energy-producing technology exists, and, more serious, possibly that its application would bring us to the threshold of an irreversible change in climate as a consequence of the enormous addition of man-made heat to the atmosphere.

It is this last problem that poses the most demanding and difficult of the challenges. The existing pace of industrial growth, with no allowance for increased industrialization to repair global poverty, holds out the risk of entering the danger zone of climatic change in as little as three or four generations. If that trajectory is in fact pursued, industrial growth will then have to come to an immediate halt, for another generation or two along that path would literally consume human, perhaps all, life. That terrifying outcome can be postponed only to the extent that the wastage of heat can be reduced, or that technologies that do not add to the atmospheric heat burden—for example, the use of solar energy—can be utilized. The outlook can also be mitigated by redirecting output away from heat-creating material outputs into the production of "services" that add only trivially to heat.

All these considerations make the designation of a timetable for industrial deceleration difficult to construct. Yet, under any and all assumptions, one irrefutable conclusion remains. The industrial growth process, so central to the economic and social life of capitalism and Western socialism alike, will be forced to slow down, in all likelihood within a generation or two, and will probably have to give way to decline thereafter. To repeat the words of the text, "whether we are unable to sustain growth or unable to tolerate it," the long era of industrial expansion is now entering its final stages, and we must anticipate the commencement of a new era of stationary total output and (if population growth continues or an equitable sharing among nations has not yet been attained) declining material output per head in the advanced nations.

These challenges also point to a certain time frame within which different aspects of the human prospect will assume different levels of importance. In the short run, by which we may speak of the decade immediately ahead, no doubt the most pressing questions will be those of the use and abuse of national power, the vicissitudes of the narrative of political history, perhaps the short-run vagaries of the economic process, about which we have virtually no predictive capability whatsoever. From our vantage point today, another crisis in the Middle East, further Vietnams or Czechoslovakias, inflation, severe economic malfunction—or their avoidance—are sure to exercise the primary influence over the quality of existence, or even over the possibilities for existence.

In a somewhat longer time frame—extending perhaps for a period of a half century—the main shaping force of the future takes on a different aspect. Assuming that the day-to-day, year-to-year crises are surmounted in relative safety, the issue of the relative resilience and adaptive capabilities of the two great socio-economic systems comes to the fore as the decisive question. Here the properties of industrial socialism and capitalism as ideal types seem likely to provide the parameters within which and by which the prospect for man will be formed. . . .

No developing country has fully confronted the implications of becoming a "modern" nation-state whose industrial development must be severely limited, or considered the strategy for such a state in a world in which the Western nations, capitalist and socialist both, will continue for a long period to enjoy the material advantages of their early start. Within the advanced nations, in turn, the difficulties of adjustment are no less severe. No capitalist nation has as yet imagined the extent of the alterations it must undergo to attain a viable stationary socio-economic structure, and no socialist state has evidenced the needed willingness to subordinate its national interests to supra-national ones.

To these obstacles we must add certain elements of the political propensities in "human nature" that stand in the way of a rational, orderly adaptation of the industrial mode in the directions that will become increasingly urgent as the distant future comes closer. There seems no hope for rapid changes in the human character traits that would have to be modified to bring about a peaceful, organized reorientation of life styles. Men and women, much as they are today, will set the pace and determine the necessary means for the social changes that will eventually have to be made. The drift toward the strong exercise of political power—a movement given its initial momentum by the need to exercise a much wider and deeper administration of both production and consumption—is likely to attain added support from the psychological insecurity that will be sharpened in a period of unrest and uncertainty. The bonds of national identity are certain to exert their powerful force, mobilizing men for the collective efforts needed but inhibiting the international sharing of burdens and wealth. The myopia that confines the present vision of men to the short-term future is not likely to disappear overnight, rendering still more difficult a planned and orderly retrenchment and redivision of output.

Therefore the outlook is for what we may call "convulsive change"—change forced upon us by external events rather than by conscious choice, by catastrophe rather than by calculation. As with Malthus's much derided but all too prescient forecasts, nature will provide the checks, if foresight and "morality" do not. One such check could be the outbreak of wars arising from the explosive tensions of the coming period, which might reduce the growth rates of the surviving nation-states and thereby defer the danger of industrial asphyxiation for a period. Alternatively, nature may rescue us from ourselves by what John Platt has called a "storm of crisis problems." As we breach now this, now that edge of environmental tolerance, local disasters—large-scale fatal urban tempera-polemics against growth are exercises in futility today. Worse, they may even point in the wrong direction. Paradoxically, perhaps, the priorities for the present lie in the temporary encouragement of the very process of industrial advance that is ultimately the mortal enemy. In the backward areas, the acute misery that is the potential source of so much international disruption can be remedied only to the extent that rapid improvements are introduced, including that minimal infrastructure needed to support a modern system of health services, education, transportation, fertilizer production, and the like. In the developed nations, what is required at the moment is the encouragement of technical advances that will permit the extraction of new resources to replace depleted reserves of scarce minerals, new sources of energy to stave off the collapse that would occur if present energy reservoirs were exhausted before substitutes were discovered, and, above all, new techniques for the generation of energy that will minimize the associated generation of heat.

Thus there is a short period left during which we can safely continue on the present trajectory. It is possible that during this period a new direction will be struck that will greatly ease the otherwise inescapable adjustments. The underdeveloped nations, making a virtue of necessity, may redefine "development" in ways that minimize the need for the accumulation of capital, stressing instead the education and vitality of their citizens. The possibilities of such an historic step would be much enhanced were the advanced nations to lead the way by a major effort to curtail the enormous wastefulness of industrial production as it is used today. If these changes took place, we might even look forward to a still more desirable redirection of history in a diminution of scale, a reduction in the size of the human community from the dangerous level of immense nation-states toward the "polis" that defined the appropriate reach of political power for the ancient Greeks.

All these are possibilities, but certainly not probabilities. The revitalization of the polis is hardly likely to take place during a period in which an orderly response to social and physical challenges will require an increase of centralized power and the encouragement of national rather than communal attitudes. The voluntary abandonment of the industrial mode of production would require a degree of self-abnegation on the part of its beneficiaries—managers and consumers alike—that would be without parallel in history. The redefinition of development on the part of the poorer nations would require a prodigious effort of will in the face of the envy and fear that Western industrial power and "affluence" will arouse.

Thus in all likelihood we must brace ourselves for the consequences of which we have spoken—the risk of "wars of redistribution" or of "preemptive seizure," the rise of social tensions in the industrialized nations over the division of an ever more slow-growing or even diminishing product, and the prospect of a far more coercive exercise of national power as the means by which we will attempt to bring these disruptive processes under control.

From that period of harsh adjustment, I can see no realistic escape. Rationalize as we will, stretch the figures as favorably as honesty will permit, we cannot reconcile the requirements for a lengthy continuation of the present rate of industrialization of the globe with the capacity of existing resources or the fragile biosphere to permit or to tolerate the effects of that industrialization. Nor is it easy to foresee a willing acquiescence of humankind, individually or through its existing social organizations, in the alterations of lifeways that foresight would dictate. If then, by the question "Is there hope for man?" we ask whether it is possible to meet the challenges of the future without the payment of a fearful price, the answer must be: No, there is no such hope.

At this final stage of our inquiry, with the full spectacle of the human prospect before us, the spirit quails and the will falters. We find ourselves pressed to the very limit of our personal capacities, not alone in summoning up the courage to look squarely at the dimensions of the impending predicament, but in finding words that can offer some plausible relief in a situation so bleak. There is now nowhere to turn other than to those private beliefs and disbeliefs that guide each of us through life, and whose disconcerting presence was the first problem with which we had to deal in appraising the prospect before us. I shall therefore speak my mind without any pretense that the words I am about to write have any basis other than those subjective promptings from which I was forced to begin and in which I must now discover whatever consolation I can offer after the analysis to which they have driven me. . . .

Let me therefore put these last words in a somewhat more "positive" frame, offsetting to some degree the bleakness of our prospect, without violating the facts or spirit of our inquiry. Here I must begin by stressing for one last time an essential fact. The human prospect is not an irrevocable death sentence. It is not an inevitable doomsday toward which we are headed, although the risk of enormous catastrophes exists. The prospect is better viewed as a formidable array of challenges that must be overcome before human survival is assured, before we can move *beyond doomsday*. These challenges can be overcome—by the saving intervention of nature if not by the wisdom and foresight of man. The death sentence is therefore better viewed as a contingent life sentence—one that will permit the continuance of human society, but only on a basis very different from that of the present, and probably only after much suffering during the period of transition.

What sort of society might eventually emerge? As I have said more than once, I believe the long-term solution requires nothing less than the gradual abandonment of the lethal techniques, the uncongenial life-ways, and the dangerous mentality of industrial civilization itself. The dimensions of such a transformation into a "post-industrial" society have already been touched upon, and cannot be greatly elaborated here: in all probability the extent and ramifications of change are as unforeseeable from our contemporary vantage point as present-day society would have been unimaginable to a speculative observer a thousand years ago.

Yet I think a few elements of the society of the post-industrial era can be discerned. Although we cannot know on what technical foundation it will rest, we can be certain that many of the accompaniments of an industrial order must be absent. To repeat once again what we have already said, the societal view of production and consumption must stress parsimonious, not prodigal, attitudes. Resource-consuming and heat-generating processes must be regarded as necessary evils, not as social triumphs, to be relegated to as small a portion of economic life as possible. This implies a sweeping reorganization of the mode of production in ways that cannot be foretold, but that would seem to imply the end of the giant factory, the huge office, perhaps of the urban complex.

What values and ways of thought would be congenial to such a radical reordering of things we also cannot know, but it is likely that the ethos of "science," so intimately linked with industrial application, would play a much reduced role. In the same way, it seems probable that a true post-industrial society would witness the waning of the work ethic that is also intimately entwined with our industrial society. As one critic has pointed out, even Marx, despite his bitter denunciation of the alienating effects of labor in a capitalist milieu, placed his faith in the presumed "liberating" effects of labor in a socialist society, and did not consider a "terrible secret"—that even the most creative work may be only "a neurotic activity that diverts the mind from the diminution of time and the approach of death."

It is therefore possible that a post-industrial society would also turn in the direction of many pre-industrial societies—toward the exploration of inner states of experience rather than the outer world of fact and material accomplishment. Tradition and ritual, the pillars of life in virtually all societies other than those of an industrial character, would probably once again assert their ancient claims as the guide to and solace for life. The struggle for individual achievement, especially for material ends, is likely to give way to the acceptance of communally organized and ordained roles.

This is by no means an effort to portray a future utopia. On the contrary, many of these possible attributes of a post-industrial society are deeply repugnant to my twentieth-century temper as well as incompatible with my most treasured privileges. The search for scientific knowledge, the delight in intellectual heresy, the freedom to order one's life as one pleases, are not likely to be easily contained within the tradition-oriented, static society I have depicted. To a very great degree, the public must take precedence over the private—an aim to which it is easy to give lip service in the abstract but difficult for someone used to the pleasures of political, social, and intellectual freedom to accept in fact.

These are all necessarily prophetic speculations, offered more in the spirit of providing some vision of the future, however misty, than as a set of predictions to be "rigorously" examined. In these half-blind gropings there is, however, one element in which we can place credence, although it offers uncertainty as well as hope. This is our knowledge that some human societies have existed for millennia, and that others can probably exist for future millennia, in a continuous rhythm of birth and coming of age and death, without pressing toward those dangerous social tensions, that threaten present-day "advanced" societies. In our discovery of "primitive" cultures, living out their timeless histories, we may have found the single most important object lesson for future man.

What we do not know, but can only hope, is that future man can rediscover the self-renewing vitality of primitive culture without reverting to its levels of ignorance and cruel anxiety. It may be the sad lesson of the future that no civilization is without its pervasive "malaise," each expressing in its own way the ineradicable fears of the only animal that contemplates its own death, but at least the human activities expressing that malaise need not, as is the case in our time, threaten the continuance of life itself. . . .

When men can generally acquiesce in, even relish, the destruction of their living contemporaries, when they can regard with indifference or irritation the fate of those who live in slums, rot in prison, or starve in lands that have meaning only insofar as they are vacation resorts, why should they be expected to take the painful actions needed to prevent the destruction of future generations whose faces they will never live to see? Worse yet, will they not curse these future generations whose claims to life can be honored only by sacrificing present enjoyments; and will they not, if it comes to a choice, condemn them to nonexistence by choosing the present over the future?

The question, then, is how we are to summon up the will to survive—not perhaps in the distant future, where survival will call on those deep sources of imagined human unity, but in the present and near-term future, while we still enjoy and struggle with the heritage of our personal liberties, our atomistic existences.

At this last moment of reflection another figure from Greek mythology comes to mind. It is that of Atlas, bearing with endless perseverance the weight of the heavens in his hands. If mankind is to rescue life, it must first preserve the very will to live, and thereby rescue the future from the angry condemnation of the present. The spirit of conquest and aspiration will not provide the inspiration it needs for this task. It is the example of Atlas, resolutely bearing his burden, that provides the strength we seek. If, within us, the spirit of Atlas falters, there perishes the determination to preserve humanity at all cost and any cost, forever.

But Atlas is, of course, no other but ourselves. Myths have their magic power because they cast on the screen of our imaginations, like the figures of the heavenly constellations, immense projections of our own hopes and capabilities. We do not know with certainty that humanity will survive, but it is a comfort to know that there exist within us the elements of fortitude and will from which the image of Atlas springs.

Ways To Turn Back the Nuclear Tide

George Kennan

In 1946 and 1947 George Kennan played a critical role in shaping American foreign policy regarding the Soviet Union. As a veteran of years in the American Embassy in Moscow, Kennan had the opportunity to experience first hand the difficulties of dealing with Russian politics and culture. At the time, he concluded that Russian suspicions of the West, together with Soviet commitment to world-wide revolution, made it incumbent on the United States to "contain" Soviet aggression. Kennan's eight-thousand-word telegram to the State Department in 1946 helped to crystallize the thinking of the Truman administration toward the Cold War, and his famous "Mr. X" article in Foreign Policy *in 1947 provided an explicit intellectual justification for that policy. (The Clifford memorandum reprinted here in Part I is largely a recapitulation of Kennan's 1946 telegram.) Almost immediately, however, Kennan began to regret the way in which his words were used. In particular, he opposed the military aspects of the Truman Doctrine, and warned against the rigid polarization that resulted from a Cold War mentality that saw every event in the world as either pro-Russian or pro-American. Here, in a speech given in 1981, Kennan asks us to reconsider some of the assumptions that have guided our foreign policy during the past thirty-five years. With passion, he urges that we have the courage to entertain new thoughts—about nuclear armament, our attitudes toward the Soviet Union, and our responsibility toward future generations of humankind.*

The recent growth and gathering strength of the antinuclear-war movement here and in Europe is to my mind the most striking

Excerpted from George Kennan, "Ways To Turn Back the Nuclear Tide," reprinted from *Christian Science Monitor.*

phenomenon of this beginning decade of the 1980s. It is all the more impressive because it is so extensively spontaneous. It has already achieved dimensions which will make it impossible for the respective governments to ignore it. It will continue to grow until something is done to meet it.

This movement against nuclear armaments and nuclear war may be ragged and confused and disorganized; but at the heart of it lie some very fundamental, reasonable, and powerful motivations: among them a growing appreciation by many people for the true horrors of a nuclear war; a determination not to see their children deprived of life, and their civilization destroyed by a holocaust of this nature; and finally, as Grenville Clark said, a very real exasperation with their governments for the rigidity and traditionalism that causes those governments to ignore the fundamental distinction between conventional weapons and the weapons of mass destruction and prevents them from finding, or even seriously seeking, ways of escape from the fearful trap into which the nuclear ones are leading us.

Such considerations are not the reflections of communist propaganda. They are not the products of some sort of timorous neutralism. They are the expression of a deep instinctive insistence, if you don't mind, on sheer survival—on survival as individuals, as parents, and as members of a civilization.

What is involved for us in the effort to turn these things around is a fundamental and extensive change in our prevailing outlooks on a number of points, and an extensive restructuring of our entire defense posture.

What would this change consist of?

We would have to begin by accepting the validity of two very fundamental appreciations. The first is that there is no issue at stake in our political relations with the Soviet Union—no hope, no fear, nothing to which we aspire, nothing we would like to avoid—which could conceivably be worth a nuclear war, which could conceivably justify the resort to nuclear weaponry. And the second is that there is no way in which nuclear weapons could conceivably be employed in combat that would not involve the possibility—and indeed the prohibitively high probability—of escalation into a general nuclear disaster.

If we can once get these two truths into our heads, then the next thing we shall have to do is to abandon the option of the first use of nuclear weapons in any military encounter.

We might, so long as others retained such weapons, have to retain them ourselves for purposes of deterrence and reassurance to our people. But we could no longer rely on them for any positive purpose even in the case of reverses on the conventional battlefield; and our forces would have to be trained and equipped accordingly.

But there is something else, too, that will have to be altered, in my opinion, if we are to move things around and take a more constructive posture. . . . I find the view of the Soviet Union that prevails today in our governmental and journalistic establishments so extreme, so subjective, so far removed from what any sober scrutiny of external reality would reveal, that it is not only ineffective but dangerous as a guide to political action.

This endless series of distortions and oversimplifications; this systematic dehumanization of the leadership of another great country; this routine exaggeration of Moscow's military capabilities and of the supposed iniquity of Soviet intentions; this monotonous misrepresentation of the nature and the attitudes of another great people—and a long-suffering people at that, sorely tried by the vicissitudes of this past century; this ignoring of their pride, their hopes—yes, even of their illusions (for they have their illusions, just as we have ours; and illusions, too, deserve respect); this reckless application of the double standard to the judgment of Soviet conduct and our own; this failure to recognize, finally, the communality of many of their problems and ours as we both move inexorably into the modern technological age; and this corresponding tendency to view all aspects of the relationship in terms of a supposed total and irreconcilable conflict of concerns and of aims: these, believe me, are not the marks of the maturity and discrimination one expects of the diplomacy of a great power; they are the marks of an intellectual primitivism and naïveté unpardonable in a great government. I use the word naïveté, because there is a naïveté of cynicism and suspicion just as there is a naïveté of innocence.

And we shall not be able to turn these things around as they should be turned, on the plane of military and nuclear rivalry, until we learn to correct these childish distortions—until we correct our tendency to see in the Soviet Union only a mirror in which we look for the reflection of our own virtue—until we consent to see there another great people, one of the world's greatest, in all its complexity and variety, embracing the good with the bad—a people whose life, whose views, whose habits, whose fears and aspirations, whose successes and failures, are the products, just as ours are the products, not of any inherent iniquity but of the relentless discipline of history, tradition, and national experience. Above all, we must learn to see the behavior of the leadership of that country as partly the reflection of our own treatment of it. If we insist on demonizing these Soviet leaders—on viewing them as total and incorrigible enemies, consumed only with their fear or hatred of us and dedicated to nothing other than our destruction—that, in the end, is the way we shall assuredly have them—if for no other reason than that our view of them allows for nothing else—either for them or for us.

Suggestions for Further Reading

The best one-volume work on the sources of the Cold War is John L. Gaddis, *The United States and the Origins of the Cold War, 1941–1947* (1972). Gaddis' most recent book, *Strategies of Containment, A Critical Appraisal of Postwar American National Security Policy* (1982), assesses America's Cold War policies through the 1970s. Provocative interpretations of the Cold War are found in Stephen Ambrose, *Rise to Globalism: American Foreign Policy 1938–1980* (1980); Herbert Feis, *From Trust to Terror: The Onset of the Cold War, 1945–1950* (1971); Gabriel Kolko's *The Politics of War* (1968) and *The Limits of Power* (1972); Walter LaFeber, *America, Russia, and the Cold War* (rev. ed., 1980); Thomas Paterson, *On Every Front: The Making of the Cold War* (1979); Adam Ulam's *Containment and Coexistence* (1967) and *Expansion and Coexistence* (1974); and Daniel Yergin, *A Shattered Peace: The Origins of the Cold War and the National Security State* (1977). Dean Acheson offers a first-person perspective in *Present at the Creation: My Years In the State Department* (1969), as does George Kennan in his *Memoirs: 1925–1950* (1967) and *Memoirs: 1950–1963* (1972). Excellent discussions of the economic issues dividing the Soviet Union from the United States are contained in George Herring, *Aid to Russia, 1941–1946: Strategy, Diplomacy, The Origins of the Cold War* (1973), and Thomas Paterson, *Soviet-American Confrontation: Postwar Reconstruction and the Origins of the Cold War* (1973). Martin Sherwin's *A World Destroyed: The Atomic Bomb and the Grand Alliance* (1975) should be compared with two conflicting assessments of the decision to drop the atomic bombs: Gar Alperovitz, *Atomic Diplomacy: Hiroshima and Potsdam* (1965), and Herbert Feis, *The Atomic Bomb and the End of World War II* (1966).

Richard Rovere, *Senator Joe McCarthy* (1960), is a pungent account. More scholarly are Richard Fried, *Men Against McCarthy* (1976); Alan Harper, *The Politics of Loyalty: The White House and the Communist Issue, 1946–1952* (1970); and Earl Latham, *The Communist Controversy in Washington: From the New Deal to McCarthy* (1966). Their interpretations clash with those of David Caute, *The Great Fear: The Anti-Communist Purge Under Truman and Eisenhower* (1978); Michael Rogin, *The Intellectuals and McCarthy: The Radical Specter* (1967); and Athan Theoharis, *Seeds of Repression: Harry S. Truman and the Origins of McCarthyism* (1971). American Communism is fairly treated by Vivian Gornick, *The Romance of American Communism* (1977), and Joseph Starobin, *American Communism in Crisis 1943–1957* (1972). HUAC's probes are dissected by L. Ceplair and S. Englund, *The Inquisition in Hollywood: Politics in the Film Community 1930–1960* (1980); Victor Navasky, *Naming Names* (1980); and Allan Weinstein, *Perjury: The Hiss-Chambers Case* (1978).

Alonzo Hamby, *Beyond the New Deal: Harry S. Truman and American Liberalism* (1973) is a solid introduction to postwar domestic politics. Insight into specific presidencies is provided by Robert Donovan, *Conflict and Crisis* (1977); Charles Alexander, *Holding the Line: The Eisenhower Era, 1952–61* (1975); Herbert Parmet, *Eisenhower and the American Crusades* (1972); Henry Fairlie, *The Kennedy Promise* (1973); Bruce Miroff, *Pragmatic Illusions* (1976); Eric Goldman, *The Tragedy of Lyndon Johnson* (1969); and Doris Kearns, *Lyndon Johnson and the American Dream* (1976). Revealing are Harry Truman, *Memoirs* (2 vols., 1958); Dwight Eisenhower, *Mandate for Change* (1963) and *Waging Peace* (1965); and Lyndon Johnson, *The Vantage Point* (1971). Arthur Schlesinger, Jr., *A Thousand Days* (1965) and Theodore Sorenson, *Kennedy* (1965) offer the perspective of sympathetic insiders. Also see Otis Graham, Jr., *Toward a Planned Society: From Roosevelt to Nixon* (1976); S. Levitan and R. Taggart, *The Promise of Greatness* (1976); and James Sundquist, *Politics and Policy: The Eisenhower, Kennedy, and Johnson Years* (1968). Especially illuminating are Edwin Dale, *Conservatives in Power* (1960); Samuel Lubell, *The Future of American Politics* (rev. ed., 1956); C. Wright Mills, *The Power Elite* (1956); Heinz Eulav, *Class and Party in the Eisenhower Years* (1962); and Robert Wood, *Suburbia: Its People and Their Politics* (1959).

The literature on the Black struggle is particularly rich. Legal developments culminating in the *Brown* decision are brilliantly described in Richard Kluger, *Simple Justice: The History of Brown v. Board of Education and Black America's Struggle for Equality* (1976). Harvard Sitkoff presents a comprehensive overview of the civil rights movement in *The Struggle for Black Equality* (1981), while individual organizations are analyzed by Clayborne Carson, *In Struggle: SNCC and the Black Awakening of the 1960s* (1981); A. Meier and E. Rudwick, *CORE* (1975); and Howard Zinn, *SNCC: The New Abolitionists* (1964). The best biography of Martin Luther King, Jr., is David Lewis, *King: A Critical Biography* (1970). It should be augmented by David Garrow, *The FBI and Martin Luther King* (1980), and Vincent Harding's essay in Michael Namoroto, ed., *Have We Overcome?* (1979). For a case study of the Movement in one community see William Chafe, *Civilities and Civil Rights: Greensboro, North Carolina, and the Black Struggle for Freedom* (1980). Also see David Garrow, *Protest at Selma* (1978). S. Carmichael and C. Hamilton, *Black Power: The Politics of Liberation in America* (1967), and Julius Lester, *Look Out Whitey! Black Power's Gon' Get Your Mama!* (1968) are enlightening explanations of this divisive phenomenon. Revealing first-person accounts are Malcolm X, *The Autobiography of Malcolm X* (1964); James Forman, *The Making of Black Revolutionaries* (1972); and Cleveland Sellers, *River of No Return* (1973). Powerful oral histories are Howell Raines, *My Soul is Rested* (1977), and J.L. Gwaltney, *Drylongso* (1980).

William H. Chafe, *The American Woman: Her Changing Social, Political, and Economic Roles, 1920–1970* (1972) offers an overview of changes in the status of women during the 20th century, as does Lois Banner, *Women in the 20th Century* (1974); Sheila Rothman, *Woman's Proper Place: A History of Changing Ideals and Practices, 1870 to the Present* (1978); and Mary Ryan, *Womanhood in America* (1975). Gerda Lerner, *The Majority Finds its Past* (1980) presents a collection of articles on women's history, as well as a theoretical interpretation of the study of women. Sara Evans, *Personal Politics: The Roots of Women's Liberation in the Civil Rights Movement and the New Left* (1979) is the best study of the origins of the women's liberation movement, while Jo Freeman, *The Politics of Women's*

Liberation (1975), and Barbara Deckard, *The Women's Movement* (1979) are important political analyses. Much of the most brilliant literature on women's experience appears in anthologies of writings by and about women, particularly A. Koedt, E. Levine, and A. Rapone, eds., *Radical Feminism* (1973); B. Moran and V. Gornick, eds., *Woman in Sexist Society* (1971); Robin Morgan, ed., *Sisterhood is Powerful* (1970); and Sheila Ruth, ed., *Issues in Feminism: A First Course in Women's Studies* (1980). Alice Walker's novel *Meridian* (1976) discusses the experience of women in the civil rights movement, and Michele Wallace focuses specifically on black women in *Black Macho and the Myth of the Superwoman* (1979).

The Pentagon Papers (1971) is *the* indispensable source on the causes and conduct of American intervention in Vietnam, and the best single-volume history of the conflict is George Herring, *America's Longest War: The United States and Vietnam 1950–1975* (1979). Varied explanations for the deepening involvement of the United States are offered by Frances Fitzgerald, *Fire in the Lake* (1972); David Halberstam, *The Making of a Quagmire* (1965) and *The Best and the Brightest* (1972); Robert Shaplan, *The Road from War: Vietnam 1965–1971* (1971); Arthur Schlesinger, Jr., *Bitter Heritage: Vietnam and American Democracy* (1967); and Guenter Lewy, *America in Vietnam* (1978). The escalation of the war is analyzed in Dennis Bloodworth, *An Eye for the Dragon: Southeast Asia Observed, 1954–1970* (1970), and E. Weintal and C. Bartlett, *Facing the Brink: An Intimate Study of Crisis Diplomacy* (1967). Some of the tragic consequences are chillingly told in Frank Harvey, *Air War— Vietnam* (1967); Richard Hammer, *One Morning in the War: The Tragedy at Son My* (1971); Seymour Hersh, *My Lai 4: A Report on the Massacre and Its Aftermath* (1970); Jonathan Schell, *The Military Half: An Account of Destruction in Quang Ngai and Quang Tin* (1968); and Michael Herr, *Dispatches* (1977). Also see Gloria Emerson's absorbing *Winners and Losers* (1977); Philip Caputo's personal *A Rumor of War* (1977); and a former State Department official's insider account, Chester Cooper, *The Lost Crusade: America in Vietnam* (1970). W.W. Rostow, *The Diffusion of Power* (1972) is a comprehensive defense of American policy.

The student revolt of the 1960s is the subject of S. Lipset and S. Wolin, eds., *The Berkeley Student Revolt* (1965); P. Jacobs and S. Landau, eds., *The New Radicals* (1966); S. Lipset and P. Altbach, eds., *Students in Revolt* (1969); Kiripatrick Sale, *SDS* (1973); and Irwin Unger, *The Movement: A History of the American New Left, 1959–1972* (1974). Kenneth Kenniston's *The Uncommitted* (1965) and *Young Radicals* (1968) offer a sympathetic analysis of the revolt by the young. The most important works on the counterculture include Theodore Roszak, *The Making of a Counter-Culture* (1969); Philip Slater, *Pursuit of Loneliness* (1970); Charles Reich, *The Greening of America* (1970); and Lewis Yablonsky, *The Hippie Trip* (1968). The connections between culture and radicalism are analyzed quite differently by Ronald Berman, *America in the Sixties* (1968), and Morris Dickstein, *Gates of Eden: American Culture in The Sixties* (1977). Todd Gitlin, *The Whole World is Watching: The Mass Media in the Making and Unmaking of the New Left* (1980), and Milton Viorst, *America in the 1960's* (1980) offer stimulating explanations on the demise of the revolt. The backlash is chronicled in Richard Lemons, *The Troubled American* (1970). Two perceptive anthologies are Murray Friedman, ed., *Overcoming Middleclass Rage* (1971), and Louise Kapp Howe, ed., *The White Majority* (1970). They may be augmented by the less critical Arnold Beichman, *Nine Lies About America* (1972), and B. Wattenberg and R. Scammon, *The Real Majority* (1970).

Indispensable for understanding the Watergate crimes are the President's memoirs, *Six Crises* (1962), and *RN: The Memoirs of Richard Nixon* (1978), and those of his co-conspirators, especially John Dean, *Blind Ambition: The White House Years* (1976); H.R. Haldeman, *The Ends of Power* (1978); and Maurice Stans, *The Terrors of Justice: The Untold Side of Watergate* (1979). The prosecution's story is best told by Leon Jaworski, *The Right and the Power: The Prosecution of Watergate* (1976), and John Sirica, *To Set the Record Straight: The Break-in, the Tapes, the Conspirators, the Pardon* (1979). Stimulating speculations on the causes and meaning of Watergate are John Lukas, *Nightmare: The Underside of the Nixon Years* (1976); Jonathan Schell, *The Time of Illusion* (1976); Theodore White, *Breach of Faith: The Fall of Richard Nixon* (1975); and

L. Evans and A. Myers, *Watergate and the Myth of American Democracy* (1974). Changing political trends in the 1970s are discussed by Alan Crawford, *Thunder on the Right: The "New Right" and the Politics of Resentment* (1980); Everett Ladd, Jr., *Transformations of the American Party System: Political Coalitions from the New Deal to the 1970s* (1978); Kiripatrick Sale, *Power Shift: The Rise of the Southern Rim and Its Challenge to the Eastern Establishment* (1975); Peter Steinfels, *The Neoconservatives: The Men Who Are Changing America's Politics* (1979); and Donald Warren, *The Radical Center: Middle America and the Politics of Alienation* (1976). Also see Faustine Jones, *The Changing Mood in America: Eroding Commitment?* (1977).

The debate on the meaning of equality in America can be traced through the following: John Rawls, *Theory of Justice* (1971); Herbert Gans, *More Equality* (1973); Nathan Glazer, *Affirmative Discrimination: Ethnic Inequality and Public Policy* (1976); and Arthur Okum, *Equality and Efficiency* (1976). On class, race, and ethnicity see Sidney Aronowitz, *False Promises: The Shaping of American Working Class Consciousness* (1973), and Richard Polenberg, *One Nation Divisible* (1980). Ben Wattenberg, *In Search of the Real America: A Challenge to the Chaos of Failure and Guilt* (1976); Christopher Lasch, *The Culture of Narcissism: American Life in an Age of Diminishing Expectations* (1979); and Landon Jones, *Great Expectations* (1980); are divergent efforts to explain contemporary predicaments.

The major environmental questions are raised by Barry Commoner, *The Closing Circle* (1971); Paul Erlich, *Population Bomb* (1968); and Frank Graham, Jr., *Since Silent Spring* (1970). Also see Robert Jungk, *The New Tyranny: How Nuclear Power Enslaves Us* (1979). Useful guides to the maze of contemporary disputes over nuclear weaponry are Fred Kaplan, *Dubious Specter: A Skeptical Look at the Soviet Nuclear Threat* (1980); Gerard Smith, *Doubletalk: The Story of Salt I* (1981); and James Fallows, *National Defense* (1982). Two fictional jeremiads, Ray Bradbury, *Farenheit 451* (1972), and Joseph Heller, *Something Happened* (1975), ought to be read with Robert Heilbroner, *An Inquiry into the Human Prospect* (1975), and Paul and Anne Ehrlich, *The End of Affluence* (1974).